THE STORY OF NIGERIA

THE STORY OF
NIGERIA

by
MICHAEL CROWDER

FABER AND FABER
3 Queen Square
London

First published in 1962
by Faber and Faber Limited
3 Queen Square London W.C.1
Revised and expanded edition 1966
Reprinted 1967 and 1968
Third edition, revised, 1973
Printed in Great Britain by
Latimer Trend & Co Ltd Plymouth
All rights reserved

ISBN 0 571 04799 8
(Hardbound Edition)

ISBN 0 571 04800 5
(Faber Paper Covered Editions)

For
Laz Ukeje
and
Onuora Nzekwu

Contents

PREFACE TO THE THIRD EDITION _page_ 9

PREFACE TO THE SECOND EDITION 12

PREFACE TO THE FIRST EDITION 18

I. THE BIRTH OF NIGERIA 21

II. SUDANESE STATES 35

III. KINGDOMS OF THE FOREST 53

IV. THE ATLANTIC SLAVE TRADE 66

V. NIGER DELTA STATES 79

VI. THE HOLY WAR OF USMAN DAN FODIO 90

VII. YORUBA CIVIL WARS 108

VIII. THE SUPPRESSION OF THE SLAVE TRADE 124

IX. EXPLORERS AND MISSIONARIES 134

X. THE GROWTH OF LEGITIMATE TRADE 150

XI. THE BEGINNINGS OF ALIEN RULE 173

XII. COMPANY AND CONSULS 188

XIII. EMIRS AND MAXIMS 210

XIV. THE UNIFICATION OF NIGERIA 231

XV. THE RISE OF NIGERIAN NATIONALISM 253

XVI. THREE CONSTITUTIONS 273

XVII. INDEPENDENCE ACHIEVED 289

APPENDIX A: SUMMARY OF MAJOR EVENTS FROM INDEPENDENCE TO THE DISSOLUTION OF THE FEDERAL PARLIAMENT IN DECEMBER 1964 316

Contents

APPENDIX B: DYNASTY OF THE SHEHUS
OF BORNU   *page* 328

APPENDIX C: THE SOKOTO DYNASTY   329

APPENDIX D: ALAFINS OF OYO   330

APPENDIX E: BRITISH GOVERNORS OF
NIGERIA, 1900–60   332

APPENDIX F: NATIONAL MINISTRIES TO 1960   333

APPENDIX G: A NOTE ON MAJOR CON-
TRIBUTIONS TO THE STUDY OF NIGERIAN
HISTORY SINCE 1965   337

NOTES   344

BIBLIOGRAPHY   389

INDEX   401

LIST OF MAPS

General map: Nigeria 1970   *pages* 16–17

1. Nigeria's major ethnic and linguistic divisions   25

2. States of the Niger-Chad region in the sixteenth
   century   38

3. Nigeria's slave-trading ports, sixteenth to eighteenth
   centuries   67

4. The Sokoto Caliphate and Bornu, *circa* 1850   91

5. Metropolitan Oyo and Yorubaland in the middle of
   the eighteenth century   109

6. Niger Delta oil markets in the nineteenth century   151

7. The growth of British influence in Nigeria   189

8. Proposed administrative reorganizations of Nigeria,
   1914   242

9. The various proposed political reorganizations of
   Nigeria, 1945–60   297

10. Nigeria's economy in 1960   302

Illustrations

1. Nok terracotta: 'The Jemaa Head'   *facing page* 64

2. Ife bronze: head of an Oni of Ife   64

3. Benin bronze: a Portuguese soldier   64

4. Igbo bronze: detail of drinking vessel   64

5. Captain Hugh Crow: a Liverpool slaver   65

6. Survival of the Slave Trade   65

7. Reception of the Denham-Clapperton Mission   80

8. The Habe Tower in Katsina   80

9. Nigerian warriors in chain mail   80

10 (*a*), (*b*). Nigerian Explorers: Clapperton and Crowther   81

11. Al-Kanemi, the ancestor of the present rulers of Bornu. From a drawing by the explorer Denham, 1825   81

12. James White preaching before King Akitoye of Lagos   176

13. Ibadan, 1854. From Anna Hinderer, *Seven Years in Yorubaland*   176

14. King Jaja of Opobo   177

15. King Pepple of Bonny   177

16. King Obie of Aboh visiting the steam vessels *Alburkah* and *Quorra*   177

17. Makers of modern Nigeria   192

18. Sunset at Port Harcourt Oil Refinery   193

19. Modern Ibadan, capital of the Western State   193

The author and publishers are grateful to *Nigeria Magazine* for plates 2, 3, 4, 8, 9, 14 and 17; to the Federal Information Services of Nigeria for the various portraits on plate 16; to Mr. Bernard Fagg for plate 1; to Monsieur Pierre Verger for plate 6; and to the British Petroleum Company Ltd for plate 18.

For information on the Nigerian Stone Age pebble tools shown on page 22, the reader is referred to pages 14 and 30.

Preface to the Third Edition

It is now seven years since I revised the first edition of *The Story of Nigeria* in 1965. The decision to revise the first edition only four years after it was published was taken as a result of the considerable amount of significant research that had since become available on Nigerian history. If there was justification for revision then, there is even greater justification today. Since 1965 not only has there been a vast addition to our knowledge of Nigerian history, but there has been considerable re-orientation of our perspectives on the past of the Nigerian peoples. There has been greater concentration on the period before the Europeans became an important factor in the history of Nigeria; there has been a healthy development of interest in the history of those peoples of Nigeria who did not form part of the great states which in the past have produced the stuff of pre-colonial Nigerian history; and the colonial period of Nigerian history itself has been increasingly looked at from the point of view of those who were subjected to it rather than in terms of the problems confronting the colonial administrators. In part this re-orientation has been due to the sheer number of research workers who, sometimes with generous grants from the Ford Foundation, sometimes with meagre postgraduate scholarships from Nigerian universities, have immersed themselves in the archives of Ibadan, Enugu and Kaduna or recorded literally miles of tape of oral traditions given them by elders who are still one of the major, though fast disappearing, sources of African history.

Perhaps the most significant development in the historiography of Nigeria since 1960 has been the great contribution to research by Nigerians themselves. Before independence Nigerians who had published scholarly works on their history could be counted on one hand; now they are the dominant factor in the study of their history and the monopoly of foreign scholars no longer exists. Nigerian participation in, and now domination of, the re-creation of the past of their peoples has been more than anything else responsible for the re-orientation that has taken place in our views of Nigerian history. This is not to say that major reassessments have not resulted from the works of non-Nigerian scholars in the fields of history, anthropology, archaeology and political science. One calls to mind here the immense impact of a historian like Jan Vansina in the use of oral tradition for the reconstruction of African history; the vital impact of an archaeologist like Thurstan Shaw on our understanding of that shadowy period when the prehistory of Nigeria merges into its history; the important contribution of Robin Horton, an anthropologist, to our understanding of the processes of state formation.

But all would agree that the most significant contribution has been the Nigerianization of Nigerian history, through the development of the virile postgraduate school at the University of Ibadan, first under the leadership of K. Onwuka Dike, then under J. F. Ade Ajayi. No less important, particularly with regard to the history of the northern areas of Nigeria, has been the more recent development of a post-graduate school at Ahmadu Bello University under the leadership of Abdullahi Smith, an Englishman who is himself now a Nigerian citizen.

In the face of all these developments it became clear that *The Story of Nigeria* needed drastic revision. I recall, when I was first drafting the history in 1960, discussing my fears about its inadequacies with Professor Harry Rudin of Yale, one of the pioneers in the teaching of African history. At the time he reassured me by saying one could at that stage of knowledge produce little more than a synthesis of what was known, which would be bound to be criticized, but at least would provide a datum-line. When I was preparing the second edition I bore his words of encouragement in mind. But today, when I contemplate the vast bibliography of works that would have to be taken into account to provide another revised version of *The Story of Nigeria*, I realize that the book would have to be completely rewritten. And, knowing how much work on Nigerian history is presently going on, or is being actively planned, I realize that even a completely rewritten book would rapidly become out of date. Indeed it seems doubtful if in the immediately foreseeable future any one man will be able to write a satisfactory history of Nigeria. It would rather be the work of a group of scholars. I have therefore contented myself with some minor revisions to the first chapter, to take into account the new twelve-state structure of Nigeria. I have not written a chapter on the decade since independence: the events of this decade are still too close, it seems to this author, to be treated in proper historical perspective. Nor have I updated Appendix A, 'Summary of Major Events from Independence to the Dissolution of the Federal Parliament in December 1964', for the six years from the Federal Election of 1964 to the end of the civil war in January 1970 are far too complex to reduce to the short diary form used in this Appendix. I have, however, added a bibliography of the books I consider best for a study of this tragic period of Nigeria's history.

What I thought would be most useful would be to add a bibliographical essay on the most important works on Nigerian history which have appeared since I completed the revised edition in 1965. This appears as a new Appendix, G, and I hope it will be useful to teachers and students who continue to use *The Story of Nigeria*.

I am very grateful to Mr. John E. Lavers for checking Appendix A and for his suggestions for the revision of Appendix B, 'Dynasty of the Shehus of Bornu'; and to Professor Robert Smith for letting me publish his revised version of the list of Alafins of Oyo (Appendix D) which he helped me prepare for the Second Edition.

I am also grateful to Professor J. F. Ade Ajayi, Dr. R. J. Gavin and Mr. John E. Lavers for their advice on the bibliography in Appendix G.

In conclusion, I hope that, despite the vast addition to our knowledge of Nigerian history, *The Story of Nigeria* will continue to be of use to those who require a short introduction to the history of the greatest nation in Africa. May I add that I have spent most of my adult life in Nigeria?

Tarauni Village   MICHAEL CROWDER
Kano
2nd April 1972

Preface to the Second Edition

The decision to publish a revised and expanded version of *The Story of Nigeria* so soon after the appearance of the first edition is in part a tribute to the great progress that has been made in the study of Nigerian history in recent years. Some of the works that have been published since the manuscript of the first edition went to press four years ago are of such importance that I felt that any new printing of the book must be one that took them into account. A further motive for the preparation of a new edition was the fact that many people had expressed regret that the text of the first edition did not include notes indicating sources, since they felt that notes would have increased the value of the book when used for teaching purposes. The publishers have therefore agreed that this edition of the book should contain end-notes, even though it is their policy to keep notes of any kind to a minimum in the series in which this book appears. Supplying end-notes to the text was a very arduous task for I had mislaid nearly all the notes I used for the original edition, and in one or two instances I have been unable to track down my original sources.

The main revisions and expansions of the text occur in the earlier chapters. The publication of G. I. Jones's *The Trading States of the Oil Rivers* has permitted me to remedy one general criticism of the book that there was insufficient material on the early history of the Eastern Region. I have now added a new chapter on the relations between the Delta states and the peoples of the Eastern Nigerian hinterland before the nineteenth century. I have also revised my interpretation of the Yoruba civil wars in the light of J. F. Ade Ajayi and Robert Smith's *Yoruba Warfare in the Nineteenth Century* and I. A. Akinjogbin's provocative paper on 'The Prelude to the Yoruba Civil Wars of the Nineteenth Century' in *Odu*. My earlier chapter on 'The Forest States' has been substantially revised in view of the work of Peter Morton-Williams and Robert Smith, both of whom made unpublished material available to me. One important new book has recently appeared, which was fortunately available to me in thesis form when I was writing the first edition: J. F. Ade Ajayi's *Christian Missions in Nigeria; 1841-1891. The Making of an Educated Elite*.

Many other books and articles that have appeared since the first edition went to press and which I found useful for the purposes of revision are noted in the text or included in the Select Bibliography. I would however like to mention Ronald Robinson and John Gallagher's *Africa and the Victorians* which was particularly useful to me for the purposes of revising and reassessing my conclusions about nineteenth-century British policy in West Africa. For the nineteenth century I also found Adu Boahen's *Britain, the Sahara, and the Western Sudan 1788-1861* very helpful; so too was C. C. Ifemesia's paper on 'The "Civilising" Mission of 1841' *J.H.S.N.*, II, 3, December 1962.

I was very fortunate in being able to attend the Postgraduate Seminar of the Department of History at Ibadan University in the first and second terms of the academic year 1963-64, as a result of which I was able to reconsider a number of my earlier judgements about Nigerian history.

Errors in the first edition that were pointed out by reviewers have been corrected in this edition.

To increase the potential value of the book for reference purposes I have added a number of appendices, including a summary of the main political events that have taken place in Nigeria from Independence up to the Federal General Election of December 1964. I have inserted a number of dynastic lists as appendices: that of the Alafin of Oyo is largely based on the list appearing in Samuel Johnson's *History of the Yorubas*, but with certain changes and additions following suggestions made by Robert Smith. The dynasty of the Sultans of Sokoto is based on that appearing in D. J. M. Muffet's provocative *Concerning Brave Captains*, London, 1964. For Bornu I have only reproduced the dynasty of Al-Kanemi, because that of the preceding dynasty, the Saifawa, is still very confused as between the various versions that have been published. I am grateful to Professor

Cohen for supplying me with the information from which I was able to prepare the dynastic table for the Al-Kanemi dynasty. Those interested in the King List of Benin should read that in Chief Jacob Egharevba's *Short History of Benin* in conjunction with R. E. Bradbury's 'Chronological Problems in Benin History', *J.H.S.N.*, I, 4, 1959.

A number of people have very kindly given their time to reading the revised versions of individual chapters, and I would like to thank them very much indeed for their useful comments and suggestions: namely, Professor J. F. Ade Ajayi, Professor Daryll Forde, Mr. John Hunwick, Professor Thurstan Shaw, Dr. David Brokensha, Miss Lalage Bown, Professor R. G. Armstrong, Mr. Robert Griffeth, Mr. Robin Horton, Mr. Martin Doornbos and Mr. Peter Morton-Williams. I owe a particular debt of gratitude to Mr. Robert Smith who made his paper 'The Alafin in Exile' available to me in advance of its publication in the *Journal of African History*, VI, 2, 1965; and to Dr. A. I. Akinjogbin for letting me see a copy of his article on the 'Prelude to the Yoruba Civil Wars' in advance of its publication in *Odu*. Professor Thurstan Shaw kindly drew the plate of Nigerian Stone Age tools on page 22. Professor Desmond Clark's comments on the first chapter of the School Edition of this book, *Nigeria: A Modern History for Schools*, of which Rex Akpofure is joint author, were very helpful to me in revising the first chapter of the present edition. I am also very grateful to Mr. Akpofure for agreeing that a slightly revised version of the appendix on a summary of recent events in Nigerian history which we prepared together for the Schools Edition should appear as Appendix A of the present edition.

Owing to the fact that sales of the first edition were more rapid than had been anticipated, this revised edition had to be delivered to the publishers five months earlier than originally scheduled. This would have been impossible to achieve but for the untiring assistance of Miss Rita Abel. I cannot thank her enough for her assiduity in tracking down sources and for her editorial work on the revised portions of the manuscript. Some of the sources I used for the first edition were not available here and I am very grateful to Miss Yvette Lane for her work on checking these for me in London. I would also like to thank Mr. Iain Scarlet and Mrs. Neil Leighton for editorial assistance.

Preface to the Second Edition

Finally I would like to thank my publisher, Mr. Alan Pringle, for agreeing in the interests of meeting a new deadline, to accept a manuscript that was to say the least scrappy, and often written in my nearly illegible handwriting.

M.C.

Berkeley, California, U.S.A.
15th March 1965

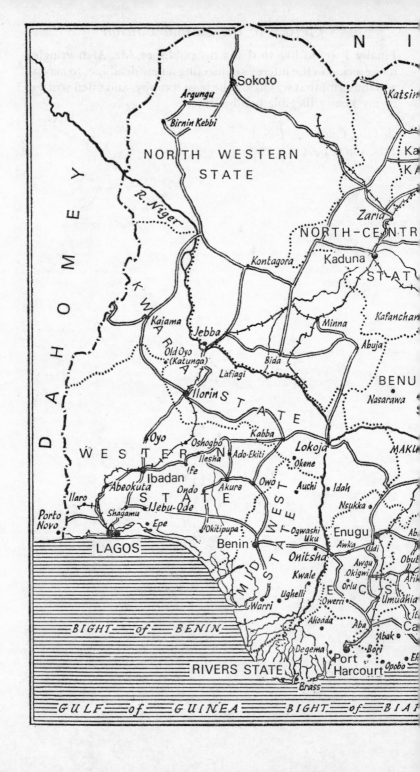

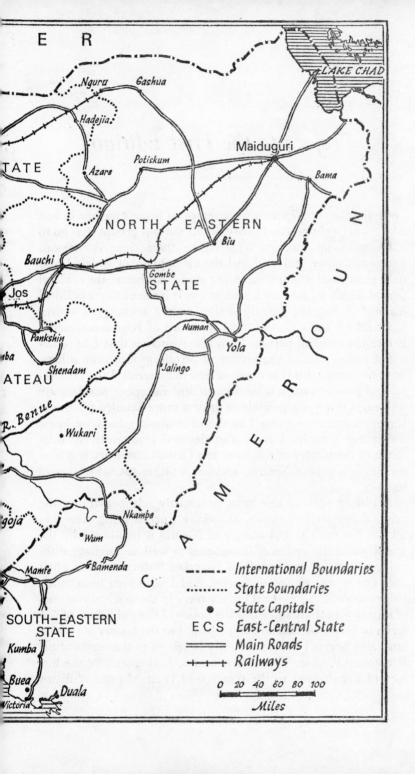

E R

NORTH EASTERN

STATE

LAKE CHAD

Nguru
Gashua
Hadejia
Potiskum
Maiduguri
TATE
Azare
Bama
Bauchi
Biu
Gombe
STATE
Jos
Numan
Pankshin
Yola
Shendam
Jalingo
ATEAU
R. Benue
Wukari

C A M E R O U N

Nkambe
goja
Wum
Mamfe
Bamenda

C

SOUTH-EASTERN
STATE
Kumba
Buea
Duala
Victoria

------- International Boundaries
.... State Boundaries
● State Capitals
E C S East-Central State
═══ Main Roads
+++++ Railways

0 20 40 60 80 100

Miles

Preface to the First Edition

The Story of Nigeria is an attempt to bring together in one short volume the history of the various groups that go to make up modern Nigeria, to trace their connexions with each other and to dispel the assumption of which I was once guilty and which is still often made that before the colonial period Africans had very little history. It is essentially a political history of Nigeria, largely owing to the scarcity of source material on the economy and structure of Nigerian societies before the colonial period. I am also conscious that I have devoted more space to the history of certain groups than others, but once again this is because of lack of material. When the results of present research by African and European scholars are published it may be possible to draw a more detailed picture of these communities as well as the ones about which we know something already. I have also devoted comparatively little space to the history of the Southern Cameroons, since it is now no longer a part of Nigeria, and has a rather special history of its own.

A history such as this must necessarily rely heavily on the original research of others, especially since investigation into all but the most recent history of Nigeria is hampered by the sparsity and dispersion of documents as well as language difficulties. For certain periods of Nigerian history there is often only one source or one authority, and I wish here to acknowledge the debt this general history owes to the original research of others, especially since it is the policy of the publishers of this series to keep footnotes to a minimum. For the history of Hausaland and Bornu I am particularly indebted to the works of Sir Richmond Palmer, Yves Urvoy and S. J. Hogben; for the history of Yorubaland to the research of Peter Morton-Williams and Dr. Peter Lloyd, as well as to Samuel Johnson's compendious *History of the Yorubas*; for the history of Benin, the work of Chief Jacob Egharevba and Dr. R. E. Bradbury has been indispensable. I have drawn heavily on the research of Pierre Verger into contact between Nigeria and the New World for my chapter on the Atlantic slave trade. The whole history of nineteenth-century Yorubaland has been made simpler to follow by Dr. S. O. Biobaku's *The Egba and their Neighbours 1830-72*. My understanding of missionary factors in Nigeria has been much increased by Dr. J. F. Ade Ajayi's thesis on this subject. Invaluable to an understanding of nineteenth-century trade on the Niger has been Dr. Kenneth Dike's admirable work, *Trade and Politics in the Niger Delta 1830-85*. For more recent history I have relied heavily on Margery Perham's biography of Lugard, on James Coleman's *Nigeria: Background to Nationalism*, and Dr. Kalu Ezera's *Constitutional Developments in Nigeria*. I owe Miss Perham a particular debt of gratitude, for she very generously allowed me to see page proofs of the second volume of her biography of Lugard several months before its publication. This enabled me to complete the last few chapters of this book much earlier than would have otherwise been possible, since her work was indispensable to any serious study of the years 1900-18. There is a full list of books that I have considered essential to an understanding of Nigerian history at the end of this book.

It is impossible to acknowledge all the help I have received in writing this history, but I should especially like to thank Mr. Robin Horton for his valuable advice on the history of the Niger Delta and his more general criticisms of the rest of the book, as well as Dr. David Bivar who has provided me with much material for my chapters on the history of Hausaland and Bornu, and has offered many valuable criticisms. Mr. Kenneth Post has made many valuable suggestions about the period 1900-60 and saved me from a number of factual errors. Individual chapters have been read by several people and I should like to thank the following for their help: Mr. Peter Morton-Williams, Dr. R. E. Bradbury, Mr. Akin Mabogunje, Professor James Coleman, Dr. Peter Lloyd, M. Pierre Verger, Mr. Thomas Hodgkin, Mr. George Vellacott, Mr. A. I. Akinjogbin, and Mr. Bernard Fagg. Of course none of them is any

Preface to the First Edition

way responsible for any of the opinions I have expressed.

I must also thank the staff of the following libraries in which most of my reading was carried out for their considerable help: the Africana section of the Library of University College, Ibadan, the Library of the Nigerian Museum, Lagos, the Library of the School of Oriental and African Studies, and the Library of the International African Institute.

Finally, I should like to thank Mr. Roland Brown who has read the manuscript for textual inconsistencies and stylistic infelicities; Mr. Alan Pringle of Fabers, who has had the hard task of preparing a slipshod manuscript for the printers; Dr. J. F. Ade Ajayi, of University College, Ibadan, for reading the final page proofs and eliminating hitherto undiscovered errors of fact and opinion, and Mr. Solomon Awosile who typed most of the manuscript.

M.C.

Lagos, March 1961

CHAPTER I

The Birth of Nigeria

N igeria, the most populous country on the African con-
tinent, only came into being in its present form in
1914 when the two protectorates of Northern and
Southern Nigeria were amalgamated by Sir Frederick Lugard.
Sixteen years earlier, Flora Shaw, who later married Lugard,
first suggested in an article for *The Times* that the several
British Protectorates on the Niger be known collectively as
Nigeria.[1]

Although Nigeria[2] was the creation of European ambitions
and rivalries in West Africa, it would be an error to assume that
its peoples had little history before its final boundaries were
negotiated by Britain, France and Germany at the turn of the
twentieth century. For this newly created country contained
not just a multiplicity of pagan tribes, but also a number of
great kingdoms that had evolved complex systems of government independent of contact with Europe. Within its frontiers
were the great kingdom of Kanem-Bornu, with a known history
of more than a thousand years; the Sokoto Caliphate which for
nearly a hundred years before its conquest by Britain had ruled
most of the savannah of northern Nigeria; the kingdoms of Ife
and Benin, whose art had become recognized as amongst the
most accomplished in the world; the Yoruba Empire of Oyo,
which had once been the most powerful of the states of the Guinea
Coast; the city states of the Niger Delta, which had grown in
response to European demands for slaves and later palm-oil; as
well as the politically decentralized but culturally homogeneous
Ibo peoples of the south-east and the small tribes of the
Plateau. Between these very diverse groups there was much
more commercial and cultural contact than has usually been

21

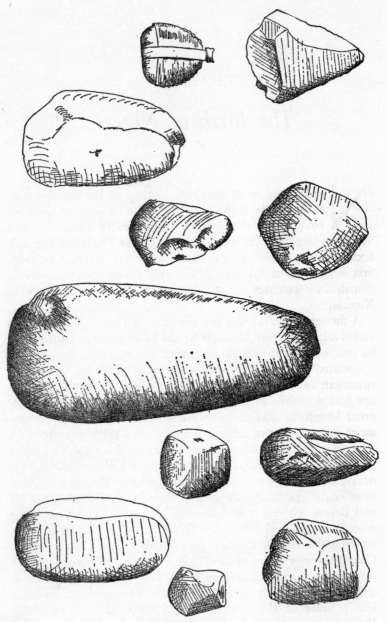

Nigerian Stone Age Tools

appreciated, and only recent research has begun to reveal how much the superficially disparate peoples of Nigeria have in common.

Any country is, in a sense, an artificial creation. In the case of Nigeria, however, union was so sudden, and included such widely differing groups of peoples that not only the British, who created it, but the inhabitants themselves have often doubted whether it could survive as a political entity. Fortunately, on 1st October 1960, despite many difficulties, focusing mainly on the differences among its various component groups, Nigeria became a sovereign federation. The pages that follow, starting with the earliest known history of its various inhabitants, tell the story of the young country of Nigeria. They may serve to illustrate some of the difficulties that impeded progress towards independence, as well as the common factors in the past of its people which are so vital to its success. And if the term Nigeria may appear anachronistic in reference to ancient Kanem-Bornu and Ife, one must remember that the histories of Mercia and Wessex are considered just as much a part of the history of the British Isles.

The Federal Republic of Nigeria covers an area of 356,669 square miles and according to the 1963 census has a population of 55,600,000 people, an increase of 20,000,000 people over the 1953 census.[8] The coastline stretches for 500 miles from Badagry in the west to Calabar in the east, and includes the Bights of Benin and Biafra. Its borders are contiguous with Dahomey to the west, Niger Republic to the north and the Federal Republic of Cameroon to the east.

Nigeria is now divided into twelve States: Lagos, Western, Mid-West, East-Central, Rivers, South-Eastern, Kwara, Benue-Plateau, North-Western, North-Central, Kano and North-Eastern. It falls more naturally into four geographical regions: a dense belt of mangrove forests and swamps stretching along the coast and often as much as sixty miles wide; the mangrove belt gives way to a forest belt which covers much of the present Western, Mid-West, East-Central and South-Eastern States; the northern savannah; and the great Jos Plateau. The northern savannah, which lies on the marches of the Sahara, stretches from Sokoto to Lake Chad, and in parts reaches as far south as Oyo in the Western State. This great plain, punctuated by occasional outcrops of granite rock, or inselbergs, forms the basis of the wealth of northern Nigeria, producing groundnuts and cotton. It is densely populated and, in parts, as heavily cultivated as Holland. In Kano State certain areas support as many as 1,300 inhabitants per square mile: from the air the land is a jigsaw of fields and irrigating rivers. The main subsistence crops of the north are guinea corn, bulrush millet, peas, beans and, of late, cassava introduced from the south. Specialized crops include tomatoes, onions, maize, sweet potatoes, sugar-cane, rice, wheat and tobacco. Groundnuts and cotton are the main crops grown for export. Goats are reared to provide the superb leather known to the outside world as Morocco leather, because before the British occupation the north exported most of its goods destined for the outside world by caravan across the Sahara to the countries of the Mediterranean littoral. The southern edge of this great plain is bounded for the most part by the great Jos Plateau which merges with it in sparsely populated Bornu. The plateau is generally very poor in agricultural resources producing mainly subsistence crops. It is, however, rich in tin and also produces columbite.

Below the confluence of the great Niger and Benue rivers lies the forest belt which covers much of the south. The subsistence crops of this area are yams, coco-yams, cassava, maize, plantains, palm produce and rice as well as secondary crops of citrus fruits, pineapples, bananas, tomatoes, and vegetables including sweet potatoes and ochra. The principal exports of the south are palm produce, cocoa, mainly from the Western State, and rubber, timber, oil and some cotton, mainly from the Mid-West, Rivers and East-Central States. The East-Central State has important coal deposits providing fuel for the Nigerian Railways, which, however, increasingly uses diesel locomotives. Over the past decade there has been rapid industrialization of the country, particularly in the fields of textiles, petrol refining, groundnut-oil extraction, soap manufacture, assembly of vehicles and electrical goods, shoes and clothing.

Nigeria today is inhabited by a large number of tribal groups ranging in size from a few thousand to many million, speaking between them several hundred languages. Though at first their variety of customs, language and social organization is bewildering they can be classified into a number of linguistic

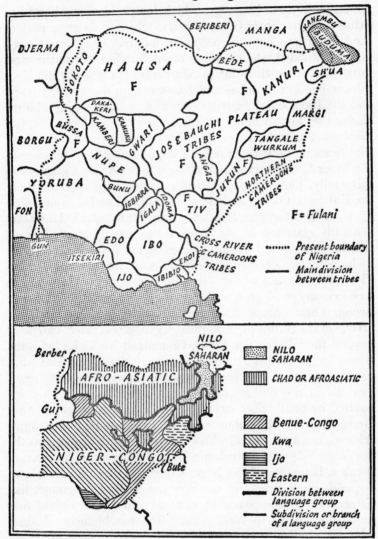

1. Nigeria's major ethnic and linguistic divisions

groups which give a fairly good indication of their wider cultural
affiliations. Of course linguistic affiliation does not necessarily
imply common descent, since contact between two very different
groups can result in the assimilation of the linguistic system of one
by the other. The majority of Nigeria's inhabitants speak one of

the large group of languages which Joseph H. Greenberg[4] has defined as the Niger-Congo family, which is in turn part of the still larger Congo-Kordofanian family.[5] The Niger-Congo family is divided into a number of sub-families, one of the most important of which as far as Nigeria is concerned is the Kwa sub-family. The Yoruba- and Edo-speaking peoples, the Nupe and the Ibo speak languages classified as Kwa, which also includes the Twi-speaking people of modern Ghana. The Ijo, the fishing population of the Niger Delta, speak a language that bears no immediate relationship to any other language in the Niger-Congo group, but which is nevertheless a member of this family. The Ijo include about twenty groups, amongst them the Kalabari, Okrika and Nembe peoples. The Efik and Ibibio of what is now the South-Eastern State speak languages generally classified in the Cross River group, which in turn falls into a huge sub-family defined as the Benue-Congo. This includes many of the major groups of the present Benue-Plateau State, such as the Tiv, who number over a million, as well as many small groups like the Batu who are but a thousand strong. These groups share the common factor that until the arrival of the British their political organization rarely extended beyond the village. The Benue-Congo sub-family includes the Bantu languages predominant in Equatorial Africa and what used to be called the Semi-Bantu languages. The Cameroons foothills in the old Benue and Adamawa provinces are inhabited by small tribes most of whom speak languages of what Greenberg calls the Adamawa-Eastern sub-family. The light-skinned, nomadic Fulani who graze their cattle throughout the north and appear to contain a large Caucasoid admixture speak a language of the Niger-Congo family, though it corresponds more closely to the Western Atlantic languages like Serer and Wolof spoken in Senegal where the Fulani first made their home in West Africa. The neighbouring Hausa, who are physically clearly of Negro stock, by contrast speak a language which is connected with the Hamitic languages spoken in North Africa, mainly by people of Caucasoid stock; whilst the Kanuri, who inhabit north-eastern Nigeria, speak a language classified by Greenberg as Nilo-Saharan, linking them with Fezzan and Darfur. With certain qualifications, which will soon become apparent, the ethnographic pattern of Nigeria has remained roughly constant for the past 800 to 1,000 years, and many linguistic experts would say longer.

The story of Nigeria as it is known today goes back more than two thousand years. Much of the earlier history of its peoples is contained in myths and legend, for only in the north, where the Kanuri and Hausa came into contact with the Arabs, are there any extensive written records before the nineteenth century. We can, of course, reconstruct something of the history of Africa and its contemporary political divisions from botanical evidence and the distribution of cultivated plants;[6] from archaeological research which is still in its infancy in Nigeria;[7] from linguistic relationships and ethnographic distribution. But for the present until archaeological investigation is undertaken on a wider scale we must still rely on oral tradition and on a few chronicles whose veracity we have few means of checking.

A proper appreciation of the difficulties of interpreting oral tradition of African societies is essential to a realization of the approximation which colours most dates and most statements of fact until the beginning of the nineteenth century. In a number of societies which had no written languages, there were certain members of the community whose duty it was to remember the history of the tribe, or of the rulers of the tribe. Thus in a Yoruba court a professional oral historian was retained by the Oba, and he was usually responsible for reciting dynastic lists. In an illuminating article on the problems of recording oral history amongst the Bakuba,[8] Vansina has listed the six sources of oral tradition available amongst these people. In Nigerian tribes, too, these are the commonly available sources: formulas including titles and names; poetry; lists including genealogies; tales; commentaries; and precedents in law. It can be readily appreciated that for a proper interpretation of oral traditions a thorough knowledge of the indigenous language is necessary. But there are greater difficulties in interpretation itself. Since so much of oral tradition is intimately bound up with the socio-political relationships of the tribal group, it is often in the interests of factions to distort it. The most common motive for distortion is occasioned by dynastic disputes, and if the party with the weakest claim to the throne succeeds, it is certain that it or its court historian will immediately modify history to create an air of legitimacy around the new régime. There is also the basic distortion of memory, even though the memories of non-literate people are often less fallible than those of a literate people. The dynastic list of the Yoruba kingdom of Ketu in Dahomey, where an individual was responsible for reciting the full rote, and suffered death if he made a mistake, is obviously more reliable than one where no such penalty was imposed. There is also a tendency to telescope early history. Kings drop out of the list if they achieved nothing of significance in their reigns, or else a single heroic act by one may be attributed to another with a fuller list of memorable deeds. There is thus an immense task before the historian who has to compare different versions of the same tradition, and take into account all these possible sources of distortion wilful or otherwise. It will need many years of patient work before more definite statements on early Nigerian history can be made. Fortunately two major research schemes investigating the history of the Yoruba and of Benin have already been undertaken. Their findings may radically change the present picture we have of the past of these two groups. Two further research schemes treating eastern and northern Nigerian history respectively are under way. It is also very important in talking of the history of Nigeria to appreciate Vansina's warning: ' "Written sources are better than oral ones," is the maxim of a non-historian. For the practitioner sources are sources. They can be good or bad, but there is nothing intrinsically less valuable in an oral source than in a written one.'[9]

In northern Nigeria we are fortunate in the number of documents available to us on the history of Bornu and Hausaland. But these, too, are subject to many limitations. Some have been copied and may have been changed. For instance, in one copy of a treatise by the Moslem reformist Usman dan Fodio, his attack on the use of titles is tactfully left out by the copyist in deference to his titled master. Naturally there were often the same political motives for distorting history as there were in non-literate societies. The Kisra legend which traces the origin of the peoples of Hausaland and Bornu to the Near East is supported by local as well as Arabic documents, which may seem to lend it greater credibility. However this may well be an attempt by Moslem Arabs to rationalize the origin of the peoples they encountered in northern Nigeria, for the North African

Arabs lived in societies in which all relationships with other people were conceptualized in lineage terms. The Kisra legend might therefore be an attempt to place the Negro peoples in relationship to themselves. A more recent example of this can be found among the Tiv, who also place great emphasis on their genealogical relationship with each other. Theoretically all Tiv can trace their ancestry back to Adam, who it is said had one son, Tiv, the ancestor of the tribe, and another from whom all foreigners including white men are descended.

Finally, we find that the early records of traditional history made by British District Officers and anthropologists and published in book form have come to be the 'official history' of a particular people. Thus an investigator is likely to have Meek's, Talbot or Palmer's version of tribal history given to him as the authoritative version.[10]

All these factors necessarily mean that for the present we must treat the early periods of Nigeria's history with considerable circumspection. The broad outlines may be there, but they may yet be subject to radical changes in the light of research being carried on at the present time.

In Nigeria, as in the rest of Africa, there is evidence of social change and cultural development during the Old and Middle Stone Age which lasted from about one million to about 5,000 years B.C. It is probable that the African continent played a significant role in man's early social and physical development, especially in the neolithic revolution. One authority, G. P. Murdock, has suggested that there was a spontaneous development of agriculture in the region of the Upper Niger between 5000 B.C. and 4000 B.C.[11] He believes that among other things these West Africans were the first to cultivate cotton. He bases his theory on botanical evidence, but it must be stressed that at the moment there are few botanists who support his hypothesis. Whatever the origin, there is no doubt that during the years from 5000 B.C. to A.D. 1 African tribes in the Sahara regions, and probably many of those inhabiting modern Nigeria, started to practise settled agriculture. In the north-east of the continent Egypt developed a powerful monarchy and an impressive civilization. Trade was carried on across the Sahara desert by the Berbers who introduced domesticated animals and plants of the South-West Asian agricultural complex to the Negroes of the

Sahara fringe. In the millennium of 2000–1000 B.C. the influence of Egypt extended to Nubia and Ethiopia where monarchical states developed. Indeed some writers believe that the Egyptian conception of monarchy was the inspiration not only for the states in East and Central Africa, but also as far distant as ancient Ghana in the Western Sudan. They base their argument on the striking similarities between the role of the monarchy in Egypt, particularly with reference to its divine aspect, and such Western Sudanese states as Kororofa (Jukun) and Yoruba, to take Nigerian examples, and the Akan of modern Ghana.

Unfortunately, research has not yet gone far enough for us to determine whether these similarities are purely fortuitous, the result of long-term culture contacts right across the Sudan, or the outcome of migrations from north-east Africa to the western Sudan which certain authors believe took place during the first millennium A.D.

The thousand years before the birth of Christ witnessed some of the major changes of the African continent. The North African coast was colonized by the Phoenicians and the Greeks. At the same time the decline of Pharaonic Egypt was paralleled by the rise of the Meroitic civilization of Nubia in the eastern Sudan. Here, many believe, may lie the solution to the problem of the Egyptian influence in the Western Sudan for Meroë may well have been one of the crossroads of African culture. On the south-east coast trade was carried on with Indonesia and crops of the Malaysian complex were introduced. Some, like yams, quickly spread across Central Africa to the Guinea Coast, showing the long distances over which agricultural, if not political, ideas could travel.

Against this general setting we can now take up the history of Nigeria. As yet we know very little about the Stone Age in Nigeria, though archaeologists have made great progress in its study in recent years.[12] Near Bussa pebble tools from the Earlier African Stone Age have been discovered (see p. 22)—the oldest known tools made by man in Nigeria. A later stage of the Earlier African Stone Age, known as the Acheulean period, is well represented by hand-axes from the Jos plateau, for one of which a radio carbon date of more than 39,000 years B.C. has been obtained. Tools used by Sangoan man, who came after

Acheulean man and who probably knew how to make fire, have been found in the upper valley of the River Sokoto and in the Abuja-Kebbi region as well as round Bussa.

The African Middle Stone Age is sparsely represented in Nigeria. Its typical artefacts—'short pointed knife-blades struck from a prepared platform, triangular points, large side scrapers and hollow scrapers, piercing tools and a few crude burins'[13]— have been found on the Jos plateau.

The Neolithic period is well represented in Nigeria by ground stone axes that are to be found in many parts of the country. They are frequently to be seen in shrines where they have attained sacred status as thunderbolts. As a result many axes that geologically could only have originated in northern Nigeria have been found in southern Nigeria, suggesting that early on there was probably contact between north and south. The wide distribution of stone axes in Nigeria indicates that there was a wide distribution of population in Late Stone Age times. On the Jos plateau there are ancient fortified villages and (possibly) Stone Age footbridges still in use. At Birnin Kudu rock paintings which may be more than two thousand years old have been discovered.[14]

A major change in the population pattern of Nigeria seems to have taken place from about 2000 B.C. onwards. The Sahara was beginning to dry up because of increasing misuse of land resources by its predominantly pastoral populations, many of whom were forced to turn south in search of new grazing lands.[15] These Sahara pastoralists, who if we judge by the paintings on the Tassili frescoes were both of Berber and Negro stock, already knew how to cultivate wheat and barley. When they moved into what is the savannah of the Western Sudan, they were unable to grow these crops since they depend on winter rain and do not grow easily in the tropics. In this area, then, on the margins of the forest, they came across Negro populations who did not practise settled farming, but did practise vege-culture. The result was the development of settled farming of a whole new range of crops, made the more necessary since the old food gathering techniques of the original inhabitants could not provide enough food to sustain both themselves and the immigrants. Thus must have developed the late Stone Age culture of Nok.

The Birth of Nigeria

Over the past twenty years more and more evidence has been collected of what must have been an exceptionally vigorous late Stone Age culture in the area to the south and west of the Jos plateau. In 1936 a small terracotta head of a monkey was found in a tin mine south-west of Jos, in the village of Nok. Eight years later a beautiful terracotta head was found at Jemma, and was immediately linked with the monkey head found at Nok. Subsequently the name of Nok was given to a widespread culture that seems to have flourished on the plateau some time between 900 B.C. and A.D. 200.[16] It spread over an area 300 miles long by 100 miles wide, stretching diagonally from Katsina Ala in the south-east to Kagara in the north-west. These Nok terracottas are generally of a high technical standard, and some of them rank as considerable works of art.

There is one remarkable fragment showing half an eye of what must have been an enormous head, since the eye alone is three inches wide. Apart from their artistic and technical accomplishments, these figurines tell us much about the people who made them. They were apparently agriculturalists, and some of the more recently discovered fragments suggest that they kept cattle. They were certainly interested in the animal world around them, for elephants, monkeys and other animals form the subject of a number of their studies. They were fond of ornaments, for not only do many of the figurines wear necklaces and bracelets, but a number of tin and quartz beads have been found in the tin mines of the plateau. Other evidence suggests that they knew how to work iron, though the frequency of stone implements shows either that they were only in the early stages of this development or else iron was scarce. The sophistication of the sculpture of these people suggests that it was a long-established tradition. Nok does not appear to have been a cultural dead end, for recent comparisons of the Nok figurines with those of later West African art reveal striking similarities in style and technique. It is too early yet to establish any direct relationships, but Bernard Fagg, who has been responsible for the recognition of the Nok culture, has suggested that it appears to show many of the cultural characteristics of later West African art. 'But by far the most striking similarities of style and subject matter', he has written, 'can be seen in a comparison of the Nok figurines with Yoruba art, which seems to indicate a profound influence on Yoruba art tradition.'[17] Recent discoveries of Nok type terracottas at Abuja only two hundred miles from Ife, the seat of Yoruba art, add weight to this hypothesis.

For the first thousand years A.D. we have almost no knowledge of the history of Nigeria. It was this period that saw the spread of Malaysian food plants throughout the Guinea Coast, amongst them yams, rice, bananas, mangoes, coconut palms and sugar-cane. People from the Nigerian plateau, almost certainly as a result of population pressures from the north, moved south-eastwards through the Cameroons into Equatorial Africa where they displaced the local pygmy hunters, overcoming them with their superior iron weapons.[18] This theory would certainly account for the close linguistic relationship of the people of the plateau with those of Equatorial Africa. In connection with this a fertile, though as yet unproved hypothesis, has been put forward that there are close similarities between the art of Nok and that of the Congo basin.

Though we know little that could be called specific about the period A.D. 1–1000 we can fill in a rough picture of what Nigeria might have been like in those days. The first major division between the peoples of Nigeria a thousand years ago was that dictated by geography. In the forest belt of the south the people were largely dependent on root crops, fruits and a few domestic animals for their food. Weaving was of a rudimentary kind using local raffia and was not general. The only well-developed crafts were pottery, basketry and wood carving. Iron smelting tended to be restricted to particular centres, and iron was generally scarce. The social organization of the peoples of the forest belt was generally small in scale, bsaed largely on local and kinship ties, contained within small villages rarely exceeding a thousand inhabitants. There was usually contact between neighbouring groups either through kinship, or for co-operation in times of need. 'Nowhere', as Daryll Forde has written, 'except where the extraneous influence of invading minorities is both traditionally asserted and intrinsically probable were politically centralized states with an administrative and territorial government established.'[19] It seems fairly clear from an examination of the legends and myths of various peoples of the Nigerian forest belt that the immigrant minorities, who are believed to have been responsible for the foundation of centralized states in this area, came originally from the north. This is not surprising when one considers that conditions in the open savannah of the north compared with the dense forests of the south were more conducive to the state-forming process. Denser population and the absence of wild fruits and tubers in the same abundance to be found in the forest zones encouraged not only the practice of agriculture and irrigation, but also the consolidation of groups to protect their farmlands. Cattle, and later the horse, which could not survive in the south because of the tsetse fly, provided the northern communities with an important source of meat and transportation. Grain grew easily in the savannah; there was always the possibility of irrigation; there was even enough food to provide sufficient surplus to allow for the specialization of other sections of the community in crafts like leather working, weaving, and smithing, and in the various tasks of large-scale government such as soldiering and policing. Cotton flourished and stimulated the use of the loom. Movement in the savannah areas was much freer than in the forest. Thus conditions were altogether more favourable in the north, and the people early on developed a more complex economy than in the south. Although the organization of the northern peoples 1,500 years ago was probably on as small a scale as that of the southerners, the pattern in the north was changed by the growth of centralized states, ruled by powerful monarchs, and based on the agricultural and physical advantages of the northern savannah.

CHAPTER II

Sudanese States

(c. 800—1600)

From the eighth century A.D. onwards there flourished in the Western and Central Sudan a succession of states and empires, the last of which only came to an end with the colonial occupation of Africa. In what is now northern Nigeria, a number of these states developed, the most important of which was the empire of Kanem-Bornu. Only Kanem-Bornu rivalled in extent and power the great empires of the Western Sudan, Ghana, Mali and Songhai. The more southerly Sudanese states of Nigeria, such as Kororofa and Nupe, were probably at least as powerful as Kano and Katsina, but because none of the Moslem scholars and travellers who wrote about the states of the Sudan visited them, we know much less about them.

Our knowledge of the early history of all these states is still very vague and often dependent on one authority, the reliability of whose evidence we have no means of ascertaining. It seems, therefore, difficult at this stage to generalize about the inspiration for the state-forming process in the Western and Central Sudan as some historians have tried to do in recent years.[1] However one of the most important factors in the growth of all Sudanese states was certainly the opening of regular trade relations with the Moslem states of North Africa. Ghana, Mali, Songhai and Kanem-Bornu might more aptly be described as market empires, since the basis of their prosperity lay not so much in what they produced themselves, which was primarily foodstuffs and local cloth for internal consumption or export to their immediate neighbours, but in their position as middlemen in the exchange of products between North Africa

35

and areas to the south of them. The most important items they procured in trade from the south were gold, slaves and ivory, which were exchanged for salt, cloth, beads, horses and swords and even some European goods. Slaves were acquired either by purchase in the markets in the south, or were prisoners taken in wars which were often conducted for the sole purpose of obtaining slaves. One of the most extraordinary achievements of these empires, from the accounts of Arab travellers, was their maintenance of security of trading conditions over vast areas of West Africa.

The second most important factor in the development of these states was their contact with the world of Islam through the trans-Sahara trade. Though Islam was accepted only by a small minority, mainly among the ruling classes, it became the imperial cult for most of these states. Many kings became Moslem, even if only nominally so, and a few even made the pilgrimage to Mecca. One of the main benefits of this contact, and clearly one of the major reasons for the adoption of Islam as an imperial cult, was the introduction of literacy into the Sudan. Literate Moslems became indispensable to the administration of these empires. Literacy also facilitated trade. Many of the states adopted elements of Moslem law and system of administration. However the great mass of the population remained attached to their traditional religions, even though a number of groups did assimilate some of the rituals of Islam.[2]

The social organization of the peoples living on the southern fringes of the Sahara in the Lake Chad region was radically altered during the seventh and eighth centuries A.D. by the arrival of groups of nomads known as Zaghawa. These were almost certainly a Negro[3] people who were being forced towards Lake Chad both by the shifting desert and the Arab invasion from North Africa. In A.D. 666–7, Okba ben Nafi, one of the Arab leaders, raided Fezzan, which lies to the north-east of Lake Chad and was at that time inhabited by Negroes.

The Zaghawa appear to have established themselves as the ruling group in the region north of Lake Chad as well as in other parts of the Western Sudan. We know very little about these people, who today are only identifiable as a group of Negroes in Wadai. The peoples over whom they assumed leadership were probably the same as the Sao people who lived

in the region south of Lake Chad. The Sao had an advanced
material culture which has become known to us through the
work of the French archaeologists Lebeuf and Masson-Détourbet.[4] They worked in metals, such as iron and bronze, and were
skilled potters. They lived in fortified villages which were
capable of withstanding siege. On the other hand they do not
seem to have been united politically, but rather appear to have
lived in a series of culturally similar but politically separate
walled village-states.[5]

At the time of the Zaghawa domination of the Chad region
the Arab historian Muhallabi[6] described their land as a great
kingdom among the kingdoms of the Negroes. It was bounded by
Nubia to the east and from there to its western frontier was a
twenty days' journey. The kingdom consisted of many tribes
and was ruled by a divine king, worshipped by his people, who
believed not only that he was the giver of life and death, but
that he existed without food. He imposed taxes on the peasantry
and was at liberty to take their goods or domestic animals for
his own use. The subsistence crops of the people at that time
were millet and beans.

The shadowy Zaghawa kingdom is believed to have been the
precursor of the Kanem Empire about which we have a little
more information. Until the sixteenth century the material is
very sparse and inaccessible to those who do not read Arabic,
except through the work of Sir Richmond Palmer,[7] many of
whose theories are open to question, and the works of Yves
Urvoy, whose history of the Kanem-Bornu Empire is still the
most comprehensive available.[8]

Before outlining the early history of the Kanem Empire, it is
important to consider in what way desert nomads were able to
take over control of the sedentary agriculturists of the Western
Sudan. Obviously in the lands of the Chad Basin the desert
nomads, used to wandering from oasis to oasis, found what was
by comparison a fertile paradise where the local inhabitants,
though organized only into small village groups, lived a life of
considerable agricultural prosperity. At first they probably
lived peacefully alongside the indigenous inhabitants, pasturing
their goats and sheep. However, these nomads through the
harsh force of circumstance were rigidly organized in their
tribal groups, acknowledging a chief and a hierarchy of leaders,

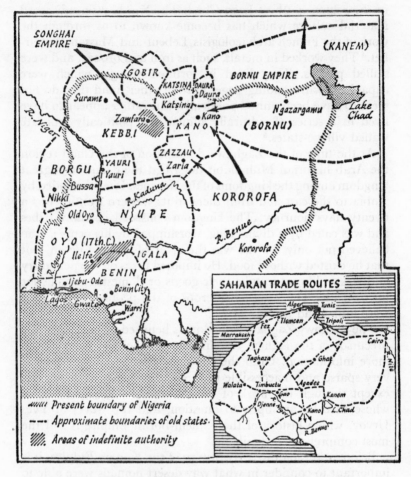

2. States of the Niger-Chad region in the sixteenth century*

whilst the local inhabitants were organized politically only at the village level, sharing no centralized authority. Thus when some of the nomadic groups tried to take control of the land it was probably difficult to resist them for long.

It is reasonable to suppose that in the early stages this pattern of conquest was not restricted to one or two tribes for it appears

* Based on R. Mauny *Tableau Géographique de l'Ouest Africain au Moyen Age.* Dakar, 1961, map on p. 436, Fig. 77, J. O. Hunwick (correspondence), and Thomas Hodgkin *Nigerian Perspectives*, London, 1960, Map No. 3.

that during the seventh and eighth centuries many different nomadic groups from all parts of the Sahara moved southward or westward to the more fertile lands of the Central and Western Sudan. And it is possible that the later break-up of the Zaghawa kingdom into several states followed original tribal divisions. One of these nomadic groups, the Beni-Saif, under its leader Dugu, a figure with one foot in history and the other in legend, set up a small state east of Lake Chad some time in the eighth century. This state, later to become the Empire of Kanem, started from rudimentary beginnings but, whilst other states faded into obscurity, Dugu's dynasty, known as the Saifawa dynasty, was to last a thousand years, one of the longest known to history. At first these nomads brought no cultural revolution, for the agricultural prosperity of the indigenous inhabitants was far in advance of the hard life they had led in the desert.

The first capital of Kanem was established at Njimi, whose location has not yet been settled satisfactorily. Palmer places it variously just east or north-east of Lake Chad.[9] Urvoy placed it at Tié, some twenty miles east of Mao in Kanem. Though ruins of some brick buildings remain there, it seems far too small to have been the capital of any kingdom, and was more probably just a desert fort. Urvoy provided the ingenious theory[10] that the nomadic rulers lived outside the settlement in tents, which is a possible answer, but based on no definite evidence. The Kanuri today say that the old capital of Njimi is in Niger not far from N'Guigmi. In fact, there is a large site with walls 800 yards by 1,600 yards, 10 miles south of N'Guigmi, but the likelihood of their story is reduced by the fact that in the reign of Mai Idris, about A.D. 1600, there were several large towns in that region. Other alternatives present themselves. On some contemporary maps there is an Njimi on the south-west end of Lake Fitri. There are three or four ruins of baked bricks in fields round Mussoro in Chad. Possibly one of these marks the site of the ancient capital. Unfortunately Arab historians and geographers who refer to Njimi are not very helpful since their other reference points are unknown to us.[11]

Whatever the location of the capital, by the end of the first millennium, the kingdom of Kanem was beginning to take shape. There was considerable contact across the desert and during the eleventh and twelfth centuries we may be sure Islamic ideas filtered through to Kanem, followed by the slow introduction of elements of Koranic Law and the Moslem administrative system. But the basic political system had been laid down by the non-Moslem rulers, known by the title of Mai. Indeed the first ruler to be converted to Islam, according to tradition, was Mai Ume,[12] who is said to have ruled from 1085–97.[13]

The Mai was the central authority in the state, probably having some degree of divine authority over his subjects. Control of outlying lands was in the hands of relatives. There was a court, with counsellors to advise the king, buttressed by a petty aristocracy. There was probably rudimentary taxation levied on the products of the peasants. There were sharp status divisions, with slaves at the basis of society. Indeed the wealth of Kanem depended largely on the export of slaves, which it obtained from the countries to the south either in exchange for salt or by raids, to the markets of the North African littoral. Within the next two centuries Kanem was to become one of the most important kingdoms in the Sudan. In the thirteenth and fourteenth centuries, however, accounts of Arab travellers who had visited the capital, Njimi, in the twelfth century, described it as a miserable place.[14]

Under the Moslem kings succeeding Mai Ume—Dunama (c. 1097–1150), who made the pilgrimage to Mecca three times, Biri (c.1150–76), Bikorom (c. 1176–93)—there was a gradual extension of the power of Kanem over the Chad basin. By the thirteenth century the influence of the new kingdom was being felt as far afield as Egypt, Tunis, Fezzan and the middle Niger, which had already seen the rise of the great Negro empire of Ghana and its successor Mali. Under Mai Kashim Biri (1242–62) a hostel for students and pilgrims from Bornu was built in Cairo, and at the same time religious leaders from Mali visited the court. Ibn Khaldun even records the receipt of a giraffe by the Hafsid prince of Tunis, sent by 'the King of Kanem and Master of Bornu'.[15]

As the kingly title implied, the empire was already expanding south of Lake Chad into modern Bornu, where the people of Kanem, particularly the Kanuri, were moving in search of new lands. Thus, with its influence stretching north to Fezzan,[16]

control of which was necessary to secure the Sahara trade route
to the Mediterranean seaboard, and south into the largely un-
tapped lands of the Negroes, Kanem was an impressive political
entity. The Mai now ruled through a council of twelve, which
had considerable control of his policy. This council was made
up of free and slave-born members. The provinces were ruled
by four provincial governors, the most important of whom were
the Yerima, controlling the lands of Yeri against attacks from
the Tuareg, and the Galadima who controlled the lands of the
west. These governorships were always in the hands of members
of the royal dynasty. That the political system was a compromise between Moslem requirements and the dictates of
earlier practices is most obvious from the important role women
played in the state. This was undoubtedly a legacy of the
matriarchal system of the original nomadic rulers. The Magira
or Queen Mother, for instance, had enormous influence and
one Magira even imprisoned a Mai for not enforcing Moslem
law correctly. This had parallels in many later African kingdoms, particularly those of Benin, Jukun and Ashanti. Again,
the senior wife of the Mai was honoured with the title of
Gumsu and apparently exercised great power. The Mai himself was treated as a divine monarch. The army, which was reported by contemporary travellers to be very extensive, was
under the control of the Kaigama or Generalissimo. The
break-up of the empire in the early fourteenth century can in
part be attributed to the main defect of this system, which was
the entrusting of the important posts of provincial governors to
members of the royal family, who constantly intrigued against
the Mai. For to rule the expanding territories of Kanem-
Bornu, which included Fezzan to the north and the young
Hausa states to the west, necessitated the delegation of considerable powers to these provincial governors who, if minded
to revolt, had remote and secure footholds from which to
organize their rebellions. In the reign of Mai Dunama Dibbalemi (*c.* 1210–24), which marked the apogee of old Kanem,
there were a number of revolts by members of the royal family.
Though these were put down and three relatively peaceful
reigns followed, by the end of the century the royal house was
divided in a bitter struggle for control of the empire.

From the end of the thirteenth century and throughout the

fourteenth century the chief preoccupation of the Saifawa dynasty was to stave off attacks by a neighbouring and related tribe of nomads, the Bulala. The struggles for power within the royal family only added to a rapidly deteriorating situation. The northern parts of the empire came under Bulala control during the first half of the fourteenth century, forcing the Saifawa to look increasingly towards the south for expansion. The climax of the wars between the ruling Saifawa and the Bulala came in *c.* 1393 under Mai Umar ibn Idris who abandoned Kanem for the lands of Bornu, west of Lake Chad, occupying land belonging to the Sao peoples.

It took nearly a century for the Saifawa dynasty to re-establish its old power, since the new state had not only to contend with the resistance of the Sao but was still troubled by dynastic disputes. Yet as early as 1391, Mai Abu Amr Uthman b. Idris was in correspondence with the Mamluk Sultan Barquq in a long diplomatic letter which still survives.[17] By the middle of the century the new state was powerful enough to exact tribute from the rising city state of Kano under its king Abdullahi (1438–52), with whom it carried on an extensive trade.[18] But it was only with the accession of Mai Ali Gazi (1473–1501), son of a preceding Mai, that an end was put to these civil wars and the occupation of Bornu completed. He built the new capital of N'gazargamu on the south bank of the river Yobe.[19]

While Kanem was being transformed into the new kingdom of Bornu, significant developments had been taking place in the savannah lands to the west of the new home of the Saifawa dynasty. Between the ninth and tenth centuries A.D. it seems that immigrants entered what is now Eastern Hausaland from the Chad basin, and settled among the local population, which appears to have been fairly sparse at the time and may have been culturally similar to the Sao.[20] As a result of the contact between these two groups, whether the contact was peaceful or one of aggression, there developed a number of small states, centred on walled cities known as *birni*. Among these states, seven eventually became pre-eminent, namely Daura, Kano, Zazzau (Zaria), Katsina, Gobir, Rano and Biram. M. G. Smith has suggested that the development of the states in this area resulted from a happy conjunction of political and geographical circumstances. Geographically it was remote from the lands where the Sudanese states had tended to flourish, in the Chad basin and on the bend of the Niger, lying happily mid-way between the two. Kanem-Bornu, which might have presented the greatest threat to their political development as separate political entities, had its political centre of gravity considerably to the north of Hausaland during this period, and for much of the time was too preoccupied with internal dissension to contemplate westward expansion. Though it appears that Mali at one time exercised political sway at least over Western Hausaland, it tended to look to the north and west for expansion. Thus, up until the fourteenth century these states were relatively untroubled by external pressures.[21]

The traditions about the foundations of these states are very coherent. A certain man, Bayajidda (Abuyazidu), son of Abdulahi, King of Baghdad, after quarrelling with his father journeyed to Bornu with his followers. There he debated attempting to overthrow the Mai and establish himself as ruler of Bornu. The cunning Mai, apprised of his intentions, first sought Bayajidda's friendship by giving him his daughter in marriage, and then isolated him from his followers by giving them chieftaincies in newly conquered towns. Bayajidda, realizing the Mai's true intentions, fled to the west, leaving his wife at Biram, where she bore him a child who became founder of the state of Biram. Bayajidda reached Daura where he killed the snake that had long prevented people from drawing water at the well.[22] The Queen of Daura then married him and they had a son called Bawo. When his father died, Bawo ruled in his place, and had six sons who became the kings of Daura, Kano, Zazzau (Zaria), Gobir, Katsina and Rano. These were known as the Hausa Bakwai, or Seven Hausa States, for to their number was added the state of Biram. In addition there were the Banza Bakwai, or seven 'bastard' Hausa states, which probably represented states which came under the Hausa influence, namely: Zamfara, Kebbi, Nupe, Gwari, Yauri, Yoruba and Kororofa.

Several versions of this legend exist. For instance, Sultan Bello of Sokoto wrote that Bayajidda was a slave from Bornu. The versions that speak of Bayajidda coming from Mecca, or the Middle East, may well be later in origin, probably influenced by the Moslem *mallams*. The traditional histories of both Kano and Katsina[23] claim that both were inhabited before the 'Bayajidda invasion'. Kano and Daura already had a large colony of ironworkers. It seems very likely that, in fact, the 'Bayajidda immigrations' took place over a fairly long period of time, and this myth merely telescopes the events into a convenient explanation of the cultural unity of Hausaland. The origin of the immigrants is also obscure. Tradition ascribes it to nomadic desert tribes, though Sultan Bello's explanation that Bayajidda was a slave from Bornu, as well as the tradition that he sojourned in Bornu before reaching Daura, might connect it with political events in Kanem at that time. It is also not clear whether they arrived and settled in Hausaland, later taking over control of the existing towns, or whether the legend of Bayajidda represents acts of simple conquest.

Chronicles of the history of the various states exist, the most notable of which is the Kano Chronicle. Both Kano and Katsina record events in their local histories dating back to 1100,[24] although there is little of significance in their local history until after 1300. Kano and Katsina seem to have assumed early preeminence among the seven Hausa states, which were said each to have a specific duty: Gobir on the fringes of the desert was the northern outpost of Hausaland, guarding it against the Tuaregs; Zaria to the south was the slave raider; Kano and Katsina were occupied with trade; Rano was an industrial centre; whilst Daura remained the spiritual home of the Hausa. In the fourteenth century the chronicles are much more detailed in their accounts of each reign. Islam appears to have trickled through to Hausaland at that time from Bornu and Mali which were at their apogee.[25] Mali may have held sway over some of the Hausa states at this time. Two important kings are recorded as having been converted to Islam during the fourteenth century, Mohammed Korau of Katsina, who is variously dated as acceding to the throne in 1320 and 1380, and King Yaji of Kano whose successor, King Kanajeji, is said to have reverted to paganism. In 1353, Ibn Battuta gave a brief description of Gobir, locating it roughly where it is now. A measure of the growth of these cities is the recording of wars between Katsina and Kano, and Katsina and Gobir, undoubtedly centred on the struggle to hold the position as terminus for the trans-Sahara caravan routes, a factor that was to dominate the politics of Hausaland, particularly those of Katsina and Kano, throughout the century.

During the fifteenth century, legend has it that Zaria achieved considerable influence in Hausaland under its queen, Amina, who is said to have taken lovers in every city, and executed them when she had done with them.[26] She was also supposed to have built fortified walls all over Hausaland like the great earthworks round Katsina. The new powers of Kororofa and Nupe, a shadowy but influential state to the south of Hausaland, as well as most of the Hausa states were said to be her tributaries.

Zaria, as the southernmost of the Hausa states, was the chief source of supply of slaves for the markets of Kano and Katsina, where many of them were bought up by Arab and Berber merchants for sale in the markets of North Africa. The wide diffusion of Negro peoples in the Maghreb and north-east Africa today is partly a result of a trade that was fundamental to the Sudanese states and was encouraged and indeed legitimized by the spread of Islam which stated that it was lawful to enslave the infidel. Ahmed Baba has left us a short treatise discussing which peoples of the Sudan were Moslem, and which were not, and hence could be legitimately enslaved. In his treatise he makes it clear that slavery is meet only for unbelievers, and that whatever a man's racial origin, he cannot be enslaved if he is a Moslem.

The fifteenth century saw the apogee of Kano; although tribute was paid to Bornu, trade was also opened between the two. During the reign of Yakubu (c. 1452–63) divines from Mali visited Kano, bringing with them books on divinity and etymology, and later under Kano's greatest king, Muhammad Rimfa (1463–99), Islam reached its zenith in Kano. He was advised by the itinerant North African theologian Al-Maghili on how to run his state according to Islamic principles.[27] Mosques were built, learned men visited the court, Koranic law was established and the administration of the state improved. Though Islam gained a foothold in all the Hausa states, and though most of the rulers officially accepted it, it was constantly challenged by the recrudescences of the traditional religions until the Holy War of Usman dan Fodio at the beginning of the nineteenth century.

The spread of Islam was accompanied by a rise of Arabic learning in northern Nigeria and the whole of the Western Sudan: witness the works of Ahmed Baba; of Al-Maghili whose work, the so-called *Obligations of Princes*[28] was read by Hausa monarchs and is still read in northern Nigeria today; of the Hausa (?) historian Baba Goro b. al Hajj Muhammad b. al-Hajj al-Aminu of Kano; of Muhammad Ibn Masanih from Katsina and Ibn al-Sabbagh from the same city. As in Europe at that time, learning was restricted to the aristocracy, scholars (*mallams*) and the merchant classes. Yet there is no doubt that a substantial number of men and women in sixteenth-century Hausaland and Bornu were in touch with the ideas of the Islamic world.

Agriculture was the main source of wealth for Kano, as it was for most of the Hausa states, though Kano itself became an international mart and commercial centre for the trans-Saharan trade. Over the ordinary peasant farmers, some of the most diligent in the Sudan, was placed a hierarchy of village heads and fief-holders who were responsible for collecting taxes for the support of the central administration of the king. The royal authority does not appear to have been absolute, but limited by the power of certain hereditary officials resident in the capital. It is significant that Muhammad Rimfa of Kano offered titles to eunuchs and slaves, undoubtedly to check the power of the hereditary aristocracy. Though the political system of the Hausa states approximated to that prescribed by the Koran, it still contained many traditional practices. Rimfa's successor, Abdullahi, was dominated by his mother who managed to extend her influence through to the reign of his grandson Kisoki. There were also numerous non-Moslem rituals surrounding the enthronement of Hausa kings.

By the end of the fifteenth century the Hausa states were becoming known to the outside world, and were increasingly influenced by the politics of the Western and Central Sudan. By the sixteenth century the history of Hausaland had become inextricably involved in that of the two leading powers of the Sudan, the Songhai Empire of Gao and the reconstituted empire of Bornu.

Sixteenth-century Bornu regained most of the power it had lost after the conquest of Kanem by the Bulala. In the reign of

Mai Idris Katakarmabe (1507–29), the Bulala of Kanem were
defeated at Garni Kujala north of Lake Chad. The strength of
Mai Idris was borne out when, in an attempt to throw off the
Bornu yoke, the Bulala were again defeated in the battle of
Lada. Bornu now became quasi-overlord of Hausaland, which
was subject also to the great power of Songhai in the Western
Sudan. Songhai had originally formed part of the Empire of
Mali, but during the decline of the latter it had asserted its
independence. Based on the river port of Gao on the Niger, it
had developed into as powerful an empire as Mali under the
leadership of Sonni Ali (1464–92). His successor, Askia Muhammad I, extended its boundaries as far west as the Senegal, north
into the Sahara desert and east to Hausaland. In 1504, Askia
Muhammad invaded Illo and Bussa in Borgu; and in 1513 his
armies attacked Katsina. Leo Africanus, the famous Maghribi
traveller, who later made reports on Africa for Pope Leo X,
visited Kano, Katsina, Zamfara and Zaria in 1526 and recorded that all were desolate from Songhai invasions. Kano had
sadly declined in power since the days of Muhammad Rimfa.
'The inhabitants are rich merchants and most civil people.
Their king was in times past of great puissance, and he had
mighty troops of horsemen at his command, but he has since
been constrained to pay tribute to the kings of Zaria and
Katsina.'[29] Spurred on by his success in Hausaland the Askia
turned his attention to Air, gaining assistance from a vassal king,
the Kanta of Kebbi,[30] who had already made incursions into
Hausaland on his own account. After conquering Air (1514–15)
the Kanta and the Askia quarrelled over the division of tribute
and the Kanta revolted against Songhai[31] which, according to
Leo Africanus, 'had mightly oppressed and impoverished the
people that were before rich'. The Kanta defeated a punitive
expedition by the Songhai army, and proceeded to subject
much of Hausaland to his authority. Bornu feared the growing
authority of Kebbi, probably preferring a divided Hausaland
as a buffer state between itself and Songhai, and after conquering Air, marched on Kebbi, but was defeated. Twelve
years later Bornu again tried to assert its authority over
Hausaland when it came to the rescue of Air, its temporary fief,
which was being attacked by the Kanta. There followed a tremendous battle which ranged over the present borders of

Northern Nigeria, ending with the defeat of the Bornu army at Nguru, their western provincial capital, and seat of the Gala-dima. The Kanta, returning to Kebbi in triumph, was killed by the people of Katsina Laka, which may have been the old state of Guangara, about which contemporary writers talk, but which has not survived today.

Despite the success of the Kanta against the Songhai, the latter's armies still made expeditions to Hausaland. In 1554 Askia Daud, who restored some order to the Songhai Empire, invaded Kano, and a year later sacked Bussa, taking away a female slave who became mother of the next Askia of Songhai. On the other hand Bornu seems to have been weakened through its defeats by the Kanta, for it maintained its authority over the Bulala of Kanem only with difficulty. If they did nothing else these wars brought Hausaland into the forefront of Sudanese affairs and in particular drew attention to the wealth of the commercial centres of Katsina and Kano, conveniently situated at the terminus of the trade routes both to the Maghreb and Tripoli through Ghat and Zawila, and to Egypt through Bornu and Nubia.[32] Mauny has suggested that Kano may have had a population of over 75,000 at this time.[33] Katsina was divided into many quarters, including those for people from Songhai, Mali and North Africa, as well as a special quarter for students. There were twelve gates to the city walls. In 1529 the distinguished Moslem divine, Muhammad b. Ahmad, from the Sankore university-mosque of Timbuktu, passed his last years in Katsina as Cadi, indicating the high prestige of Islam in that city. Barbary merchants were settled in all the important towns of Hausaland.

In 1591 Songhai's influence was brought to an end when the Moroccans under Judar Pasha invaded Timbuktu, and with the advantage of firearms were able to drive Askia Ishaq II out of his kingdom. He was succeeded first by Muhammad Gao, and then by Nuh who retreated towards Borgu where in the marshes of Dendi he was able to keep the Moors at bay. While the power of Songhai declined, that of Bornu rose under a brilliant ruler Mai Idris Alooma, who was fortunate enough to have his own chronicler Imam Ahmed ibn Fartua.[34] Under Mai Idris, Bornu was completely reunified and Kanem brought to heel.

Idris Alooma had only attained the throne of Bornu with difficulty. On the death of his father the throne had gone to his cousin, Mai Dunama, who ensured that his own son, Dala, succeeded him. Dala likewise tried to keep the kingship within his own section of the family, but died without issue. At that time Idris Alooma was in Kanem, and the throne was taken over by Dala's sister, Ais Kili N'guirmamaramama, who held power for seven years before handing over the throne to Idris Alooma; that she was able to do so is evidence of how powerful women still were in the state.

Idris Alooma undertook the unification and pacification of Bornu in a series of extensive wars against the peoples of the south, conquering the Marghi, Gamergum and Mandara. He also established some sort of sovereignty over Wadai in the east.

Despite close relationship through his mother with the ruling family of Kanem, he was forced to undertake war against them when they refused to recognize his sovereignty over certain border villages. He defeated them in a number of great battles so that, by the end of his reign, Bornu had become as powerful as it had ever been. He died in 1617 in a battle against rebellious subjects in the south of his empire.

Idris Alooma was a devout Moslem, trying to extend the Shari'a in place of customary law throughout his kingdom. He built mosques in brick, and established a hostel for pilgrims in Mecca. Indeed some authorities believe that Idris Alooma was more significant as an Islamic reformer than as an empire-builder.[35]

The basis of Idris Alooma's power was his army, of which we get a vivid picture from Ahmed ibn Fartua's chronicles of his reign. It differed little from other Sudanese armies, except in its efficacy. The vanguard of the army was the cavalry of the nobility, superbly caparisoned, both horse and rider in armour, bearing decorated shields, feathered lances, a riot of colour in the fierce Sudanese sun as drummers urged them on and slaves sang their praises to a cacophony of brass trumpets. Behind them followed the infantry, the peasants sparsely armed with bows and arrows or spears. The rear was brought up by women carrying loads, or possibly by some ferocious-looking group of naked pagan warriors, called in from the outskirts of the empire.

Idris Alooma's army benefited by the presence of a band of musketeers, trained by Turkish instructors and selected from among his household slaves, but the army as a whole was ill-disciplined and incoherent, relying as much on numbers as anything else. Its recompense was pillage or slaves, and it was more often deployed against defenceless villages than against formidable enemies like Kanem or Kano. Yves Urvoy, in a brilliant description of this Sudanese army, sums it up thus: 'This braggart and anarchic cavalry, the despised and badly organized plebeian infantry, the surprise raids, the pillaging of hamlets, the rare and brilliant battles, the confused multiplication of individual combats, is our own feudal army of Crécy and Agincourt.'[36]

There were few significant changes in the organization of the empire: the central administration still subsisted on tribute from outlying states, the income from slave raids, and the taxes collected by the local administration in Bornu itself. Slaves or members of humble families, who owed their all to the ruling Mai, were made governors of the provinces instead of members of the Mai's family who were given honorific titles and kept safely at home, no Mai caring for a repetition of the events that led to the break-up of the old Kanem Empire.

Mai Idris left a secure state for his successors, but after forty years, on the succession of Mai Ali (1657–94), the state began to weaken under attacks from the Tuareg in the north and Jukun in the south. The Jukun kingdom of Kororofa was based on the Benue near Ibi.[37] The Jukun themselves claim affinity with the Kanuri, stating that they came from Yemen with them, and parted ways in Bornu. It is possible that the founders of Kororofa were either another group of nomads, settling in Nigeria about the same time as the Beni-Saif, or else a dissident group from the Bornu Empire. Alternatively they might represent one of the large tribes who were driven south by the Kanuri when they moved into Bornu.

Not much is known about their early kingdom. The Kano Chronicle states that Yaji, King of Kano (*c.* 1349–85), attacked Kororofa for refusing to pay tribute to him; Amina, Queen of Zaria, is said to have conquered Kororofa in the fifteenth century. In the reign of Muhammad Zaki of Kano (1582–1618)

Kororofa forced the people to flee to nearby Daura. They made another major attack on Kano in the reign of Muhammad Kukuna (1652–60). It is evident that by the end of the sixteenth century Kororofa was becoming a power of great influence.

The main strength of the Jukun of Kororofa lay in their cavalry, and one suspects that they made highly mobile and lightning raids on the northern cities, terrorizing the countryside but rarely occupying it effectively. They were ruled over by a divine king, who was surrounded by an elaborate and complex round of ceremonial. Much in their ceremonial has led early anthropologists to seek connections with Egypt. It is possible that the Aku, as the king was known, held authority over local tribes largely through his divinity and magical powers; for though the Jukun had some spectacular successes in their expeditions to the north, they do not seem ever to have been many in number. Today they are not even classified separately as a Nigerian tribe.[38]

The Jukun first started to be a serious factor in northern Nigerian politics in the reign of Mai Idris Alooma of Bornu. Zaria had become tributary to them at the end of the sixteenth century, and throughout the seventeenth century raids were made on the walled cities of the north. In 1653 they invaded Kano, and in 1671 they attacked both Kano and Katsina. They even besieged Mai Umarmi of Bornu in 1680. Later, however, in a great battle the Bornuese king drove off the Jukun, and a peace treaty was signed between the two powers, whereby a permanent Jukun representative was sent to N'gazargamu, whilst Bornu sent a Zanna to Kororofa. This title of Zanna is significant; it was usually given to a representative sent to a tributary state and may indicate the beginning of the Jukun decline.[39]

In Hausaland the city of Kano, worn out by a century of wars with Kororofa and Katsina, and having lost control of the trans-Saharan trade route to the latter, declined in importance. It was Katsina that profited from the break-up of the Songhai Empire, quickly establishing itself as the leading city of Hausaland, and all were subjected to the occasional incursions of the Jukun. The next century was to see the rise of two other Hausa states, Zamfara and Gobir, and the conflict between them was to have monumental consequences for the future of northern Nigeria.

CHAPTER III

Kingdoms of the Forest

South of the Niger there flourished the related states of Ife, Oyo and Benin. These do not appear to have been the first states to have developed in this area, but they are the first of which we have any definite knowledge. Legends of the Yoruba tell of migrations from the north or north-east. It is possible that the growth of the highly centralized kingdoms of Ife, Oyo and Benin in the forests of the south were associated with those of the north.[1] The establishment of Oyo and Benin could hardly have been the result of mass migrations from the north, since the Yoruba and Edo (Benin) languages bear no relation to Hausa or Kanuri. It may well have been the result of incursions by small groups who imposed their ways on the indigenous population but were linguistically if not culturally assimilated by them. What does seem clear is that some time during the first millennium strangers from the north-east either invaded or settled at Ile Ife, establishing a kingdom there.

The Yoruba creation myth that probably parallels this event talks of Ile Ife as the origin of life. In the beginning the earth was covered with water. Olorun, the supreme god, let his son Oduduwa down a chain carrying a handful of earth, a cockerel and a palm nut. Oduduwa scattered the earth over the water and the cockerel scratched it so that it became the land on which the palm tree grew. Its sixteen branches represented the sixteen crowned heads of Yorubaland, probably the heads of the main settlements established by the newcomers.[2] Unfortunately we still know very little about ancient Ife, which is revered today as the original home of the Yoruba.

A second version of the myth of origin recorded by Samuel Johnson tells that Oduduwa was an eastern prince driven out of his kingdom.³ After long wanderings he conquered the local inhabitants of Ife where he settled. He had seven children who were the ancestors of the Oba of Benin and the six crowned rulers of Yorubaland, namely the Olowu of Owu, the Onisabe of Sabe, the Olupopo of Popo, the Orangun of Ila, the Alaketu of Ketu and the Alafin of Oyo. In this story the non-Yoruba kingdom of Benin is included and both Benin and Yoruba traditions agree on the circumstances. Oduduwa sent his son or grandson Oranmiyan to rule over Benin, a task which the latter found impossible, deciding that only a prince of Benin blood could rule that kingdom. He therefore fathered a child by a Benin woman and left him as ruler. He then founded a new kingdom at Oyo, which he made his capital. Adimu, who was either a slave or the original ruler of Ife, was left there to guard its national treasures.

This myth and its variants seem to describe a second invasion of Yorubaland, and suggest that at the time Ife, and probably Benin, were well-established states. The date of this invasion is usually placed at the beginning of the present millennium.

There are at present no means by which the history of this very early period can be checked, but as Chief Egharevba has shown, there are many traditions and sayings associated with the first period of the Benin 'Empire'.⁴ The rule of the Ogiso or early kings was apparently so unsatisfactory that the Bini tried to set up an alternative, non-hereditary 'republican' type of government, but the first of their leaders, Evian, immediately nominated his own son, Ogiamwe, as his successor. It was at this stage that Benin sent to Ile Ife for a prince to rule over them. The coincidence of the decline of the first Benin state and the arrival of Oduduwa is significant, as indeed is the request of the Bini to a foreign people to come and rule over them. This could either be a convenient legend to disguise what in fact was a conquest by Oduduwa's party or alternatively it may represent a not uncommon occurrence in Africa. There are several examples of centralized states ruled over by a chief invested with supernatural powers and surrounded by a large number of small, headless communities, constantly feuding and in daily terror of death and disorder, beset by droughts and other misfortunes. For these people the sacred kingship of their neighbours often seemed the source of good order, regular rain-

fall and other benefits. So they grouped together and demanded
a prince of the royal blood to rule over them or sent a leader to
be initiated into the mysteries of sacred kingship.

Though very little is known for certain about the early history of Oyo and Benin, there have fortunately survived from
the ancient kingdom of Ife some remarkable and very beautiful
bronzes[5] and terra-cottas, some of which rank among the
masterpieces of world sculpture. They give evidence of great
technical accomplishments and the elaborate regalia of the Oni
or kings of Ife, whom many of the bronzes portray, indicate a
complex society.[6] Their naturalism still remains a puzzle for
historians of West African art, most of which has been more
formalized, more abstract and more symbolic than Ife art.[7]

The bronzes were probably cast some time around the
twelfth century or even earlier,[8] though it is not clear whether
they preceded or followed the founding of Oyo. Mr. Peter
Morton-Williams in a paper read to the Historical Society of
Nigeria suggests that Oyo was founded at the earliest in 1390 or
at the latest in 1440.[9] References in legends to Adimu who was
left to guard the National treasures suggest that sacred cult
objects already existed, and these were very probably the
bronzes and terra-cottas dug up at Ife. The fact that Benin history records the introduction of bronze casting in the time of
Oba Oguola, who probably reigned in the early fifteenth century, would roughly tally with Professor A. W. Lawrence's
opinion that if Benin style is derivative of Ife naturalism then
the latter must have flourished some three centuries earlier.
The conquest of Ife by Oduduwa's party might explain the
apparent discontinuance of the Ife naturalistic style. The odds
then seem to be in favour of Ife art's preceding the second
invasion.

Even though the supposed invasions of Ife and Benin were
associated, they would obviously have been invasions of a small
group of people, for the languages of Benin and Yorubaland,
though related, are very different. The languages of the indigenous people obviously survived that of the invaders.

Oranmiyan must have chosen Oyo as his capital because it
was in a fertile sector of the savannah belt, with good access to
the Niger and caravan trails leading both from north to south
and east to west.[10] It was also strategically placed to defend the

new kingdom against the neighbouring powers of Borgu and Nupe, and probably was one of the terminations of the caravan trail from the north. This invasion, then, led to the establishment of twin kingdoms, Oyo and Benin, which up until the establishment of the British Protectorate at the end of the nineteenth century were to remain two of the most powerful kingdoms on the west coast.

Unfortunately little is known about the early history of Oyo, for there was no written language, and unlike Benin which was first visited by Europeans at the end of the fifteenth century, it appears in European descriptions of the coast only as the vague but powerful kingdom of 'Katunga' in the interior. For our information we have to rely on tradition and the compendious *History of the Yorubas* by the Rev. Samuel Johnson. Not until the end of the seventeenth century are there any definite dates for the history of Oyo. It was during the preceding century that Oyo appears to have begun its expansion into an empire that eventually controlled most of Yorubaland. It was probably at this period, too, that Oyo developed its force of light cavalry which was the key to its military success.[11]

At its height the new empire of Oyo covered a huge area, bounded to the north by the Niger, to the east by Benin, to the west by the frontier of modern Togo and to the south by the mangrove swamps and lagoons that form a barrier between the sea and the interior. The kingdom founded by Oranmiyan was based on Oyo, commonly referred to as Old Oyo as a result of its abandonment and transfer in *c.* 1837 to a new site, which lies about sixty-five miles to the south of Ilorin. The King of Oyo, known as the Alafin, became the supreme ruler of much of what is now called Yorubaland.[12] Under him ruled a number of provincial kings, the most powerful of whom was the Onikoyi of Ikoyi. The Alafin, as supreme monarch, ruled over other monarchs whose powers and independence varied according to his calibre and their own proximity to his capital. The Oyo kingdom was divided into a number of provinces, comprising Yoruba proper, and possibly even including the important town of Ife, the traditional birth-place of the tribe. To the south-west lay the Egbado, closely controlled by Oyo, and the semi-independent Egba; to the south were the Ijebu, who were practically independent, and may have been subject to Benin at various times; and to the east, the Ekiti, who appear always to have been independent of Oyo. In this complex organization only Oyo proper can be said to have been completely under the rule of the Alafin. The remoter provinces were almost completely independent and, despite its early connections with Ife, Benin soon achieved its independence.

It is not clear at what stage the political organization of Oyo developed into that described by Johnson, but from early times Oyo developed a complex political structure of title grades and palace societies through which government was exercised. This differed considerably from the system generally obtaining in other Yoruba kingdoms.

To begin with, it appears that the rule of primogeniture obtained in Oyo, but that was abandoned in favour of selection from among members of the royal family by the Oyo Mesi.[13] There were seven principal councillors of state, though the number and composition of this group varied over the centuries. They were also the ward heads of the city of Oyo and were presided over by the Basorun, or Prime Minister. The eldest son of the Alafin was appointed Aremo, or Crown Prince, and from the early eighteenth century onwards he was forced to commit suicide on the death of his father,[14] an arrangement that safeguarded the Alafin from plots by an over-ambitious son. The Aremo was placed in charge of the royal children and was also responsible for some of the vassal kingdoms.

The Alafin was considered *Ekeji Orisa*, that is Companion of the Gods, as well as Owner of the Land and Lord of Life.[15] He administered the empire* through three eunuchs, one the Osi Efa, the Eunuch of the Left, who was responsible for political affairs and died with the Alafin, one the Ona Efa, the Eunuch of the Middle, who performed the Alafin's judicial tasks, and one the Otun Efa, the Eunuch of the Right, who performed the Alafin's religious duties. The Alafin rarely appeared before the people in person and spent most of his time in his huge palace.[16] The main check on the power of the Alafin was held by the Oyo Mesi who, if they felt the Alafin had exceeded his powers, could divine that all was not well between the Alafin and his spiritual double and force him to commit suicide by presenting

* See map on p. 38.

him with an empty calabash or parrot's eggs, or more directly by informing him that he had failed to conform to precedent. However the Oyo Mesi were restrained from abuse of this power by the fact that one of their number had to die with the Alafin. Another restraining influence was the Ogboni Society, which was a secret society to which the Oyo Mesi and the heads of important families and religious cults belonged. The Ogboni Society discussed among other things political affairs and its decisions were binding on all its members, including the Oyo Mesi, even if they disagreed with them.

The Oyo empire was administered by officials called Ajele or *Asoju oba*, meaning one who was the king's eyes. The Ajele resided in the vassal kingdoms to supervise payment of tribute to Oyo. They had the same status as the kings they supervised, controlling them through the authority of the royal cult of Sango, a deified Alafin. Since Sango was the god of thunder and lightning they could threaten recalcitrant kings with his wrath.

Government at Oyo was a delicate balance of power between the Alafin and his palace administration on the one hand and the Oyo Mesi and the more representative Ogboni Society on the other. The division of power in Oyo is nowhere better illustrated than in the composition of the army. The head of the army was an ilari or titled slave called the Are Ona Kakanfo, and was directly responsible to the Alafin, whilst the army was raised by the Oyo Mesi as ward heads. The Alafin himself was represented in battle by the Osi Efa.

There was only one Kakanfo at any one time, and if he were to suffer defeat as leader of the Oyo army, then he had to commit suicide, which is certainly one explanation for the success of the Oyo army.

Ife retained its constitutional and spiritual importance for Yorubaland, and to a lesser extent for Benin, but its power as a state clearly declined for the important cities of Owu and Ilesha, neither of which owed allegiance to the Oni, were able to establish themselves within thirty miles of its city walls. Bradbury has suggested that the rise of Benin and Oyo coincided with the decline of Ife 'as an effective political empire, though it has retained its primacy as a religious metropolis and the source of true divine kingship to the present'.[17] In Benin to this day on the coronation of an Oba, his cheeks are chalked with Yoruba tribal marks, which are subsequently erased, whilst the Oba of Benin were given token burial in Ife. Willett recently excavated the 'graveyard' of the Oba of Benin, in Ife, known as 'the heaven of the kings of Benin'. Even the Alafin of Oyo, as Akinjogbin has shown, was sanctioned in office by the Oni of Ife (see page 115).

The provincial kingdoms and towns differed somewhat in their organization from that of Oyo. Each town was an entity in itself, ruled by an Oba who was supplied by one of the sections of the ruling lineages. In the smaller towns, all the non-ruling lineages supplied chiefs, who together with heads of various cults and societies formed a council which exercised considerable control over the acts of the Oba. Since most lineages as well as associations, whether political or religious, were represented on the council the people of the town had a voice in their government.[18]

The history of the Yoruba before the eighteenth century is extremely vague, the only available source for it at present being Johnson's *History of the Yorubas*, written at the end of the nineteenth century. It is said that there is a Hausa history of the Yoruba extant in Katsina, but as yet this is not available. It would provide interesting material for checking the validity of Johnson's statements about the period before the eighteenth century, since it was written at that time. What follows is necessarily a paraphrase of Johnson's record of the Alafins of Oyo.

The first period of the Oyo Empire deals with what must be termed the legendary kings. Its history is further obscured by the fact that several of the early Alafins were deified, and new, more dramatic legends woven around them.

Oranmiyan, founder of Oyo, son or grandson of Oduduwa, and direct ancestor of the present Alafin who is forty-third in line of succession,[19] was succeeded by his son, Ajaka, who was so mild a ruler that the provincial kings encroached on his lands, and the people dethroned him. His successor Sango is one of the most glamorous figures in Yoruba tradition. He brought ruin on himself and his family by playing with magic. At the time of Sango's reign the supremacy of Oyo was by no means recognized by the other Yoruba kings, particularly the Olowu of Owu, and it was Sango who apparently subjugated this important monarch. Sango's downfall came through his fascination with magic. One day, so the story goes, he used a preparation to summon lightning, and thereby destroyed his own house and most of his wives and children. Either because of discontent among the people about his dangerous interferences with the forces of magic, or because of his desolation at the loss of his family, he hanged himself. He was then deified as the God of Thunder and Lightning, and today is recognized as one of the most important gods with followers all over Yorubaland.

Ajaka came out of retirement to rule once more. He is said to have waged war against the Nupe, as well as against many of his provincial kings. It is interesting that Yoruba tradition tells of contact between these early kings and both Nupe and Hausa. Indeed there is strong reason to suppose that from an early stage Hausa and Yoruba traded with each other. Johnson himself writes that 'Light and civilization with the Yorubas came from the North . . . the centres of life and activity of large populations and industry were in the interior'.[20]

Johnson writes that the Alafin who succeeded Ajaka can be described as 'historical'. However, we are still very much in the realm of legend. An important successor of Ajaka was Kori who was responsible for the founding of the large town of Ede. The Ijesha were interfering with his subjects, on the borders of their own territory, so Timi, a famous hunter, was sent almost as a marcher lord to defend the Alafin's interests, which suggests that the outlying Yoruba provinces were far from being subject to the Alafin at that time. Timi established himself successfully at Ede, but refused to send Kori his rightful dues on the caravans trading with Benin. He therefore sent the Gbonka, one of his army commanders and a leading member of the Esho, or praetorian guard, to deal with Timi, in the secret hope that Timi would kill him. However it was the Gbonka who killed Timi and on his triumphal return he forced Alafin Kori to commit suicide.

The first king whose reign can be placed with any degree of probability in relation to other known events in the history of Nigeria is Onigbogi. It was during his reign that Nupe invaded Yorubaland and actually destroyed Old Oyo. Dr. S. F. Nadel in his study of the Nupe people says that the reign of Tsoede, who conquered and refounded Nupe, can be placed about

1531, though this date has no definite accuracy, especially since he is said to have reigned for 128 years.²¹ Mr. Morton-Williams has suggested *c.* 1516 on the long scale and *c.* 1549²² on the short scale for the destruction of Old Oyo by Nupe, which is usually credited to Tsoede. So with some certainty the reign of Onigbogi can be placed in the first half of the sixteenth century. Even before Tsoede's reign Nupe appears to have been a powerful state. Tsoede was supposed to have been a son of the Ata of Igala whose capital, Idah, was on the river Niger.²³ Bronze casting is said to have been introduced by him from Idah, where the art had been learnt from Benin. However, the famous Tada (Nupe) bronzes which Tsoede is said to have brought with him from Idah, are stylistically closer to those of Ife, and the seated figure is probably the finest work of art to have been found in Nigeria.²⁴

It was left to Onigbogi's successor, Ofinran, to lead his people back towards Oyo. His son, the Aremo, Egunoju, continued the return from exile, for Ofinran died *en route*. It seems fairly evident that Oyo was destroyed by the Nupe for Egunoju founded a new town called Oyo Igboho, where he buried his father.²⁵ Four kings reigned at the new capital over a period of some fifty years or more. Evidently life was not very secure there, for these kings were all engaged in continuous wars with the Nupe and Borgu. However, Egunoju's successor, who was his brother, Orompotu (who may possibly have been a woman) defeated Borgu decisively. It was left to his successor, Ajiboyede, a son of Egunoju, to drive back the Nupe in a battle in which the Oyo captured the Nupe Etsu. During his reign there was celebrated the first recorded 'Bere' or festival to mark a long and successful reign after which peace should be maintained for a period of three years in Yorubaland. Unfortunately the king's favourite son died shortly after the end of this festival. Stricken with grief the king received the sympathies of his courtiers and nobles only to find them with hands fresh from eating. He accused them of feigning their condolences, since he, the king, had not eaten for days, and ordered their execution. The people were angered by this tyrannical act and only the intervention of a Moslem preacher from Nupe saved him from insurrection. The impact of the remonstrances of the Moslem priest was apparently so effective that the king apologized to

61

the people publicly for his wickedness. Reference to the presence of a Moslem preacher from Nupe may be significant, for Islam had first penetrated Hausaland on a large scale in the fifteenth century and was probably spreading southward by the end of the sixteenth century.

Abipa, who succeeded Ajiboyede, was also a son of Egunoju. It was he who moved the capital to Oyo against opposition from those who had by now established themselves firmly on the farms of the new land. But Abipa was adamant, and the capital was transferred to its original site, where it remained until its abandonment in *c.* 1837.

Little of interest is recorded about the Alafin who ruled at Oyo until the reign of Ojigi, ninth Alafin to rule there after the return from exile. It may have been he, or one of his predecessors called Ajogbu, who made war on Dahomey and attacked Porto Novo in 1698.[26] With him we enter a phase of Oyo history about which it is possible to write with more certainty (see Chapter VII).

Like Oyo, the new Benin kingdom developed its own complex administration of title-holders and palace officials. There was undoubtedly contact between Oyo and Benin, if not through their marcher towns, certainly through Ife, which they both treated as their spiritual home. Caravans probably moved from Benin up to Oyo and the north, or westwards along the edge of the forest belt.

The first king of the Ife dynasty in Benin was Oranmiyan's son, Eweka I, whose reign probably commenced in about 1300.[27] At that time Benin was administered by a group of chiefs or Enogie, with direct responsibility to the Oba. This was obviously part of the indigenous system of administration, for the father of Eweka's mother was a powerful Onogie. Eweka consolidated his hold on the land by appointing his children Enogie in the various villages of the Benin kingdom. He also set up a state council of six hereditary members who became, in effect, kingmakers. At first, the principle of succession by primogeniture was not established in Benin as it is today,[28] and Eweka I was succeeded by one of his elder sons, who was in turn succeeded by his brother. It was his son Ewedo who decided to transfer the capital from Usama to its present site, so as to be rid of the councillors of state, whose powers were becoming almost as great as his own. When he reached the city of Benin he was attacked and prevented from entering it by Ogiamwe, a successor of the administrator of Benin who had reluctantly allowed Oranmiyan to rule over Benin. A battle ensued in which the new Oba overcame Ogiamwe. This victory is celebrated in a Benin coronation ritual, where the Oba and the representatives of Ogiamwe do mock battle.[29] This evidence could bear out the theory that the tradition which portrays the people of Benin inviting the Oni of Ife to send over a ruler was mere convenience to disguise conquest as more dramatically represented by the Oba's defeat of Ogiamwe, possibly a later leader of resistance to the new dynasty. Installed in his new palace, the Oba gradually but effectively reduced the power of the kingmakers. It is said that he changed the name of the country from Ile-Ibinnu to Ubini (Benin). Ewedo was succeeded by his second son Oguola. To him is attributed the introduction of the practice of making brass castings for the preservation of the record of events. Little is known of the reigns of his two eldest sons Edoni and Udagbedo. Ohen, his third son, succeeded him. It is said that he was paralysed, and to conceal this from his councillors, he was carried into the council chamber before meetings and always left last. However, the Iyase, through whom he made all communications to his councillors and subjects, discovered this, and since a crippled Oba could not reign the Iyase was murdered lest he divulge the secret. This angered the people, who rebelled and eventually stoned the Oba to death.

Benin reached its apogee in the fifteenth and sixteenth centuries. In A.D. *c.* 1440 Uwaifiokun usurped the throne from Ogun, the rightful heir. Ogun murdered him shortly after, and took the title of Ewuare. He extended the empire to the west banks of the Niger and became known as Ewuare the Great. He also enlarged the city of Benin. His rule was unpopular and many citizens are said to have migrated to other lands beyond his jurisdiction. This is possibly the source of some of the traditions of Benin origin of neighbouring tribes like the Urhobo, Western Ijaw, Western Ibo and Onitsha Ibo. An examination of the form of monarchy of these states suggests close relationship with Benin which could have come about through migration, culture contact or through the installation of a ruling class from Benin.

Ewuare it was who changed Benin's name to Edo in memory of a faithful slave who had saved him from being murdered when Uwaifiokun usurped the throne. Under Ewuare, carving in both ivory and wood was greatly encouraged. Indeed his reign, the last before the arrival of the Europeans, is remembered in Benin as one of the greatest in its long history. The kingdom was highly organized, backed by a large and efficient army, which gave it control of a large area of the coast.

The Oba was the focus of both the political and religious life of the empire, participating in an incredible number of elaborate rituals,[30] considering that he also had to govern an increasingly more powerful empire. Checks to the Oba's power came from two groups, the Uzama, or hereditary kingmakers, and the town chiefs. The Uzama were either descendants of the original chiefs who invited Oranmiyan to become King, or those followers who came with him. The Town Chiefs were led by the Iyase, who acted as the Oba's chief adviser. There was frequent friction between the Oba on the one hand and the Town Chiefs and the Uzama on the other. It appears that the Palace Chiefs were created as a counterbalancing force that would remain dependent on the Oba, though they did not often attend the Council.

It is interesting to note how the Obas of Benin solved the problem of administering the outlying parts of the Empire through chiefs without encountering the problem of disloyalty as did so many other African kings. Chiefs were not given single blocks of territory, but a series of villages scattered in different parts of the Empire, so that they could not build a coherent base for revolt.[31]

Benin's influence extended as far as Idah and Lagos, which was a Benin colony. Its economy was such as to allow not only for the production of sacred carvings such as one finds in the small headless societies of Nigeria, but for a great deal of secular art, such as superbly carved ornaments, bells, lamp-holders, doors and pillars, many of which are now scattered throughout the museums of the world.[32] It seems then that Benin city, with its complex system of defensive walls,[33] its large army, its hierarchy of chiefs, its elaborate court ceremonial, must have been based on something more than subsistence agriculture. It probably carried on considerable trade with its immediate neighbours, as

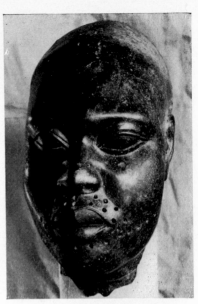

1. Nok terracotta: 'The Jemaa Head'

2. Ife bronze: head of an Oni of Ife

3. Benin bronze: a Portuguese soldier

4. Igbo bronze: detail of drinking vessel

5. Captain Hugh Crow: a Liverpool slaver

6. Survival of the Slave Trade: a priestess of the Yoruba god
Shango in Bahia, Brazil

well as Oyo and the northern states. Possibly it supplied slaves for the Hausa markets, though we have no definite evidence of this. What is remarkable about Benin, and indeed Oyo, is that both of them were purely African states, whose growth was stimulated neither by contact with Islam nor Europe.

CHAPTER IV

The Atlantic Slave Trade

Ewuare the Great may have been the first Oba of Benin to meet a European. According to Antonio Galvão, Ruy de Sequiera reached Benin in 1472 during his reign. However, it is more likely that the first European to visit Benin was João Affonso d'Aveiro who reached Benin in 1486. Whichever was the first, the encounter marked a turning-point in Nigerian history. Until the arrival of the Europeans the coast had been of little significance in the politics of West Africa. Benin and Oyo both looked to the interior for their trade. The creeks of the Atlantic littoral had been inhabited only by a few small fishing communities. Contact with the outside world was across the great Sahara desert. Benin and Oyo were probably the ultimate destinations of the trans-Sahara caravans. The arrival of the Portuguese in Benin marked the first stage in the complete reorientation of the economy of Nigeria, culminating in the establishment of the British Protectorate over Northern Nigeria in 1900–6 when trans-Saharan trade gave way to the speedier export of goods by road and rail through the ports of the Atlantic coast.

Until the fifteenth century Africa, south of the Sahara, had remained unknown to Europe. Nevertheless, in classical times there are references to voyages beyond Cape Bojador. Herodotus recorded that Phoenician mariners successfully circumnavigated the continent, returning through the Pillars of Hercules *c.* 612 B.C. He also mentions Carthaginian trade in gold with West Africa. There are references made to a visit of Hanno the Carthaginian to West Africa in *c.* 500 B.C.

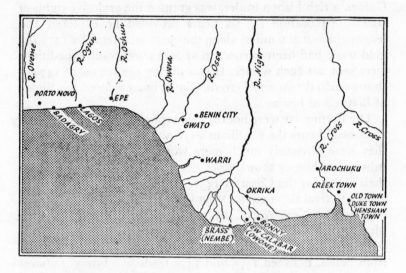

3. Nigeria's slave-trading ports, sixteenth to eighteenth centuries

These voyages are all of historical interest but had little bearing on Portuguese decisions to venture beyond Cape Bojador.[1] It was known even before the fifteenth century that somewhere in the hinterland of the Maghreb gold was obtained by the Arabs from Negro peoples. This gold was then sold on the European markets. Not unnaturally Europeans wanted to gain direct access to the source of supply so that they could avoid using the Arabs as middlemen. Furthermore, nations like Portugal and Spain were interested in finding a sea route to India, which would likewise save them from trading for Indian goods through Arab intermediaries. These two economic motives, combined with the hope that a Christian king would be found in tropical Africa as an ally in the struggles against Islam and the desire to further geographical understandings, led Prince Henry of Portugal, known better as Henry the Navigator, to equip expeditions to sail beyond Cape Bojador and attempt to discover a new route to India. By 1462 as a result of his enthusiasm and imagination most of the coast from Senegal to Sierra Leone had been opened up to trade with Europe. After his death in 1462 Portuguese enthusiasm for exploration lost something of its initial ardour. In 1469, however, Fernão

Gomes, a rich Lisbon trader, was granted the exclusive rights of coastal exploration for six years provided he explored 100 leagues (about 400 miles) along the coast each year. By 1471 the gold trade had been opened up at Mina and trade expeditions were sent out each winter. It was during the winter of 1472–3 that Fernão do Po and Pero de Cintra first explored the Bights of Biafra and Benin.

The Portuguese were not the sole explorers of the Coast, since their neighbours the Castilians were always on their heels. And they were obviously much more worried by this rivalry than subsequent history shows, since they secured Papal Bulls about their rights on the Coast in 1451, 1455 and 1456. Castile only ceased to rival them on the West Coast after Columbus had discovered the New World. By 1480 the Portuguese had completed their exploration of the West Coast and were able to settle down to its fruits, mainly in gold from Mina and peppers from Benin. Between 1475 and 1479 trade was brought almost to a standstill by the war between Portugal and Castile. England also appears to have profited from this, for in 1481 an embassy was sent by John II of Portugal to Edward IV of England to request that he restrain his subjects from trading in West Africa, over which Portugal had a monopoly by virtue of its Papal Bull.

In 1483 John II declared himself Lord of Guinea, but in reality his hold over the lands to which he so proudly claimed title was non-existent. The Portuguese were only established at strategic points on the Coast by virtue of treaties with local kings. Apart from hostility on the part of these kings to any penetration inland, there were all the difficulties of climate and disease that were to make later attempts at penetration of the interior so hazardous. Furthermore the Portuguese, hotly rivalled by other European powers, found it easier to concentrate on the erection of stout forts, at which goods could be received and defended against marauders, rather than acquire extensive territory which they were in no position to defend.

Portuguese trade with Benin was largely effected from the small island of São Thomé, where a Portuguese settlement was established. Indeed as early as 1485 John II gave authority to the people of São Thomé to trade with Benin, where peppers were a much-prized commodity. São Thomé, where early attempts at settlement were far from successful, found that Benin could supply its greatest want: a labour force, for it had no indigenous population. Soon Benin was exporting Negroes to work on the plantations of São Thomé. Later it was discovered that by exporting slaves from Benin to Mina huge profits could be made, since gold merchants were prepared to pay for them at twice their original cost. The demand for slaves on São Thomé increased after 1493 when colonization of the island was started with deported Portuguese Jews, exiles and convicts. Thus began one of the most remarkable forced migrations in history, whereby the pattern of the world's population was radically altered. The slave trade which followed close on the first visits to West Africa—slaves were on sale in Lisbon as early as 1441—was to make the Negro race second only to the Europeans in their dispersion over the world's surface.

The Portuguese built a factory, as trading stations on the Coast were known, at Gwato, the port of Benin, to handle the pepper trade and to purchase slaves. Fortunately through the establishment of this factory we have some amount of information about ancient Benin, though it is often far from accurate. Benin was quickly recognized by the Portuguese as one of the most important kingdoms on the Coast and the King of Benin sent an ambassador to Portugal in the reign of King John II (1481–95). In return Portugal sent missionaries and factors (trading agents), together with many presents for the King. The King himself showed little enthusiasm for the new religion, though he ordered his son and some of his chiefs to become Christians. He also ordered a church to be built.

Pina, a contemporary chronicler, records the visit of the Benin ambassador thus:

'This ambassador was a man of good speech and natural wisdom. Great feasts were held in his honour, and he was shown many of the good things of these kingdoms. He returned to his land in a ship of the King's, who at his departure made him a gift of rich clothes for himself and his wife: and through him he also sent a rich present to the king of such things as he understood he would greatly prize. Moreover, he sent holy and most catholic advisers with praiseworthy admonitions for the faith to administer a stern rebuke about the heresies and great idolatries and fetishes, which the Negroes practise in that land.'[2]

Early optimism about the value of the pepper trade with Benin was damped and by 1510 trade with Benin was almost exclusively in slaves. This was to be the pattern for the next three hundred and fifty years, when trade in the natural products of West Africa finally ousted that in humans. Slaves were normally sent over to São Thomé where they joined large caravels, packed with men from the Congo and Mina, and sailed to their destinations.

From the start, however, there was considerable intercourse between the Bini and Portuguese. The Portuguese taught some of them to read, and in 1553 Captain Windham was surprised to find that the King of Benin 'could speak the Portugal tongue, which he learned of a child'.[3]

To this day a section of the Benin royal palace speaks a language quite unintelligible to the ordinary Bini, which is allegedly derived from Portuguese. That the King of Benin greatly impressed the Portuguese is clear from the report of the Portuguese representative, Duarte Pires, to King Manuel from Benin, 20th October 1516.

'. . . he pays us high honour and sets us at table to dine with his son, and no part of the court is hidden from us but all the doors are open. Sir, when these priests arrived in Benin, the delight of the king of Benin was so great that I do not know how to describe it, and likewise that of all his people; and he sent for them at once; and they remained with him for one whole year in war. The priests and we reminded him of the embassy of your highness, and he replied to us that he was very satisfied with it; but since he was at war, that he could do nothing until he returned to Benin, because he needed leisure for such a deep mystery as this; as soon as he was in Benin, he would fulfil his promise to your highness, and he would so behave as to give great pleasure to your highness, and to all your kingdom. So it was, at the end of one year, in the month of August, the king gave his son and some of his noblemen—the greatest in his kingdom—so that they might become Christians; and also he ordered a church to be built in Benin; and they made them Christians straightway; and also they are teaching them to read, and your highness will be pleased to know that they are very good learners. . . .'[4]

Some twenty-five years later, a Portuguese navigator wrote

that the men taken as slaves were mainly captives of war, or sometimes children sold by their parents in the hopes that they might find a more profitable life elsewhere. He also gives an interesting account of the burial of the King of Benin, though its accuracy cannot be vouched for since he states in the same account that most Negroes live to 100 years old. He was also quick to observe the divine status of the Benin kings:

'The Kings are worshipped by their subjects, who believe they come from heaven and speak of them always with great reverence, at a distance and on bended knees. Great ceremony surrounds them, and many of these kings never allow themselves to be seen eating, so as not to destroy the belief of their subjects that they can live without food. . . .'[5]

After 1520 few Portuguese lived for any length of time in the Niger region, and their agencies were held by half-castes or Africans able to speak Portuguese. The main reason for decline in direct trade with Benin was the growth of Asian trade and the creation of better bases at Fernando Po and São Thomé.

The hazards of West African trade are well brought out in Richard Eden's account of Windham's voyage to Benin in 1553,[6] at a time when Portuguese monopoly of the West Coast trade was already being whittled away by rival European powers. Eden describes a visit to the King of Benin. 'They were brought with a great company to the presence of the king, who being a black Moore (although not so black as the rest) sat in a great huge hall, long and wide, with walls made of earth, without windows, the roofs of thin boorde, open in sundry places, like unto lovers to let in the aire.'

They traded successfully with the king, who straight away offered them the thirty to forty hundredweight of peppers in his own store, and promised to gather enough to fill all their ships within thirty days. He did this, collecting the phenomenal amount of eighty tons. But the crew drank too much palm wine and caught fevers. Most of them died. So Windham sailed without out the pepper, full haste to avoid further disaster, leaving several of his crew behind including one Nicholas Lambert, a son of the Lord Mayor of London. This was one of the last of the major pepper expeditions. It also marked the end of Portuguese monopoly of trade on the West Coast.

From then on England was to establish herself not only as a

leading trader on the Coast, but as one of the chief exporters of slaves, a trade profitable both to Africans and Europeans, though bringing with it untold human misery and degradation.

Conservative estimates put the total number of slaves exported from West Africa and Angola as high as 24,000,000, of which probably only 15,000,000 survived the notorious Middle Passage across the Atlantic.[7] In the sixteenth century about 1,000,000 slaves were transported to the Americas, in the seventeenth century, some 3,000,000, and in the eighteenth century some 7,000,000 or 70,000 a year. Of these about 22,000 were shipped annually from ports in Nigeria. Benin and its colony of Lagos sent about 4,000 and the ports of Bonny, New Calabar and Old Calabar, which grew up directly in response to European demands for slaves, together with the Cameroons sent some 18,000. Even in the nineteenth century, when many major European powers had abolished slavery, and when the British Navy patrolled the coast of Africa, another 4,000,000 slaves were taken across the Atlantic. Many of these came from Yorubaland, where civil war produced thousands of captives to be sold into slavery.[8]

The stimulus to this colossal traffic in human beings was the discovery of the Americas and the realization of their mineral and agricultural wealth. In 1580 the union between Portugal and Spain opened up the West Coast, hitherto a Portuguese monopoly, to the country with a monopoly of the New World. Spain's policy of settling and developing the New World and her stake in West Coast trade greatly stimulated the sale of slaves in West Africa. Both in the West Indies and on the mainland the Spaniards found that the indigenous inhabitants, with the exception of the Indians of Mexico and Peru, were unable to adapt themselves to the new conditions imposed on them by their conquerors, particularly by succumbing to newly introduced European diseases. In the West Indies the establishment of Spanish rule led to the extinction of nearly the entire indigenous population. This was repeated on the mainland to which the Spaniards moved after the exhaustion of the West Indies mines. There was not enough labour available or willing to leave Europe and live in these new lands, so that when it was found that Africans survived well in the climate, and moreover were adaptable both to working in mines and on plantations, the slave trade that had been carried on in a desultory way at the beginning of the sixteenth century received tremendous new impetus. The settlement of North America and the West Indies in the early seventeenth century by Britain and France led to further demands for slaves, especially with the development of sugar-cane plantations in the mid century. In 1637 the Dutch, who had thrown off the Spanish yoke in 1572, conquered Brazil, and in order to supply the already established Portuguese planters with slaves, set about capturing West Coast slaving forts. In addition to these major slaving powers, supplying slaves to their own colonies, there were the purely commercial slavers like the Brandenburgers and Danes who sold to the highest bidders. During the seventeenth century the Dutch were the leading slavers, followed by the Portuguese. But after the Treaty of Utrecht in 1713 Britain and France took control of the traffic, the French mainly operating on the upper Guinea Coast. The British who had acquired the Spanish monopoly of the slave trade under the terms of the treaty were rivalled by the Dutch on the lower Guinea Coast. The British were particularly strong in the Niger Delta ports, where a corrupt form of English became the language of the slave dealers. Liverpool and Bristol owe their growth at that time to the profits of the slave trade.

Thus in the seventeenth and eighteenth century the West Coast of Africa became a centre of European enterprise and rivalry with slaves as the prize. There was only one means by which the Europeans could ensure the supply of slaves, and that was to obtain the co-operation of the local population. In certain instances it was feasible to make raids on sea and riverside villages, but the small number of slaves captured by these methods never justified the huge expenditure in fitting up a ship to go to the West Coast. It was impossible for the Europeans to penetrate inland, not only because of the tight control the local rulers had on their territories, but also because of the diseases to which they were subjected. It was also in the interests of the coastal middlemen to prevent the European from penetrating inland and trading direct with the slave-supplying areas. African chiefs were not only reluctant to hand over land to European traders, but were also prevented from doing so by customary law whereby, in most cases, land belonged corporately to the people. In such circumstances the European and

African slave dealers soon established friendly relations to further their mutual interests.

The slave traffic raised surprisingly few objections in the minds of either Africans or Europeans. The Europeans, of course, conveniently salved their Christian consciences by suggesting that in fact they were saving 'heathens' for Christendom. Anyway, on many occasions they had profits of the order of £5,000 to £10,000 a trip to dispel any qualms they might have felt. Moreover, the horrors of the Middle Passage were far from the sight of ordinary civilized people. To the African the idea of slavery was not foreign. Most tribes had some form of domestic slavery, though this was very different from that proposed by the Europeans. In the African system slaves, though of inferior status, had certain rights, whilst their owners had definite and often onerous duties towards them. In Bornu, for instance, the kings often sent slaves out to govern their provinces; Hausa kings often ruled through slaves; and in Yorubaland slaves of the Oba attained great power and were much feared by his subjects. In these states slaves had a special usefulness as recruits to high office, since they had no influential lineages behind them, and hence no pressures on them that could be potentially opposed to their ruler's interest. They were also utterly dependent on their ruler, and as slaves could attract no following among the freeborn. In some states eunuchs held similar positions.

Once slavery had been instituted it was hopeless to expect those Africans who profited from it to have any more conscience about it than the Europeans who bought slaves, especially since in this case the Africans were not usually selling their own people, but members of other tribes whom they often considered not only inferior, but also only fit to be slaves. When they did sell their own people it was usually because they were criminals. Thus thieves in Iboland were usually punished by being sold into slavery. A parallel to this can of course be seen in the English system of transporting convicts to Australia. Normally prices for slaves were high, since demand invariably exceeded supply, though occasionally when there were few ships, the price of slaves dropped. The slavers usually anchored some distance away from the slave port, and most of the negotiations were conducted on board after customary presents had been given to the local chief. Slaves would be brought out by canoe and the traders would then present them to the ship's surgeon for inspection; those rejected were as often as not murdered on the spot.

In exchange for slaves the Europeans brought a large and varied list of goods, whose popularity differed along the Coast. James Welsh, who visited Benin in 1588 on a trading voyage, lists the following items they carried for trade: linen, woollen cloth, iron bars, copper bracelets, or manillas, glass beads and coral.[9] This was not a slaving voyage, and they bought in exchange ivory, palm oil, pepper, cotton cloth. He also reported that cowries were the local form of currency. A century or so later James Barbot visited Bonny where the rate of exchange for slaves was thirteen iron bars for a male slave, nine for females.[10] In 1703–4 the price of slaves in nearby New Calabar was twelve bars for a man and nine for a woman. Often media for the purchase of slaves were copper bars, beads of various sorts, brass belts, cloths, ox horns for drinking cups, pewter tankards, spirits and blue linen.[11]

On board ship the lot of the slaves was terrible. Crammed into the holds of the ships, men slaves were shackled to each other by chains. There was hardly room to move. It was almost impossible for them to excrete, other than where they were lying, so that dysentery soon became rife. Each day the slaves were taken on deck for exercise and left there till evening. The women, boys and men were all separated. The ship's officers had the right to use any woman slave. Strongest precautions were made against attempts at suicide by jumping overboard. If conditions were frightful for the slaves they were almost as bad for the wretched sailors, many of whom were press-ganged into service on the slavers with contracts that forbade them to complain subsequently about their ill-treatment. About a sixth of the slaves transhipped died; probably a greater proportion of the sailors did, being whipped for the slightest fault by sadistic captains who seemed to make a speciality of the slave trade. Not all slaving captains were of this character. For instance, Captain Hugh Crow from Liverpool was a more thoughtful master, priding himself on delivering his slaves all fit and alive. He was a close friend of King Pepple of Bonny.[12]

The English captains did not always have it their own way. On many occasions slaves revolted on board, for they often outnumbered Europeans ten to one. On the Bonny River a group of slaves just carried aboard an English ship took advantage of the bargaining between the captains and the local chiefs for further supplies of slaves, seized the ship's arms and over-powered the crew. This is one reason for the barbarity of the instruments of torture or discipline kept on the ship. The men were usually all chained together, though on one occasion women, who were allowed the freedom of the deck, saw the armoury unlocked and swiftly passed arms to their men, and together they seized the ship. The lot of the slave was little improved when he reached his destination, especially in the British West Indian colonies, where many of the slaves from the Delta ports were sent. The method of sale today seems almost comic, except when one puts oneself in the place of the slave. Those who looked about to die were quickly sold at cheap prices to surgeons; the healthy ones were often sold at what was called a 'scramble'. They were enclosed in a pen, obscured from the public view. Prospective buyers paid an agreed price, and were then let into the pen to seize the best they could. The terror of the wretched negroes as a horde of white men rushed amongst them, grabbing them as quickly and in as great a number as they could, can easily be imagined. No one ever thought to warn them of the method of their sale, which, compared with that of the African markets, must have appeared utterly bar-baric. Indeed the barbarism of the West Indian colonies was incredible; for misdemeanour on these islands the slaves were subject to the most inhuman of punishments. Trivial offences might mean an ear lopped off, a hand axed, a tongue or nose slit. 'No slave to be buried after sunset,' reads one of the laws. 'Nor in any other than a plain deal board coffin, without covering; nor shall scarfs and favours be worn at any of their funerals. The punishment for transgressing to be 50 lashes, and the scarfs, etc., to be forfeited.' Of course, such laws were largely a result of fear of slave revolts such as took place in Brazil, Havana, some of the French West Indian colonies and Jamaica itself.

It is interesting to follow up what happened to the many Nigerians who were forcibly settled in the New World. On the whole they soon lost their tribal identities, especially in those territories where families were broken up indiscriminately and where no consideration was given to the welfare of the slaves. It was difficult for a group in the British West Indies to retain its identity when, as we have seen, common participation even in a funeral, was forbidden. Different tribes reacted differently to the new situation. The Ibo, for instance, were not highly organized like the Yoruba. Their largest unit of government was the village group, and though the domination of the Aro Chukwu oracle gave them some political and religious unity, there was little common ground between Ibo from villages fifty miles apart. It must be remembered, too, that a large number of slaves from Ibo territory were already slaves, who had offended their masters and been sent to the Aro Chukwu oracle or else were outcasts from their own societies. It was almost impossible to take Ibo of high status with the Ozo title as slaves, since they always committed suicide. Thus it is not surprising that a decentralized people like the Ibo did not retain their cultural individuality under the oppressive slave system. This was not the case with the Yoruba, who were not usually captured individually as in the east but as the result of wars, which might cause a large number from the same town to be transported. It must be remembered also that they were shipped through the ports where the Portuguese and Spanish purchased their slaves, and many of them found their way to Brazil, Cuba and Trinidad, where their masters were less oppressive in their attitude, especially with regard to the possibility of slaves practising their own religions. This was far from being an altruistic concession in Brazil, for the government permitted and indeed encouraged the maintenance of cultural traditions, thinking that thus, on the classic formula of divide and rule, they could preserve the ethnic identity of various groups and prevent Africans of various tribes uniting in their misery against them. The Governor of the state of Bahia, writing in the early nineteenth century, said: 'These feelings of animosity between tribes may be regarded as the best guarantee for the security of large towns in Brazil.'[13]

This finds a modern parallel in South Africa, where the official policy of the Nationalist Government has been to emphasize tribal differences to prevent Africans uniting against them.

On the other hand the African as such was not despised by the Latin races, and indeed many slaves attained their freedom and became powerful traders long before the eventual abolition of the trade there in the late nineteenth century. Miscegenation frowned on in British and French territories, was the general rule in Brazil where, as to a lesser extent in Cuba, traditions of the Yoruba in particular survived, since they were one of the major ethnic groups there. Today there has developed in Bahia and other towns that were based on a slave economy a syncretistic religion combining elements of the Catholic and Yoruba religion. Yoruba from Nigeria can still recognize the religious ceremonies practised by their cousins in Brazil. In Cuba, Efik and Ibibio slaves re-created Egbo, whose membership included both black and white. In Haiti Voodoo is a survival of traditional African religions.[14]

A further feature of this cultural interchange between Nigeria and Brazil was the repatriation of large groups of slaves who revolted against the government. Between 1807 and 1813 the Moslems, chiefly Hausa, revolted against not only their white masters but also fellow-Africans who were not Moslems. This was undoubtedly an extension of the Holy War being fought in Northern Nigeria at that time by the Fulani, and is an indication of the close contacts between Nigeria and the New World. Moslem Africans who had been liberated and had become wealthy also joined the revolt. The last of these revolts took place in 1835 and resulted in the expulsion of all the Moslem freed slaves, many of whom returned to Lagos. This started a more general return movement which included Christians too. Verger has written: 'These were those who established themselves in those parts of Lagos still known as the Brazilian Quarter ... where ... they built houses like those they used to build in Brazil. ...'[15]

CHAPTER V

Niger Delta States

The slave trade had marked effects on the political structure of the Niger Delta and its hinterland, where a large proportion of the slaves exported from Nigeria were procured. Before the arrival of the Portuguese the Delta seems to have been inhabited mainly by the Ijo peoples, who lived in small, scattered fishing villages in the tidal zone. Most of these Ijo communities have a history of moving down from the northwest, several claiming that they migrated from Benin, or rather away from Benin domination. But these legends refer to a period well before the opening up of coastal trade. These early southward movements, whatever their causes, were unrelated to the slave-trade; possibly they referred to some upheaval in the early Benin Empire.

The arrival of slave-traders in the Delta stimulated the growth of a number of trading states, which were in effect expanded versions of small Ijo fishing villages that happened to occupy favourable positions on the creeks of the Niger Delta.[1] The most important among these were Bonny, Owome (New Calabar), Okrika, whose origins can be traced to the early seventeenth century, and Brass (Nembe), which only became a major slave-trading state in the early nineteenth century.[2] Farther down the Coast at the mouth of the Cross River, the Efik trading state of Old Calabar was also organized to meet European demands for slaves. In the western Delta the Itsekiri kingdom of Warri, closely related to Benin, became another major source of supply for slaves.

Before the arrival of the Europeans the Ijo of the Eastern Delta lived in villages ranging from two hundred to about a thousand inhabitants. Their villages were divided into a number of wards or 'houses', each representing a patrilineage.

The 'head' of the village was the *amanyanabo*, title to which was usually vested in one particular lineage, though in some villages the amanyanabo was elected by the ward heads. The amanyanabo's functions were largely ritual, though he did preside over the village assembly, which consisted of all adult males. The ward heads were usually chosen on the grounds of age, but ward members of exceptional political or economic ability could aspire to the office over someone of greater age. Cutting across allegiance to the house were such ties as membership of age-sects and dancing societies, and relationship with kin outside the patrilineage.

The Ijo traded with the peoples of the hinterland who were mainly Ibo and Ibibio. The Ibibio, like the Ijo, lived in villages usually consisting of about five hundred inhabitants. Likewise they were presided over by a ward head whose election was determined by seniority. The Ibo lived in federated village groups numbering some five thousand inhabitants and the head of the ranking village was the 'president' of the group.[3] Some Ibo, however, lived in larger communities with more centralized political structures, such as Onitsha, which had come under the influence of Benin. Some, too, had attained high technological skill to which the beautiful Igbo bronzes bear witness. These are associated with the Eze of Nri, or priest-king of the Umieri clan, and have tentatively been dated as artefacts of the sixteenth or seventeenth century.[4]

The Ijo exported dried fish and salt, which they panned in the salt water creeks, to the peoples of the hinterland in exchange for vegetables and tools, particularly those made of iron. The pattern of this relationship was radically altered by the advent of the slave trade. The sparsely populated Ijo could not find slaves from among their own communities in sufficient quantities to satisfy European demands, even if they had been prepared to sell their own kin. They therefore looked to the more populous tribes of the hinterland, in particular the Ibo, as a source of supply. They not only brought slaves from Iboland and beyond for export, but also for use in their own communities. One of the most dramatic changes in these fishing villages was the rapid expansion of their population through the importation of slaves who were quickly assimilated into the community. Ijo culture was not, however, markedly affected by

7. Reception of the Denham-Clapperton Mission by the Sultan of Bornu

8. The Habe Tower in Katsina

9. Nigerian warriors in chain mail

10 (a), (b). Nigerian Explorers: Clapperton and Crowther, who later became Bishop on the Niger

11. Al-Kanemi, the ances of the present rulers of Bo nu. From a drawing by t explorer Denham, 1825

these involuntary immigrants because the trading states operated a ruthless system of assimilation whereby those slaves of ability could gain great power and prestige in society by observing its rules, whilst those who were unable to assimilate were relegated to the most menial tasks, were ill-treated and subject to severe punishments. Such arrangements have led Horton to describe Ijo society as a 'carrot and stick society'.[5]

The slave trade also changed the pattern of trade between the Ijo and their hinterland neighbours.[6] In exchange for the slaves the Europeans brought salt, used as ballast on the way out from Liverpool and Bristol, dried fish which came from Norway and new consumer goods such as cloth and tools. Probably most important of all, however, they brought firearms which enabled the Ijo states and their neighbours to dominate the trade. The peoples of the hinterland no longer sent their crafts down the coast in the same quantities as before, since tools from Europe were cheaper and better made. They did increase their sale of vegetables, however, since these were needed in greater quantities by the expanding fishing villages and by the European slavers to feed the slaves on the Middle Passage across the Atlantic.

Those Ijo fishing villages which were successful in gaining control of the slave trade with the Europeans underwent considerable internal changes in their social organization. First, their population expanded from small villages of a thousand inhabitants to sizeable towns of between five and ten thousand inhabitants. The new function of the community as an exporter of slaves in considerable quantities to the Europeans provided an increasing emphasis on individual economic ability as a means of achieving status in the system. Economic achievement rather than traditional status became the basis of political power in the community. While government in the fishing village had been carried on by an assembly of all adult males under the presidency of the amanyanabo, it was now effectively concentrated in the hands of the amanyanabo and the leading traders of the state. The amanyanabo, whose functions in the former order had been largely ritual, was now transformed into a hereditary monarch[7] and leading trader of the state. The most significant alteration in the Ijo community was the emphasis laid on the role of the house. In the fishing village loyalty to the house or ward did not exclude loyalty to other groups. But success in the slave trade necessitated the concentration of the loyalties of the people to their houses, for it was this unit which became the basis of productive activity in Ijo society.

The development of the importance of the house, and of house rule, which according to G. I. Jones[8] crystallized in the eighteenth century, is a striking example of the adaptability of an African society to a new economic and political situation. The house which has been named the canoe house to distinguish it from the house or ward of the fishing village was, as its new name suggests, based on the possession of a canoe, though one equipped for war. The house also possessed ordinary trading canoes for bringing slaves down from the markets of the interior. The canoe house consisted of a wealthy trader who was the head of the house, his children and all the slaves he owned. All his lineal descendants and slaves were members of the house. When he died, preference of succession was given to one of his own children, though a remarkable feature of these Ijo states was that a slave of outstanding ability could succeed to leadership. The new head of house was chosen by all freeborn and slave members of the house. The head of house exacted tax from other traders in the house. With this he was able to run the house and equip the war canoe, paddled by fifty men and with muskets and canon tied fore and aft. A great deal of capital was needed to maintain a canoe house because the head of house had not only to equip this war canoe but maintain the trading canoes which supplied his income. Because of the large amount of capital necessary to sustain this canoe house, there was a tendency to the concentration of economic and therefore political power in the hands of a few. The financial ability to equip a war canoe allowed a man to found a new canoe house. The head of an existing house always encouraged his members to branch off on their own, since this would give him extra voices in the assembly for these traders remained politically dependent on him, even though they now had their own voice in the affairs of the assembly. The head of house had a great deal of authority over his members, in certain cases even being able to settle cases of homicide. Any inter-house dispute became a matter for the town assembly.

The amanyanabo was the initiator of policy. He decided on the conduct of war, and led the battle fleet. He was expected to pay for the conduct of war, and to defray these expenses the town assembly agreed that from time to time he should have a complete monopoly of a particular trading article.

The system of house rule was encouraged by the European traders who preferred to trade through a few men with established reputations who could also vouch for the honesty of their subordinates. Some of these traders took on trust several thousand pounds' worth of goods to exchange for slaves in the interior.

This pattern of house rule was the most characteristic feature of these new trading states, including the non-Ijo states of Old Calabar and to a lesser extent Warri.[9] The organization of each state, however, differed considerably. Bonny, New Calabar and Warri were under a strong monarchical system, whilst political authority in Brass and Old Calabar was divided.

In Old Calabar, for example, there was no one supreme person, and ascendancy in the community shifted from the leading house of Duke Town to that of Creek Town. The real power in the community was the Egbo Society. This was a secret society to which only those of age and wealth could belong. Membership cost a considerable sum, but, once admitted, members shared in the proceeds of payments by other initiates. It gave out laws, settled disputes between various branches of the houses and collected debts. It was, thus, Egbo which in 1850, under European pressure, passed a law forbidding human sacrifices.

As G. I. Jones has written: '. . . Egbo was the sole authority capable of maintaining peace between the different groups or stopping fights and disturbances once they had broken out, since it alone could apply effective sanctions against offenders.'[10] In Bonny and New Calabar, by contrast, political authority lay with the king in council with his chiefs. In Bonny the monarchy dated back probably to the fifteenth century, and at the height of slave traffic in the eighteenth century the state was under the remarkably capable Pepple dynasty. However, his power was not absolute and, like most African kings, he was bound by restrictions of other important members of the community, in this case the house heads. The power of the various Delta states depended on their fast large war canoes.

The economy of all the Delta states was based on slaves not only for export but as the workers within the state. However, there was a considerable difference in the attitudes of the various states towards slaves. Old Calabar and New Calabar make a striking contrast in this respect. In New Calabar as we have already noted the main emphasis for membership of the state was acculturation, rather than descent from the founding ancestor of the house as it was amongst the Efik. Thus a slave who was successfully integrated into New Calabar could rise to the highest position of state. It was a capital offence to refer to a man as of slave origin. Again, the competition between the three Ijo trading towns of New Calabar, Bonny and Okrika, forced them to lay emphasis on ability as the major criterion for leadership if they were to survive in the fierce struggle for control of markets. Thus, at a later date in Bonny, when there was strife between two major factions in the state, a slave, Jaja, was able to establish a rival state of Opobo. In the New Calabar state the slaves lived in their masters' compounds, giving them little chance to organize themselves; in Old Calabar they were relegated to plantations, whilst the freeborn stayed in the towns, giving them ample opportunity to organize revolt. In New Calabar there were no slave revolts for only those slaves who were idle or stupid suffered oppression. In Old Calabar there was oppression of the slaves, not only through refusing to admit them to high status in the community, but also by excluding them from any participation in society. In addition once Egbo, the main instrument of government in Old Calabar, had unified the Efik settlements at the mouth of the Cross River the geographical insulation of their route to the markets eliminated the cut-throat competition with other states which would otherwise have turned attention to ability rather than pedigree in the selection of leaders.

James Barbot gives a good picture of trade conditions in the Delta states.[11]

'On the first of *July*, the King sent for us to come ashore, we staid there till four in the afternoon, and concluded the trade on the terms offered them the day before; the King promising to come the next day aboard to regulate it, and be paid his duties. . . .

'The second, heavy rain all the morning. At two o'clock we

fetch'd the King from shore, attended by all his *Caboceiros* and officers, in three large canoes; and entring the ship, was saluted with seven guns. The King had on an old fashion'd scarlet coat, laced with gold and silver, very rusty, and a fine hat on his head, but bare-footed; all his attendants showing great respect to him and, since our coming hither, none of the natives have dared to come aboard of us, or sell the least thing, till the King had adjusted trade with us.

'We had again a long discourse with the King and *Pepprell* his brother, concerning the rates of our goods and his customs. This *Pepprell*, being a sharp blade, and a mighty talking *Black*, perpetually making objections against something or other, and teasing us for this or that Dassy, or present, as well as for drams, etc., it were to be wish'd, that such a one as he were out of the way, to facilitate trade. . . .

'Thus, with much patience, all our matters were adjusted indifferently, after their way, who are not very scrupulous to find excuses or objections, for not keeping literally to any verbal contract; for they have not the art of reading and writing, and therefore we are forced to stand to their agreement, which often is no longer than they think fit to hold it themselves. . . .

'We gave the usual presents to the King, etc. . . . To Captain Forty, the King's general, Captain Pepprell, Captain Boileau, alderman Bougsby, my lord Willyby, duke of Monmouth, drunken Henry and some others two firelocks, eight hats, nine narrow Guinea stuffs. We adjusted with them the reduction of our merchandize into bars of iron, as the standard coin, viz: One bunch of beads, one bar. . . .

'The price of provisions and wood was also regulated.

'Sixty King's yams, one bar; one hundred and sixty slave's yams, one bar; for fifty thousand yams to be delivered to us. A butt of water, two rings. For the length of wood, seven bars, which is dear; but they were to deliver it ready cut into our boat. For a goat, one bar. A cow, ten or eight bars, according to its bigness. A hog, two bars. A calf, eight bars. A jar of palm oil, one bar and a quarter.

'We paid also the King's duties in goods; five hundred slaves, to be purchased at two copper rings a head.

'We also advanced to the King, by way of loan, the value of a hundred and fifty bars of iron, in sundry goods; and to his principal men, and others, as much again each in proportion to his quality and ability. . . .'

By the end of the eighteenth century, as Jones has shown,[12] the pattern of trade between the Ijo and the Europeans had become better regulated. The 'breaking of trade' or negotiation of terms had become a ritual since the system had over the years become standardized. Customs or 'Comey', paid by the Europeans to the Delta kings, had also become standardized, and by the beginning of the nineteenth century it had for example at Bonny been fixed at £150 per vessel, and at Old Calabar at £250. Even the ubiquitous dash, payable to various groups involved in the trade, had a fixed rate and was taken into account by buyer and seller when the price of exchange was settled.

Receipts from customs levied were shared among the amanyanabo, his chiefs and the villages along the creeks which connected it with its hinterland trading market, which also received a portion. The Ijo states therefore compromised not only the trading town, but also nearby dependent fishing villages, the villages along its trading creek, as well as the hinterland market, which was peopled by the Ibo or the Ibibio.

The supply of slaves to the Delta ports was controlled by the Aro of Arochuku, and in a land of politically decentralized people, they maintained a highly complex and centralized system of trade, coupled with religious-political domination. The power of the Aro, a sub-section of the Ibo peoples, was based on the universal respect of the peoples of Eastern Nigeria for the oracle known as the Long Juju, which was said to be Chukwu, the Ibo supreme deity.[13] Thus the Aro, who controlled the oracle which resided in a cave in their territory, commanded great respect among the Ibo and the Delta states. The Aro as representatives of the oracle settled in small colonies throughout the region, ostensibly as mediators between other tribes and the oracle. These colonies very quickly became trading colonies, hedged with religious sanction. In loosely organized Iboland the Aro were the only people who could safely travel from village to village unharmed. Thus Aro hegemony over Iboland, which was directly founded on the proceeds of the slave trade, provided the mechanism of communication over long distances in Iboland where none had existed before: one could now travel in the company of a recognized Aro agent, a guarantee of safe conduct. The Aro colonies were sited on the main trading routes, and along them passed slaves for the Delta ports. The Delta rulers found the oracle a convenient buttress to community discipline. Slaves would be threatened with being sent to the oracle, where it was believed certain death would follow, though, in fact, the cunning Aro rarely killed a man, but sold him into slavery. In New Calabar it was common for one chief to accuse another of witchcraft, so that he would be sent for 'trial' by the oracle. To avoid certain enslavement the chief would have to pay the oracle keepers most of his fortune, which would consist largely of slaves. He would return a broken man, without followers (i.e. slaves) and therefore without status. The Aro backed up the efficacy of the oracle by hiring mercenaries to raid those who would not respect it. Fines from big men had to be paid in slaves who were supposed to be eaten by the oracle, but in fact were quickly exported.

West of the Aro sphere of influence, the hinterland was unified by the migration eastward from Benin to the Niger of people who drew the indigenous population together into sizeable states. The classic example is the migration of the Onitsha people to the Niger, which is generally believed to have taken place in the seventeenth century. Though classified as Ibo, the Onitsha, as do many other Ibo groups along the Niger, have strong Benin influences in their political structure. They had a monarch, which most Ibo societies did not; and many of their chiefs bear Benin titles.

Benin was the most important slave mart west of the Niger. The port for Benin was Gwatto, where factors of the King exercised his monopoly on trade. Olfert Dapper, writing at the end of the seventeenth century, remarked that: 'As soon as a ship has anchored on this coast, the King is informed, and he summons two or three Fiadors, and twenty or thirty merchants to whom he gives authority to go and do business with the Whites.'[14] Benin traders were interested in cloths of all descriptions, brass armlets, looking-glasses, iron bars, fine coral, cowries from East India, beads and perfumes. In exchange they exported slaves, local cloths, pepper, jasper stones, leopard skins and ivory.

At that time Benin appears to have been very prosperous,

with a large well-disciplined army. But at the beginning of the eighteenth century when Van Nyendael visited Benin, he remarked:[15] 'Formerly this village was very thick and close built, and in a manner over charg'd with inhabitants, which is yet visible from the Ruins of half remaining Houses. . . .' Benin seems to have overspent itself by the eighteenth century, its constant slaving wars ultimately impoverishing the kingdom. Van Nyendael was nevertheless impressed by its organization. He describes the honesty of the traders, the just code of law, the lack of beggars, and the civility of his own reception.

By the end of the century, Captain John Adams, writing in the period 1786–1800, remarked the decline of the slave-trade in Benin and its concentration farther down the coast in the Delta ports. Significantly for the future he observed: 'Human sacrifices are not so frequent here as in some parts of Africa; besides those immolated on the death of great men, three or four are annually sacrificed at the mouth of the river, as votive offerings to the sea, to direct vessels to bend their course to this horrid climate.'[16]

The last of the great slave ports was the Itsekiri state of Warri, which according to both Benin and Itsekiri tradition was founded towards the end of the fifteenth century by a Benin prince. By the end of the seventeenth century it was a powerful trading state almost independent of Benin. 'The King of Ouwerre is the ally and in some manner the vassal of the King of Benin, but in other respects he is absolute in his dominions,' Dapper wrote.[17] There appears to have been considerably more contact between the Portuguese and the Itsekiri of Warri than with Benin, for he records that Antonio Domingo, Olu of Warri in 1644, was a mulatto, his father having been educated in Portugal where he married a Portuguese lady.[18] In 1682 Father Jerom Merolla da Sorrento recorded that the reigning Olu of Warri was married to a Portuguese woman of São Thomé.[19] He had married her according to Catholic rite, and many of his subjects had apparently followed his example in adopting the Catholic faith.

P. C. Lloyd has written that the 'development of the new kingdom . . . and its independence from Benin must certainly owe much to Portuguese influence, for all mission activity was centred here when Benin itself seemed to be fruitless soil for

proselytising'.[20] Indeed Warri was the only town connected
with the slave trade which came under strong missionary influence. Dapper recorded that 'the King himself and most of his
inhabitants have some leaning towards the Roman religion'.
Elsewhere slave traders were not concerned with the propaga-
tion of their culture.

In Nigeria, as elsewhere on the Coast, the first effect of the
slave trade was depopulation, though this is exaggerated when
one considers that probably during the early eighteenth century
no more than 11,000 people were sent abroad annually from
Nigeria, and that even in the heyday of the slave trade at the
turn of the eighteenth century Captain John Adams estimated
that in twenty years between 1800–22 probably some 370,000
Ibo had been sold into slavery.[21] This may seem a tremendous
figure, but it certainly had its economic *raison d'être* since then,
as now, Iboland's chief problem was overpopulation.

The slave trade tended to bring some equilibrium to the
Eastern region which, in parts, was intensely overpopulated, in
other parts sparsely populated. There is sufficient evidence to
suggest that in fact most slaves came from the overpopulated
areas where there was land hunger, being exchanged with the
agriculturally richer areas for yams and other farm products.[22]

Though the slave trade brought great suffering to many
Africans, both on their way to the coast where they were roughly
handled, and on the Middle Passage to the Americas, it did not
in the case of the Delta bring the political instability that is
usually described. Kidnapping and raiding in Iboland were the
exception rather than the rule, and in many ways the governments that evolved on the coast were admirably suited to their
new economy. One authority has written, probably with more
enthusiasm than is justified by the facts: 'From the contemporary personal reports of English Port-Governors and employees,
of slaver captain surgeons and ships' officers, it is evident that
the African chiefs had a highly developed system of government
and a rigid code of laws and that, influenced largely by super-
stition as they were, they yet lived in ordered communities and
were as far removed from the "barbarian brutish nations" of
the Liverpool merchants' conception as their cruel witchcraft
trials were akin to the religious inquisitions and pogroms of
civilized Europe.'

CHAPTER VI

The Holy War of Usman dan Fodio
(1804—30)

Hausaland and Bornu were at first unaffected by the arrival of the Europeans on the coast; their economy remained firmly orientated towards the Sahara desert. Even in the eighteenth century when the Hausa states were sending slaves to the markets of the south, their main concern was still with the desert trade.

By the beginning of the eighteenth century Katsina had won the long struggle for control of the caravan routes from Hausaland to North Africa and for a hundred years she was to remain the leading commercial and cultural centre of the Western Sudan. Bornu lived in the shadow of its former glories, retaining control over its vassal states, but being constantly threatened on its northern borders by desert nomads and on its southern borders by the sedentary tribes that served as its slave reservoir. The standard of learning in the state rose, and a number of Mais, ruling in the second half of the eighteenth century were noted for their scholarship. Intellectuals now played an important role in the court, whose structure had become more elaborate, especially since princes who in ancient days would have ruled provinces were kept under surveillance in the capital or in the nearby summer palace of Gambarou. The new nature of the court appears to have been ideal for court intrigue, and the Mais seem to have lost much of their control of political affairs as a result. The growing weakness of the empire was made clear towards the end of the eighteenth century when the Bornu army suffered a disastrous defeat at the hands of the Mandara, a subject tribe.

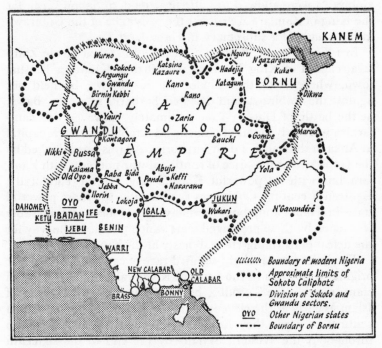

4. The Sokoto Celiphete (or Fulani Empire) and Bornu, *circa* 1850

The first half of the eighteenth century witnessed the rise to power of Zamfara which, though one of the oldest of the Hausa Banza Bakwai states, was only now becoming of major importance in the politics of the Western Sudan.[1] In 1700, however, Zamfara conquered Kano, and by the middle of the century she was rivalling Katsina's supremacy in Hausaland. At the same time the Hausa state of Gobir which, despite the importance of its frontier position on the desert, had remained rather remote from the general trend of affairs in Hausaland, began to assert its power, and from 1731–43 engaged Kano in a series of hard battles. The Gobirawa were at the time being pressed back on their northern frontiers by desert tribes and were looking for expansion to the fertile lands of Zamfara on their southern borders. At first they infiltrated peacefully into Zamfara, and Barbari, King of Gobir, gave his own sister in marriage to Marroki, King of Zamfara. A treaty was drawn up whereby the

Gobirawa were allowed to settle near modern Sabon Birni, for the King of Zamfara welcomed the assistance of the Gobirawa in his struggle for supremacy in Hausaland.

In 1764, however, Barbari attacked and sacked Birnin Zamfara, capital of King Marroki, who fled to Kiawa, a Katsina town, where, with the help of the Katsinawa, he held out against the Gobirawa and defeated Barbari's successor, Bawa, at the battle of Dutsin Wake. Ultimately, however, the Zamfarawa were driven out of Kiawa and established a new capital at Anka in the south of their territories. All this was achieved by the Gobirawa at the price of continual war not only with Zamfara but with its powerful Katsina ally. At the end of the eighteenth century Gobir was superficially the most powerful state in Hausaland, but internally it had been considerably weakened by these prolonged wars which prepared the way for the defeat of its ruling Habe dynasty at the hands of the Fulani.

The Fulani were a light-skinned race of cattle nomads whose original home was in the Senegal River valley. Several Fulani clans, notably the Torodbe, had come under the influence of Islam as early as the eleventh century, and from the fourteenth century onwards they had been proselytes of their religion throughout the Western Sudan. By the end of the sixteenth century both the Torodbe and the cattle-herding Fulani, who had remained animist, were established throughout Hausaland and as far east as modern Adamawa.[2] In the courts of the kings of the Western Sudan, the Moslem Fulani played important roles as administrators, much as the clerics did in the courts of the kings in mediaeval Europe. Some of the kings by whom they were employed were themselves ardent Moslems, but the majority were either avowedly animist or mixed traditional practices with their observance of Islam. After the collapse of the Songhai empire at the end of the sixteenth century and its division into its constituent parts, Islam, in so far as it was upheld by the rulers of the Western Sudan, saw a general decline. Its main standard-bearers remained the Fulani, who found their position in the courts of the traditionalist kings increasingly more difficult, for the kings began to fear the power of this group upon whom they were so dependent for the conduct of the affairs of state. Some even actively persecuted the Moslem Fulani minorities in their states.

The Holy War of Usman dan Fodio

Under such conditions, the Moslem Fulani were increasingly drawn to the idea of revolt against their 'pagan' masters. For according to the Shari'a or Moslem law, revolt against the state is legitimate if the ruler is 'pagan' or mixes Moslem and pagan practices. If Moslems are persecuted, a flight from the land of the pagan or the *hijra* is decreed to be followed by the declaration of Holy War or *Jihad*.[3] Thus the Fulani rose in rebellion against the Mandingo authorities of the Futa Djallon in the highlands of Guinea in 1725 and the pagan Fulani rulers of the Futa Toro in the upper Senegal valley in 1768.[4]

The aim of these rebels was to establish states governed in accordance with the Shari'a. The importance of these Jihads, taking place so far away from Nigeria, was that they served as inspiration for Usman dan Fodio in his own Jihad against the rulers of Hausaland.

The Fulani were established in Gobir, as in the rest of Hausaland, not only as cattle-herders but also as officials in the courts of the Habe kings, many of them occupying high positions. Others were teachers and traders many of whom became very wealthy. By the turn of the eighteenth century their increasing political and economic influence in the northern states gave the local rulers considerable cause for disquiet, especially since they formed a class at the vanguard of movements for religious and intellectual reform. They openly criticized what they described as the religious laxity and the decadent standards of learning in the Hausa states. In some areas they were openly asserting themselves, as in the Benue where the Fulani were attacking the Jukun even before 1800.[5]

The general unrest amongst the Fulani living in the towns was focused on a famous Moslem scholar in Gobir, Usman dan Fodio.[6] He was born at Marata in Gobir in December 1754, a Fulani of the Torodbe clan which had migrated fourteen generations before from Futa Toro. His education was broad, consisting of the traditional Islamic sciences of Grammar, Law, Exegesis, Theology, Rhetoric and Prosody. He had several teachers, two of whom were inspired by the reformist ideas that were stirring throughout the Moslem world at that time. One of them was his uncle, Binduri, with whom he studied for two years, the other, the famous Mallam Jibril of Agades who had already preached an unsuccessful Jihad against the Hausa kings. On completing his education he returned to Degel in Gobir where he became a teacher and itinerant preacher carrying his message of religious and social reform to the peoples of Gobir, Zamfara, and Kebbi.[7] He even travelled beyond the Niger. His sermons appear to have attracted large crowds for his fame was already widespread when Nafata, King of Gobir, sought him out to become tutor to his own children. As a result he gained considerable influence in the court both with the king and the nobility. In 1802 Yunfa, who had been his pupil, succeeded to the throne of Gobir. He was deeply resentful of the power of his old tutor in the court, and particularly concerned about his radical reformist ideas. He even took drastic measures against the further conversion of his people to Islam. The wearing of the turban was forbidden to men, and the veil to women. This interference, as Hiskett has written, was almost entirely political for it was these customs which gave to the Shehu's party the cohesion and sense of common identity which the Habe kings feared.[8]

The Fulani justified their Jihad against Yunfa and the other Habe kings on the grounds that though they professed Islam, in mixing traditional practices with their observance of the 'true faith' they were juridically pagans against whom it was legitimate to rebel.[9] And it is clear that in many respects Islam, as it was practised in Hausaland where it had been established for three hundred years, made concessions to the indigenous religion of the Hausa. Indeed, as far as the Habe monarchs were concerned, they practised a calculated syncretism whereby their authority as Moslem monarchs was boosted by, and to a considerable extent depended on, their respect for Habe religious rites and social practices. Thus the Fulani attack on their 'reversion to paganism' was an attack on the very authority by which they ruled. Though the Habe kings made such political concessions, Islamic learning flourished in their courts. They maintained around them a small circle of Moslem divines and scholars. At the court of Gobir, Usman dan Fodio had been amongst the most respected of such scholars.

It becomes clear in this light that the attacks of Usman dan Fodio struck at the very heart of Yunfa's power, and Yunfa's anti-Islamic measures were undoubtedly designed to prevent Usman, the reformer, from gaining more adherents. The antagonism between the two was not really that between believer and infidel, even though the Fulani were able by their own definition to depict Yunfa as an unbeliever. It was rather between a radical reformer and a conservative willing to compromise in pursuit of stable government.

In the *Kitab al-Farq*, a work on the Habe kingdoms attributed to Usman dan Fodio, and translated by Hiskett, the writer accuses the Habe rulers of imposing illegal taxation on the population of their states.[10] Taking into account any natural prejudice that might come into the writings of one attacking the established régime, there was no doubt much truth in his charges. In the Habe kingdoms *gaisuwa*, or the giving of bribes to superiors, was common; judges were open to bribery; Moslems were pressed into military service; illegal market taxes were imposed. Undoubtedly the indiscriminate, oppressive and frequently excessive imposition of taxes was one of the sorest grievances of the people against their rulers. In particular the Fulani nomads bitterly resented the taxes on their cattle, and here, as much as in the violation of the principles of the Sharia, we may look for the motives which brought both the Hausa commoners and the Fulani nomads into Usman dan Fodio's camp.

Usman dan Fodio argued that Holy War became obligatory under three conditions. 'Firstly on the orders of the [Moslem] ruler. . . . Secondly, if the enemy launch a sudden counter-attack on Moslem territory. . . . Thirdly, to rescue captured Moslems from the hands of the heathen.'[11] The second two of these three conditions were soon fulfilled as a result of actions by Yunfa. First he forced Usman to leave his court for Degel, his home town, where he became so outspoken against the Habe régime that it is said Yunfa even planned to have him killed. Then Yunfa attacked Gimbana where one of Usman's disciples, Abd al-Salam, had refused to bless some Gobirawa troops passing through the town. Yunfa took prisoner some of Abd al-Salam's disciples who were freed by Usman's troops. Yunfa then threatened to destroy Degel and thus heralded the general persecution of the Shehu's followers. Usman emigrated from Degel to Gudu in February 1804 (i.e. performed the *hijira*), recalling the emigration of the Prophet from Mecca to Medina. The Shehu's brother, Abdullahi, said at the time, according to Usman dan Fodio in *Tanbih al-ikhwan*: 'Truly this matter has become intolerable; recourse must be had to arms. There can be no doubt that the situation demands a prince to manage our affairs, for Moslems should not be without government'. Usman dan Fodio was therefore elected Caliph and leader of the revolt against the Habe King of Gobir, and his followers did 'homage to the Sheik, as is directed by the Kuran and Sunna[12] in such circumstances, and made him leader of the Holy War'.[13]

Thus in early months of 1804 the fifty-year-old Moslem scholar and reformist preacher, Usman dan Fodio, found himself at the head of a great Jihad, or Holy War, that within a few years was to sweep most of the Hausa kings off their thrones, and during the next thirty was to establish Fulani hegemony throughout all Northern Nigeria with the exception of Bornu and certain pagan areas inaccessible to the Fulani cavalry.

The causes and motives of this Jihad are extremely complicated. As far as it concerned Usman dan Fodio, who was given the title of Amir al-mu'minin or Commander of the Faithful in acknowledgement of his religious leadership of the revolt, it was a Holy War to establish a purer form of Islam in what he considered a predominantly corrupt and decadent society. This fits into the pattern of reformist movements taking place throughout Africa at that time. As Thomas Hodgkin has written of Usman dan Fodio: 'His ideas and achievements have to be understood in the context of the succession of reforming movements which profoundly affected the Moslem world during the latter part of the eighteenth and nineteenth centuries—beginning with Muhammad Ibn Abd Al-Wahab in Saudi Arabia, and including Muhammad ibn Ali al-Sanusi in Cyrenaica (Barka), Shehu Ahmadu and Al-hajj Umar ibn Said in the Western Sudan and Muhammad Ahmad ibn Abdullah (the Mahdi) in the former Egyptian Sudan. These movements, though differing from one another in many respects, had a common objective—"a return to the pure and primitive faith of Islam, purged of heresies and accretions". This implied the attempt to restore the original model of the Islamic State, as it was believed to have existed in the time of the Prophet and the first four Caliphas: a State in which social justice, administered in the light of the Shari'a by God-fearing rulers, took the place of the arbitrary decisions of irresponsible—and effectively non-Moslem—despots.'[14]

The initial motive force of the rebellion came from a small

cultured group of Fulani, mostly religious leaders and teachers who, as Hiskett has written, 'were able to carry their Jihad to a successful end . . . due to their sense of cohesion and intellectual superiority over the surrounding Hausa. This gave them a degree of organizing ability and political acumen above that of the Hausa aristocracy'.[15]

Beyond the primary religious motive lay many political and economic factors. Group feelings were of dominant influence. The Fulani were a small minority amongst the Hausa, and some authorities have sought to explain the Jihad as a war between Fulani immigrants and Habe Hausa rulers, although this is too clear cut an explanation, for many of the Hausa *talakawa* or common people joined the Shehu's revolt, whilst as Abdullahi, the Shehu's brother, complained bitterly, many Fulani remained on the side of Yunfa. Certainly the cattle Fulani (*Bororoje*) who joined the Shehu did so largely out of tribal loyalty,[16] for many of them were certainly not Moslems. However it is again difficult to know whether tribal loyalty or resentment of Habe taxation and raids on their cattle was the more important motive for supporting the Shehu's *Jihad*. (See p. 100.)

Most significant was the large number of talakawa to join forces with the Shehu, who was preaching not only religious reform but a reform of the political affairs of the kingdom, particularly the oppressive system of taxation and the despotic administration of its ruler. Economic fears were also involved; the town Fulani were in many cases extremely wealthy, and this, combined with their political influence, aroused considerable jealousy. Ultimately it is impossible to say whether religious or economic motives, class feelings or tribal loyalties, played the largest part in the revolt.

In its later stages the Jihad seems however to have become increasingly political and correspondingly less religious in its character. Zamfara, for instance, had considerable cause to regret its early assistance to the Fulani against Gobir when its towns were sacked by Abdullahi and Bello, the son of the Shehu. Later Al-Kanemi who, as we shall see, effected a religious revival in Bornu similar to that in Hausaland, was to write to Bello asking him why he should want to carry the Jihad into Bornu, which was a Moslem state under himself, a reformist ruler. He also accused the Fulani of seizing political power in the guise of a religious revolt. Al-Kanemi's letter, and the reply made to it by Bello, not only illuminate the arguments for and against a Jihad, especially when this concerned attacking avowedly Moslem states, but serve as an excellent illustration of contemporary diplomatic correspondence.[17]

Perhaps the harshest critique of the revolution came from one of the Shehu's earliest disciples. Abd al-Salam, who it will be remembered had precipitated Yunfa into attacking the Fulani after his refusal to bless the Gobirawa soldiers, had sought refuge afterwards with the Shehu, where he became one of his closest lieutenants. His initial fervour for the Shehu's Jihad declined in later years, and he took up arms against Bello. The reason he gave for this was that the Jihad had lost its early reformist character. He cited the fact that the best posts in the administration had gone to the Shehu's brother and son, whilst he, an early disciple, had been given nothing.

If anything, its complexity of motives gave the Jihad added force. The old régime crumbled before the Fulani armies which fought vigorously though they were hastily drawn up.

The actual history of the Jihad can be divided into three phases: the consolidation of power in Hausaland and the establishment of the Fulani Empire; the attack on Bornu; and the southward expansion of the Fulani Empire.

Once it became apparent to the King of Gobir that the Fulani were proving a real danger to his own security, he sent out forces to attack them. The Fulani retaliated by raiding outlying Gobirawa villages. The first engagement between the two forces occurred on 21st June 1804 at Tabkin Kwatto where the Fulani, assisted by the Zamfarawa, defeated the Gobir army. It would seem that this was achieved against great odds for Bello records that the Fulani had only twenty horse, whilst those of the Gobirawa were 'numberless'.[18] This was decisive in its effect on the discontented Fulani throughout Hausaland. The Shehu had demonstrated that Habe kings could be overthrown, and despite his subsequent defeat at Tsuntsuwa he was able to keep the loyalty of his forces. In July 1804, hot from victory at Tabkin Kwatto, he sent what amounted to declarations of intended war to the Habe Hausa kings, urging them to purify their religion.

The Holy War of Usman dan Fodio

In 1805 he built a permanent base camp at Sabongari, twenty miles north of the Zamfara capital of Anka. Here he received delegations of Fulani from all over the north. He gave a flag to the leaders of each delegation, blessing them and calling on them to rid the country of unbelievers and to establish Islam throughout Hausaland. The Shehu himself was no soldier and entrusted the army to his brother Abdullahi and his son Bello. The ranks of his army were swollen by the faithful as well as the usual band of adventurers that followed any Sudanese army. This curious admixture of religious fanaticism and opportunism accounts for the charges of mass slaughter and plunder that accompanied most Fulani victories. The Shehu was quick to condemn such actions on the part of his followers.

Zamfara, which had been alienated by the attacks on its villages by Fulani forces, joined its old enemy Gobir, together with Kebbi and the Tuareg, in an attempt to suppress the rebellion. The alliance very nearly succeeded when it defeated the Fulani at Alwassa and all but took Gwandu, which had become the Fulani headquarters. However, after these initial successes the Habe kings seemed unable to resist the Fulani forces.

What was the secret of the Fulani strength? How was a scattered immigrant minority able to overthrow the powerful Habe states, with their large standing armies? These are questions to which satisfactory answers will not be forthcoming until further research is made into Jihadi documents. One important factor was the lack of unity among the Hausa kings. Even so, it is remarkable how the Fulani succeeded. As Bello wrote, 'We had none of the *Soudanese* on our side except the people of Zamfara, and the reason for their being so was their enmity to the people of *Gobir*.'[19] Yet the town Fulani were able to organize their own army in such a way that they could defeat the formidable alliances of the 'Soudanese' kings. In the first place there was close contact between the town Fulani and the cattle Fulani. The town Fulani were often the representatives of a large clan, acting on its behalf in the capital of the kingdom in which they were accustomed to pasture their herds. Very often the leading town Fulani owned large herds, and therefore indirectly controlled the considerable number of their nomadic brethren involved in their care. Since the cattle grazed right across Northern Nigeria it was not difficult for the Shehu in remote

Gobir to the north-west to have close contacts with town Fulani in Adamawa far to the south-east.

The call to revolt was quick to spread, for there were stronger loyalties between town and cattle Fulani in those times than is the case today. Granted these close connections, how were these nomads formed into the formidable fighting force they later became? In the eighteenth century, the social organization of the Fulani differed considerably from that of the small groups which we are accustomed to see nowadays wandering freely over Nigeria. In those days the Fulani sacrificed considerations of good pasture in order to live in semi-permanent settlements. In their migrations eastward to Nigeria they had been sub-jected to frequent attacks by local kings, particularly the pagan Bambara kings and the Tuareg. In Hausaland they were not infrequently the object of cattle raids by the Habe kings. Their encampments were organized on a defensive basis,[20] and each group had its own militia to guard it in times of attack. Thus, when Usman dan Fodio called on the Fulani to join his Jihad he was not calling on loosely organized peoples, untutored in the art of disciplined warfare, but men who had long experience of fighting in their own defence. What is more these nomads had certain advantages over the standing armies of the Habe kings: in particular their light cavalry was far superior to the heavy cavalry of the Hausa.

By 1808 the Fulani army had brought most of Hausaland under control, though right up to the 1820's there were pockets of resistance to Fulani rule. One of their earliest and most important successes was in Zazzau (Zaria) which at first sub-mitted peacefully. Here the Habe ruler, Isiaka Jatau, Sarkin Zazzau, heeded Usman dan Fodio's call to religious reform and was installed as first Emir of Zaria.[21] His son, M. Makau, when he succeeded to the throne in c. late 1804, did not accept the authority of Usman dan Fodio. According to the Fulani he reverted to the traditional religion, or at least mixed the obser-vance of it with his observance of Islam. Thus as far as the Fulani were concerned he was a 'pagan', a description con-tested by implication in The Chronicle of Abuja.[22] A flag was thus given to a Mallam Musa, who joined forces with a Bornuese Fulani called Yamusa, and attacked Zaria either in late 1806 or early 1807.[23] Almost as soon as they reached the city, the 'pagan' king, M. Makau, with all his subjects fled southwards to what has since become Abuja. Today the kings of Abuja are still referred to as Sarkin Zazzau, the name of the state of which Zaria was the capital.

In 1805 Muhammad Fodi, King of Kebbi (1803–26), was driven out of his capital at Birnin Kebbi by Abdullahi, though from his new headquarters at Argungu he offered stubborn resistance that the Fulani were never to overcome. He was eventually killed by the Fulani twenty-two years later, but he succeeded in maintaining the great Kebbi dynasty, descended direct from Kanta, for his brother Karari became the first Kebbi King of Argungu. Hadeija, north-west of Kano and on the borders of Bornu, submitted to the local Fulani leader Umaru without resistance. And shortly afterwards the neighbouring towns of Kazaure, Garin Gabbas, Gatarwa and Auyo surrendered.

The great Hausa cities of Katsina and Kano both fell to the Fulani in 1807. The local leader of the Fulani in Kano sent to the Shehu for a flag in that year, and though the King of Kano was able to control his eastern territories, the Fulani conquered the west with ease. When they met in battle at Dan Yahaya the Fulani triumphed and the Habe king fled. The victorious Kano Fulani sent to the Shehu to choose a ruler, since there were several factions among them, making choice difficult. The saintly Shehu asked who was the wisest man among them, and when they replied Sulumannu, servant of their general, the Shehu declared that he should be their Emir.

In Katsina three Fulani leaders, Umaru Dumyawa, Na Alhaji and Umaru Dallaji, went to the Shehu for a flag. All three were given flags, though after quarrels between them Umaru Dallaji took over leadership of the Fulani revolt against the King of Katsina, who fled with many of his people to Maradi, some fifty miles north. From there he and his successors were to harass the Fulani for many years to come. Umaru Dallaji became first Emir of Katsina, whilst the son of Na Alhaji became ruler of the Yandaka area, and Dumyawa overlord of Sandam, to which Maradi paid tribute. All three rulers owed allegiance directly to the Shehu. Throughout Umaru Dallaji's reign, which ended in 1835, he was threatened by the Habe kings of Maradi who had Agades and Zamfara as allies.

Indeed, until the separation of Maradi and Katsina by the effective establishment in the 1900's of the Franco-British boundary between Niger and Northern Nigeria, there was no peace between the two. In 1808 Yunfa, King of Gobir, died in battle outside his capital of Alkalawa. This marked the end of the Jihad in Hausaland.

With all the important Hausa states under Fulani domination the foundations of the great Fulani Empire had been laid. In the fighting the Shehu had taken little part; he was rather the philosopher of the revolution, whilst Abdullahi and Bello were its executives. The new empire was divided into two: the Western Sector with headquarters at Gwandu came under the administration of Abdullahi; the Eastern Sector was placed under Bello, who ruled it from Sokoto which the Shehu had made his home. The administration was devolved on these two men, whilst the Shehu returned to his studies.

The first serious check to Fulani expansion eastward came from Bornu. In 1805 the Fulani of the Western Province of Bornu rebelled and were attacked by Mai Ahmed, who at first drove back their leader Ardo Lerlima, but finally, when other Fulani groups joined the attack, was defeated at Nguru, the Galadima's capital, which the Fulani sacked. This led to a general uprising of the Fulani and a number of small emirates were carved out of Bornu by their leaders. Ibrahim Zaki, who came from an old-established family in Bornu, founded the emirate of Katagum on the eastern frontiers of Hausaland. Buba Yero, who was given a flag by the Shehu in return for his help against Zamfara in the early days of the Jihad, set himself up in southern Bornu in the emirate of Gombe. The most serious threat came from within Bornu. In 1808 the Fulani led by Gwoni Mukhtar drove the Mai out of his capital of N'gazargamu, which they sacked. At that time it seemed as though Bornu would quickly fall under Fulani domination.

The Fulani were eventually repelled by the leader of a similar cattle-owning, nomadic people, the Kanembu, who came from the old kingdom of Kanem. Under the leadership of Al-Kanemi they had already formed a small army which attacked the Fulani wherever they seemed strongest. This was a curious situation for their acts were apparently quite unofficial, having no sanction from the Mai of Bornu though they were clearly in his interest. It seems that a possible explanation was jealousy between the two nomadic groups. The Kanembu were as reluctant to be ruled by the Fulani as was the Mai. Al-Kanemi absorbed the remnants of the defeated royal army into his own, and marched on N'gazargamu, retaking it and killing Gwoni Mukhtar. In 1810 Mai Ahmed died and was succeeded by Dunama. A period of peace ensued whilst the Fulani consolidated their position in the small frontier emirates. In 1811 Ibrahim Zaki was given a flag with the right to take whatever parts of Bornu he could conquer. In a brilliant campaign he took N'gazargamu once again, but Mai Dunama's forces joined with those of Al-Kanemi and drove him back to Katagum. Despite succeeding wars the *status quo* in Bornu was fixed by the outcome of this campaign.

Al-Kanemi had thus become the saviour of Bornu. He established himself near Mai Dunama's new capital, enjoying great wealth as well as the devotion of the masses.

In 1814, Dunama, in an attempt to shake off this shadow ruler, undertook what Urvoy has described aptly as 'a flight to Varennes', intending to establish himself at a firm base in some distant province.[24] He was caught and deposed, and though the Saif dynasty ruled until 1846 this marked the real end of their power. Al-Kanemi now exercised all the powers of the old Mai. As Clapperton, who visited Bornu in 1821, remarked, 'The Sultanship of Bornu, however, is but a name; the court still keeps up considerable state, and adheres strictly to its ancient customs, and this is the only privilege left them. When the sultan gives audience to strangers, he sits in a kind of cage, made of the bamboo, through the bars of which he looks on his visitors, who are not allowed to approach within seventy or eighty yards of his person.' Denham and Clapperton were most impressed by the ascetic Al-Kanemi, effective ruler of Bornu. '. . . no one could have used greater endeavours to substitute laws of reason for practices of barbarity, and, though feared, he is loved and respected. . . . Compared to all around him, he is an angel, and has subdued more by his generosity, mildness and benevolent disposition, than by the force of his arms. . . .'[25]

Al-Kanemi's first task after repelling the Fulani was to consolidate the greatly weakened empire. Between 1815 and 1824 he re-established his suzerainty over Kanem and the growing state of Bagirmi.[26] By 1826 Bornu was once more a powerful state, deprived only of its former territories of Gombe, Hadeija, Misau and Katagum. Al-Kanemi was succeeded by his son Umar, who like his father took the title of Shehu, and ruled through the puppet Mai Ibrahim. In 1846, after a relatively peaceful reign the small state of Zinder revolted and Mai Ibrahim and his followers took advantage of the situation by calling on the Sharif of Wadai to help them throw off Sheikh Umar. The latter so manœuvred his troops that he was able to put down both revolts and Mai Ibrahim was executed, his sons having perished in battle. Thus came to an end one of the longest and most distinguished dynasties in African history.

South of Bornu the Fulani were more successful. Buba Yero in Gombe subdued all the surrounding tribes and even made expeditions into Jukun country. Yakubu, Emir of Bauchi, who was the only non-Fulani flag-bearer, likewise subdued all the pagan tribes in the Bauchi area, founding the town of Bauchi as his headquarters in 1809.[27] Friction occurred between him and Buba Yero when the latter pushed his frontiers westwards, and Yakubu had to check him at Beri-Beri. Buba Yero was more successful to the south where for a time even the Fulani of Muri came under his jurisdiction.

The farthest the Fulani Empire extended eastward was Adamawa where two important emirates were established, those of Yola and Muri.[28] In 1806 Moddibo Adama travelled to Sokoto to receive a flag from the Shehu; on his return he quickly rallied around him the many Fulani who had settled in the area. He overcame the local pagan tribes with little difficulty. Meanwhile, the Fulani Emir of Muri made more inroads into the territory of the once powerful Jukun Empire, and hastened its already rapid decline, which had been assisted by the ravages of the invading Chamba people from the south-east.

The Fulani faced much greater difficulties in the southward expansion of their empire into Nupe and Yorubaland. In both areas they gained footholds only after years of patient intrigue in local politics.

At the time of the Jihad, Nupe was involved in bitter civil war. Muhammad, the Etsu or King of Nupe, had just died, and his son Majia succeeded him, only to find himself rivalled by his cousin Jumada, who had established himself with his followers at Rajada on the Niger, opposite the Nupe capital of Rabba.[29] As in all northern territories, the Fulani had settled in Nupe, and a certain Mallam Dendo took up the position of leader of the Jihad in Nupe. He had, however, to work with great care. His opportunity came soon after Etsu Majia had defeated and killed Jumada. Mallam Dendo straightway offered his support to Jumada's son Idris, and together they drove Majia out of his capital of Rabba. Mallam Dendo then established henchmen as emirs of Lafiagi and Agaie. Idris soon found the Fulani an embarrassment and attempted to drive them out. The Fulani, ever skilful at intrigue, then joined forces with Majia who routed Idris, gaining himself recognition as Etsu Nupe at Jengi. The Fulani remained at Rabba.

Mallam Dendo never took the title of Etsu Nupe, though he was effective ruler of much of Nupeland. At his death in 1832 the Fulani were still far from secure in Nupe, and their position was made the more precarious by strife between their various factions. These disputes necessitated the intervention of the Emir of Gwandu on two occasions. Eventually the rival Nupe Etsus were pushed back to two small towns, Zuguma and Pategi, whilst the title of Etsu Nupe was taken over by Mallam Dendo's successors, who ruled from Bida.

In Ilorin, the Fulani gained their foothold by similar methods.[30] The great Empire of Oyo had since the end of the eighteenth century lost most of its control over Yorubaland. Afonja, the Governor of Ilorin and Are-ona-Kakanfo of Oyo, had successfully asserted his independence from the Alafin of Oyo, but to achieve and maintain this, he had to join forces with Solagberu, the leading Moslem of Ilorin, and use Hausa and Fulani mercenaries. Afonja's revolt, as will be seen in the next chapter,[31] resulted from internal difficulties in the Oyo empire, and was not in its origin an extension of the Fulani Jihad. However because he was forced to rely for his supply of mercenaries on a certain learned Fulani scholar, Mallam Alimi, who arrived in Ilorin around 1817–18, his rebellion was to give the Fulani a foothold in Yorubaland. Mallam Alimi was not a flag-bearer of the Jihad, nor indeed were any of his sons, whom Afonja asked him to bring in to assist him in his struggle with Oyo around 1821. However it was one of these sons, Abd al-Salam, who, as Ajayi has written, 'converted Afonja's secessionist movement into an outpost of the Fulani Jihad'.[32] After the death of his father, Abd al-Salam sought to seize power from Afonja, and teamed up with Solagberu against him. Afonja was defeated in battle and his body, pierced with arrows, was publicly burnt in the market-place. One tradition says that he committed suicide. The victorious Abd al-Salam soon turned against his ally Solagberu, and made himself sole master of Ilorin, thus establishing it as the southern outpost of the Jihad. It seems that he was not confirmed as Emir of Ilorin, that is given a flag by Sokoto, until c. 1829.

By 1830 the Fulani were masters of most of what until the creation of the twelve states was the Northern Region of Nigeria. Only Bornu, parts of Kebbi and Gobir, the hill areas of the Jos Plateau and the Tiv and the Idoma did not come under their control. Much has been written of the decadence and corruption of the Sokoto Caliphate in its later years. There is, as we shall see (Chapter XIII), some truth in these assertions, which have unfortunately obscured the real virtues of the early years of the Sokoto Caliphate. Probably its greatest achievements were first the establishment of a uniform system of government through a vast area of Nigeria which for centuries beforehand had been torn by internecine wars; and second the stimulation of commerce under what might be called the Pax Fulani; and finally, and in many ways most significant of all, the literary revolution which it stimulated.

Even though the Fulani were accused of destroying the books of the Habe, a much-debated accusation, there was a great revival of learning under Bello. Moslem divines came from far afield to the court at Sokoto. Al-Haji Sa'id lists among the learned of his reign several women: 'Of women—Zani Gharka, mother of Al-Bukhari; Inna Gharka, mother of Bello and others.' This was apparently true of the following reigns, for under Aliu Baba he lists 'Nanna son of Fodio, Uthmanu his son-in-law, who had married his daughter Miriam, his mother Ladi, his daughter, Miriam, who knew the Koran by heart....'[33]

One noteworthy aspect of the Shehu's reformist ideas was his insistence on the education of women in the tenets of Islam. One of dan Fodio's accusations against the society of the Habe kings in the *Nur al-Albab* was that 'men treat these beings [women] like household implements which become broken

The Holy War of Usman dan Fodio

after long use . . . this is an abominable crime. Alas—how can they thus shut up their wives, their daughters, and their captives in the darkness of ignorance while daily they impart knowledge to their students?'[34] At heart the Fulani revolution was a revolution of radical intellectuals. Inevitably after the first ardour of revolution wore off it became increasingly materialistic in outlook. Slave-raiding became more frequent, and certain areas were devastated of human beings. Corruption was rife in many emirates. Nevertheless, when the British occupied the north in 1900, they took over the administrative system adapted by the Shehu from the old Habe kingdoms to suit the needs of his vast empire and made it the basis of their system of indirect rule.

CHAPTER VII

Yoruba Civil Wars

The dramatic collapse of the authority of the Alafin of Oyo over his provincial kings and tributary states at the beginning of the nineteenth century was touched off by the revolt of Afonja, in Ilorin, aided by the Fulani, and resulted in civil wars that were to last throughout the century. The speed with which the Alafin lost control of the situation was the result of much deeper causes than this simple rebellion.

It has been suggested that by 1700 the Oyo Empire was already in decline.[1] This does not appear to be true for the eighteenth century marked the height of Oyo's conquests of her neighbours and control of the trade routes to the coast. Throughout the preceding century Oyo had been dogged by political instability and burdened by excesses of tyranny for which the unwritten constitution of Oyo did not provide. King after king was rejected by the Oyo Mesi. The probable cause of this state of affairs was the increasing rivalry between the Oyo Mesi and the palace administration which the Alafin was strengthening in order to secure his control of the expanding empire and its trade routes. Furthermore, the people themselves were probably in sympathy with the Oyo Mesi in their attempts to check the growing power of the Alafin, for the Yoruba expect unchecked power to be oppressive.[2] Thus, by the middle of the eighteenth century, Oyo was ready for the seizure of power made by the newly appointed Basorun, Gaha, who proved equally as tyrannous as the Alafins from whom he snatched control of Oyo, but who did at least provide some stability for the empire.

During the eighteenth century Oyo's authority stretched south-west to the Ashanti states and Dahomey, and north-east

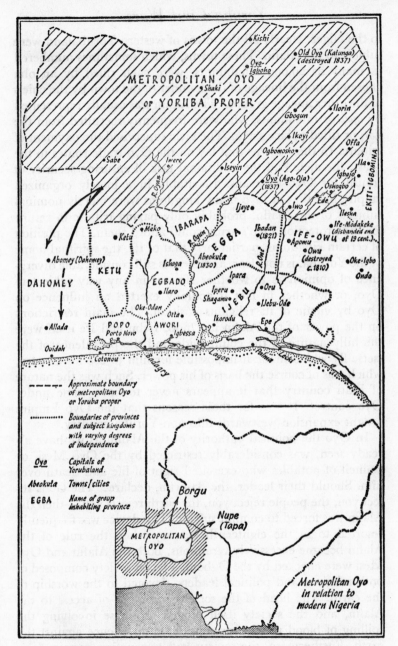

Kishi

Old Oyo (Katunga)
(destroyed 1837)

Oyo-
Igboho

METROPOLITAN OYO

Shaki

or YORUBA PROPER

Ilorin

Gbogun

Ikoyi

Offa

Ogbomosho

Sabe

Iwere

Ila

R. Oyan

Igbajo

Iseyin

Oyo (Ago-Oja)
(1837)

Oshogbo

Ede

Ijaye

Iwo

Ilesha

IBARAPA

R. Ogun

Ketu

Meko

Ibadan
(1821)

IFE-OWU

Ife-Modakeke
(disbanded end
of 19 cent.)

EGBA

Apomu

Owu
(destroyed
c. 1810)

Abeokuta
(1830)

Abomey (Dahomey)

Ishoga

KETU

Oke-Igbo

EGBADO

Ondo

Ipara

DAHOMEY

Ilaro

Iperu

Oru

R. Oni

Shagamu

IJEBU

Oke-Odan

Ikorodu

Ijebu-Ode

Otta

Allada

POPO
Porto Novo

AWORI

Igbessa

Epe

Ouidah

Cotonou

Badagry

Lagos

Palma

EKITI-IGBOMINA

— — —   Approximate boundary
          of metropolitan Oyo
          or Yoruba proper

·········   Boundaries of provinces
          and subject kingdoms
          with varying degrees
          of independence

<u>Oyo</u>   Capitals of
          Yorubaland.

Abeokuta   Towns/cities

EGBA   Name of group
          inhabiting province

Borgu

Nupe
(Tapa)

METROPOLITAN
OYO

Metropolitan Oyo
in relation to
modern Nigeria

5. Metropolitan Oyo and Yorubaland in the middle of the
eighteenth century[3]

to the Niger. Nearly all the towns of western Yorubaland were subject to the Alafin. These towns, which sometimes numbered as many as 20,000 inhabitants, were each ruled by an oba chosen from the lineage of the founder of the town by the chiefs of the other lineage groups.[4] The Alafin was usually represented by *ajele* or intendants, who were frequently recruited from the *ilari* or titled palace slaves. The ajele supervised the payment of tribute. In those towns that lay on the Oyo trade routes to the coast, the ajele had the additional task of ensuring security of transit for Oyo caravans. Inevitably in a loosely organized empire like that of Oyo many kingdoms were merely nominal subjects of the Alafin, probably only paying tribute in return for the protection Oyo's army could afford them. The position of certain kingdoms, particularly that of Ife, the spiritual home of the Yoruba, is not clear, and there is still considerable divergence of opinion as to whether Ife was in any way subject to Oyo, or whether in fact it actually exerted an influence on Oyo by virtue of its religious position. The main restrictions on the power of the Alafin in Ondo, Ijebu and Ife itself were the hilly nature of the countryside and the prevalence of the tsetse fly which made it impossible for him to use his cavalry, which was of course the basis of his power. Such was the nature of Ekiti country that it appears never to have come under Oyo control. It was for these reasons that the Oyo Empire sought expansion westwards into non-Yoruba country.[5]

In Oyo the political authority of the Alafin, as we have already seen, was considerably restricted by the Oyo Mesi, or council of notables who exercised right of life and death over him. Should their leader, the Basorun, declare: 'The Gods reject you, the people reject you, the earth rejects you'—then the Alafin was forced to commit suicide. This device was frequently resorted to in the eighteenth century when the rule of the Alafin became excessively tyrannous. Both the Alafin and Oyo Mesi were checked by the Ogboni, a secret society composed of both religious and political leaders, devoted to the worship of the earth. The head of the society had right of access to the Alafin, and the society itself judged any case involving the spilling of blood which was considered an offence against the earth. Furthermore, the society had to sanction certain decisions of the Oyo Mesi, including the rejection of the Alafin.

The Alafin represented authority only in so far as his decisions were arrived at after a complicated series of negotiations with the Oyo Mesi and other factions of society. Thus in no sense could the Alafin be compared with the Habe Hausa kings or the northern emirs as a fulcrum of power. Attempts to rule on their own, as we have seen, were the most frequent cause of rejection of the Alafins.

In the eighteenth century Oyo's main problem was the maintenance of its authority over the young kingdom of Dahomey, founded about 1625. Its authority depended on its formidable standing army, whose efficacy was described by the Dutch merchant William Bosman in 1698. In that year Alafin Ojigi made war on the tributary state of Great Ardra. Bosman described the army that attacked Porto Novo, the territory's capital, thus: 'These being all Horsed, and a warlike Nation, in a short time mastered half the King of Ardra's territories, and made such a slaughter among his subjects, that the Number of the Dead being innumerable, was commonly express'd by saying, "They were like the Grains of Corn in the Field. . . ." This Nation strikes such a terror into all the circumjacent Negroes, that they can scarce hear them mention'd without trembling: And they tell a thousand strange Things of them.'⁶

Dahomey first defied the authority of the Alafin in 1724 when it invaded Great Ardra in an attempt to gain access to the sea. The Alafin promptly despatched an army, backed up by cavalry, which after initial successes was defeated by the Dahomeyans. Dalzell described the ruse by which Dahomey gained this impressive victory: 'In the morning the Eyeos, seeing the enemy fled, secure of victory, began to burn and plunder the town and to indulge themselves very freely with the treacherous liquor: this soon intoxicated and spread the ground with the major part of their army. At this juncture, the Dahomians, who had timely information of the enemy's disorder, fell upon them with redoubled fury, destroyed a great number, completely routed the rest; and those that escaped owed their safety to their horses.'⁷

The Dahomeyans were nevertheless frightened of the consequences of this victory and sent presents to appease Oyo. However, in 1727, Dahomey attacked Wydah in another attempt to gain access to the sea.⁸ Wydah, which had aided Oyo in its attack on Great Ardra in 1698, appealed to the Alafin for help and a second army was despatched against Dahomey. It swept through Dahomey, ransacking its villages, and in 1729 the King of Dahomey sued for peace and promised to pay tribute. This was not paid, and in 1738 Oyo once again invaded Dahomey, laying siege to Abomey the capital. The Dahomeyans tried to make peace, but the Oyo terms were: 40 men, 40 women, 40 guns and 4,000 loads of cowries and corals a year to date with effect from the defeat of 1728. The Dahomeyans would not accept this, but such was the pressure exerted by Oyo that in 1747 Dahomey agreed to pay tribute on these terms.

The subjugation of Dahomey coincided with the appointment of Gaha as Basorun by Alafin Labisi who ascended the throne in 1754.[9] Gaha immediately murdered the new king's two chief supporters, so that Labisi was forced to commit suicide. Each succeeding Alafin came increasingly under the influence of this ruthless but capable Basorun. It was not until the accession of Abiodun as Alafin that Gaha met opposition from his nominal master. At first Abiodun accepted his position as figurehead, but quietly plotted against the Basorun with the army commander, Kakanfo Oyabi. On a fixed day all members of the Basorun's family in Oyo and its tributary states were murdered, and the Basorun himself was seized and burnt. According to Dalzell, the king's supporters 'ripped open the bellies' of the pregnant women of the Basorun's family, 'and cut to pieces the immature fruit of their womb'.[10]

Abiodun became Alafin in fact as well as in name in 1774. His reign is remembered by the Yoruba as one of the most peaceful in their history, but with his death in 1789, as Johnson writes, ended 'the universal and despotic rule of the Alafins of Oyo in the Yoruba country. He was the last of the kings who held the different parts of the kingdom together in one universal sway and with him ended the tranquillity and prosperity of the Yoruba country. The revolution ensued, and the tribal independence with the loss to the Yoruba of the Tapa and Bariba, and Dahomey provinces, and the Popos later on, which had continued to our own day. In a word, with Abiodun ended the unity of the Yoruba kingdom.'[11]

In fact, as Akinjogbin has shown, an important part of the empire had already gained its independence.[12] In 1783 the

Bariba of Borgu soundly defeated the Oyo army, and Oyo was subsequently never able to bring them back into tributary relationship. Biobaku has suggested that the Egba obtained their independence from Oyo under their leader Lishabi between 1775 and 1780,[13] though it has been suggested that this may have taken place later.[14] Johnson does not mention it as occurring in Abiodun's reign, nor as one of its immediate sequels. Dahomey, under King Adahoozu, whilst not obtaining its independence from Oyo, failed to pay tribute twice during Abiodun's reign, in 1781 and 1784. The Nupe, after two centuries of subjection to Oyo control, defeated the Oyo army only two years after Abiodun's death and declared their independence.

Despite these disastrous events, the collapse of the Oyo Empire was staved off for another twenty-five years. If we accept Biobaku's dates for the Egba revolt, then at first appearances no further inroads were made into the authority of the Alafin until 1818 when King Gezo of Dahomey declared his independence. Two years later the outbreak of the Owu wars heralded the impending disintegration of the empire. This was impossible to stave off for Afonja, the Alafin's own army commander, had already rejected his authority and set himself up in alliance with the Fulani as an independent ruler over the important Oyo province of Ilorin which was virtually at the doorstep of the imperial capital. (*See map p. 109.*)

The reasons for the break-up of the Oyo empire are many and complex. One of the chief causes of collapse was that the traditional political institutions were not suited to running an empire as large and prosperous as Oyo had become by the eighteenth century. The elaborate constitution which allowed for maximum participation of all sections of society in the decision-making process had to give way to the concentration of power in the hands of a single person or group that could make rapid decisions. Thus in the late seventeenth and early eighteenth centuries the Alafin became increasingly despotic. Reaction to this was the elimination of the power of the Alafin by the Oyo Mesi led by Basorun Gaha, who, far from returning to the traditional political system of Oyo, likewise concentrated power in his own hands. Nor did Abiodun's deposition of Gaha and his followers resolve the situation. There remained a basic tension in Oyo between on the one hand the need for concentration of power in the hands of one man or group if the empire was to be efficiently managed and on the other the traditional Yoruba dislike of such acquisition of unchecked power by one individual or group.

Furthermore the military strength of Oyo, hitherto unchallenged, had weakened seriously under Abiodun. The defeat of the Oyo army by Borgu and Nupe within the space of eight years was not only a great humiliation but cut off Oyo from her northern trade contacts, and in particular, as Akinjogbin has shown, her main supply of slaves for export to the coast.[15] Since it appears that slave-trading was becoming increasingly important for Oyo at the end of the eighteenth century, she had to turn elsewhere for slaves, without which she had nothing to exchange for guns with the European traders, guns which were vital to her army and thus the maintenance of the empire. She was forced to look towards her tributary kingdoms to the south as a new source of slaves, thus creating increased tension among the Yoruba-speaking peoples. It has been argued that the desire of the provincial and tributary kings to share in the profits made by Oyo from the slave trade was one of the principal causes of the break-up of the empire.[16] However Ajayi has insisted that there is little evidence for this view, since the great expansion of the slave trade in this area, which only took place in the 1820's, was a consequence rather than a cause of the civil wars.[17] Ajayi's interpretation would seem to be substantiated by the sequence of events between the death of Abiodun and the Owu wars as outlined by Akinjogbin. This interpretation is complemented by the fact that it was not until the 1820's that the British naval patrol was beginning to check the export of slaves from the Niger Delta, forcing the European traders to seek elsewhere to satisfy their needs.

It was therefore not until about the 1820's that the Europeans began appreciably to increase their demand for slaves in the Dahomey ports, through which Oyo exported her slaves. Indeed Akinjogbin points out that at the time when he suggests Afonja, the army commander, and the leading provincial kings were breaking away from the control of the Alafin, there was actually a decline in demand for slaves in the Dahomey ports because of the banning in 1794 of the slave trade by the

French, who at that time were the main traders in the area. The law against the slave trade was not repealed until 1802 and French interest in the slave trade in this area never really revived.

It was at the end of the eighteenth century that the effective breakdown in the authority of the Alafin over his provincial kings took place, and not in 1817 as is usually assumed. One of the main causes of this breakdown was Oyo's need for an alternative source for the supply of slaves. Her cavalry could not operate in the Ondo-Ekiti area. Dahomey to the west was too powerful and too sparsely populated to be used as an alternative. There remained the densely populated Yoruba provinces to the south: Owu, Ife, Ijebu and the possibly independent Egba. The main problem of raiding in this area, Akinjogbin argues, was that Oyo might come into conflict with Ife with which spiritually and constitutionally it had a special relationship. The Alafin of Oyo, whilst the ruler of the Yoruba Empire, could not be installed without the formal sanction of the Oni of Ife as king of the spiritual home of the Yoruba.[18] The Alafin-elect had to obtain the *Ida Oranyan* from the Oni, for without it Akinjogbin argues he could have no authority over the empire. In order to obtain this sword he had to promise that he would never attack Ife or its neighbouring territory. This ceremony is still observed by the Alafin today.* Thus in 1793 when Awole ordered the army to take the market town of Apomu in Ife territory, allegedly to avenge a grievance against the Bale of the town, though probably more in order to gain slaves, he violated the terms of his accession. Afonja was reluctant to attack an Ife town in view of the special position of Ife, and thus refused to undertake the expedition. It would seem that all the other important chiefs of Oyo refused to support this attack, and there appears to have been a complete breakdown in the authority of Awole as Alafin. In 1796 when he ordered the army to take Iwere, it killed his supporters and forced him to commit suicide, though not before he had uttered a curse that has become memorable in Yorubaland. From the palace forecourt he shot three arrows, one to the north, one to the south and one to the west, crying: 'My curse be on you for your disloyalty and disobedience, so

---

* In Oyo, however, today the ceremonies in the Sango shrine are considered much more important.

let your children disobey you. If ye send them on an errand, let them never return to bring you word again. To all the points I shot my arrows will ye be carried as slaves. My curse will carry you to the sea and beyond the seas, slaves will rule over you, and ye their masters will become slaves.' Then he smashed an earthenware dish, shouting: 'Broken calabash can be mended but not a broken dish; so let my words be irrevocable.'[19]

From then on there seems to have been a complete breakdown in the authority of the Alafin, a situation which was to lead to civil war in Yorubaland for nearly eighty years. Afonja, the army commander, and the important provincial kings, such as Opele, Bale of Gbogun, and Adegun, the Onikoyi of Ikoyi, set themselves up as semi-independent rulers within the empire.

Thus, if Akinjogbin's chronology is correct, the Oyo Empire had effectively come to an end by 1797. However it was not until the Owu wars of 1821 that the full impact of the collapse of Oyo authority was felt throughout Yorubaland.[20] Insecurity in Oyo itself, occasioned by the internal political situation, the economic depression that had taken place as a result not only of the decline in the slave trade, but in the loss of traditional sources of supply of slaves, the presence of hostile Nupe and Borgu not far from the capital, together with fear that the Fulani revolution in Hausaland might extend itself southwards towards Yorubaland, led to the emigration of many Oyo to the south. One of the factors in the collapse of the Oyo Empire which is impossible to assess is the influence of Islam. The new religion had undoubtedly made its influence felt in Oyo even before the eighteenth century, but it probably only became important as a political factor towards the end of the century, with the preachings of reforms by Usman dan Fodio. The Shehu undoubtedly travelled south out of Gobir. Whether his preachings had any repercussions in Oyo politics is difficult to tell. But the Fulani revolution itself, particularly when after 1808 it began to expand beyond Hausaland, certainly presented itself as a menace to the security of Oyo.

The cause of the outbreak of the Owu war is not at all clear. Johnson says that the Onikoyi, the leading provincial king, ordered the Owu to attack some Ife towns that had been engaging in indiscriminate slave trading with the Ijebu.[21] This naturally incurred the anger of the Oni of Ife who, thinking that he would easily conquer the Owu, marched against them only to be severely defeated. However, there was some altercation between the Owu and some powerful Ijebu traders, as a result of which the Owu took and destroyed Apomu. The Ijebu then joined forces with the remnants of the Ife army and Oyo refugees fleeing from the Fulani and, armed with guns, drove back the cutlass-swinging Owu. They laid siege to their town and destroyed it (1827).[22]

This would suggest that the Ife were trying to break into the monopoly of Oyo in the slave trade, which as Ajayi and Akinjogbin have stressed, remained intact until after the Owu wars. The war may have been the first open expression in Yorubaland of the breakdown in the authority of the Alafin and the empire, a situation which had been a reality for the past twenty years.

Though the political difficulties in Oyo might of their own have led to the long series of civil wars that raged through Yorubaland in the nineteenth century, it is just possible that if the various factions in Oyo had sunk their differences, the situation could have been saved. But the fact that Afonja, the Are-ona-Kakanfo, had, in his attempt to consolidate his secessionist movement, decided to rely on the Fulani meant all hope was lost for the maintenance of the integrity of the empire, for Afonja had brought into play a new political force, which it was clearly impossible for the Alafin to control, with one part of his army in rebellion under Afonja, and the other tied down in Owu. Normally Afonja, as Are-ona-Kakanfo, would have been a slave, which would have made it difficult to understand how he could, given his servile status, have mustered sufficient support from the freeborn. However he was a royal prince through his mother, and, after unsuccessfully contesting the throne of Oyo, gained the position of Are-ona-Kakanfo.[23]

Afonja's rebellion and the Owu wars led to a series of conflicts between the various Yoruba kingdoms and sub-groups that lasted for the rest of the century, and saw the obliteration of some of the most important provincial kingdoms of Oyo.

Owu was laid siege to by the Ife, Ijebu and Oyo forces, and finally invested in 1827. Oyo was itself taken by a force led by the only surviving son of the Basorun Gaha, showing how strong the rift between the Alafin and the Basorun had been and how long it had persisted. Gaha's son, who formed his army in Borgu, might even have taken Ilorin, had he not been deserted at the last minute by the Onikoyi. Alafin Adebo died while his army was trying to take rebellious Gbogun. His successor, Maku, was the author of the famous message to Afonja: 'The new moon has risen', to which the latter replied impertinently: 'Let that new moon quickly set.'[24] Ironically soon afterwards Maku waged unsuccessful war against Iwo and had to commit suicide.

The success of Afonja's revolt encouraged every provincial king to seek his independence from Oyo. Afonja was now the only man with anything like the power of the former Alafin, but to obtain this he played into the hands of the Fulani. With the Fulani established in Ilorin, the Yoruba were completely cut off from their traditional source of supply of slaves. Oyo, as a result of the loss of Nupe, had had to turn towards the southern parts of the empire for a new supply. Now with the collapse of Oyo authority, coupled with the general increase in demand for slaves both for export and for domestic purposes, the civil wars between the various sections of Yorubaland were given added impetus. The increase in the demand for slaves by European traders in the Dahomey ports and at Badagry and Lagos was a reflection not only of the rising demand for slaves in the Americas, but of the increasing difficulty in obtaining them in the Delta ports where the British Anti-Slavery patrol was having some success in controlling export of slaves from Old Calabar and Bonny. The stretch of coast from Lagos to Togo, known as the Western Slave Coast, was more difficult to control.[25] At the same time the development of legitimate commerce in Yorubaland was also to increase the demand for slaves for use as head-porters and farm-labourers.[26] Consequently what had started as civil wars arising from the break-up of the Oyo Empire increasingly took the character of slave-raising wars. In these circumstances it is at first sight perhaps surprising that during this long and vicious series of wars, whose motives and complexities are often difficult to follow, people managed to carry on farming their land, that the unity of Yoruba culture was not destroyed and that indeed the Yoruba remained the vigorous progressive people they are to-day. Of course it must be remembered that comparatively few people were involved in the fighting. However, in the case of the sack of Old Oyo, and the obliteration of Owu, Ikoyi and many other important towns in northern Yorubaland, there were thousands of refugees.

For a simpler understanding of the complex wars that lasted from 1821 to 1893 it is convenient to name the chief participants. To the north was Ilorin, outpost of the Fulani Empire, intent on carrying the Jihad into Yorubaland. Close by was Oyo, ancient imperial metropolis seeking both to reassert its former authority, and later, after its people were forced to move south, to re-establish itself. To the west was Dahomey, now a great military power, participating in any war which provided opportunities for capturing slaves. To the south and bordering on the coast were the Egba and Ijebu, now placed in a strategic position to act as middle-men for the export of slaves to the coast and for the import of firearms with which to continue the wars. In the east lay many kingdoms, some of which were now independent of the Alafin, some of which had never been under his influence. These, too, became embroiled in the general holocaust, both as slave-raiders and sources of supply for slaves. In the course of the war there emerged two major cities, one of them, Ibadan, destined to be the saviour of Yorubaland from the Fulani, the other, Abeokuta, destined to be the stepping-stone for Christian influence in Yorubaland.

After the fall of Owu, its inhabitants were chased into Egba territory, where for nearly ten years there ensued a series of battles, invariably alleged to have begun because of some injustice, but more often than not inspired by the desire for slaves. Egba towns were destroyed willy-nilly as undisciplined freebooting armies rampaged across the countryside and thousands were rendered homeless or taken as slaves.

In about 1829 the Ijebu, Ife and Oyo forces settled at the small Gbagura town of Ibadan, into which some of the homeless Egba also moved.

The chief of this mixed settlement was Maye, an Ife man. He was a considerable leader but was jealous of the Oyo whose leader, Lakanle, was fortunately able to stand up to him. It is not surprising therefore that civil war soon broke out, and when an Egba leader had shot an Ife chief, the Egba decided to leave for what was to become Abeokuta, or 'the town under the Rock', led by Sodeke, a hunter. The new town, probably founded in 1829 or 1830, comprised several communities: the

Egba-Alake, the Egba-Oke-Ona, the Gbagura and the Owu refugees. They set up a federal form of government, in which the chiefs of each community participated, though Sodeke remained their acknowledged leader. Both the Ibadan and the Ijebu did their best to destroy this new settlement, the Ijebu being particularly jealous of this potential rival to their monopoly as middlemen in trade with the coast. In Ibadan itself there were further disputes, from which the Oyo section emerged supreme. Maye was executed and a civil government instituted. From then on Ibadan grew to be the most important town in Yorubaland, closely associated with Oyo, but though it acknowledged the Alafin as titular ruler of the Yoruba and did not demand a crown for its own chief, it was never subordinate to it.

The Yoruba might well have defeated the Fulani and driven them out of Ilorin, if only they had not been so divided amongst themselves. They were never able to unite against the enemy. Indeed, if the three powerful rulers of Ikoyi, Gbogun and Ago-Oja had for once combined they might have stemmed the Fulani menace, but they chose to make alliances where they saw the greatest opportunity of personal aggrandizement. It was not a paying policy, for very shortly Ikoyi, once the premier provincial kingdom, was captured by Ilorin. The succession in Ikoyi was disputed, the Alafin supporting one claimant, the Ilorin the other. The result was that the Ilorin attacked and killed the Onikoyi approved by the Alafin and appointed their own candidate, Soyenbola, as his successor. The only town now powerful enough to resist the Fulani was Gbogun but the Fulani soon took it, forcing Edun, the greatest Yoruba general of his day, to flee.

Ilorin was thus able to subjugate many of the important towns of Yorubaland. Abd al-Salam, the Emir, tried to make inroads into Ijeshaland, but he was unsuccessful, since the Fulani horse could not operate easily in the hilly and wooded country of that area. Refugees from the northern towns and from Oyo flooded south to Ife, and such was the apparent folly of the civil conflict at the time that the Oni of Ife, with the Fulani at his back door, insisted on humbling the Oyo by making them undertake the most menial of tasks and selling them into slavery. A later Oni however permitted them to settle outside Ife, and there they built the town of Modakeke, defended by a huge wall. With reason, the Ife were furious with their Oni for allowing the Oyo to build a town which they realised might soon become a menace to their own security. They poisoned the Oni and set out against Modakeke, but were repulsed. Once again the Ife attacked, this time to be so severely defeated that Ife, original home of the Yoruba, was deserted.

It is almost impossible to outline the tangled skein of civil strife at this time. The most important event in the decade 1830–40 was the destruction of Old Oyo. Oluewu became Alafin in succession to Amodo who, it is said, died of a broken heart when fire destroyed the Afin (palace) and all its treasures. When Abd al-Salam tried to force Oluewu to become a Moslem, the latter secured an alliance with Borgu in a final and bitterly unsuccessful effort to throw off the Fulani yoke. In *c.* 1835 Old Oyo was sacked, and today almost nothing remains of 'Katunga', the great metropolis of Yorubaland.[27] Once again the failure of Yoruba chiefs to support the Alafin in his hour of crisis ruined his chances of success even before he had started fighting. Oluewu, himself, was captured and put to death. The new site for Oyo was chosen by Atiba, son of Abiodun, who, after a successful career as a freebooter, had become too powerful to be denied the crown. He selected Ago Oja (Oja's camp) where he had lived probably since *c.* 1830. He collected all the Oyo refugees around him, and on pain of death forced all the villages for miles around Ago Oja to move into the new capital. Oluyole, ruler of Ibadan, also as Oyo, was made Basorun out of deference to his city's immense power. The Ibadan were to protect the north and north-east and were given a free hand in Ekiti and Ijesa. Ijaye was to protect the south-west, whilst the Alafin, who was no longer to go personally to the wars, was responsible for Iluku, Igboho, Kisi and Saki, where many Oyo refugees were living. Kurunmi, chief of Ijaye, was made Kakanfo. By thus conferring these important titles on the leaders of what were now the most important Oyo towns, Atiba hoped both to secure their loyalty and lessen their rivalry.[28]

With the foundation of New Oyo, a turn in the fortunes of Yorubaland became evident. The Ibadan defeated the Ilorin at Gbodo and again at Oshogbo, *c.* 1840, when the latter were laying siege to that town. This latter victory in fact halted the

Fulani advance to the sea, and though there were many battles in the following fifty years, the Fulani were never able to make the easy inroads into Yoruba territory that they had made in the previous decades. The Alafin failed to follow up this success and even in the hour of triumph civil war broke out once more. Finally the only people who had been able to live in peace in these troubled times, the Ekiti, were brought into the war, when Ilorin attacked them. At the same time the powerful Basorun at Ibadan began plotting to wrest the throne from the Alafin. Though the Alafin was apparently not perturbed by this, Kurumi, the Are of Ijaye,* greatest Yoruba general of the day and a man intent on carving out a kingdom for himself, resented any further increase in the strength of the Basorun, and it was hardly surprising that a move on the part of some Ibadan to occupy a ruined town between Ijaye and Oyo provoked war between the two cities of Ibadan and Ijaye in 1844. This war, known as the Batedo war, lasted two years, and so deep were the internal divisions in Yorubaland that even the Ibadan at one stage called on their enemies the Ilorin as allies.

In the south-east the Dahomeyans, once tributaries of the Alafin, were expanding their vigorous kingdom, whose main source of revenue came from the sale of slaves. They attacked Otta in 1845. Three years later they captured the town, carrying off its inhabitants as slaves. But their first serious invasion of Yorubaland was the 1851 attack on Abeokuta.[29] Taking advantage of Ibadan's preoccupation with the north in a war against the Ilesha that did not finally come to an end until 1854, the Dahomeyans marched on Abeokuta, a column of Amazons at their head. The Dahomeyan Amazons, a unique feature in the history of West African armies, were originally superfluous wives of the King used first as bodyguards and then to swell the ranks of the army.

During the nineteenth century there were usually as many as from 3,000 to 8,000 Amazons, and in the army that attacked Abeokuta 6,000, out of a total strength of 16,000, were women. At the time Abeokuta was not in a particularly good state to resist this impressive army, and without the aid of the cunning Oba of Isiaga, an Egbado town on the Dahomey route to

* Kurumi was usually known as the *Are* of Ijaye, from his title as Kakanfo, Are-ona-Kakanfo.

Abeokuta, the city might well have fallen. The Dahomey army had been informed by an Egba spy which were the weakest points of the Abeokuta defences. When they attacked Isiaga the Oba quickly submitted advising the Dahomeyans to attack the south-western wall of Abeokuta and then sent a messenger to inform the Abeokuta leaders of the probable Dahomey approach. The Egba immediately set about strengthening this section of the wall and prepared their army of some 15,000 men, most armed with guns, to meet the Dahomey attack.

At first the Dahomeyans appeared as if they would take the town, and it was really only the discovery that they were fighting women that spurred the Abeokutans into the final resistance that drove off the Dahomeyan army. However, the most significant factor in this was the part played by Britain. Not only had the British Consul, Beecroft, visited King Gezo of Dahomey in an attempt to persuade him to give up slaving, but he had also issued ammunition to the Egba army through the missionaries stationed there. Indeed, without the aid of the British Consul and the missionaries it is doubtful whether the Egba could have saved Abeokuta from destruction by the far better equipped Dahomeyans. British intervention in the first Dahomeyan invasion of Abeokuta marked the beginning of a new era in the history of the civil wars in Yorubaland.

CHAPTER VIII

The Suppression of the Slave Trade

The abolition of the slave trade by Britain in the first half of the nineteenth century was to make a profound impact on the peoples of what is today Nigeria, for it laid the foundations of her legitimate commercial relations with West Africa, and eventually led her to establish herself politically along the West African coast, the most important stretch of which was the one they inhabited. The abolition of the slave trade by Britain in 1807 may appear somewhat paradoxical when it is remembered that at the turn of the century she was the chief carrier of slaves from West Africa.

The decision of 1807 was the climax of thirty years of agitation in Britain against the slave trade.[1] Before 1772 few people had had any conscience about it. So far removed was the common Englishman from the conduct of the slave trade with the attendant horrors of the Middle Passage and the cruel system of labour in the plantations that it is hardly surprising that he rarely questioned its morality. In 1729 the question of the rights of slaves on British soil had been considered by the Solicitor General and the Attorney General, whose opinion was that a slave did not become free by coming to Britain, and remained the property of his master. However, there were a few people in Britain who were not content with this interpretation of the law. And in 1772, as a result of Granville Sharp's one-man crusade against the institution of slavery, a test case was brought before Lord Chief Justice Mansfield to establish whether a slave had freedom under the laws of Britain. This was the case of *Somersett* v. *Knowles*. Somersett, a Negro, had run away from his master, who recaptured him and clapped him in irons on board a ship bound for the West Indies. Granville Sharp learnt of this and took out a writ of habeas corpus for Somersett, which was heard by Lord Chief Justice Mansfield, who ruled that once a slave set foot on British soil he became free. This was the starting-point of the movement for the abolition of the slave trade which had for years been fundamental to the plantation economies of the colonies of the great European powers.

In 1776 a motion was moved in the House of Commons that 'the slave trade is contrary to the laws of God and the rights of man'. It failed, and it was left to ardent social reformers like William Wilberforce, M.P., Thomas Clarkson and Granville Sharp to carry on the struggle against this long-established trade. In 1787 they formed the Society for the Abolition of the Slave Trade, and with Wilberforce as their agent in Parliament began to lobby for abolition. Though Wilberforce gained the sympathy of William Pitt and Charles James Fox, it took him twenty years to secure a majority in the House.

Before it the society had the formidable opposition of the vested interests in the slave trade. Liverpool and Bristol both depended largely on it for their income, and many members of the government were deeply involved in it. Indeed, eighteenth-century economists believed that the wealth of the West Indies, which depended on the slave trade, was fundamental to the strength of the British Empire. Certainly the triangular trade between Africa, the West Indies and Britain supplied some of the necessary capital to finance the industrial revolution.[2]

How then did the abolitionists persuade Parliament to do away with what was apparently a vital factor in the British economy? The end of the eighteenth century was a time of new ideas in Europe. America had just broken away from England. The foundations of the French Revolution were being laid by the radical and revolutionary ideas of Liberty, Equality and Fraternity. The rights of the individual, as in Thomas Paine's *The Rights of Man*, were being bandied about in pamphlet and newspaper. Not unnaturally a public receptive of such arguments was also likely to be receptive of the idea that Negroes were also men and that the slave-trade was wrong. Certainly they were shocked to read of its brutality in accounts like that of Falconbridge, who had been a surgeon on a slaver.[3] But even then the entrenched interests seem too great to have been overcome by the zeal of Wilberforce and his small but ardent band of abolitionists. Did Wilberforce really succeed in changing the attitude of a nation? Did he really touch the conscience of Parliament? It hardly seems possible in a nation that carried on public executions of children for petty theft right up till the middle of the century and instituted a system of child factory labour whose conditions, in many cases, were far worse than those for the slave on the sugar plantation. It is not to belittle Wilberforce and the humanitarians to suggest that in fact by the time of his campaign the odds against him were not so overwhelming as has commonly been suggested. The fact is Britain was really economically ready for this change-over from an economy of mercantilism, based largely on the Indian trade and slave-carrying between Africa and the West Indies, to that of the first industrial nation in Europe. A good example of this change-over is Liverpool which, at the time of abolition, was already diverting many of her ships to trading in cotton with America. As a new industrial nation Britain had greater interests in the opening of markets for her manufactured goods than in retaining a slave trade that was not necessarily conducive to the expansion of the West African market. Significantly the hostility of the British Government to trading in slaves by other nations did not prevent it from allowing Manchester goods to be used by such nations as their main means of exchange for slaves. Britain had another great interest in stopping the slave trade: she needed palm oil as a lubricant for her factories, for soap and for lighting. While slave trading continued, production in the oil-growing areas of the interior of West Africa would always be hampered. It was therefore very much in the interests of Britain to check slavery in order to permit the economic exploitation of the Coast.[4]

It is significant also that neither Bristol nor Liverpool collapsed as a result of the cessation of the slave trade; and relatively few English ships found it worth while to engage in privateering as slave-dealers after abolition. One notorious French slaver, Théodore Canot, complained that the British combined suppression of the slave trade with the promotion of their own commerce in adulterated Manchester goods.[5] Despite these commercial motives, 'the unweary, unostentatious and inglorious crusade of England against slavery', as the historian Lecky has written, 'may probably be regarded as among the three or four perfectly virtuous pages comprised in the history of nations'.[6]

It was one thing for Britain to proclaim the legal abolition of the slave trade, quite another to persuade other nations to follow suit. Britain tried to bring the slave trade to an end both by treaty with other powers and by seizing ships actually carrying slaves. In certain cases other nations followed Britain by abolishing the slave trade. Denmark had actually declared it illegal in 1804. The U.S.A. abolished it in 1808, Sweden in 1813, and the Netherlands in 1814. But official abolition did not stop slavers from operating on the Coast. In defiance of the law many American ships crossed the Atlantic with human cargo over the next fifty years. Thus Britain had to undertake the establishment of an anti-slavery patrol on the West Coast to capture slaving-ships. In 1817 she secured from Spain[7] and Portugal treaties which agreed to the reciprocal rights of search and the subsequent condemnation of ships if they were found with slaves on board. This often had horrific results, since slavers were liable to discharge their human cargo into the ocean if capture seemed imminent. Later, fortunately, treaties were secured which allowed the condemnation of ships if slaving equipment was found on board. Even so the patrol was largely ineffective in its early years and the figures of slaves exported from West Africa, far from decreasing, actually rose steeply.[8]

Two problems therefore confronted Britain. First was the difficult diplomatic tangle over the right of search; second was the smallness of the patrol for so lengthy a coastline. For operational purposes the Coast was divided into three strips: from Senegal to Sierra Leone; from Sierra Leone to Cape Coast Castle; and from Cape Coast Castle to the Line (Equator) beyond which treaty powers ceased. This last was known as the Bights Division. The Coast was an unpopular station, and to encourage the anti-slavery patrol the 1807 Act provided for generous rewards for the capture of slavers. But by 1824, when abolitionist enthusiasm was waning under the mistaken impression that the slave trade was dying a natural death, the bounty was reduced from £60 for a rescued male slave to £10. In 1830 it was further reduced to £5. Nevertheless, the Navy did capture a large number of slavers, towing them to Freetown where they were brought up before the Court of Mixed Commission which was empowered to condemn them. Freetown had been established by the Society for the Abolition of the Slave Trade as a settlement for freed slaves. Despite the inconvenience of taking ships from the Bights of Benin and Biafra on the long leg up the coast to Freetown the British government insisted on keeping it as its base for the suppression of the slave trade.[9]

The abolition of the slave trade by the country that hitherto had been its chief practitioner came as a profound shock to many African chiefs who had looked to Britain as their best customer. When the kindly and successful British slaver, Captain Hugh Crow, arrived in Bonny on his last visit, he informed his old friend King Opobo Pepple of Britain's decision to abolish the trade. Pepple replied, 'We tink trade no stop, for all the Ju-Ju men tell we so, for demn say you country can niber pass God A'mighty.'[10] And as late as 1842 Lieutenant Levinge of the West African Naval Squadron said that Africans in the Delta often asked him whether England was at war with the other nations of Europe. 'They cannot understand why we take them [the slavers]. We carried on the slave trade so shortly before ourselves, that I do not think they clearly understand why we should be so anxious to suppress it now.'[11]

It was hardly surprising that few of the chiefs took much notice of Britain's change of heart. There were other customers. Indeed, in the ensuing economic war between the slavers on the one hand and the British legitimate traders on the other, 'what determined the side the Africans took', as Dr. Kenneth Diké has written, 'was the importance or otherwise of the trade to the economy of the country'.[12] Certainly the presence of the naval squadron at the various mouths of the Niger did not at first deter Bonny, which had become the leading slaving port on the Coast, from dealing with Spaniards, Portuguese and American slavers, as well as a polyglot bunch of pirates and privateers. Bonny was the chief offender, though even she tried to get the best of both worlds. In 1826 12 slavers and 12 British merchantmen were reported in Bonny waters.[13]

Inevitably there was bitter competition between the slavers and the legitimate traders. Life was difficult for the latter, for whenever a slaver arrived, even in Calabar which by the 'twenties had largely devoted itself to trade in palm oil and timber, everyone rushed to meet the slavers' requirements.[14]

Farther up the coast Lagos and Badagry flourished as they had never done before on the profits of the slave trade. Civil war amongst the Yoruba, wars between Yoruba and Fulani, Egba and Dahomeyans kept a plentiful supply of slaves for the markets of Brazil and Cuba. Even here the rivalry between legitimate traders and slavers was keen.

These attempts at the suppression of the slave trade, despite their early inadequacy, were to bring about a complete revolution in the economy of the African slaving states. A new economic order based on trade in the products of the West African forests was ushered in. However, the old trading organization that was built up to deal with the slave trade was taken over unmodified to cope with the new trade in palm-oil. Many of those who would have been exported as slaves were now employed as porters. While Bonny rose to the position of chief slave port on that part of the coast, Calabar compensated for her loss by exporting palm-oil. In 1828 she exported 2,000 tons whilst Bonny exported almost none. However, by the 1830's Bonny, which was still the chief slaving state, was whittling away Calabar's early lead. Her traders switched from slaves to oil as the markets demanded. New oil markets were developed by the coastal traders, who usually exercised a monopoly over them. In addition to palm-oil these traders sold timber, ivory and bees-wax to the British ships.

Britain's growing interest in the promotion of legitimate trade saw a gradual change of both official and commercial attitudes towards the local rulers, who in the past had been accustomed to having their sovereignty completely respected by the European slave-traders. In 1824 Captain Owen, who was significantly given the task of surveying the coast of Africa by the British Admiralty, anchored in Bonny waters, and sent a junior officer to tell King Opobo he had arrived. The King was furious at this breach of etiquette, and resented deeply the fact that British ships had anchored in Bonny waters without his permission. In retaliation he ordered the complete cessation of trade with the British.[15] Though the affair was ultimately settled amicably, it indicated a new trend in British attitudes to West African chiefs. Later in 1836 the Navy, now backed up by the Equipment Treaty which allowed them to take Spanish and Portuguese ships as slavers if they were carrying the appropriate equipment, seized some Spanish ships waiting for slaves in Bonny. A tremendous dispute over this infringement of sovereignty arose between the responsible naval officer, Lieutenant Tryon, and the Regent of Bonny, who was naturally supported by the Spaniards. He ordered the arrest of Lieutenant Tryon and threw him into jail. The Navy promptly sailed into Bonny and forced the Regent to sign a treaty ensuring the protection of life and property of British subjects.[16] This was the thin end of the wedge. Legitimate trade was becoming so important that the British Government in order to make it secure was prepared to usurp the power of the coastal chiefs.

In 1834 Britain's trade in palm-oil was worth £500,000, a huge sum for those days, and she was not going to be without control of its source. Such was the concentration of naval force at the mouth of the River Bonny by the end of the thirties that Bonny was compelled, at least outwardly, to cease her traffic in slaves. Indeed Britain's treatment of Bonny may be taken as typical of her new attitude to African states.

After the death of King Opobo Pepple, the date of which is uncertain but which has been placed in 1830, there was an interregnum in Bonny. There appears to have been a struggle for power between the two main houses of Bonny, the Manila house and the Anna Pepple house. Since they could not agree on a mutually acceptable candidate, there was a regency under the control of the Anna Pepple chiefs. Eventually the Anna Pepple house had to accept William Dappa Pepple, candidate of the Manila house, but it appears they held on to the regency, on the grounds that he was too young to rule on his own. The Regent, as we have seen, had supported the Spanish slavers against the British Anti-Slavery patrol. Though he had signed a treaty with the British assuring them security of trade, the Regent continued to support the Spanish slavers, and within a month of signing the treaty, a British trader was detained by him contrary to Article I. Thus in March 1837 the Anti-Slavery patrol was sent to depose the Regent and install William Dappa Pepple as the King of Bonny in fact as well as name.

The new King, it was felt, would be more favourable to British trading interests. In 1839 a treaty abolishing the slave trade was signed with Bonny; but it was never ratified since the Navy believed that the compensation offered for the loss of trade would in fact be used to finance it further. In 1841 a new treaty was negotiated abolishing the slave trade with the important proviso that 'if at any future time Great Britain shall permit the slave trade to be carried on, King Pepple and the Chiefs of Bonny shall be at liberty to do the same'.[17] This treaty, too, was not ratified and King William Dappa Pepple never received his compensation. The existence of the patrol at the mouth of the River Bonny made it difficult for him to carry on the trade openly, but he and his chiefs cunningly diverted their trade to the small, concealed state of Brass which exported hundreds of slaves to Brazil and Cuba.[18] By 1844 such were British encroachments on Bonny that even King William Dappa Pepple, who owed his position to the British, was complaining of their interference. That same year a treaty abolishing the slave trade was ratified on the spot, the only condition under which he would sign.

It is significant, too, that in 1842 Palmerston tried to reacquire Fernando Po as a base to watch over the oil river ports and to give British traders protection. The earlier settlement there had been abandoned at a time when legitimate trade was not so important.

By the 1840's a large section of the British fleet was engaged in the anti-slavery patrol in West African waters. The ensuing decade, 1840–50, was critical both for the suppression of the slave trade and the establishment of British interests in Nigeria. The growth of legitimate trade during the period in which Britain was busily suppressing slavery is most significant. In 1820 there were 38 British merchantmen trading in the Bights of Benin and Biafra. In 1840 there were 134. Oil exports had increased from 200 tons in 1808 to 13,945 in 1834 and 25,285 in 1845. It is apparent that Britain was looking increasingly towards West Africa as a profitable area for trade.

Despite Britain's growing commercial interest in West Africa, the suppression of the slave trade nearly suffered disastrous setbacks in the decade 1840–50. In 1839 an English captain and ardent abolitionist called Denman actually destroyed a slaver's barracoon in an attempt to attack the slave-traders at the very source of their supply. In 1841 Captain Nurse followed suit and razed a barracoon on the Rio Pongos, but in the process he destroyed a considerable amount of foreign property. The foreigners declared themselves legitimate traders, and in England, the country of merchants *par excellence*, there was an outcry against Nurse's action on the grounds that it endangered the growth of legitimate trade. Aberdeen, the British Foreign Secretary at the time, then decided that the Navy should refrain from such actions unless the chiefs in whose waters these barracoons were sited agreed by treaty to their destruction. This, then, marked the beginning of a new phase in the suppression of the slave trade. The Navy started to make treaties with the coastal chiefs to gain their consent to the suppression of the slave trade. Later this system of treaty-making was to be used in the establishment of the British Protectorate over Nigeria.

All was not well for the abolitionists. In 1846 Peel's Tory Government reduced the import duty on sugar which in effect increased demand for it in England and therefore the demand for slaves to work on the sugar plantations of Cuba. Statistics bear this out: it is estimated that in 1842 only 24,800 slaves were exported from West Africa. By 1847 there were 84,356.

In the mid-nineteenth century there was a sharp conflict between humanitarians and traders. All went well when their interests coincided; but when, as in the case of the Sugar Act, they conflicted, humanitarian interests suffered. During the forties the West African Squadron came under frequent criticism, particularly because of its cost. Even those with humanitarian interests attacked it, because at times it apparently worsened conditions for slaves, who would be thrown overboard the moment a ship of the squadron gave chase to a slaver. There was a strong commercial faction that felt that British trade with Brazil would be seriously endangered if Brazil did not obtain slaves, the main prop of her plantation economy. A Member of Parliament called Hutt led these diverse factions in an attempt to have the squadron withdrawn, and in 1849 his Select Committee decided by one vote that the squadron should be called off and diplomatic pressure and missionary enterprise should be used to check the slave trade in its stead. In the Lords, Bishop Wilberforce managed to set up a rival committee which rejected Hutt's decision. When the reports of both Houses came up before the Commons Lord John Russell made it a vote of confidence in his Government to reject Hutt's motion for the withdrawal of the squadron, so that it was defeated.

The Suppression of the Slave Trade

The result of the defeat of Hutt's motion for the abolition of the slave squadron was, in fact, an increase in zeal for the cause of suppression. There were fresh diplomatic approaches to foreign powers and an increasing number of treaties were made with West African chiefs. One naval captain considered that without a naval squadron on the West Coast 'the coast would become a nest of pirates; the number of slaves exported would be enormous; all legitimate trade would cease, and in a very short time we would have to increase the squadron for the protection of what trade remained'.[19]

By the 1850's slave-trading had largely been abolished in Old Calabar, with whom official treaties had been negotiated. In Bonny, which was increasingly subjected to British political pressure, it had gone under cover. Farther up the coast, Lagos was still a sore spot. By the mid century the slave squadron had completed much of its work. Britain had supplied the slave ports with an alternative trade—that in palm oil. Between 1830 and 1850 legitimate trade had increased by 87 per cent. But the traders in palm oil, known as the palm-oil ruffians, were little different from the slavers themselves. They lived the same precarious existence on the fringe of Africa. They never penetrated inland. A great new field of commerce in the interior still remained to be exploited. This was the result of the enterprise of explorers, missionaries, and traders, African and European. The next three chapters will deal with the role of these three groups—explorers, missionaries and traders—in laying the foundation on which the British government was to build modern Nigeria.

CHAPTER IX

Explorers and Missionaries

T he movement in Britain for the abolition of the slave trade was accompanied by the desire to find markets for the products of Britain's new industries. At first the marketing of these goods was handled entirely by the African middlemen of the coastal kingdoms, who secured their monopoly on the basis of their exclusive knowledge of conditions in the interior and the fact that the climate was too unhealthy for Europeans to penetrate beyond the coastal fringe.[1] However, as Britain's trading interests grew in Nigeria, so did the desire of her merchants to trade direct with the markets of the interior. Much of the history of Nigeria in the nineteenth century concerns the resistance of African kings and middlemen to penetration of the interior by European traders. That these traders did in fact overcome this resistance was in the first instance largely due to the pioneer work of explorers and missionaries.

It is not surprising when one considers Britain's needs for overseas markets in the first half of the nineteenth century that many of the leading names in the history of the exploration of the West African hinterland should either be British or those of men like the German, Barth, who were sponsored by the British Government. The pioneers of inland trade were the great explorers like Mungo Park, Clapperton, the Lander brothers, Barth and Baikie. Their main problem was to discover an inland highway for trade into West Africa. Their attention was focused on the still legendary Niger.

The exploration of this great river dates from the founding of the African Association in 1788. This association represented a multiplicity of interests, such as politicians, scientists, indus-

trialists and humanitarians. But the chief object of the society
was initially, as Adu Boahen has shown,[2] the promotion of
scientific knowledge about Africa. However it was significant
that one of its founder-members was Josiah Wedgwood, an
architect of the industrial revolution in Britain. The Association
was to show great concern with the opening up of Africa to
legitimate trade. However, though humanitarians were
strongly represented on the board by Fox, Wilberforce and
Clarkson, the Association showed no open concern with abolition as such. As Boahen points out its founder, Sir Joseph
Banks, was against abolition, as were its second secretary, Bryan
Edwards and his successor, Sir William Young.[3] There was no
direct reference to the abolition of the slave trade in the objectives of the Association. Nevertheless the humanitarians intended to use it to further their own ends, for they believed that
promotion of legitimate trade was necessary to fill the vacuum
that would be left by the suppression of the slave trade.

The importance of the African Association, which was given
the backing of Pitt, must be seen against contemporary political
developments in the British Empire. Britain had just lost her
American colonies, and was looking to India as an alternative
outlet for her economic expansion. Australia had just been discovered and British interests in the Far East were increasing.
Geographically Africa lay in the path of the main axis of
British trade. It was thus of a high strategic interest, heightened
twelve years later by the Napoleonic Wars. It was not surprising, then, that the British Government gave the African
Association its unofficial support.[4]

The specific object of the Association was to organize the
exploration of the interior of Africa. At the time West Africa
was, as far as Europe was concerned, almost a *carte blanche* and
had been used as such by the more imaginative pictorial geographers of the preceding centuries, who dotted the land with
mythical cities, and often more mythical lakes and seas that were
to confuse considerably the determination of the source of the
Niger, which, because it was hoped it might prove a major
highway of trade into Africa, became one of the chief objects of
the Association's attentions.[5] In 1788 it was believed that the
Niger flowed to the west, as Leo Africanus had reported over
two centuries before.[6] The Gambia and Senegal rivers therefore

appeared as its most obvious outlets. In an attempt to discover the Niger, the Association equipped expeditions to cross the desert, all of which were tragically unsuccessful. Others were sent to the West Coast to attack the problem, as it were, from its southern side. Tragedy also struck the first explorer on this route, Major Houghton, who was either murdered by Moors or died of hunger as a result of being deserted by them,[7] but not before he had sent back sufficient information to suggest that the Niger might flow to the east.[8] It was left to Mungo Park, a young Scotsman, whose two journeys into the interior of West Africa have earned for him next to Livingstone the most celebrated place in the history of the European exploration of Africa, to tell Europe for certain which way the Niger flowed. Inspired by an incredible determination, which allowed him to suffer the unendurable in the firm belief it was predestined by God, he succeeded in reaching the Niger. Even when he had been robbed of all his belongings, and was sick with fever and deserted by his followers, he did not give up his quest for the Niger. Finally, after a hellish journey, he came 'through some marshy ground where, as I was anxiously looking around for the river, one of them called out *geo affili* (see the water); and looking forwards, I saw with infinite pleasure the great object of my mission; the long sought for, majestic Niger, glittering to the morning sun, as broad as the Thames at Westminster, and flowing slowly to the *Eastward*. I hastened to the brink, and having drunk of the water, lifted up my fervent thanks in prayer, to the Great ruler of all things, for having thus far crowned my endeavours with success.'[9]

This information was to set the world of armchair geographers abuzz. Hitherto it had been taken for granted that the Niger flowed to the west.

Major Rennell propounded the theory that the Niger flowed into a great lake—the sink of Africa—where it simply evaporated.[10] However his theory, which gained wide recognition, was opposed by the German geographer Reichard, who correctly stated that the huge delta of rivers in the Bight of Benin was the Niger's outlet into the sea.[11]

The African Association declared that as a result of Park's discovery 'a gate is opened to every commercial nation to enter and trade from the West to the eastern extremity of Africa'.[12] Therefore when Park, who had subsequently become a doctor

in Peebles, volunteered to return to the Niger and seek its outlet, the Association accepted his services eagerly and the British
Government put up the money for a lavishly and, as it eventually turned out, farcically equipped expedition. Park set off this
time not alone but with a band of forty-five Europeans, fully
equipped to construct a boat in which the party would sail
down the Niger to its source. The expedition was a disaster, a
monument to bad organization. Park, brave and capable of
much suffering himself, was incapable of understanding the
needs of others, and before he himself was murdered on the
Bussa rapids in Northern Nigeria, every man in his party but
his Mandingo servant Isaaco had died. Fortunately the devoted
Isaaco made his way back to the coast and delivered up Park's
manuscript to the British Government.[13] At the time Park's
achievement of travelling eight hundred miles from Timbuktu
to Bussa was not appreciated, since contemporary geographers
estimated it at only a tenth of the actual distance,

The problem of the Niger was left aside during the Napoleonic Wars. However, the end of those wars saw a revival of
interest in the termination; but an unsuccessful expedition by
Major Peddie following Park's old route dampened the British
Government's enthusiasm, which only really revived in 1821
when Denham, Clapperton and Oudney left for Nigeria across
the Sahara. That same year a West Indian planter named
M'Queen became a champion of the theory that the Niger's
outlet was in the Bight of Benin, deducing this from reports his
slaves had given him.[14] Crossing from Tripoli, the Denham-
Clapperton expedition at first seemed to justify Rennell's theory,
for in 1823 they discovered Lake Chad, supposedly 'the vast
sink of Africa'. However, when they followed the river that fed
this lake they found that it dwindled to a mere trickle after a
short distance.

In Bornu, Denham and Clapperton were received by Al-
Kanemi, who actually wrote to King George IV saying that he
would welcome four or five traders from England in his country:
'The Rayes Khaleel (Major Denham travelled under this name)
desired of us permission, that merchants seeking for elephant-
teeth, ostrich feathers, and other such things, that are not to be
found in the country of the English, might come among us. We
told him that our country, as he himself has known and seen its

state, does not suit any heavy (rich) traveller, who may possess great wealth. But if a few light persons (small capitalists), as four or five only, with little merchandize, would come, there will be no harm. This is the utmost that we can give him permission for; and more than that number must not come.'[15]

The party was greatly impressed by the vast array of chain-mailed horsemen under the command of the Shehu.[16] Clapperton and Oudney, who died shortly after, moved on into Hausa country. Clapperton arrived at the great metropolis of Kano eager with anticipation. He was extremely anxious to look his best on entering this city which frankly, after the tales he had heard from Arab traders, disappointed him. He dressed in his best naval uniform but 'not an individual turned his head round to gaze at me, but all intent on their own business, allowed me to pass without notice or remark'.[17] In Kano he noted that the only foreign goods on sale were French, German and Italian.

Clapperton moved on to Sokoto, the capital of the great Fulani Empire, ruled over by the scholarly Sultan Bello, who was able to tell him much about the country.[18] Though he would not allow Clapperton to leave for the Niger, he expressed a desire to establish commercial relations with the British, and asked that a consulate be established in Sokoto. Clapperton left a happy man and joined Denham, who had gone south along the Shari River which he confused with the Benue, the main tributary of the Niger. Clapperton had every reason to be pleased with himself. He had been promised commercial relations with Sokoto; he had been told by Sultan Bello that he would have no difficulty in reaching the sea by the Niger; and a consulate had been established in Bornu. The party left a Mr. Tyrwhitt, who had joined the expedition in May 1824, as consul in Kuka, the capital of the Shehu of Bornu.

The British Government was well pleased with the expedition. The prospects of trade with the interior seemed about to be realized at last, for Clapperton had even been told by Sultan Bello the name of the port at the mouth of the Niger. Clapperton's return to England seemed to herald the end of the long quest for the termination of the Niger. The Government promptly equipped a second expedition to be led by Clapperton with the object of reaching the interior from the seaboard, preferably up the Niger.

But on his return to the coast to discover the port, which Sultan Bello had called Rakah, Clapperton met with disappointment. No one had ever heard of such a place. So he decided to trek overland from Badagry to Sokoto, where instead of friendliness he met with considerable hostility from the Sultan. There was now no question of trade, and certainly no question of giving up slave-dealing. It seemed that a rival economic interest, that of Arab merchants from Tripoli and Morocco, had persuaded the Sultan that trade with the Europeans would be foolish. The Sultan also had suspicions about Clapperton's friendly relations with his enemy, the Shehu of Bornu.[19] Bitterly disappointed, and making no headway against the Sultan's new position, Clapperton became ill and died in April 1827. Richard Lander, his Cornish servant, tried to reach the coast along the River Niger, but at the confluence of the Niger and Benue he was captured by the local inhabitants and forced to make his way back by land. On his return to England Lander persuaded a reluctant government, which had now come to believe that trade with the interior would never be possible because of the high incidence of disease, to make him a grant to return once more to the coast. He was given £100 for himself and his brother, who was to accompany him, and a further £100 to keep his wife in his absence.

In 1830 the Lander brothers trekked overland from Badagry to Bussa where Mungo Park had met his death.[20] There they were able with much difficulty to secure two canoes. They sailed down the Niger through the confluence with the Benue until at Asaba they were taken captive by local Ibo. Eventually their captors agreed to deliver them to the master of an English brig anchored at Brass on the mouth of the Niger. They were taken downstream and were overjoyed to learn that they had at last discovered the mouth of the Niger. At Brass, Richard Lander was allowed to go on board the brig to negotiate the ransom with its captain, Thomas Lake. At first Lake was most reluctant to pay up, but eventually agreed to do so on delivery of John Lander. No sooner was John Lander on board than he set sail without paying a penny. Thus in 1830, in melodramatic circumstances not untypical of trade in those days, the quest for the Niger was ended by the efforts of Richard Lander, a 'gentleman's gentleman' turned explorer. A new phase of exploration had opened. The route to the interior was known. Now the great question, of such great import for the future of Nigeria, was whether life was possible for Europeans in the interior.

Once the mouth of the Niger had been discovered, it was not long before this new knowledge was put to commercial use. With British naval supremacy on the coast, the Niger opened up tremendous and unexplored possibilities to British trade. It was significant that shortly after the return of the Landers a Liverpool trader, Macgregor Laird, financed a commercial expedition to the coast in 1832, though at the time he was virtually the only merchant interested in opening up interior African trade. His two ships, the *Alburkah* and *Quorra*, were the first two iron steamships ever to be built as ocean-going vessels. Commercially, however, the expedition was a disaster, accompanied by a heavy death toll from malaria. Only nine of the forty-eight Europeans on the expedition survived. Nevertheless, it did sail up the Niger as far as the confluence and beyond.[21] The failure of this expedition postponed further attempts to penetrate the interior for commercial purposes until 1841.

Now a new element was brought in as the motive force behind the development of internal trade: the humanitarians and their delegates, the missionaries.

The humanitarians had quickly come to realize that the prohibition of the slave trade was not enough. Certainly, as we have seen, the British Navy was not sufficiently strong to prevent traders obtaining slaves for export to the Americas. The answer, they maintained, was not only to increase the size of the Anti-Slavery patrol but to attack slavery at its economic root—that was, to show Africans an alternative method of obtaining money with which to buy European goods. The natural, not the human products of Africa should form the basis of exchange. This was the view put forward by Sir Thomas Fowell Buxton in his book *The African Slave Trade and its Remedy*.[22] The only way to save Africa from the evils of the slave-trade, he insisted, would be to call out its own natural resources. At the same time every effort should be made to save the souls of those whom they were rescuing from slavery. Already missionaries had established a settlement for freed slaves in Sierra Leone, and with the growing militancy of Christian sects in England, thoughts began to turn towards the evangelization of the whole

West Coast. Africa seemed an excellent missionary target for it was considered in the words of Eugene Stock in his *History of the C.M.S.*, published in 1897, 'one universal den of desolation, misery and crime'.[23]

Thus early missionaries in West Africa had a dual purpose: to promote legitimate trade between African and European, and to convert Africans to their own religion. This came out clearly in the expedition up the River Niger in 1841. The object of this expedition, sponsored by the Society for the Extinction of the Slave Trade and for the Civilization of Africa, of which Buxton was a leading member, was to promote trade in the interior, to conclude treaties with local chiefs and to establish a model agricultural farm. This farm, originally the idea of Commander William Allen who had travelled with Laird's expedition in 1832, was to serve as an 'exhibition centre' for the surrounding people. The expedition, consisting of 145 Europeans, was given an official send-off at Exeter Hall by no less a person than Prince Albert, Consort of Queen Victoria.

The expedition was the brain-child of men who were almost entirely ignorant of conditions in the interior of the Niger region. One of its members, W. Simpson, carried letters from the Chief Rabbi and the Rabbi of the Portuguese Community in London, in case they were to encounter Jews.[24] The expedition came under heavy fire in England. Robert Jamieson, in *An Appeal Against the Proposed Niger Expedition*, [25] protested to the Government against humanitarian interference in commerce, pointing out that its experiment in Sierra Leone had already proved a failure. Merchants also objected to interference by the Government in trade.

Nevertheless the expedition set sail in three ships: the *Albert*, *Sudan* and *Wilberforce*. On board were two missionaries, the Rev. J. F. Schön and Samuel Crowther, a freed slave who later became Bishop on the Niger.[26] He had been taken as a slave during one of the Yoruba inter-tribal wars in 1822. The slaver on which he was being transported across the Atlantic was intercepted and taken to Freetown. On his release he was sent to the C.M.S. school where his great intelligence soon caught the attention of the missionaries. In 1825 he was baptized Samuel, though he always kept his native name Ajayi, which means one born with his face to the ground and destined for a remarkable future. He was then sent to the Parochial School in Liverpool Street, Islington, in London. He took the name Crowther from a distinguished member of the Church Missionary Society.[27]

Crowther and Schön were charged with pursuing the new policy of 'Bible and Plough' on the expedition. From now on missionaries were to play a major role in the exploration of the interior. Hitherto their influence and interest in Nigeria had been marginal, largely because the local chiefs did not permit penetration of the interior, and also because of the difficult living conditions under which most Europeans succumbed to malaria. Furthermore, European slaving interests had naturally been hostile to missionary penetration.

The 1841 expedition was superficially a disastrous failure and set back the promotion of commercial enterprise ten years, for on the expedition over a third of the members of the expedition died of malaria.[28] Ironically the expedition carried plenty of supplies of the one thing that could have cured them: quinine. But they used it only when a patient showed signs of recovery. The model farm, purchased from the powerful Ata of Idah, was a failure, and the expedition returned to England with little to show for their early optimism and enthusiasm.

The Times and the *Edinburgh Review*, both of which had criticized the expedition, wrote self-satisfied editorials that prevented its repetition for another decade. And though the foundations of the Niger mission had been laid in 1841, it would hardly have survived as a concept had not Henry Venn been made Hon. Secretary of the C.M.S. in that year. He it was who had such faith in the Yoruba ex-slave Ajayi Crowther, who became the first black bishop of modern times. He it was who took the Rev. J. F. Schön's advice, based on his experiences on the expedition, that since Europeans could not easily survive the climate, Nigeria must be evangelized by Africans themselves, of whom there were large numbers ready to offer themselves in the Sierra Leone settlement. As a result of the failure of the 1841 expedition the Niger mission was to start predominantly as an African mission.[29]

Despite the setback which the 1841 expedition represented at the time, missionary penetration of Nigeria really dates from then. As C. C. Ifemesia observes: 'Whatever were the opinions of Buxton's critics, the British missionaries (especially the Church Missionary Society) never believed that the expedition was a total failure.'[30] They believed that as a result of the mission they had learned much, both about the country and its peoples and how best to organize their subsequent efforts. Missionaries were to become latter-day, less spectacular explorers, pushing into the remotest corners of the country to spread the Gospel, and thereby to make the hinterland accessible to government and trading interests. Missionary enterprise in Nigeria took the form of a three-pronged attack: the Church of Scotland mission occupied itself with Calabar; the Church Missionary Society established missions in the Niger Delta and up the Niger; the Methodists, the Church Missionary Society, and the Baptists advanced into Yorubaland. In all three areas freed slaves and Africans played an important role in the evangelization of Nigeria.

Africans were very much in the vanguard of missionary activity in Badagry and Abeokuta. In the late 1830's a number of freed slaves from Freetown returned to their original homes in Lagos, Badagry and Abeokuta. As a result of trade between Badagry and Freetown, some of the Aku (Yoruba) Creoles learnt of the great Yoruba cities of Abeokuta and Lagos and decided to return there. Two parties left Sierra Leone, one for Lagos, the other for Abeokuta. The Lagos expedition finished with all 300 members being robbed of their possessions. By 1842 over 500 returned slaves were resettled in Abeokuta. Their appeals to the Church Missionary Society in Sierra Leone to open a mission in Abeokuta brought down Henry Townsend, who had been preceded in the missionary field in Nigeria by a half-caste, Thomas Birch Freeman, head of the Gold Coast Methodist mission. He had opened a station at Badagry in 1842 and had already established cordial relations with Sodeke, the founder and leader of Abeokuta. Townsend actually met Freeman while he was on his way back from Abeokuta, where the immigrants from Sierra Leone had been well received.

A year later an important event took place in London. Samuel Ajayi Crowther, whose journal of the 1841 expedition had greatly impressed the C.M.S., was ordained a priest. Afterwards he preached before Sir Thomas Buxton. When, later, as a result of Townsend's visit to Abeokuta, the Yoruba mission was established, it was only natural to make the Yoruba-speaking Crowther one of its members. Together with the German missionary Gollmer, Townsend, two catechists and an interpreter, Crowther set off for Abeokuta, only to learn with distress that Sodeke had died. This meant not only that the new mission would be without the protection of this sympathetic ruler, but also that the one unifying force amongst the Egba sub-tribes and immigrants that went to make up Abeokuta had been removed. Matters were further complicated by the dispute over the chieftancy in Lagos, where Kosoko, a well-known slaver, had usurped the throne of his uncle Akitoye:[31] Some Egba war chiefs had given their support to Kosoko, so it became impossible for the missionaries, enemies of slavery, to reach Abeokuta. Further, Gezo, the slaving king of Dahomey, had control of the Badagry–Abeokuta road. The missionaries therefore contented themselves with opening a mission at Badagry. Schools were built, an experimental farm was established and a steel corn mill introduced to stimulate legitimate trade. Not until 1846 were they able to leave for Abeokuta, where they were well received by the people. Again a church was built and schools established. However, their work did not easily survive the death of their first convert in 1848. Funeral rites in most indigenous African religions are of deepest significance to their adherents. When, therefore, on the death of an indigenous convert the mission attempted to bury him according to Christian rites there were naturally many relatives anxious that he should be buried according to native custom. Feeling ran high and riots followed, together with a general persecution of the Christians.

Perhaps one of the most significant results of the establishment of the mission at Abeokuta was the visit four months later of the representative of the large trading firm of Thomas Hutton and Co., with a view to establishing a factory or trading store. Soon afterwards factories were opened at Abeokuta as well as Badagry which had become an important trade centre both for slaves and legitimate commerce.

The prestige of the missionaries in Abeokuta, both Baptists and C.M.S., rose as a result of their close co-operation in 1851 with the Abeokutans in the defence of the city against the Dahomeyans. The Amazon vanguard of the Dahomeyan invaders was repelled with Townsend of the C.M.S. and Bowen of the Baptist mission offering advice. Bowen had in fact been a contemporary of Davy Crockett, fighting Indians in Texas and Alabama, before becoming a missionary.

The C.M.S. in London felt optimistic enough to expand its activities beyond Yorubaland. Hinderer, together with his wife, who became a great missionary in her own right, arrived initially with the intention of going to Hausaland but, because of the civil wars, remained in Yorubaland travelling extensively and gaining warm receptions everywhere except in Ijebuland.[32]

The emphasis in any history of early missionary activity in Nigeria must be on the C.M.S., since as an offshoot of the Anglican Church it had official sanction in days when Nonconformism was still a social disadvantage. No better illustration is given of this than the close interest of Queen Victoria in the mission's work. She sent two Bibles to the mission, one in English and one in Arabic; and Prince Albert, a year before his Great Exhibition of 1851, not surprisingly made it a gift of a steel corn mill. Later, when Crowther went on leave, he was received by Lord Palmerston, the Foreign Secretary, and had an audience of Queen Victoria, at which he read the Lord's Prayer in Yoruba, described later by the Queen as soft and melodious.[33]

The political influence of the Church Missionary Society, therefore, was much greater than that of any other group. Indeed, as we shall see in the next chapter, one of the main factors behind Britain's decision to depose King Kosoko of Lagos in 1852 was pressure from the missionaries at Abeokuta, who found his slave trading prejudicial to the development of legitimate trade in Egbaland. And as they were prepared to lobby the British Government in furtherance of their policy of 'Bible and Plough', so too they were willing to interfere in local politics. Townsend, for instance, was largely responsible for the introduction of the new supreme ruler of Abeokuta, the Alake, preferring one sovereign chief, with whom he could deal direct, to a multiplicity of chiefs without real power. Later on, as we shall see, this political interference was to bring considerable tension to both Lagos and Abeokuta.

The second prong of early missionary enterprise in Nigeria was on the Cross River in the old slave-trading state of Calabar.

K   145

In 1846 Hope Waddell arrived in Calabar together with a group of Christian Jamaicans to establish the Church of Scotland Mission. In 1834, on the release of all Jamaican slaves from bondage, the Church of Scotland had established a mission in Jamaica, and it was largely through the moving spirits of these Negroes that the mission to Calabar was organized.[34]

In Calabar conditions were as bad as anywhere on the coast. We have already seen that, by contrast with Bonny and New Calabar, the Efik treated their slaves with scant consideration. Human sacrifice on a large and ostentatious scale, associated with the death of chiefs, was prevalent; twin murder was practised; and widows were often forced to remain in total seclusion without washing or changing their clothes for several years. To abolish these practices and the slave trade, as well as to evangelize the people, was the main aim of the Church of Scotland missionaries. Their mission was granted land between Duke Town and Henshaw Town by King Eyamba V of Duke Town, who with King Eyo Honesty of Creek Town was the most important ruler of Calabar at the time. Shortly after the mission's arrival a leading chief died in Duke Town, and despite the intervention of the missionaries many slaves were killed to accompany him on his eternal journey. In 1847 King Eyamba himself died—this was the signal for large-scale sacrifice.

In Creek Town the missionaries were more sympathetically received. King Eyo Honesty cleared a site for a mission house and school. Pressure from both the missionaries and legitimate traders forced the Calabar chiefs to conduct sacrifices at the death of any of their number more and more secretly. In 1850 ten ship captains, three surgeons and two missionaries met in the mission house at Creek Town to form 'A Society for the Suppression of Human Sacrifices in Calabar'. They wrote to both king and chiefs to inform them that all friendly intercourse with them would cease until the practice was discontinued. As a result an Egbo society law was passed on 15th February 1850, abolishing human sacrifice. This was not always easy to maintain. The real test was to come later in 1858 when King Eyo Honesty himself died after a long reign. Not one man was sacrificed!

The history of the Niger Mission, which was the third prong of missionary attack in Nigeria, once again illustrates the combination of commercial and philanthropic interests that so often went hand in hand in West Africa.[35] Before the highly successful expedition up the Niger in 1854, led by Dr. Baikie, little headway had been made on the Niger. In 1848 an American Negro and the principal of the Fourah Bay Institution in Freetown did lead a mission to the Delta to try and resettle 100 freed Ibo slaves. But the King of Bonny refused them permission and instead they were sent to Calabar. Baikie's expedition was to mark the foundation of one of the most successful missions in West Africa, the Niger Mission, the first to start off with an entirely African-staffed mission, following the earlier recommendations of Schön.

The background to the Niger Mission was the highly successful expedition up the Niger and Benue in 1854. The British Government, whose appetite for expeditions up the Niger had been damped by the 1841 failure, was stimulated to a further trial by despatches sent by the great German explorer, Heinrich Barth. Still interested in the country around the Niger, and hoping that it would be possible to open up trade across the Sahara in sufficient volume to supplant the trans-desert slave trade estimated at 10,000 per year,[36] the British Government had sent James Richardson with two Germans, Barth and Overweg, across the desert for reports on the general conditions in these countries on what was known as the Central African Mission. Richardson and Overweg died, but Barth covered hundreds of miles in Northern Nigeria and wrote eventually a voluminous and fascinating book describing with remarkable observation and scholarship the geography, history and ethnology of the peoples he encountered.[37]

In 1852 a despatch from Barth informed the British Government that he had crossed the Benue. He speculated that this was the same river as the Tschadda that flowed into the Niger at Lokoja. To ascertain this, and to promote once more trade with the interior, the government financed an expedition to sail up the Tschadda to see if in fact it was the Benue. The expedition originally mooted by Barth[38] was of deepest significance for the future of European commercial interests in West Africa, for not one European died on the 900 miles' journey into the interior to Yola.[39] The use of quinine as a prophylactic against malaria showed that life was possible for Europeans in the interior of

Africa. From this date, as much as any other, can be traced the growth of effective British interest in the hinterland of Nigeria, which was eventually to lead to the establishment of a British protectorate over Nigeria and the loss of sovereignty by the various African kingdoms and states that comprised it.

While Baikie and other members of the expedition occupied themselves with the more mundane tasks of the expedition, Crowther set about reconnoitring the sites for the future Niger Mission, at Onitsha and Lokoja amongst others. The subsequent history of these missions and their associated trading stations belongs to the next chapter.

The activities of these early missionaries were to have the most profound influence on the future of Southern Nigeria. In the North, of course, they came up against the barrier of Islam, and were able to make little progress except in non-Moslem areas.

Before the arrival of these missionaries, traders, the only other representatives of European culture, had made remarkably little impact on the societies with which they conducted their commerce. New consumer habits were naturally developed as a result of both the slave and the oil trade, but even with the new economic régime brought about by the commercialization of palm-oil, the Delta societies remained fundamentally the same. Certainly the traders never sought to alter this situation. The missionaries, by contrast, came out with the deliberate intention not only of changing the economic habits of a predominantly slave-trading society, but of converting it to a completely new way of life: that of Christ. These missionaries came from a society deeply convinced that their religion and their mode of life, especially with its new benefits of industrialization, were superior to anything else in the world.[40] When they arrived in Africa they quickly came to the conclusion that there was nothing good in indigenous African religion. Almost from the start they condemned the indigenous religions in all their aspects, and required of the African conversion not only to a new religion, but to a completely new way of life. For this they have been frequently attacked, for in so doing they destroyed many of the riches of African culture, in particular ritual art and dancing, with the result that many Africans take as scathing a view of their own traditional society today as the most prejudiced Europeans. On the other hand, it must be said in defence of the missionaries that they made a correct appreciation of the fact that West African religions were much more closely integrated with West African cultures than Victorian Christianity with the rest of Victorian culture. To destroy the one effectively it was essential to destroy the other. In this missionaries were later to be opposed by the administrators, with their policy of indirect rule through traditional institutions. The fact that many Nigerians today still largely retain their traditional religious world view even when they are practising Christians is in part due to the fact that the missionaries were never able fully to carry out their policy of effacing not only traditional religion, but the entire culture with which it was so intimately bound up.

The most powerful factor of change introduced by these early missionaries was Western education. In traditional society the wealth and power that education could bring introduced education as a new indicator of status. Later, when the occupation of Nigeria by the British brought about a great demand for indigenous employees for the new administration, the benefits of Christian education were seen to be very great. Christian education and knowledge of the English language also gave common ground to members of many of the widely differing groups of which Nigeria is composed. It was from these early converts that the first African élite to gain the respect of the white man emerged. It was this élite which was to provide the leading members of the professional and commercial world, and which ultimately was to produce the leaders of the nationalist movement for self-government and independence.

CHAPTER X

The Growth of Legitimate Trade

In 1851, Kosoko, King of Lagos, was forced off his throne by the British on the grounds of his slave-trading activities and replaced by his more tractable uncle, Akitoye. Three years later, *The Pleiad* sailed up the Niger without a single European member of the crew succumbing to malaria. Both these events may be taken as symbolic of the increasing attraction to Britain of the Nigerian region for trade.

In the one case the installation of a king not only sympathetic to British interests but also largely dependent on Britain for his authority, in place of one openly hostile to her, was a classic example of nineteenth-century colonial expansion; in the other it was proved that life beyond the coast was possible for Europeans and this diverted attention from the coastal states to the supposed wealth of the interior. Nigerian rulers now faced a Britain openly prepared to interfere in their politics if they proved hostile to her trading interests. This becomes increasingly clear from the activities of the British Consuls in the years between 1850 and 1865, and makes the subsequent recommendations of the famous 1865 Select Committee that the British Government should withdraw from the West Coast seem on the surface quite paradoxical.

The gradual opening-up of the interior to direct trading relations between African producer and European buyer, and the consequent breakdown of the monopoly of coastal trade held by the Delta middlemen and the Liverpool traders, were to produce a crisis in Delta politics. In this period much of the thinking of the representatives of the British on the West Coast was on the lines that if trade was to be carried on to advantage, then the highest authority in the land would have to be not the

6. Niger Delta oil markets in the nineteenth century

African chief, but the British Government. This was a view that evoked considerable opposition in Britain, not only from commercial and humanitarian circles, but also from the Government itself. The Treasury and the Colonial Office approached imperial expansion with great parsimony, agreeing to acquire colonies only if it was clear that they could support their administration from locally derived revenues. This opposition to any colonial enterprise that might prove a burden to the British budget crystallized in the findings of the Select Committee of 1865.[1]

By 1850 British trading interests were concentrating in two

regions of what is now Nigeria: Lagos, the gateway to the rich forests of Yorubaland; and the Delta ports, which were the outlet for the trade of the interior of Eastern Nigeria. The chief export was still palm-oil. The slave trade became progressively less important as the African middlemen of the Delta found it more profitable to export palm-oil.[2] Only in the area around Lagos where a steady supply of slaves, mainly prisoners taken in the Yoruba civil wars, continued to reach the coast, was it still of a serious nature. During the fifties the Delta was preeminent in the palm-oil trade, and Bonny was its richest port. However in both Yorubaland and the Delta hinterland the internal demand for slaves rose as a result of the expansion of legitimate trade. Labourers were required to gather the palmnuts, porters to carry oil to the coast. Sir Richard Burton informed the British Parliamentary Select Committee on Africa in 1864 that legitimate trade had led to an increased demand for slaves as porters. Thus legitimate trade, which the abolitionists hoped would prove a substitute for the slave trade, was actually responsible for its increase.[3]

During the fifties the Delta was pre-eminent in the palm-oil trade, and Bonny was its richest port. The oil was prepared in the markets of the interior by boiling the husks in water and skimming off the resultant oil. It was then transported to Lagos or the Delta ports. In the 1855–6 season the Delta exported 25,060 tons of oil, which was over half the total quantity of oil exported from Africa. Of this quantity, 16,124 tons were sold by Bonny and its rival New Calabar; 4,000 by Old Calabar; and 2,280 by Brass. However, by the end of the fifties Lagos, now under the docile rule of Docemo, paid off earlier British intervention by exporting over 20,000 tons.[4]

The oil trade was monopolized by the middlemen of the Delta, who prevented any contact between the producers and the white merchants who came mostly from Liverpool. These merchants supplied the middlemen with credit in the form of trade goods, which were taken up to the markets of the interior and exchanged for palm-oil, and to a lesser extent ivory, timber and bees-wax. Credit goods, which were known as 'trust', were often supplied up to the value of £5,000 to reputable middlemen for as long a period as a year. There was no real form of money though Spanish dollars were generally accepted.

The value of goods was measured variously in the different ports. In Bonny, for instance, they were equated to iron bars worth about five shillings each.[5] A wide range of goods, particularly cloths, guns, beads, lead and copper rods, were used in exchange. Vast profits were made by the Liverpool merchants through their monopoly. They fobbed off second-rate goods to the Africans who had no standards of comparison, and often sold them ridiculous second-hand clothes pretending that they were those worn by the aristocracy in England. We should not laugh therefore at the amused descriptions by contemporary travellers of the pretentious attire of many African kings, for it was as often as not encouraged by the white traders themselves with high profit as the primary motive.

Basically the control of the standards of trade was in the hands of the African authorities, though this became less and less so with the interference of the British Consuls. The palm-oil traders were as rough a lot as the old slave-traders, and well deserved their title 'Palm Oil Ruffians'. The African chiefs could not actually bring these traders before their own courts, so they resorted to the expedient of imposing collective punishment on the European community through the banning of trade. This was fairly effective, since conditions on the Coast were such that most traders were very anxious to get back to Europe as quickly as possible, and could stomach no delays. The ban on trade was always absolute because of the strict control African chiefs exercised over their subjects. There was no 'scabbing' on the African part, to use a modern trade-union term. On the other hand the Europeans found it difficult to combine effectively, since whenever a European community stuck out for lower prices, there was usually one of their number willing to trade at the African's price.

In 1854 Africans and Europeans in Bonny combined to deal with the problems of local trade by setting up a 'Court of Equity' on which both Bonny middlemen and European supercargoes were represented. Traders offending against the regulations of the court, which was presided over by a different white supercargo in monthly rotation, were subject to fines, which had to have the approval of the King of Bonny. If such a trader refused to pay, a collective boycott was placed on him until such time as he did. This court was so successful that soon similar ones were instituted at New Calabar, Akassa, Benin River, Old Calabar, Brass and later Opobo. Despite this healthy development in the regulation of coastal trade, the European traders still used the power of their local Consul to force their own terms on African chiefs. Indeed the growth of British consular power is the most characteristic trend in relations between Britain and Nigeria in this period, and is epitomized by the career of the first of Britain's consuls, John Beecroft.[6]

In 1849 John Beecroft was appointed Her Britannic Majesty's Consul for the Bights of Benin and Biafra. As Dr. Diké has written, it was he who 'laid the foundations of British power in Nigeria and initiated the politics which were to characterize the consular period of Nigerian history'.[7] His very remarkable career in West Africa began on Fernando Po, when it was occupied by Britain as a base for the suppression of the slave-trade in 1827. When it was abandoned by Britain, he stayed on to look after the interests of the liberated slaves who had been settled there. In 1843 he was appointed Governor of the island by Spain. Already he had acquired an unrivalled knowledge of the Coast. In 1835 he had travelled as far up the Niger as Idah, and not one of the Europeans on his expedition died. In 1840 he had entered the Benin River and proved that it was not the principal outlet of the Niger. In the following two years he had led further expeditions up the Cross River. He thus came to know most of the Coastal chiefs intimately, and was deeply respected by them.

From 1844 to 1849 the British Navy employed him on various political missions, so that he became the obvious choice for appointment as first British Consul for the Bights of Benin and Biafra. During his six years as Consul he was to wield immense influence in the Delta and farther up the coast in Lagos. From the outset he was bent on involving Britain in the affairs of the coastal states, for as he saw it important British interests were at stake. He therefore interfered constantly in local politics and advocated the eventual take-over of the Coastal states by Britain.

Soon after he was appointed Consul, English traders in Bonny complained to him about their treatment at the hands of King William Dappa Pepple.[8] Beecroft himself was in favour of putting an end to what he considered to be Pepple's persecution of British traders, some of whom had actually been murdered on their way up the New Calabar River in 1847. Pepple argued that he had nothing to do with these murders nor the insecurity on the New Calabar River, for both were the responsibility of an important priest, Awanta, who was 'jew jew' and therefore outside his jurisdiction.[9] Beecroft paid little attention to Pepple's complaints about the series of treaties he had signed with Britain agreeing to the abolition of the slave-trade and the protection of British interests; these had not been ratified nor, more important, had the subsidy promised him been paid. In the case of Calabar and the Cameroons, Pepple complained that those treaties had been ratified and the subsidies paid. Why not his? His bitterness was increased by the fact that his rival and neighbour, New Calabar, was still trading in slaves and making a profit out of it. Whereas warships could block the Bonny River with ease, New Calabar, like Brass, was concealed in the creeks.

In these circumstances British traders feared a recurrence of past disturbances, so Beecroft came in to settle the dispute. He summoned Pepple to come on board his warship, which Pepple naturally refused to do, inviting Beecroft to come to his own palace, an invitation Beecroft eventually accepted. Though a treaty was signed between the King and the Consul on 3rd October 1850, regulating conditions of trade[10], no real improvement in relations resulted from this visit. Rather did it make Pepple deeply suspicious of British intentions. He was in a difficult position, faced with threats of British intervention from without, and the hostility of the party backing Alali, the former Regent, from within. Alali was only too eager to exploit any difficulties that might come King Pepple's way. The net result of this show of force on the part of the Consul was merely to increase Pepple's antagonism towards the British.

The following year Beecroft took what was to prove a crucial step in Britain's involvement with Nigeria and deposed Kosoko, the slave-trading King of Lagos. Kosoko's uncle, Akitoye, was placed on the throne after having guaranteed to suppress the slave trade in Lagos. The British Government took this dramatic step largely because Kosoko was proving one of the major obstacles to the suppression of the slave trade on that part of the Coast. Furthermore his neighbour, King Gezo of Dahomey, had told Beecroft that he would not give up slave-trading while

Kosoko still indulged in it. The missionaries at Abeokuta had exerted great pressure on the home government in favour of deposing Kosoko, for while he reigned there was little hope of legitimate trade through the port of Lagos.

The Kosoko dispute has usually been painted as one between a bad slave-trading king and his peace-loving Uncle Akitoye whose throne he had usurped.[11] This is an oversimplification of a very complex dynastic dispute, which dates back to 1811 when the Oba of Lagos died and his second son Adele succeeded him instead of Esilogun who, as eldest son, felt himself to be the rightful heir. This led to a series of disputes and the eventual expulsion of Adele by Esilogun in 1821. Adele turned to the British at Badagry, and in 1825 tried to effect his return with the help of the Navy. It was not until 1833, however, that Adele actually became king again, this time with the aid of the Oba of Benin, his overlord. He died the next year and was succeeded by his son Oluwole, who died in 1841 without issue. This led to rival claims, chiefly between Oluwole's cousin Kosoko and his uncle Akitoye. As it was, Akitoye was crowned King of Lagos by the Oba of Benin. Naturally Kosoko resented this and worked hard to undermine the power of Akitoye, and in 1845 he expelled him. Akitoye made an alliance with Abeokuta, in an effort to re-establish himself, and was financed by a well-known slave-trader, Domingo José, which, as Ajayi rightly points out,[12] destroys the picture that Akitoye was an anti-slaver. Had he been King of Lagos at the time when the missionaries and British traders were trying to promote trade between Abeokuta and the coast, he would just as likely as Kosoko have been an instigator of the slave trade. As it was, both missionaries and Consul saw in him their main hope for establishing a friendly ruler at Lagos.

The missionaries lobbied Palmerston at home, and in due course instructions were sent to Beecroft to deal with the situation in Lagos. He visited the missionaries in Abeokuta, and then went to Badagry, where he held discussions with Akitoye, who was already growing unpopular with the local chiefs. Indeed by this time most of Badagry's chiefs were on Kosoko's side, so that Beecroft was able to take Akitoye to Fernando Po on the grounds that he would otherwise be attacked by the Badagry people. In Fernando Po, Akitoye agreed that if he were restored he would outlaw slavery in Lagos. In 1851, on Bee-croft's return, Kosoko's guns fired on a ship flying a flag of truce, and in retaliation Beecroft attempted to seize Lagos with a small naval force, but Kosoko was too well defended and com-pelled him to retreat. This premature invasion infuriated the British Government, particularly Palmerston, the Foreign Secretary, who had already written: 'If Lagos, instead of being a nest for slave-traders, were to become a port for lawful trade, it would become an important outlet for the commerce of a large range of country in the interior, and instead of being a den of barbarism, would become a diffusing centre of civiliza-tion.'[13] Instructions had already gone out to the Commodore of the West African Squadron to effect the capture of Lagos, and to have Beecroft instigate a half-cock invasion was humiliating to Palmerston, who was already under fire from Parliament over his West African policy. Fortunately for Palmerston the squadron retrieved the situation by taking Lagos. A month later Kosoko was expelled and Akitoye installed. The latter signed a treaty abolishing slavery, guaranteeing missionary activity and according Britain most-favoured-nation terms. His power was considerably reduced compared with that of Kosoko, and what amounted to a British Protectorate was in fact established. A vice-consul was appointed to supervise the execution of the treaty and the Navy promised support if Kosoko should attempt to recapture Lagos, as seemed very probable at the time.

In the same year Beecroft found cause to intervene in the slave rebellion in Old Calabar. The Efik, unlike the Ijo states, treated their slaves harshly, and excluded them entirely from participation in the politics and commerce of their community. The majority were relegated to plantations in the interior, from which they might be seized at any time for sacrifice. However, the preachings of the missionaries instilled in them a desire for freedom, and in one plantation on the Qua River, to which all in trouble with Egbo fled, a political organization called The Blood Men sprang up among the slaves. Several of its members were arrested in Duke Town in 1851. This was the signal for the first of a number of uprisings. The slaves ravaged the plantations and threatened to invade Duke Town itself un-less they were released. The white supercargoes, fearing a stop-page in trade if there were no authority in Duke Town, called in Beecroft, who effected a settlement that modified certain aspects of Egbo government, but certainly did not put an end to the slaves' grievances. His contention was that without Egbo there would be chaos, and chaos would of course impede the trade of British merchants. The following year Beecroft even presided over the election of the new King of Old Calabar.

In 1852 an event of momentous importance took place. It was also one that was later to necessitate the increasing attention of the Consul. The British Government agreed to subsidize a small fleet of steamers owned by Macgregor Laird, which were to form the basis of a regular mail service between Liverpool and West Africa. The introduction of this new service had two important consequences. First, it allowed a large number of small traders to come out to West Africa, who would otherwise have been unable to, since they would never have had the capital to finance a ship. Secondly, it introduced into the Delta competition against the great Liverpool houses. The small traders found that they could undercut the established and highly monopolistic prices of the old firms; furthermore the African middlemen found it cheaper to export oil direct to Liverpool on the mailships, rather than through the old Liverpool firms. By 1856 there were nearly 200 firms operating in the Delta in place of the few houses trading before the inauguration of this service. This caused great bitterness amongst the old-established trading houses who had sunk much capital into their West African trade; it also opened the eyes of the African to the extortionate profits and shoddy goods these houses had so long palmed off on them. Relations between the African middlemen and Liverpool traders were never amicable again.

In 1853 Beecroft's jurisdiction as Consul was restricted to the Bight of Biafra, since there was now a Consul permanently resident in Lagos. He soon had business in Bonny again. The story of the exile of King William Dappa Pepple is a long and complicated one.[14] Its broad outlines, in so far as it affected trade relations with Britain, must suffice here, for this incident confirmed that Britain was prepared to use action such as she had employed in Lagos to further or secure her trading interests. In May 1852, King William Dappa Pepple had a stroke. He then appointed the two senior chiefs of the Manila Pepple house, his main basis of support, as regents. The supercargoes agreed to recognize their authority, but the Anna Pepple house immediately protested at this delegation of power. The British Consul was then brought in to settle the dispute and after meeting with the chiefs and the supercargoes, approved the regency. Pepple soon recovered and resumed his powers. However he now antagonized not only the Anna Pepple house, who were naturally hostile to him, but also the supercargoes and some of his own supporters, through his policy of forcing Bonny traders to take goods on trust from him at excessive rates before he would let them trade in the interior, where he himself as a result was able to trade on more favourable terms. This also antagonized the white supercargoes who had lost business through it. Tension rose so high in Bonny that some European gigs were attacked and considerable property destroyed. The supercargoes were now suspicious that Pepple himself had engineered these attacks. Pepple now faced a divided kingdom and hostile supercargoes. He attempted to divert their attention by an attack on his powerful and prosperous neighbour, Amakiri of New Calabar. This attack was a failure, since the Anna Pepple faction refused to join the war party. The supercargoes, concerned about the effects on trade, sent speedily for Beecroft who at once came to settle the dispute. Pepple was exiled through the Court of Equity over which Beecroft presided. The official British version of the event was that not only did the chiefs want him exiled, but that he himself had begged the Consul to give him safe conduct to Fernando Po. A more realistic view is that, however much even the Anna Pepple faction were opposed to him, they did not want him exiled since it was usually difficult to replace a deposed monarch, and furthermore, native traders in the interior might not trade with them once Pepple had gone.[15] A convention was signed by the chiefs and the Consul whereby it was agreed that succeeding Bonny kings should not engage in trade, thus embodying, as G. I. Jones has put it, 'the consul's conviction that the king should be concerned with government and not with trade, and that King William Dappa Pepple's downfall was due to his neglect of this principle.'[16]

Soon after Pepple's departure for England his successor died and poisoning was suspected, though an English doctor vouched that he had died of natural causes. Civil war flared up and the Anna Pepple faction took over the town, destroying in the process most of the property of the house of William Dappa Pepple. Beecroft's successor, Consul Lynslager, in a surprisingly conciliatory tone, treated with the Anna Pepple faction for the institution of a regency council of four. This was not a success. As Consul Hutchinson wrote later in his book *Ten Years' Wandering among the Ethiopians*: 'The experience of five years has taught the British as well as the Native Traders that this government has been no more than a mockery and delusion. . . .'[17] Co-ordination of government was so weak, and the authority of the regents treated with such contempt that very soon the European traders who had sought the removal of Pepple were demanding his return. By 1859 they were acutely aware that no one but the legitimate king would be accepted in Bonny, and arrangements were made for his restoration. In 1861 he returned to Bonny having been paid compensation of £4,520. He was accompanied by a number of English men and women who had accepted positions in his court, but since they were not paid they soon left! The British Consul and the supercargoes had learnt that they had to be careful about interfering with the institutions of African government, unless they were prepared to take them over altogether.

In 1855 a critical situation developed in Calabar as a result of the introduction of open competition into local trade. The Christian Africans who had come from Sierra Leone to settle there attempted to help the local middlemen avoid the extortionate trading terms of the Liverpool supercargoes, who complained about this to the new Consul Lynslager (Beecroft died in 1854), saying that King Eyo and the Sierra Leoneans were shipping oil direct to England before paying the 'trust' they owed them. Consul Lynslager warned King Eyo to pay off his 'trust' before he shipped oil to England on his own account.

The next year the Consul destroyed Old Town Calabar on the grounds that it had broken the law against human sacrifice. In Old Town, where the Church of Scotland had established a mission station, the Chief, Willy Tom Robins, had ordered a large number of people, including his wives, to be put in chains as hostages for what seemed to be his impending death. When he did die many people were sacrificed, and, since this was a breach of the agreement between Calabar and the Consul, Lynslager effected the complete destruction of the town. This incurred bitter protests from the Church of Scotland missionaries, who believed that the white traders had merely wanted to make an example of Old Town, where they had no trading posts, so as to bring Duke Town and Creek Town into line. However, Lynslager sent despatches to say that he had destroyed Old Town on the invitation of the missionaries.

The situation in Calabar deteriorated rapidly. The antagonism between the supercargoes and the Sierra Leoneans became so acrimonious that the whites took to beating up the 'interlopers'. There was little that the divided authorities of Calabar could do. (It paid to have a centralized monarchy such as Bonny in cases like this.) Matters came to a head in 1857, when King Eyo Honesty actually chartered a boat, the *Olinda*, to ship oil direct to England. Lynslager's successor, Consul Hutchinson, prevented the ship from setting sail on the grounds that Eyo owed the equivalent of £18,000 in trust. Significantly the trust was owed to the Consul's former employers, Messrs. Hearn and Cuthbertson. The Foreign Office was annoyed by this incident, and three years later, with evidence of Hutchinson's corruption mounting, it ordered a Commission of Enquiry into his conduct, as a result of which he was dismissed. This was a severe blow to Liverpool interests in Calabar.

Despite these dramatic shows of force, the British Consuls had considerable difficulty in enforcing the punishments they chose to inflict on people who interfered with trade. The local rulers did not consider that the British Consuls had any right to force free trade on them, and merely recognized that when warships were around the safest policy was to bow to British demands. Without warships the Consuls found it virtually impossible to obtain payment of fines, as in 1862, when some Benin River tribes refused to pay a fine for damaging a trader's store. It was clear that effective regulation of trade in their favour could only be secured if some form of protectorate were established over the Coastal states. However much the Consul might desire this, there was still considerable opposition in Britain to any extension of overseas responsibilities.

So far, both in the Delta and in Lagos, European trade had been restricted to the coast. Trade with the interior remained almost exclusively in the hands of the African middlemen, and in the case of the lands beyond the Niger and Benue, no effective trade relations had been established. Baikie's voyage of 1854 changed this situation.[18] Not only did he prove that European life was possible in the interior, but he travelled as far as Yola on the Benue, a distance of over 900 miles from the coast. In 1857 the British Government made a contract with Macgregor Laird to maintain a steamer on the River Niger for five years. A subsidy of £8,000 was offered for the first year, diminishing annually by £500. Laird placed Baikie in charge of this expedition which was in fact a failure, since the *Dayspring* on which they sailed was wrecked on the Juju rock at Jebba. Nevertheless, as Diké has written: 'Just as 1854 marked the end of the era of exploration, so in 1857 the traders took over where the explorers left off. Seen in this light the voyage of the *Dayspring* marked the beginning of an era in Nigerian history.'[19]

Factories or trading posts were established at Aboh, Onitsha and Lokoja on the confluence of the Benue and Niger. Laird even issued small copper coins, very popular, to replace cumbersome cowries. Trade was not brisk to begin with, amounting to less than £9,000 in the third year. Laird had to contend with much opposition. His ventures were resented by the Liverpool supercargoes as much as they had resented his earlier introduction of the mail steamers. But whereas the latter venture benefited the African middleman, his attempts to trade direct with the markets of the interior were a deadly threat to the livelihood of the middlemen themselves. Thus Laird had ranged against him both African middlemen and Liverpool supercargoes, who now combined to wreck his commercial adventures. Attacks on the steamers by hostile 'natives' were often alleged by Laird's traders to have been instigated by the Liverpool supercargoes acting through the Delta middlemen, who had long-standing contacts with the tribes of the interior. Heavy guns were positioned at strategic points on the river, and the steamers frequently came under severe fire. Sometimes the steamers were even stopped and boarded, despite punitive measures taken by naval gunboats. In 1859 a number of villages seventy miles inland were shelled for their part in the attack on the *Rainbow* on her return from a successful voyage up the Niger.

By 1860 Laird had largely convinced the Government that

inland trade could pay, and the Government in return offered to escort his ships up the Niger. The instructions to this effect were not carried out by the local naval commander, who felt that the risks were too great to justify such a convoy. As a result Laird's expedition was a disastrous failure, involving heavy loss of capital. From then on until 1870 escorts were provided.

In the meantime Baikie, who had been wrecked in the *Dayspring* on Juju Rock at Jebba, installed himself at Lokoja near the site of the model farm, where he took on the role of unofficial consul, and set about exploring the possibilities of trade with the north.[20] His intentions are best described in his own words: 'The position I have now selected may possibly prove a permanent British Commercial site; and it is most favourably placed both as a convenient rendezvous and as a centre for trade. A direct route to Nupe is now being opened, and other roads lead also to Zaria and the interior of Hausa. As soon as I get a little settled, I shall see about the possibility of a direct route to Lagos.'[21] With the assistance of Lieut. Glover he did establish a direct route to Lagos and won the friendship of King Masaba of Nupe. Baikie demonstrated clearly that the Niger was the real highway to the interior, including Hausaland, of whose potentials Clapperton and Barth had already written. Baikie conceived his task as helping to secure for Britain a commanding position in Africa, and when the Foreign Office ordered his return home, he refused, both because he felt his work was not then complete, and also because he was in debt to King Masaba. In 1862 he trekked to Bida, Zaria and Kano, and died two years later on his way back to England.

Baikie's enterprise on the Niger together with that of Macgregor Laird reflects the vital new interest of Britain in hinterland trade, an interest that eventually led her to annex the whole of Southern Nigeria.

Throughout the lands of the Niger valley there was a growing hostility to the new-style traders, stimulated by their enemies the middlemen and Liverpool traders, though Laird's factories were attacked and destroyed, by the early sixties trade with the interior was well on its way to supplant the old coastal trade. By 1865 the executor of the will of Macgregor Laird, who had died in 1861, promoted a new Company of African Merchants to trade with the interior. The British Government even promised a subsidy. The ferocity of the attacks by Liverpool traders on this Government decision are a testimony to the seriousness of the economic threat this company and those like it represented to them. After 1865 the pattern of trade in the Delta changed radically, and penetration of the interior became more and more systematic.

Intimately bound up with this expansion of trade with the interior was the founding of the Niger Mission. The 1857 expedition led by Dr. Baikie on the *Dayspring* was again a combination of trading, government and evangelical interests. On board was the by now well-travelled Rev. Samuel Crowther, together with the Rev. J. C. Taylor and a party of catechists, bearing a commission from the C.M.S. to found the Niger Mission.[22] At Onitsha both trader and churchman negotiated with the Obi or King for land, and the Rev. J. C. Taylor, a freed Ibo slave, was left in charge of the new Onitsha mission station. Crowther sailed upstream founding small stations at both Gbebe and Lokoja, after which his work was called to a halt for a year when the *Dayspring* ran aground on Juju Rock at Jebba. The only mission station to be really successful was Taylor's mission at Onitsha where a school was opened. Soon delegates from many parts of Iboland were asking for stations to be opened in their own towns and villages. The difficulties of the early years of the Niger mission, which is remarkable as an almost exclusively African enterprise, were largely the result of its close association with trading interests. The mission was dependent on the interior traders both for transport and supplies, and inevitably in the minds of the local people it became identified with the traders they so hated. Thus, in 1859 and 1860, attacks on the trading posts at Onitsha brought the mission's work to a standstill. Attempts were made to make it independent of the traders, but this was almost impossible, since the mission relied on them both for supplies and communication with the outside world.

Despite these early vicissitudes, Venn, the Secretary of the C.M.S., did not lose faith in Crowther and in 1864, against considerable opposition from the Yoruba Mission under Townsend, he nominated him as Bishop of 'Western Equatorial Africa beyond the Queen's Dominions'. Crowther had been reluctant to accept this great office, but Venn was insistent despite the irate and threatening letters of a disappointed Townsend who had long and justifiably coveted the episcopate now given to Crowther. Venn was convinced that, with the heavy mortality of Europeans, an African mission was the only solution. Unfortunately Townsend's disappointment at not being selected brought into mission affairs an early element of racial bitterness. Thus whilst the Queen's Dominions such as Lagos and Freetown were excluded from Crowther's diocese, so too was the Yoruba Mission at Abeokuta as a special concession to Townsend and the European missionaries.[23]

The fifteen years from 1850 to 1865 saw a general expansion of missionary activity throughout Southern Nigeria. Though the Church of Scotland had been unsuccessful in its earlier efforts to open a mission at Bonny, it established stations up the Cross River. The Yoruba Mission opened stations at Oyo, Iseyin, Saki, Ogbomosho, Ijaye, Ilaro and Isaga. The study of indigenous languages had reached impressive proportions: by 1851 most of the New Testament had been translated into Yoruba; in 1862 Bowen of the Baptist Mission supplemented Crowther's earlier work by publishing a *Grammar and Vocabulary of the Yoruba Language*. The Reverend S. W. Koelle of the C.M.S. published in 1854 a *Grammar of the Bornu or Kanuri Language*. In 1849 Hope Waddell published his vocabulary of the Efik language which was supplemented by further studies by his colleague Goldie. In 1862 Schön revised his *Grammar of the Hausa Language*, helped by a Hausa youth whom Barth had brought back with him from Northern Nigeria. In 1864 Crowther published his *Grammar and Vocabulary of the Nupe Language*. The role of missionaries in promoting Western education was cardinal in the history of Nigeria. As early as 1859 the Yoruba Mission had published a newspaper called *Iwe-Irohin*, giving news in Yoruba.

In Lagos the overthrow of Kosoko in 1851 had been motivated largely by the exigencies of suppressing the slave trade on that part of the Coast; the later annexation of the town was undoubtedly the result of Britain's need for a stable base from which to regulate her trade with the interior. Only against the background of the internal instability of Lagos and the inter-tribal warfare in Yorubaland, which continually interfered with trade, can this expansion of British territorial interests, despite severe opposition at home, be understood.

In 1853 a full-time Consul was appointed for Lagos. Benjamin

Campbell, the first to hold this office, was certainly more than a consular representative of the British Government; he had a large say in local affairs, in which Akitoye acquiesced since he owed his position to the British. Indeed, on his arrival, Campbell found Lagos on the verge of civil war. Kosoko, through his strong faction in Lagos, was preparing insurrection against Akitoye. Campbell promised naval protection, should Kosoko attack. Cunningly Akitoye precipitated the crisis by attacking Kosoko's men, so that the Navy in effect gave support to aggression by Akitoye, when their instructions had been to offer defensive protection only. Though censured by the Admiralty, Campbell decided that the best way of defending Lagos against Kosoko was attack, and he even sent an expedition to seek out Kosoko in his retreat at Epe. A further indication of the new Consul's power was the fact that in 1853, when Akitoye died, he arranged the installation of Docemo, who was likely to prove tractable, before any of the other chiefs ever knew of Akitoye's death.

Trade with the interior prospered, though Kosoko proved a major problem through his constant interference with trading canoes plying between Lagos and Abeokuta. Such was Consul Campbell's insistence on the priority of trade that in 1854, against severe opposition from the missionaries at Abeokuta, he completed a treaty with Kosoko, allowing him the port of Palma and a subsidy of 1,000 dollars on condition that he gave up his slaving activities. He installed two pro-Kosoko chiefs at Badagry by force, despite the bitter opposition of the Egba who used the port as an outlet for their own trade. The missionaries, remembering the former role of Kosoko, could not easily contemplate any treaty made with him, especially one as advantageous to him as this. But Campbell had his reasons—Kosoko alone was sufficiently influential to extend legitimate trade beyond its present restricted frontiers with Egbaland. The C.M.S. mission lobbied against Campbell at home; Campbell in retaliation despatched a petition against the missionaries signed by leading traders and the local Methodist missionary.[24] The dispute was certainly not one-sided. Campbell, with some justification, felt that the C.M.S. under Townsend interfered too much with the politics of Egbaland and Lagos, which he considered his own proper province. The missionaries felt that their own ideal state, which was to lead the way for the regeneration of Africa through legitimate commerce, should not be sacrificed to the interests of men like Kosoko.

In Abeokuta, too, the missionaries had their own troubles. They had a slaving faction to deal with, and felt that any compromise of principles in Lagos would facilitate the slave trade. By 1856, however, relations between the missionaries and the Consul became closer, when Campbell forced Docemo to expel Madam Tinubu, a powerful middleman operating between Lagos and Abeokuta, who was suspected of being a surreptitious slave-dealer as well as a party to the 1856 rising against Docemo. Moreover, the missionaries had so encouraged the growth of cotton and palm oil in Egbaland that trade boomed in Lagos to Campbell's considerable satisfaction. In 1856 alone, 15,000 tons of oil were exported from Egbaland.

In 1857 the French launched a scheme whereby 'free' labour was exported from Ouidah to Martinique in the French West Indies. A contract had been granted by Napoleon III of France to the House of Régis Aîné allowing it to obtain labourers for work on its plantations on the condition that they should be volunteers who would be paid for their work. Payment was made to local chiefs for each labourer enlisted, and no questions were asked about his provenance. To the African this was indistinguishable from the slave trade. Both Consul Campbell and the missionaries associated this scheme with the deterioration of the situation in the interior: tension increased between the Egba and Dahomey, and in 1858 war broke out once again between Ibadan and Ijebu. On 18th April 1959 Atiba, Alafin of Oyo, died and was succeeded, contrary to custom, by his son, Adelu, the Crown Prince.[25] The powerful Are of Ijaye refused to recognize Adelu as Alafin, protesting that he should have committed suicide on the death of his father in accordance with tradition. Ibadan, anxious to curtail the power of its rival, took up Oyo's cause and recognized Adelu as Alafin. It seemed clear that war would soon break out again, with Ibadan and Oyo facing a grand alliance of Ijaye, Abeokuta, Ilesha and Ilorin. As Ajayi has shown, the issue at stake was the claim of the Are that he controlled the provinces west of the upper reaches of the Ogun river. In 1859 there had been a clash in this region in the important town of Saki, which declared its loyalty to the Alafin. When the Are sent troops to assert his authority they were defeated by the people of Saki, and a number taken prisoner. Then in January 1860, the chief of Okeho, again in this region, agreed to pay tribute to the Alafin rather than to Ijaye. The Alafin and the Are both sent troops to establish their authority in the town, and Ijaye, after initial defeat, took the town and with it several dozen prisoners, whereupon Oyo called on Ibadan for help. Ikorudu and Ijebu Remo, both placed strategically on the trade route to Lagos, declared for Ibadan, thus giving it access to the coast and supplies of arms. Fearing that this civil war would completely disrupt trade in the interior, the new Consul, Brand, sent a Lieutenant Lodder to mediate between Ibadan and Ijaye. This mission was a failure and soon after Ibadan made overtures to Dahomey to support them and thereby revenge their defeat by the Egba in 1851. War broke out at the end of March 1860.[26]

Kosoko naturally took advantage of the situation and was only kept under control by the presence of a gunboat. Trade dwindled and Consul Brand, who succeeded Campbell on his death in 1860, suggested to the Foreign Office that Britain should take over Lagos as a protectorate. The Foreign Office was not unfavourable to this suggestion, fearing that the French, who had sent a delegation to Docemo, might try to take over Lagos themselves. Brand survived only a year in Lagos, and his successor Foote went even farther by suggesting that the only ultimate solution to peace would be the introduction of troops, and the stationing of consuls at strategic towns in the interior. This was opposed by the Foreign Office which was not prepared to undertake such large territorial commitments. Nevertheless, vice-consuls were stationed at Badagry and Lagos. When, soon afterwards, Porto Novo placed an embargo on trade in oil, Foote promptly ordered its bombardment, thereby gaining a treaty guaranteeing freedom of trade for Britain.

The situation for the Egba was serious. On their western flank the Dahomeyans threatened; to the north-east the military power of Ibadan was preparing for another attack, though ominously quiescent. Abeokuta was still the main source of trade for Lagos so that plans were even mooted to supply armed defence for Abeokuta. But McKoskry, the Vice-Consul for Lagos, who succeeded Foote that same year, had a somewhat different approach to the problem, believing that trade should be extended without favour to any one section of Yorubaland. Thus when a contingent of ten men and one officer arrived in Lagos to teach the Egba the art of military defence in pursuance of Foote's policy, they were diverted to the consular guard in Lagos.[27]

Shortly afterwards the Foreign Office sent the Consul instructions to annex Lagos 'to secure forever the free population of Lagos from the slave-traders and kidnappers who formerly oppressed them; to protect and develop the important trade of which their town is the seat; and to exercise an influence on the surrounding tribes which may, it is hoped, be permanently beneficial to the African race'.[28] Comparatively little was made of Britain's interest in trade which had been paramount in the actions of all the consuls from 1851 to 1861 and which had led up to the annexation of Lagos.

Thus, on 30th July 1861, Docemo ceded Lagos to Acting Consul McKoskry in return for a pension of £1,030 a year. The handing-over ceremony was concluded by the singing of the British National Anthem by three hundred local schoolchildren, and they were conducted by two missionaries.[29] A Governor of the Colony of Lagos, Henry Stanhope Freeman, was appointed and there began a new era in the history of British relations with that part of the coast, an era which inaugurated the new territory of Nigeria. British interests were firmly established in the town. By 1862 there were sixteen British merchants to one French, two Italian, three German and five Brazilian traders. Half in the guise of humanitarian motives, Britain had gained her first foothold on the Nigerian coast primarily to secure her trade.

The history of Lagos subsequent to its annexation in 1861 is closely bound up with the opening up of the interior, largely because of its most able and aggressive administrator in the sixties, Glover, who had accompanied Baikie on the 1857 expedition organized by Laird, and shared the ideals of both concerning the penetration of the interior and its accessibility to trade.[30]

The annexation of Lagos was accompanied by a deterioration of conditions in the interior. The Ijaye wars flared up once more. Ibadan, with the assistance of Oyo and Borgu, surrounded Ijaye and cut off its supplies from the south. In this situation Freeman, as Governor of Lagos, was placed in a dilemma. He had been instructed not to extend British territory, yet he was also to look after trade interests. Freeman, who was strongly influenced by Glover, his right-hand man as Administrator, was led to believe that much of the blame lay with the Egba side, since they refused to let Ibadan have a road to the coast. He tried to force a vice-consul on them, a move that was quickly rejected by the Egba, who had already seen what happened to Lagos when a consul took up residence. The missionaries complained to the Colonial Office about this interference, and that department made it known that it was against coercion of the Egba. Freeman however pursued a contrary policy, instituting a blockade on Egba trade and annexing Palma and Lekki from Kosoko in return for a pension. He also annexed Badagry so that he could exact a 4 per cent import duty on all goods to help pay for the administration. In the interests of free trade he even destroyed Epe, where the ruler, Possoo, had established himself with the rest of Kosoko's followers who had opposed the cession of Palma and Lekki to the British.

In the interior the situation had become very tense. Kurumi, the Are of Ijaye, had died, thus depriving that town of its most able leader when it was in the direst of straits owing to the successful siege by the Ibadan. Such was their condition that people from Ijaye were even selling themselves to their allies the Egba in order to obtain food. The Ibadan attacked the Awaye people for the help they had given to besieged Ijaye; whilst the Egba attacked the Ijebu Remo for their help to the Ibadan in the Ijaye war. The Egba captured the important Remo town of Iperu, which gave its name to these new wars. They had the singular advantage of having an American sharpshooter called Pettiford, who had fought in the Ijaye wars, and was reserved for picking off Ibadan chiefs in battle. The war was only settled by the intervention of the Alafin, whose influence in Yorubaland was being rapidly reduced by the civil wars. A curious sidelight on this war was the press battle between the missionaries. Townsend championed the Egba through his *Iwe-Irohin*,[31] whilst Hinderer took the part of Ibadan in the *Anglo-African*.

Trade came almost to a standstill during these wars. The new Lieutenant-Governor, Glover, hoped to expand trade in the interior to the friendly country of King Masaba of Nupe.

But the inter-tribal wars made this impossible. A further threat came to the Egba from Dahomey in 1863, and at the instigation of Townsend and the C.M.S. prayers were uttered for their deliverance in churches as far afield as Switzerland and Syria. In 1864 the Dahomeyans did attack but were repulsed with great losses.

Peace between Ibadan and the Egba was shortlived. The Egba were jealous of and afraid of the growing power of the Ibadan. The Ibadan likewise resented the heavy tolls exacted by the Egba. In March 1865 the Egba attacked and besieged Ikorodu, a Remo town strategic for Ibadan's supplies from the Coast. This was one of the most important incidents in the long history of the Yoruba civil wars, for it was the first time the British from Lagos actually intervened in them. The Ikorodu traders appealed for help to the Governor in Lagos, who had pressures placed on him by Lagos traders to the same end. Glover had come round to the view that the only way to end civil strife and thus promote trade in the interior was armed intervention. He was also convinced that the Egba were at the root of the trouble, since they were determined to prevent Ibadan trading with the Coast. On 29th March 1865 he gave the Egba twenty-four hours to withdraw from Ikorodu, then despatched West Indian troops to deal with them. In a quick action, using screaming rockets, the Egba were defeated and British authority was by implication extended far beyond the frontiers of the colony. Not long after, the King of Dahomey sent Glover an embarrassing gift of a flag on which Dahomey was represented as about to pounce on a deer (Abeokuta), held down by Lagos and Ibadan.[32] Soon Glover found occasion to chastise the oft-bombarded King of Porto Novo. As in the Delta and in the interior, Britain was becoming inextricably involved in Nigerian affairs.

It must come therefore as something of a surprise that in 1865 the Select Committee on West Africa recommended the gradual reduction of British commitments on the Coast, and declared itself against any further territorial expansion. To understand this one must look to the history of both the West Coast and Britain. In England anti-imperialist sentiment was strong. It was backed up by missionaries like Townsend who resented the intervention of Lagos in the affairs of Abeokuta. Free trade was an article of faith for many traders, both in England and on the Coast, though often the first trader to call in the gunboat when his interest was affected would be the most convinced advocate of free trade. Liverpool trading interests were hardly happy as a result of their experience of Government interest in the Coast. Finally there was still a great gulf between the realities of life on the coast and what the Government and parliamentarians imagined it to be. If the years 1850–65 proved nothing else, they convinced Britain's representatives on the Nigerian coast that if the interior were to be opened up to legitimate trade with Britain, then British authority would have to be paramount.

CHAPTER XI

The Beginnings of Alien Rule

From 1865 until the proclamation of the British Protector-ate over the Niger Districts in 1885, British interests in Nigeria were concentrated in three separate areas. In Lagos the trading requirements of the merchants of the Colony led to constant interference by the Governor in the affairs of Yorubaland. In the Delta bitter competition for the oil markets between the various states and European traders pushed further the local consul's intervention.

It was however expanding trade in the hinterland of the Delta, with its superb river highway, the Niger, that eventually led Britain to proclaim a Protectorate over the Niger Districts, and thus lay the foundations of modern Nigeria.

Although Britain's official sentiments were against any further commitments in her West African settlements, let alone exten-sion of them, Glover was left in charge of Lagos as Lt.-Governor, and on his past record he was hardly likely to stand aloof from Yoruba politics.[1] Under his rule Lagos became increasingly important in the tribal disputes of the Yoruba, and Glover soon assumed the role of mediator-in-chief. The peace between Ibadan and her enemies, the Egba and Ijebu, was very un-easy. Glover certainly believed that the Egba bore chief respon-sibility for tension in the interior because of their persistent blocking of the roads from Ibadan to Lagos. He seemed to have little time for Egba complaints that if the warlike Ibadan received arms, they would be the sufferers. And it hardly seemed to the advantage of either the Egba or the Ijebu middlemen to keep the roads closed. Obviously their fear of arms reaching the Ibadan outweighed the economic advantages of keeping the roads open. In an attempt to force the Egba to open the roads Glover blockaded their supply lines in 1865. This policy was to suffer a reversal the following year, when the various West African settlements were amalgamated under a Governor-in-Chief in Sierra Leone to whom Glover was made responsible as Administrator. Blackhall, the new Governor-in-Chief, was much more in tune with official attitudes in Britain and called off Glover's blockade on the grounds that it constituted interference in affairs beyond the province of the Lagos Administrator. Glover went on leave that same year but returned in the autumn. In 1867 the Igbajo war broke out with Ibadan fighting its vassal town of Ilesha. Glover managed to persuade the Ibadan to withdraw from Ilesha. But for this, that town might well have been totally destroyed.

In 1867 the long-standing dispute between Lagos and Abeokuta came to a head. The Egba United Board of Management, a quasi-government of Abeokuta, in which Mr. Secretary Johnson, a Coloured British subject, was the most important figure, informed Glover that it was going to set up a customs post on the Ogun River. The E.U.B.M. had been established in 1865 in an attempt to form a compromise government in which both chiefs and educated elements would be represented. 'In fact', as Biobaku has written, 'the Board was little more than an empty bureaucracy, parading sovereign pretensions, and issuing largely idle threats. Its single positive achievement was that it established a short-lived Customs Department for levying export duties instead of customary tolls at the gates'.[2] It was this preoccupation with raising revenues from customs that was to bring Abeokuta and Lagos into dangerous conflict. Glover tried to use the decision of the E.U.B.M. to set up customs posts as the occasion for the settlement of the boundaries between Lagos and Abeokuta, but this move was rejected by the E.U.B.M. who demanded that Glover withdraw the policemen he had placed at certain points on the frontier. Shortly afterwards a messenger from Glover's old friend, King Masaba of Nupe, was murdered by the Egba *en route* for Lagos. Glover demanded an explanation which only accentuated feelings against European interference which were running high in Abeokuta. At the time Glover even feared an Egba invasion of Lagos and moved troops up to Ebute Metta. However, the Egba vented their resentment on locally stationed missionaries and European traders who were expelled from Abeokuta on 13th October 1867 after the riot called *Ifole*, or housebreaking. Several factors influenced this outbreak. The Egba still resented their defeat by Glover at Ikorodu. There was increasing resentment against European penetration in Yorubaland, and it was hardly surprising that Glover's oppression of Abeokuta should be associated quite wrongly with the missionaries. Anyway, there were factions in Egbaland who wanted the missionaries out of the way: would-be slave-traders; influential Moslems; and the Sierra Leone immigrants. In the end the Colonial Office reprimanded Glover for provoking the crisis through his expansionist aims, which ran contrary both to official British policy and the wishes of the Governor-in-Chief in Sierra Leone.

The expulsion of the missionaries from Abeokuta marked the beginning of a period of stagnation in missionary work in Yorubaland. C.M.S. headquarters were moved to Lagos Island and the Egba Christian refugees settled on the mainland. Lagos itself prospered despite the setbacks to trade brought about by the civil wars of the interior. By 1870 the colony was almost self-sufficient. Over half a million pounds' worth of goods passed through the port annually. The administration recorded a very slight excess of expenditure (£42,379) over revenue (£41,684). Furthermore it occupied a key role in the affairs of the interior; for instance, in 1868, only a year after *Ifole*, the supporters of the two rival claimants for the position of Alake of Abeokuta both sought Lagos's support in their dispute.

However, there seemed no foreseeable end to the civil wars. Indeed the Alafin of Oyo feared that they might soon lead to the extinction of the Yoruba people. After nearly fifty years of fighting, antagonisms ran very deep. The Egba and Ijebu both feared the loss of their position as middlemen. Glover was determined to secure, if not peace, at least a free road from Lagos to the interior unhampered by the interferences or exactions of the Egba and Ijebu. To this end, in July 1871, he presided over a conference of the rulers of the interior in an attempt to secure a permanent and free road for the Oyo and Ibadan. Delegates from Oyo, Ijebu, Ibadan and Abeokuta were joined by representatives from Benin, Ijo, Ilaro and Ketu. There were five major routes to the interior: the Egba route, i.e. Lagos via

Abeokuta to Ibadan; the Remo route—Lagos–Ikorodu–Ibadan; the Ijebu-Ode route—Lagos via Ijebu-Ode to Ibadan: the western route—Lagos–Igbessa–Ilaro–Ketu–Ibadan: the eastern route—Lagos–Ijo–Ondo–Oke-Igbo–Ibadan.[3] Glover's aim was to persuade the Egba and Ijebu to keep their roads open by threatening to open up an alternative route through Ijoland and Ondo to Ibadan, which would in effect deprive them of their monopoly. He was not successful in this and in 1871 the Ibadan and Egba were once again at each other's throats over the road to Lagos. Glover offered his mediation in vain, and decided to blockade Porto Novo, the main source of Egba arms supplies. If he could annex this port, so much the better, for then he could cut off all supplies for the Egba and force them to open the road. So exasperated did Glover become that he even considered closing all roads and forbidding any exports through Lagos. This naturally angered the Lagos merchants who quickly expressed their anger to the visiting Governor of the West African settlements, Pope Hennessy, when he arrived. He was instinctively hostile to Glover. Glover left Nigeria finally as a result of his alienation from the merchants. Dr. Biobaku concludes: 'Glover's departure marked the end of an era of unauthorized expansionist policies which the Egba, supported by the missionaries and later by Sierra Leone immigrants and their Ijebu allies, frustrated.'[4]

The first five years of the seventies were relatively peaceful in Yorubaland, though in 1875 the Ibadan slave-raided into Ekiti country and reached Nupeland. The Ibadan were then at the height of their power, but they still depended on Benin for their supplies of gunpowder since the direct routes to the Coast through Ijebu and Egbaland were closed. In 1877, however, a caravan under military escort was sent to Porto Novo to collect gunpowder, purchased by the Alafin Adelu shortly before his death. The expedition, which passed through Egba territory, was successful, encountering neither Dahomeyans nor Egba on the way. On receiving news of this the Egba retaliated by closing their roads completely to the Ibadan, forbidding even the passage of salt. Despite protests from some of his advisers, the Are of Ibadan closed the gates of the city to the Egba and declared war on them, with these words: 'I am going to perform a task which God has allotted me to do, and those who say that they

12. James White preaching before King Akitoye of Lagos

13. Ibadan, 1854. From Anna Hinderer, *Seven Years in Yorubaland*

14. King Jaja of Opobo

15. King Pepple of Bonny

16. King Obie of Aboh visiting the steam vessels *Alburkah* and *Quorra*

shall see that I do not accomplish it will not live to see it done, as done it shall be, and when I have finished there shall be no more wars for ever in the Yoruba country.[5] The Are then sent out raiding parties to ravage the Egba farms on the grounds that the best way to harass the Egba was to destroy their food supplies.

The war between Ibadan and the Egba had some of the elements of the strife in Eastern Nigeria between the Delta middlemen and the interior traders. Essentially what the Ibadan wanted was direct trade with Lagos. The Egba naturally wished, like the Ijebu, who soon joined them, to preserve their monopoly as middlemen and to ensure that the already considerable military power of Ibadan was not increased by the free supply of arms from the Coast. They attempted to get the Ondo road closed to the Ibadan, and to cut off their supplies of firearms and ammunition. The Ijesha who could control this route, and resented the oppressive rule of the Ibadan, their overlords, gladly joined the Egba together with the Ekiti and Ilorin in the north, who also feared the growing military might of Ibadan. By the end of the year, then, the Ibadan were surrounded by hostile armies—the Egba and Ijebu to the south; the Ijesha and Ekiti to the east; and the Ilorin to the north.

Ibadan did not succumb to this formidable opposition, but in fact drove off the members of the alliance with surprising ease, which lends credence to Egba fears of its increasing power. By 1879, however, the strength of Ibadan's enemies seemed overwhelming. The Ekiti, together with the Ijesha, Effon, Yagba and Akoko, formed the Ekiti-Parapo or Ekiti Confederation against Ibadan. Ife helped both parties, but in reality favoured the confederation. Ibadan was cut off from any source of firearms and ammunition, except through Oke-Igbo and Ondo. The chief of Oke-Igbo, the Oni-elect of Ife, tried to cut off this route, but the Oyo inhabitants of Modakeke, near Ife, managed to get supplies to them. Soon even the Dahomeyans from the west started to attack the Ibadan.

Trade in the interior was by now at a standstill, so it was not surprising that the Governor of Lagos welcomed the Alafin of Oyo's appeal to him to try and reconcile the warring parties. However, the Governor had no success since, when messages were sent to the various war camps, the Ekiti refused to give any firm reply. In 1882 the Ife came out openly against Ibadan and attacked Modakeke, but were repulsed. The combined Ibadan and Modakeke army then took Ife and destroyed it. It is remarkable how well the Ibadan survived these constant attacks. In 1882 they were engaged in battles with the Ilorin, the Ekiti, Egba, Ijebu and Ife. To the west were the Dahomeyans, ready to take advantage of Ibadan's plight and doing so by raids on their farms.

In December 1882 overtures for peace were made between the various participants. The Ijebu, contrary to the wishes of their ruler, the Awujale, actually made peace with Ibadan, and trade was opened up again with the Ilorin. But no general peace could be arranged. In 1884 the Rev. J. B. Wood of Abeokuta attempted to secure peace between the Ekiti-Parapo and the Ibadan but failed, and the following year fighting broke out again at Modakeke and Offa.

As far as Lagos was concerned the trade of the interior was by 1885 completely disrupted, though the wide area of the war did not make life impossible for the people of Yorubaland. Governor-General Rowe wrote in 1883: 'In the so-called war but little actual fighting occurs, few are killed; capture is the object of the warrior on either side. Man hunting is the real business of these fights. . . . All these tribes trade more or less with the Ibadans, notwithstanding they are at war with them; the most saleable produce the Ibadans can bring to market is slaves; to the Egbas they sell the slaves caught from Ijeshas; to the Ijeshas those caught from the Egbas.

'The Egbas, the Ijebus, the Ijeshas are middlemen. When these tribes talk of making peace with Ibadan—they mean a peace on which Ibadan shall bring its produce to their frontier market on the interior side, but no farther—no Ibadan trader must come beyond that market. On the seaboard they will exchange this produce with the Lagos traders for European goods, but no Lagos trader must come into their country beyond the market place on the seaboard. The Ijebus pay a high price for slaves. They use them for farm labourers, and if the Ibadans cease to catch slaves, the Ijebus must cease to import them. The Ibadans find that the most profitable trade article they can take to market is a slave.'[6]

By 1885 it had become abundantly clear that if the Colony of

178

Lagos were to survive, an end to the inter-tribal wars would have to be achieved. This would necessitate direct British interference in Yoruba affairs, implying a reversal of official policy on the part of the British Government.

Events in the Delta and along the Niger were, however, to place Britain in a much better position for dealing with the problems of Yorubaland, for it was there that competition between British and French merchants, and the increasing need to maintain peace in order that trade might be encouraged, led the British Government to reverse its policy of non-interference and proclaim a Protectorate over the Niger Districts.

In 1865 King William Pepple died and was succeeded by his son George, a man of weak personality. Control of affairs in Bonny thus rested with an ex-slave, Oko-Jumbo, who became chief adviser to King George. Opposing him was another ex-slave, Jaja, who became head of the Anna Pepple house on the death of Alali, the former regent. For the next twenty years Jaja was to dominate Delta politics.[7] He was a man of exceptional ability, combined with a ruthlessness that alone could ensure survival in the cut-throat competition of the palm-oil trade. He had been an Ibo slave, who, by his quick identification with Ijo customs, was readily accepted in the Anna Pepple house. From an early age he showed considerable ability as a trader and mixed well with the European supercargoes. Thus, when Alali died in 1863[8] with debts to the tune of £10,000 or more, it was difficult to find a successor to the headship of the Anna Pepple house, which also involved assuming leadership of the opposition to Oko-Jumbo. Certainly none of the senior chiefs wished to fill it, and it was with a sense of relief that they saw Jaja take the burden on. Jaja quickly paid off Alali's debts and appeared to Oko-Jumbo's party as a potentially more serious rival than Alali had been.

In Bonny the quarrels between the two factions became so intense that in 1867 King George asked the Consul to intervene on his behalf. This the Consul refused to do, reprimanding him for supporting Brass and Okrika in their attacks on New Calabar. In 1869 the supercargoes sent a message to the Consul that civil war was imminent. Oko-Jumbo was itching for an early outbreak of hostilities since the Anna Pepple house would be at a severe disadvantage because of heavy losses they had sustained in a fire the year before. On 13th September 1869, civil war broke out but came to a sudden halt when Jaja and his followers decamped to one of the outlying colonies of Bonny. Realizing his weakness he had wisely retreated to a position from which he could counter-attack with much more devastating results than the heavy guns of Oko-Jumbo could inflict on him. Jaja had chosen as his retreat a place in Andoni country from which he could cut Bonny off from its richest oil-producing areas. Jaja had been planning this manœuvre even before he succeeded to leadership of the Anna Pepple house. He did so for several reasons which G. I. Jones points out.[9] First, he saw there was little prospect of the Anna Pepple house dominating the Manila faction. Even if it succeeded in doing so there was no possibility that Jaja would be accepted as king since he did not come from royal lineage. Therefore the only alternative was to set off and found a new state. Second, now that Europeans were resistant to malaria, and ships of shallow draft, driven by steam rather than sail, could negotiate the Delta rivers, the advantages of proximity to the interior oil markets were becoming apparent. Bonny had had the advantage of being a sea-port, but was far removed from her markets. Jaja could profit from the discovery of quinine and the use of steamships by founding a new state close to the traditional markets of Bonny, to which he could deny her access. By 15th February 1870, Jaja felt strong enough to declare himself independent of Bonny. Despite warnings from the Consul and from Bonny, the supercargoes traded openly with Jaja. Bonny war canoes retaliated by firing on British ships. Consul Livingstone tried to settle matters by procuring Jaja's return to Bonny. Having failed in that, he sent a man-o'-war to Opobo, as Jaja had named his new state, to force him to open the interior markets to Bonny. After forty-eight hours' bombardment Jaja agreed to treat with Bonny under the arbitration of the kings of New Calabar and Okrika. He delayed as before until once more hostilities broke out. Earl Granville, the British Foreign Secretary of the day, wrote to Livingstone: 'It appears to me, as it did to Lord Clarendon, that the continuance of the present state of affairs is as much owing to the rivalry of the British traders as the quarrels of the natives, and that if it were not for the interference of Europeans the dispute might be easily settled.'[10] The pro-Bonny and pro-Jaja supercargoes both ensured a continual supply of arms to their respective allies. Glover in Lagos was consulted and characteristically advocated direct interference. By Christmas 1870, however, since the Foreign Office refused to countenance interference, Jaja was able to proclaim his new kingdom, which was made up of fourteen of the eighteen houses of Bonny. Jaja had broken Bonny and established what was to be the most important Delta state, until Britain finally declared its protectorate. In 1873 a peace treaty was secured between the two states by Commodore J. E. Commerell, V.C., C.B., with the aid of five warships. Britain recognized Jaja as King of Opobo, who in turn made a few small concessions to Bonny.

The Benin river and the Western Delta did not present such dramatic hazards to peaceful trading. There security of trade was guaranteed, though not always achieved by the Itsekiri Governor of the Benin river, whose authority was sanctioned by the British Consul, and recognized by the British traders.

The Governorship of the Benin river had been established in 1851 as a result of a treaty signed by Diare and other leaders of the house of Ologbotsere and Consul Beecroft who was anxious to regulate trade conditions on the river for the British.[11] Two years later he had failed to obtain a similar treaty with the other main house of Itsekiri, the royal house of Emaye. The house of the Ologbotsere, a senior Warri chief, was established on the north bank of the River Benin with its headquarters at Jakpa. Under the leadership of the Ologbotsere Eyinmisaren it had broken away from Warri at the end of the eighteenth century after a rebellion of some of the leading Itsekiri chiefs against their king. The secessionist movement was successful and as a result the royal house now only controlled the south bank.

The abolition of the slave trade had brought hard times for the Itsekiri. The oil trade was slow in developing and illicit slave traders were unwilling to risk trading with the Itsekiri because there was a great deal of difficulty involved in crossing the bar to the Benin river, behind which they might be temporarily trapped and thus become easy victims of the British Anti-Slavery patrol. With the development of the oil trade in the forties came the demands of the British traders that there be some form of regulation of trade conditions on the river. Thus Beecroft agreed with Diare and the leading chiefs of the house of the Ologbotsere, who seemed to him to control the river at that time, that they choose from among them a Governor of the Benin river, who would be responsible for securing favourable trade conditions. Diare, a rich trader, was selected, and ruled until 1870 with a short interruption when he was unsuccessfully deposed in 1858 by Consul Campbell for failing to take action against a nephew who had seized a launch belonging to one of the leading British traders. He was succeeded by Chanomi, a member of the royal house, rather than by Olumu, the richest trader on the river and also a member of the house of Ologbotsere. Lloyd suggests that he was either 'reluctant to assume office, or else it was strongly felt that the office should be held, in rotation, by the House of Emaye'.[12] Chanomi was deposed in 1879 by the British for stopping trade on the river, and was succeeded by Olumu, who had transferred his headquarters from Jakpa to Ebrohimi. Olumu ruled for only four years before being succeeded by his son, Nana, whom he had effectively designated as his heir from the time he assumed the Governorship. In 1884 Nana signed treaties with Consul Hewett bringing the Benin river, Warri and certain parts of Western Ijo under British protection, and thus establishing paramountcy of British trade in the area.

British gains in the Western Delta were paralleled by the advance of British interests in the interior. Despite the decisions of the Select Committee of 1865, a consulate was established in Lokoja and the new Consul J. M. Macleod set sail on H.M.S. *Investigator* the following year. His ship was attacked by local tribesmen and ran aground. This seemed a signal for local people to give general vent to their resentment against the incursions of the European traders. Bishop Crowther, who was busy extending the scope of the Niger Mission, was arrested by an African chief who demanded £1,000 for his ransom. He was, however, rescued in a brilliant sortie by the assistant consul at Lokoja who was himself killed in the fighting. Lokoja was blockaded for six months by hostile tribes, who were ultimately beaten off by allies of the Consul. The following year, 1869, the consulate was closed, but the Foreign Office, betraying continued interest in river trade, in 1871 sent W. H. Simpson to negotiate with King Masaba of Nupe for protection of all British traders on the river. Masaba, unlike the chiefs of the river tribes, sought the promotion of trade with the Europeans, since they could provide him with much-needed arms to ward off the many rivals to his throne,[13] and assure for him a monopoly of trade up the Benue and Niger beyond Lokoja.

The Lokoja incidents illustrate both the determination of the British to secure trade in the Niger hinterland, even if it meant placing themselves under the protection of a friendly local ruler, and the equal determination of most of the river-side tribes to keep the European traders away. Considering the vast investments of the British companies on the Bight of Biafra and along the Niger, which together accounted for over £1,000,000 worth of trade annually, it was unlikely that the British, despite the temporary setback at Lokoja, would give in to their opponents. In 1871 hinterland trade suffered another blow when the government abandoned the naval escort for vessels trading up the Niger and the steamer *Nelson*, having decided to go it alone, was fired on and sank in retreat. Yet in 1872 the consulate in Fernando Po was transferred to Old Calabar, and in 1873 the Courts of Equity, which until then had enjoyed no other sanction than the power of the local chiefs and supercargoes to enforce their decisions, and had at times had those decisions reversed by properly constituted British Courts in Accra, were regularized by an Order in Council. By this Order the consul was empowered to inflict fines of up to £200, imprisonment for 21 days, or order banishment for a year for any breach of regulation between natives and the British. It was clear that, if the British were to protect trade in the hinterland, a more stable form of administration would have to be maintained in the Delta. In 1875 and 1876 the *Sultan of Sockatoo* was so fiercely attacked that no steamer dared enter the river. Behind this concerted attack on the British was the influence of the African middlemen of the Delta ports, particularly the Brassmen, who resented these incursions into their traditional monopoly of the palm-oil markets. Slowly it was slipping into the hands of European traders, who had long since realized that direct trade with the hinterland was inevitable. Thus the temporary alliance between Liverpool traders and African middlemen in the Delta was broken, and the middlemen faced a fairly solid combination of European interests. But the general interest of the British traders was often seriously damaged by the cut-throat rivalry between the various firms. In some small trading stations as many as five firms had established themselves. By 1878 there were four major companies trading along the Niger: Messrs. Alexander Miller Brothers and Co. (Glasgow), James Pinnock and Co. (Liverpool), West African Company (Manchester) and The Central African Trading Company (London). They maintained trading posts along the river and brought in over £300,000 trade a year between them. Their main problem was the hostility of the interior tribes and their lack of common policy and direction. The old cut-throat competition characteristic of the Delta was spreading to the interior. By 1878 the three main companies had established an identical chain of trading posts on the river. Great losses were also sustained as a result of attacks by neighbouring tribes, who during the dry season took advantage of the fact that no steamers could ascend the river to execute punitive bombardments.

The worst of these attacks was on Onitsha when the trading houses and the mission station were burnt down. Bishop Crowther had had a difficult task in maintaining the work of the Niger Mission.[14] Though he had some success in the Delta, especially in Bonny where the worship of monitor lizards was officially abandoned in 1867, his missions had been subject to frequent waves of persecution. Yet by 1880 the Niger Mission, which was entirely in the hands of Africans, had eleven stations. The mission at Calabar had also extended its work. Two missionaries had reached Oban, Uyanga and Ibami in 1879; and in 1884 the Rev. Goldie established a mission station at Ikotana on the Cross River.[15] Thus whilst traders were pushing the boundaries of trade farther into the interior, missionaries were penetrating remote villages and spreading the Gospel. Most important of all, they were bringing education to an ever-increasing number of people. Traders who had for long treated missionary activity with suspicion, were soon to be thankful for the supply of clerks that the missionaries produced from their schools.

Until the 1870's trade both in the hinterland and the Delta had been almost the exclusive province of British merchants.

Indeed, surprisingly little interest had been shown in West Africa by other colonial powers. But in the 1870's both Frenchmen and Germans were looking to the West Coast for expansion. Indeed French interests were already developing their master plan for Africa whereby they could link their protectorates of the north with the West Coast and, almost more important, extend their territory from Senegal to the Horn of Africa. The contemplation of such vast possessions had been made feasible by the success of railways in Australia and America.

Thus the firms trading in the interior were threatened not only by hostile tribes but, though they did not realize it at that time, by the possibility of foreign competition. Just at this stage in Delta politics there arrived in Nigeria a man, subsequently called 'the Founder of Modern Nigeria', who dealt successfully with both these threats to the British monopoly of trade along the Niger. First he set about amalgamating the various Niger companies, impressing erstwhile rivals with the advantages of co-operation through sheer force of personality. This was George Dashwood Goldie Taubman, who had already travelled in north-east Africa, and had been fired with imperial zeal from an early age.[16] He had a shrewd appreciation of the ambitions of the French in Africa[17] and was determined that they should not carry off what he considered the main prize: the lands of the Niger basin. By November 1879 Goldie (he was later knighted as Sir George Taubman Goldie) had welded all the major companies trading on the Niger into the United African Company, having persuaded their directors that the only cure for over-competition was monopoly. All ships, stores and staff were pooled. But this monopoly was soon to be challenged by the French.

In 1878 the Comte de Semellé had visited King Masaba of Nupe's successor, Umoru, with a view to acquiring land for a trading station for his Compagnie Française de l'Afrique Équatoriale. But though Umoru granted the British a monopoly in 1879, the help given to him against the rebels by the French secured for the latter his goodwill. By 1882 this company and the Compagnie du Sénégal et de la Côte Occidentale d'Afrique, were almost of equal strength to the United African Company. Goldie tried to ward off their threat in two ways. First, he proposed that his company should become a charter company so that Britain would establish a protectorate over the Niger through his agency. In this way the British Government could secure its interests in the area without incurring the expenses of an administration that might have to be borne by the British budget. In 1882 the National African Company was formed with a view to receiving a charter, though the British Government refused at first to contemplate such a move. Secondly, he tried to persuade the French companies to join with his own. When they refused, he undertook a drastic price war against them, using most of his personal fortune and undercutting their prices by as much as 25 per cent. He forced them out of business in 1884. Goldie did not under-estimate the French menace. In 1883 Jules Ferry, with known imperialist ambitions, became Prime Minister of France, and in 1883 annexed Cotonou, Aghwey, Great and Little Popo and Porto Novo, driving a wedge between the Lagos and Gold Coast settlements of Britain. The French even sent a gunboat to Bonny in an attempt to secure a treaty by which they could establish a protectorate on the mouth of the Niger.

The Germans were active, too. G. L. Gaiser, founder of the present well-known firm, purchased Mahin beach near Lagos, though he was later forced to return it. Goldie anticipated these threats with remarkably clear foresight. The Delta he considered no problem, for with easy access to British gunboats the local chiefs and kings could easily be controlled. The hinterland was a different problem. Since it was inaccessible to warships, it would, he believed, always be possible for another power to gain the interior. Though the British Government refused to grant Goldie a charter, it conceded him the right to make treaties with local chiefs. By 1884 he had concluded thirty-seven such treaties. He formed a fleet of twenty gunboats, which proved very valuable as opposition as his company's monopoly increased. Akassa, Brass, Patani and Asaba were all bombarded for attacks on the company's trading factories. On the other hand, when Africans like the Emir of Nupe proved friendly and willing to co-operate, the company was prepared to offer its assistance, and indeed it did give the Emir very substantial help in putting down rebellions in 1881 and 1882. Goldie, in fact, behaved as though he had already been granted a charter by the British Government. In 1884, when the Germans sent

Herr Flegel to gain treaties with the Sultan of Sokoto and the Emir of Gwandu, it was Goldie through Joseph Thompson who forestalled him.

The Foreign Office also gave Consul Hewett grudging permission to make treaties in the Oil Rivers. Sometimes Consulate and Company competed for the same treaties. More serious was international competition: in July 1884 Germany hoisted her flag over the Cameroons a few days before Hewett arrived to declare a British Protectorate. The growing atmosphere of 'scramble for Africa' brought the European powers to the Conference table at Berlin to agree on their respective spheres of influence. It was here that the value of Goldie's work for Britain, on whose behalf he attended the conference as an official delegate, having broken the rival French company only a fortnight before, and armed with a sheaf of treaties with local rulers was seen. Goldie almost saw his work ruined when Germany proposed the establishment of an international commission to ensure free trade on the Niger, whatever power controlled the territory through which it flowed. However, in exchange for Britain's promise to recognize Leopold of the Belgians' Congo Association, Bismarck supported a revised Niger Navigation Act, which, while it insisted on the principle of international free trade, made no provision for a commission to ensure its observance.

As a result of Goldie's work, Britain had little difficulty in laying claims to the area around the Niger. She formally proclaimed a Protectorate over the Niger Districts, thus reversing her declared policy of 1865. The Niger Districts were proclaimed 'the territories on the line of coast between the British Protectorate of Lagos and the right or western bank of the Rio del Rey' and the 'territories on both banks of the Niger, from its confluence with the river Benue at Lokoja to the sea, as well as the territories on both banks of the river Benue, from the confluence up to and including Ibi'.[18] From now on Britain was deeply involved in the affairs of Nigeria. Any hesitation about interfering in the affairs of Yorubaland and the more remote Fulani Empire was cast aside as trading and government interests fused as a result of threatened foreign competition. No consideration to African interest was given either by Britain or the other powers attending the Berlin Conference. West Africa was parcelled out in terms of European political rivalry.

CHAPTER XII

Company and Consuls

The states of the Oil Rivers found the new British Protectorate little more effective than the consular rule that had looked after British interests until the Berlin Conference. It was rather the Niger Company which showed the chiefs of the Delta states that the Berlin Conference had changed irrevocably the *status quo* in Africa. In 1886, as a result of Goldie's determined work over the preceding eight years, the Niger Company was granted the Royal Charter that it had been refused in 1881. Under the terms of this charter the company obtained political authority over those territories with which the company's agents had signed treaties whilst those territories which had been brought under protection by the Consul became the new Oil Rivers Protectorate. The company was to 'discourage and as far as may be practicable, abolish by degrees any system of domestic servitude existing among the inhabitants'. On the other hand the company was enjoined to interfere as little as possible in the affairs of native chiefs. Most important of all were the words, 'Nothing in this Our Charter shall be deemed to authorise the Company to set up or grant a monopoly of trade.'[1] The company's subsequent failure to observe this injunction was to incur the animosity of both African and European traders.

The charter was quite explicit about freedom of trade: 'and subject only to customs duties and charges hereby authorised, and to restrictions on importations similar in character to those applicable in our United Kingdom, trade with the Company's territories under Our protection shall be free and there shall be no differential treatment of the subjects of any power as to the settlement or access to markets, but foreigners alike with British subjects will be subject to administrative dispositions in

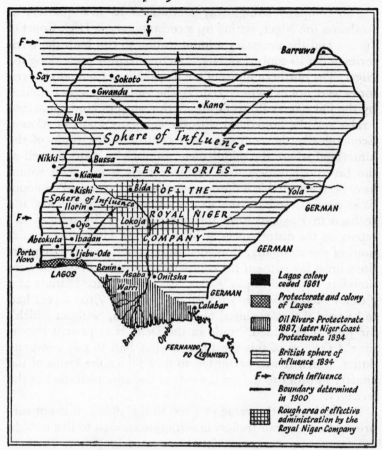

7. The growth of British influence in Nigeria

the interests of commerce and good order.' This conformed with
the condition laid down by the Berlin Conference that, while
Britain had demonstrated clearly her occupation of the lands
along the Niger, that river should be free to navigation by other
powers. The history of the administration of the Royal Niger
Company, over whose territories British Protection was officially placed in 1887, is largely that of bitter rivalry with its
African, British and foreign competitors who all justifiably
complained that the company was using its political authority
to secure a monopoly of commerce.[2]

The company straightway established its headquarters at Asaba on the Niger, setting up a constabulary, a High Court of Justice and the necessary administration to run both the territories under its control and its numerous trading posts along the Niger. The northern limits of the Royal Niger Company's territories were not in fact marked. To the south they were bounded by the Oil Rivers Protectorate. A thin strip of land connected Asaba and the hinterland with the company's port at Akassa. Economically the company now controlled the trade of the hinterland where the middlemen of the Delta states as well as the Liverpool traders used to make their living. This would have been acceptable if the company had not exercised monopolistic powers. Indeed the extent of this monopoly was not realized in England until the publication of Sir John Kirk's report on the disturbances at Brass in 1896. Under the regulations of the company, Brassmen were considered as foreigners since Brass lay without the company's territory. Brassmen were therefore required to pay £50 a year for a licence to trade and £10 for each station they traded in. A further £100 a year had to be paid if they required to trade in spirits, 'without which', Sir John Kirk added, 'trade in the Delta is at present impossible'.[3] On top of this the Brass traders had to pay company duties, which it was permitted to levy under the terms of the charter in order to defray the cost of the administration of the territory.

Remembering the value of £100 in the 1880's, it is not surprising that African traders unfortunate enough to live outside the company's territories bitterly resented its policy. Furthermore, by insisting that all trade within its territories pass through Akassa, it dealt a fatal blow to the Delta ports.

No less resentful were the Liverpool merchants in the Delta, as Mary Kingsley, who knew them well and was equally a friend of Goldie, revealed in her *West African Studies*.[4] French and German complaints not unnaturally tended to be biased since merchants of both powers were busily extending their interests in other parts of West Africa and regarded the company's territories with covetous eyes. Sir George Goldie had good reason to be suspicious of them. Free navigation of the Niger for foreign powers was all very well if such powers respected the patently tenuous hold of the company over its territories. This it was clear neither the Germans nor the French were prepared to do. In 1887 a German merchant called Hoenisberg entered the Niger with a cargo of salt, with the deliberate intention, it is said, of annoying the company and of 'busting up their Charter'. He had apparently infringed the customs regulations, so his cargo was seized. He then travelled on to Nupe, where it is alleged he intrigued against the company. He was arrested, tried at Asaba and deported. A year later Von Puttkamer, a nephew of Bismarck and German Consul in Lagos, went to Nupe to investigate the case. In fairness to the foreign traders it must be admitted that as with African and Liverpool traders, the company deliberately obstructed their activities. However, the German threat was not the most serious, and indeed boundary agreements were drawn up with Germany in 1886, 1890 and later in 1893. The constant threat to the company came from the French, still fired with the ambition of creating an enormous African empire. Indeed Sir George Goldie himself declared in an interview with Reuters in 1899: 'The only stroke of fortune that we have had throughout was the reaction of France in 1884 against colonial enterprises in consequence of those disasters at Tonking, to which M. Jules Ferry, the great Colonial Minister, owed his downfall and the nickname "Le Tonkinois". But for this reaction in France, which lasted until the Paris Exhibition of 1889, and which she had long and rightly deplored, we might have been pushed out of Nigeria.'[5] The more arbitrary interpretation of the charter by the company as regards its monopolistic control of the territory may better be understood when it is realized just what a threat to the Niger territories the French were.

The French were established on the frontiers of the territories in which the company was interested, both to the west and the north. Technically they also had free access from the south by sea. From their base on the coast of Dahomey they were already trying to establish themselves in Yorubaland.

In 1887 a French mission visited Abeokuta and alleged that it had secured a treaty, never put into effect, permitting it to build a railway from Porto Novo to Abeokuta, and thus drain away the palm-oil trade that was the life-blood of Lagos. There were indications that they were intent on securing a similar treaty with the Alafin of Oyo, so the Governor in Lagos hastened to draw up a treaty of friendship with the Alafin in 1888. In 1889 a Lieutenant Mizon, with a party of Frenchmen and Africans, actually sailed up the lower Niger on a warship armed with a Hotchkiss gun. The party was attacked by the Patani tribe and finally gained succour at Akassa. They then sailed on to Yola, where Mizon attempted to make a treaty with the Emir of Yola. On his return to France, Mizon became a national hero as a result of the attack by the Patani, which was not unnaturally attributed to the machinations of the company. Two years later he returned amidst violent protests by the company, but with permission from the British Foreign Office, to take an armed party through the company's territories. He reached Muri, where he drew up a treaty with the Emir. As an expression of gratitude, Mizon, against protests from his officers, shelled the nearby non-Moslem town of Kwana, which the Emir then raided for slaves to sell in the markets of the north. France conquered Dahomey on Nigeria's western borders in 1892, and was rapidly taking the Western Sudan under control. To stave off French colonial expansion, particularly towards the Fulani Empire which he had secured by treaty for the company, Goldie put forward the idea that a narrow triangle of hinterland extending to Lake Chad, the modern Cameroons, should be given to Germany. But the real crisis of Anglo-French relations in West Africa came in 1894 with Lugard's famous race to Nikki.

Whilst the Royal Niger Company was established firmly on the Oil Rivers, and as far up the Niger as Jebba, there was a very fluid position in what was known as Borgu. Though France and Britain had made treaties agreeing the boundary between Dahomey and Lagos, this boundary did not go effectively much farther than 100 miles inland. Far to the north a boundary marking the southernmost limit of France's North African possessions was drawn from Say on the upper Niger in a straight line eastwards to Barruwa near Lake Chad, much the same as the present boundary between Northern Nigeria and Niger. A large area of indefinition existed in Borgu, bounded to the north by the Niger, to the east by Nupeland and to the south by Yorubaland. To the west it stretched into modern Dahomey. It was not at all clear which power had rights in this area. It was also not clear whether the Say-Barruwa line merely

Glover

Goldie

Lugard

Macaulay

Macpherson

Robertson

Azikiwe

Abubakar

Awolowo

Sardauna

Akintola

Okpara

17. MAKERS OF MODERN NIGERIA

18. Sunset at Port Harcourt Oil Refinery

19. Modern Ibadan, capital of the Western State

determined the northern limits to British territory. France chose to read into it that she could expand wherever possible to the south of the line.

The Royal Niger Company was particularly anxious that France should not get a foothold in Borgu since, if she could claim territory to the south of Bussa, she could have a port on the Niger; for the Bussa rapids were the last obstacle to navigation on the river. In 1892 France had declared a protectorate over Dahomey, a development which caused Goldie considerable concern. He claimed Borgu belonged to the company since he made a treaty with the Sultan of Sokoto, suzerain of Borgu. The French, with some historical justification, denied that Sokoto controlled Borgu. Goldie countered this by producing two treaties made with the King of Bussa, who styled himself 'Lord of all Borgu'. The French quickly replied that the King of Nikki was the real suzerain of Borgu. In this there was again some truth for although Bussa was the ancestral home of the Nikki rulers, who had to acknowledge spiritual overlordship from its King, in terms of real political power Nikki was the more important.[6] At that time no European had visited Nikki or knew its exact location. It was even a possibility that the Germans, busily establishing themselves in Togoland, might make a dash to Nikki. The French rushed off an expedition under Decœur to gain a treaty with Nikki; Goldie was not caught unawares and arranged for Captain Lugard, who had already distinguished himself as a pioneer of Empire in East Africa, to make the treaty with Nikki on Britain's behalf.

Although the exact location of Nikki was unknown, the French expedition had the easier task for their base in Dahomey was a straight march to Nikki. Lugard, who arrived in Nigeria in August 1894, had to start off at a great disadvantage from the company's base at Akassa several hundred miles down the coast. (His task would have been easier if he could have left from Lagos.) With a small caravan of Hausa and Yoruba soldiers, he sailed up to Jebba thus starting what was to become a very long association with Nigeria.[7] Lugard made a quick call on the King of Bussa, feeling that if he were really the 'Lord of all Borgu', he would be able to provide an excellent introduction to the King of Nikki. After some delay Bussa promised to send envoys and letters to the kings of both Kaiama and Nikki in exchange for gunpowder. Lugard returned to Jebba to make preparations for immediate departure with a caravan for Borgu, hoping that Decœur would be delayed because of the rains which made travel extremely difficult at that time of the year. On 28th September Lugard, with a caravan of 320 carriers and soldiers, set out on what was later to be called the Nikki Steeplechase. Under appalling weather conditions, more often as not low with fever, Lugard pushed westwards to Borgu. At Kishi in the very north of Yorubaland, and but a few yards from the frontier of Borgu, he made a treaty with the local sovereign where a chief remarked to Lugard that 'the British had introduced law and order into all Yoruba and at last it had come to them'.[8] Despite descriptions of the wildness of Borgu, Lugard was given a very friendly reception by the King of Kaiama with whom a treaty was drawn up. Kaiama warned Lugard of the dangers of Borgu, and advised him on no account to travel beyond Nikki. As he neared that town a messenger arrived to say that the King had been told that if he looked at a white man he would die within three months. Lugard replied that if he did not receive a favourable message within two days he would move in another direction. The loss would be Nikki's not his. This ruse seems to have paid off, for two days later the messenger returned to say that the King would admit the strangers. His reception of them was very unfriendly. Lugard, however, was relieved to find that he had beaten the French. Eventually after much procrastination Lugard obtained the treaty, five days before the arrival of Decœur's party.

Lugard returned to London to find that his treaty was fast becoming the cause of an international incident. The French hotly contested its validity. In her biography of Lugard, Margery Perham has written of the international background: 'The European nations at this time were not unlike a lot of greedy, quarrelsome children in a school playground; none quite big enough to dominate all the others, kicking and then making up to each other, sulking, coaxing, telling each other secrets and then "splitting", combining for a moment and then breaking up. Britain was the rather aloof child in the corner, a little superior, unwilling to join wholeheartedly in the rough games and yet warily watching lest too many of these quarrelling school mates combined against her.'[9] The Nikki question very nearly developed into an international incident. Both Chamberlain, the British Colonial Secretary, and his French opposite indulged in what had by then become determined brinkmanship to ensure that they retained as much of Africa as possible.

The Royal Niger Company under Goldie extended its frontiers northwards by its conquest of the Emir of Nupe, who had been slave-raiding into the company's territories. To the west it also conquered Ilorin, which had aided the Emir of Nupe and had been a constant thorn in the flesh of the British administration in Lagos. Ilorin lay just to the south of Borgu, where France still had ambitions. The French then stationed a Resident at Ilo, on the Niger, with instructions to occupy territory as far south as Bussa. The French also took Kishi, with which Lugard had signed a treaty. They also placed Kaiama under their protection. It thus became imperative for Britain to stop France's advance along the Niger. But Britain was severely handicapped by the fact that the Government had delegated its authority to a chartered company, whilst the French could bring down the full weight of governmental administration behind their ambitions. It was clear that sooner or later a stand would have to be made against the French. Chamberlain favoured conceding the right bank of the Niger to a point thirty miles south of Bussa, which would have allowed the French their port. This Goldie hotly contested, citing his treaty with Bussa. Eventually Chamberlain decided on the creation of a military force under the command of Lugard, which would hold the position of the Royal Niger Company in the hinterland. Lugard returned to Nigeria in the spring of 1898. By 16th April he was at Lokoja where the 1st Battalion of the West African Frontier Force paraded before him.

Lugard immediately set about organizing his small force to deal with the French who were by then established at both Ilo and Bussa. Lugard's task was to take as much of the territory in this area of undefined sovereignty as he could without precipitating actual fighting. The French had been given roughly the same order—so that both sides were really playing an elaborate game of political chess. While this tense campaign of non-violence, in which any single false move might have meant war, was played out in the dry savannah of Borgu, negotiations in

Paris and London were bringing settlement closer. Chamberlain eventually secured a favourable agreement with France, gambling on the strength of Lugard's force and French reluctance to start a war. On many occasions there were very real dangers of fighting, yet by his brilliant brinkmanship Chamberlain, against the opposition of his own Prime Minister, Lord Salisbury, secured a most favourable treaty with France. The French did not get access to the navigable stretch of the Niger, although the British were pushed down the Niger 100 miles from Say to Ilo. The French were given Nikki and the northern boundary of Nigeria was determined as a slight variation on the Say–Barruwa line.

British encroachments on Nigerian territory did not go unresisted by the local population. The Delta middlemen in particular demonstrated their resentment of the increasing power of the Royal Niger Company. This opposition was epitomized by the actions of Jaja, King of Opobo. The year before the Treaty of Berlin, Jaja had made his own treaty with the British by which he placed his country under the protection of the British Crown, but he ensured that the usual clause guaranteeing freedom of trade was omitted. He had suspiciously asked for a definition of the word Protectorate. Hewett, who as Consul had negotiated the treaty, defined it thus: '. . . the Queen does not want to take your country or your markets, but at the same time she is anxious that no other nation should take them. She undertakes to extend her gracious power and protection, which will leave your country still under your government: she has no wish to disturb your rule . . .' (Letter 8th January 1884).[10] This concession was probably made because the French and Germans were also attempting to gain a foothold on territories already under British Protection.

Jaja had at first been treated with considerable sympathy by the British Consul. In 1875 he had even sent a contingent to the Ashanti war, as a result of which he was awarded a sword by Queen Victoria. On the other hand he was a bitter opponent of free trade, preventing any European trader dealing direct with his sources of supply. Indeed any tribe that dared to trade direct with the European merchants was punished swiftly, as the Kwa Ibo learnt in 1881 when Jaja captured and executed hundreds of their number. His men fell on the group of villages known as Ibuno (Ibeno). Mr. Holt, the Liverpool trader, writing to Earl Granville, described the incident thus:

'. . . at daylight on the 11th April last he suddenly invaded them with a force of about fifty fully manned canoes, armed with breech loading cannon and rifles, by means of which he bombarded seven of their villages, which he plundered and afterwards burnt, destroying their crops and stores of food, and taking prisoners upwards of 100 people, whilst the natives of Qua Eboe, unable to protect themselves, and without any means of defence, took to the woods, where many of them greatly suffered from want and exposure.

'Jaja's canoe remained in the river several days, broke into Mr. Watt's Factory, scattered his goods about, and either took away or destroyed a number of barrels and hogsheads of oil belonging to him which were in the native towns that were looted. With their plunder and their prisoners, consisting chiefly of women and children, they returned at length to Opobo, where their unhappy victims were cruelly slaughtered, Jaja's own children being made to cut off the heads of some of the Qua Eboe children, to entitle them to wear the "eagle plume" a mark of distinction bestowed only on those who have slain an enemy.'

Whatever the terms of Jaja's 1884 treaty, the international Treaty of Berlin, made far from the sombre creeks of the Oil Rivers, had handed over his country to Britain, and inevitably there was soon to be a clash. Jaja was already involved in a major trade dispute during which European traders had formed the Amalgamated Association to break his monopoly. Oil prices had risen very favourably in England in 1883 and 1884, and this had led to a rise in prices in the Delta, which trimmed the extra profits the English traders had hoped to make. Their boycott to force down Jaja's prices failed since the firm of Alexander Miller Brothers and Co. of Glasgow agreed to trade at his prices. In June 1885 Consul Hewett, who supported the Association, explained to Jaja that as a result of the 1855 Berlin Treaty freedom of trade in the Oil Rivers was now guaranteed. This encouraged the excluded firms, who bitterly resented the fact that Jaja was now shipping oil direct to England, to seek markets up-river. However, Jaja was well prepared and his agents threatened vengeance on any tribe that traded with the Europeans. This was no idle threat to anyone who remembered his expedition against the Kwa Ibo in 1881.

In 1887 the Acting Consul, H. H. Johnston, by way of retaliation, forbade Jaja to exact his 'comey' or customs duties on the grounds that his direct shipment of oil was unjust competition with those who paid the duty. Jaja protested to the Secretary of State for the Colonies, and sent a delegation of chiefs to Britain. Johnston decided to take drastic action against Jaja whom he believed to be the instigator of the attacks on English merchants in July. He threatened Jaja with gunboats unless he called off his trade war. Under such a threat Jaja agreed to open trade, but in fact did little to alter the situation. On news of trouble in the markets Johnston sailed up river only to find a boom blocking his way. He then telegraphed London for permission to deport Jaja, and on receiving what he considered an affirmative reply, which was in fact probably the reply to an earlier and quite unrelated telegram, he arranged for Jaja's expulsion. Johnston sailed to Opobo on H.M.S. *Goshawk* and invited Jaja to meet him on the beach of Messrs. Harrisons, which Jaja refused to do unless he had the Consul's pledge that he would go free after the meeting. Johnston agreed to this in these words: 'I hereby assure you that whether you accept or reject my proposals tomorrow no restraint whatever will be put on you—you will be free to go as soon as you have heard the message of the Government.'[11] But once there, Jaja was told that if he did not go to Accra for trial he would be considered an enemy and Opobo would be bombarded. Under the cover of H.M.S. *Goshawk*'s guns, there was little Jaja could do, so he sailed for Accra where he was found guilty of blocking the highway of trade, and of failing to honour Article V of his treaty of Britain whereby:

'The King and Chiefs of Opobo hereby engage to assist the British Consular or other officers in the execution of such duties as may be assigned them, and further to act upon their advice in matters relating to the administration of Justice, the development of the resources of the country, the interests of commerce, or in any matter in relation to peace, order and Government and the general progress of civilisation.'[12]

He was deported to the West Indies on a pension of £800 a year, and when at last in 1891 he was allowed to return home he died on the way.

Though it was not until 1891 that an effective government was instituted by Britain for her new Oil Rivers Protectorate, from the British point of view much progress had been made. The energetic Acting Consul felt that the deposition of Jaja was a major break-through in Britain's attempt to break the power of the African middlemen who lay between her traders and the markets of the interior. Elsewhere, as Cook points out, Johnston felt that progress had been made.[13] Johnston was on good terms with Nana, Governor of the Benin river, and he had secured an understanding with Benin. Furthermore he had avoided a clash between the Royal Niger Company and the British traders of the Oil Rivers. Thus, in 1891, when Sir Claude Macdonald, and not he, was appointed Commissioner and Consul General of the Oil Rivers Protectorate, Johnston felt justifiable disappointment. Macdonald had already gained first-hand knowledge of the Delta when he headed an inquiry into allegations made against the Royal Niger Company in 1889. His policy as Commissioner General and Consul General was to avoid the inclusion of his Protectorate in that of the Royal Niger Company. He believed firmly in free trade, and rightly deduced that the Delta kings would not tolerate government by the Company. Unlike Johnston, he believed the Delta middlemen could be used to advantage.

Thus, on 1st January 1891 Britain established an effective government for her protectorate, with a revenue in the first years of nearly £90,000 derived from import duties. In 1893 the Oil Rivers Protectorate became the Niger Coast Protectorate and included all those areas that had made treaties with Britain and were not included in the Royal Niger Company Protectorate. It was governed by a Consul General responsible to the Foreign Office, under whom served a number of vice-consuls responsible for individual areas. Its administration included customs, postal, marine and medical departments as well as a small army of 200 men. But the extension of this power, even under an enlightened administrator like Macdonald, did not go unchallenged. In 1893 an Akuna chief on the Cross River brought trade to a standstill by deliberately provoking an inter-tribal war. He had murdered some Ibo traders who had been trading with his own people. As a result the newly formed constabulary was sent to end the war, and bring the chief to trial.

He was found guilty and hanged. A much greater challenge to this newly constituted authority came from Nana, Governor of the Benin River whom the British ceased to recognize as Governor of the River after they had extended the control of the Oil Rivers Protectorate over Itsekiri country in 1891. 'However the Itsekiri still regarded him as their leader', Lloyd writes, 'and Nana contrived to use his title.'[14] At first, as we have seen, Nana co-operated with the Protectorate government. But he also created a monopoly on the Benin River and carried on a surreptitious trade in slaves. In 1894 Acting Consul General Moor informed the Foreign Office that Nana had strangled trade on the Benin River and that he had continually defied his authority. Moor sent despatches to Nana summoning him to answer charges against him, but Nana made excuses. Moor then forbade Nana's men to trade on the river, and once again summoned Nana, who not unnaturally refused to go, remembering what had happened to Jaja.

Nana defied all edicts that the river should be made free to traders and placed a bar across the creek leading to his headquarters at Brohemie. The gunboat *Alecto* was sent to blow up the barrier, but while it did so it was fired on by Nana's troops.

On the 28th H.M.S. *Phoebe* came to the rescue of *Alecto* with 200 men and 150 members of the constabulary. Nana put up so strong a fight against this new party that H.M.S. *Philomel* and H.M.S. *Widgeon* had to be brought up in support. On the 25th September 1894 a strong attack was made on Brohemie which was captured without casualties, the explanation for this being that Nana had seen the red light and tried to escape. He had even made an ingenious, if desperate, effort to cut a canal from Brohemie to a creek behind the town to evacuate all his goods. These, as the attackers found, consisted of thousands of pounds' worth of merchandise, including 8,300 cases of gin. The town was a veritable arsenal with 106 cannon, 14 tons of gunpowder, 445 blunderbusses adapted for use on war canoes, and a machine-gun. Nana gave himself up to the authorities in Lagos, where he was tried and deported to the Gold Coast. The importance of Nana at this stage of Nigerian history was considerable. Like Jaja he stands out as one of the few who was able to offer serious resistance to the encroaching British power, and, as Cook has pointed out, he established the principle of removing native chiefs who opposed British penetration, rather than seeking their co-operation.[15]

The real bitterness felt against the Royal Niger Company by those it deprived of trade did not come to a head until 1895 when the Brassmen raided Akassa, the company's port. After years of ineffective resistance to the company's authority, the Brassmen resorted to violence. This had been contemplated before, and the British Government was sufficiently aware of the fact to have sent Macdonald to investigate certain allegations made about the company's monopolistic practices. Though he sympathized with the Brassmen, he found that the company had acted within the terms of its charter.[16] The Brassmen took every measure to evade the stringent rules of the company, but by 1895 the situation had become so intolerable to them that they made a direct attack on the company.[17] On 27th January the Vice-Consul at Brass received an anonymous letter informing him that the Brassmen were to raid the company's port at Akassa. The Vice-Consul, who did not give much credence to the warning, nevertheless sent the letter on to the company's Agent General at Akassa, who likewise thought the wole affair far-fetched.

He took the precaution of sending off a patrol and setting a machine-gun at a commanding position on the river. Under cover of darkness, and cloaked by the heavy evening mists of the river, the Brass canoes by-passed the patrol, and attacked Akassa. They destroyed the stores and captured sixty men whom they took to Nembe, for which Brass was the port, eating forty-three of them. None of the European traders was taken.

Though the attack had been made on the company, Brass fell within the jurisdiction of the Niger Coast Protectorate and the Consul General was left to deal with the situation. The Brassmen, who were asked to surrender all their chiefs and armaments, refused to do so, stating that their quarrel was not with the Queen, whom the Consul General represented, but with the company. All they wanted was free access to their old markets. In effect they were complaining as bitterly about the company's monopoly as the Protectorate administration had complained of Nana's.

The Consul General then informed the Brass chiefs that if

they did not obey his orders they would be punished. They played for time whilst they prepared their defences. A naval force with a contingent of Protectorate troops broke the barrier on Nembe creek, landed on Sacrifice Island and, despite fierce resistance by the Brassmen, captured it. Another ultimatum was issued to say that the town would be destroyed if the chiefs did not comply. They continued to hedge, so the punitive force attacked Nembe and against stiff resistance captured and burnt it.

The Protectorate government had now established its authority over all the traditional centres of trade except Benin. That proud and ancient kingdom had withdrawn increasingly from overseas trade and its king had actually issued a decree forbidding his people to trade with Europeans. Furthermore, the old kingdom had gained a notorious reputation because of the prominent role human sacrifice had played in its religion in recent years. In 1862 Sir Richard Burton, the Consul at Fernando Po, had tried to persuade Oba Adolo to abolish human sacrifice, but he did not fully appreciate the very deep religious role sacrifice played in the life of the Bini. Gods had constantly to be propitiated through human sacrifice, for if this were not done disaster would follow for the kingdom. However, in 1892 Gallwey, Vice-Consul for the Benin River District, did visit Benin and persuaded Oba Ovenramwen to sign a treaty by which Benin was placed under British protection and human sacrifice and slavery were abolished. Trade was also opened. This did not last for long and in 1896 Acting Consul General Phillips decided to visit Ovenramwen to press his compliance with the treaty. Early in 1897 Phillips set off for Benin at the time of the great Ague festival during which the Oba should see no man who was not a Bini. For the Bini this was a festival of the greatest importance for it marked the time of rededication by the Bini to their king.[18] It was also a time for extensive human sacrifice.

Phillips informed Oba Ovenramwen of his intention to visit him, but did not wait for a reply. Ovenramwen was considerably embarrassed, for he knew that to refuse would be to incur the wrath of Britain, but to accept would be to incur the even more dire wrath of the gods. Phillips did not wait for a reply and set off from Gwato, the port for Benin, and was met by the

Oba's messengers, led by Ologbotsere, who ordered him and his party to turn back. In the ensuing dispute tempers appear to have been lost, and six of the British party of nine, including Phillips, were killed, together with most of their escort of about 200 men.

Within six weeks of the massacre a punitive expedition of 1,500 was sent to Benin. Ovenramwen had feared this outcome and human sacrifices were increased in a desperate attempt to ward off the inevitable. This, at least, would explain the otherwise staggering number of sacrifices described by Ling Roth, surgeon to the expedition, in *Great Benin*.[19] The Bini were conquered, the town burnt and nearly 2,500 of its magnificent bronzes taken by the British back to Europe. Ovenramwen fled, but after threats by the British he was delivered up six months later. He was tried on 1st September 1897, and deported to Calabar. The fall of Benin was the last major act in the British occupation of Southern Nigeria and marked the end of one of the greatest and most colourful of West African kingdoms.

In Lagos the Governor still viewed with considerable concern the strife in the interior which caused constant interruption to trade. By 1888 palm-oil trade was worth £1,172,840 in the first six months, three-fifths of it was in British hands and much passed through Lagos. Moreover, the French were active in Dahomey, and threatened to interfere in Yorubaland if he himself did not. In January of 1886 Lagos was detached from the Gold Coast and became self-administering. Governor Moloney almost straightway sent delegations to the various parties warring in the interior. The two delegations, led by the Rev. S. Johnson, author of the *History of the Yorubas*, and the Rev. C. Phillips, were initially successful. A cease-fire was arranged between the Ekiti-Parapo and the Ibadan, but the Ilorin were still reluctant to call off battle unless the Offa, with whom they were fighting, did so first. Johnson and Phillips then went southeast to Ife where they negotiated peace between that town and its Oyo rival and neighbour, Modakeke.

The various factions then sent representatives to Lagos where a peace treaty was signed including all Yorubaland except Ilorin, which still refused to negotiate. Under the terms of the treaty Ibadan was to be independent of Oyo, and the various members of the Ekiti-Parapo were to have their independence.

The Alafin of Oyo and the Owa of Ilesha should be as an older to a younger brother; Modakeke was to be rebuilt within Ibadan territory; and the two war camps should be disbanded. A small Hausa force, led by the Acting Colonial Secretary, Henry Higgins, and Mr. Oliver Smith, Queen's Advocate, as Special Commissioners, set off to supervise the dismantling of the war camps. Here is how the Commissioners described the last major act in the long drama of the civil wars:

'The rains ceased before the meeting took place and, the mist clearing away, the sun shone brilliantly on the scene. Thousands of people were to be seen posted on the huge boulders of rock which were scattered through the Kiriji camp, and crowned the summit of the mountain (the Oke Mesin camp was not visible from the place of meeting, there being a slight rising in the ground between) and, as we learned afterwards, the sound of the gun which was to announce that peace had been concluded, and that the people could go to their homes, was most anxiously awaited in both camps and received, when heard, with cheers and hurrahs.'[20]

The main problem of the peace settlement was Modakeke, the Oyo refugee town near Ife. This had by now grown into a huge town of 60,000 inhabitants, difficult enough to disband at the best of times, let alone at the height of the rainy season. Yet this was what the treaty implied, and it is little wonder that the Modakeke refused to move.

Peace was still not finally restored to the harassed Yoruba, for in the north the Ilorin were fighting with the Offa who were in alliance with the Ibadan. The Ibadan themselves tried to mediate a settlement, but failed, and after their withdrawal the chiefs of Offa submitted to the Emir of Ilorin who had them all murdered. He then raided south to Ikirun in search of slaves. Meanwhile, the Dahomeyans were still a menace on the western frontier, invading Oyo in 1887. To the south the Ijebu tightened their control over the roads once again. All Oyo and European traders were forbidden to enter Ijebu territory. The situation was further complicated by the arrival of a French mission in Abeokuta, where arrangements were made for a treaty whereby France would build a railway from Porto Novo to Lagos. The apparent advantages of the peace arrived at between the Ibadan and the Ekiti-

Parapo must have seemed completely lost to the Lagos Governor, especially when he heard that the French intended securing a treaty with the Alafin himself. Thus, as we have already seen, the Governor hastened to make a treaty with the Alafin by which it was agreed Oyo should cede no territory, open trade to all and levy no tolls, except with the agreement of the Governor in Lagos. All this was to be granted in exchange for 200 bags of cowries a year. Even so the war between the Ibadan and Ilorin appeared to have no end in sight. Ibadan became even more loth to call a cease-fire when she caught some Egba traders carrying arms to the Ilorin. In 1890 Governor Moloney despatched yet another mission to the Ilorin, and Samuel Johnson was sent off to see the Alafin, who gave him little co-operation. But the other Commissioners, in an attempt to get the Ibadan to agree to be more loyal to the Alafin, obtained the consent of the Ibadan that any dispute over the limits of their territory should be settled by the Alafin and the Governor. As Samuel Johnson observed, the Alafin, by agreeing to such an arrangement was in effect conceding part of his sovereign rights to the Governor.[21] The Alafin became more co-operative with the Lagos government in his attempts to stop the war as a result of the Dahomeyan menaces on his western frontier. He approached the Ilorin who indicated initial interest but carried on their raids, thereby making a settlement impossible. In the south the Egbado, long oppressed by the Egba, appealed to the Governor to place them under British protection.

Not trusting the French, who were dangerously near Egbado territory as a result of the delimitation of French and British spheres of influence reached in the 1890 agreement, Moloney established a small British garrison at Ilaro, the Egbado capital. For the first time Britain had gained a foothold in Yorubaland. So furious were the Egba that they embargoed all trade with Lagos, and for a time the city came to a commercial standstill, though eventually the Egba themselves recommenced trade, due to economic pressures in Abeokuta. Following closely on the Egba decision to reopen the roads came more trouble with the Ijebu who closed their roads in an attempt to prevent the British in Lagos trading with Ibadan, via Shagamu, which they foresaw would deprive them of their position as middlemen. This position the Ijebu abused cruelly: Johnson, who it must be remembered was an Oyo himself, described at great length the injustices inflicted by the Ijebu on the Ibadan and Oyo trading through their territory to Lagos. They were able to do this with impunity since they knew that Ibadan depended on them for its supply of arms. The Ijebu position remained intact under Governor Moloney, who, Johnson assures us, was not a man of action. 'It was said that he was too fond of writing letters to and drafting treaties for men who hardly appreciated the one or comprehended the other nor knew the force or value of their marks or signature.

'During his five years of administration he never once visited the people and scene of which he so much writes: a single visit from him would have cleared up many difficulties in his way and enabled him to understand much, and he would have acted more to the purpose. No wonder then that matters remained *in statu quo*.'[22]

On Moloney's retirement, Denton, the Colonial Secretary, became acting Governor and attempted to visit the Awujale of Ijebuland to secure a peaceful solution to the problem. The Awujale agreed to the visit, but on Denton's arrival at Ijebu-Ode he was roughly received by the chiefs, and though the Awujale showed some signs of friendliness the chiefs did not attempt to hide their deep hostility to the interference of the Lagos government, and refused to accept the customary presents the acting Governor brought them. This Denton rightly diagnosed as a calculated insult.

This incident led the British Government to decide on coercive measures against the Ijebu, and Sir Gilbert Carter arrived as next Governor, determined to bring peace to the interior once and for all. He demanded an apology from the Awujale for his treatment of acting Governor Denton. This was agreed to, as well as a treaty abolishing human sacrifices and opening trade routes in return for a subsidy of £500 a year to cover loss of revenue from tolls to the Awujale. As we have already seen, the chiefs of Ijebu-Ode were deeply opposed to any form of treaty with the British, and under their influence the roads were soon closed again, especially since the ordinary Ijebu did not benefit from the £500 paid to the Awujale in lieu of tolls. The Awujale then took action that may be construed as seeking to placate the Ijebu chiefs. The Awujale, picking a quarrel with the

Ibadan, accused the Rev. D. Olubi of the C.M.S. of bringing the Europeans into the interior, and passing European goods through Ijebu-Ode by means of his son. The Awujale demanded the heads both of Olubi and of the Rev. T. Harding, his English colleague. The Ibadan were so frightened by the Awujale's threats that it seems clear that both Olubi and Harding would have lost their lives had not Sir Gilbert Carter decided to send a military expedition against the Awujale in May 1892. The punitive force landed at the port of Epe on the 13th and with difficulty battled its way through to Ijebu-Ode which was found deserted except for the Awujale and a few chiefs. The speedy defeat of the Ijebu was the most significant step in the British occupation of Yorubaland. As Johnson wrote: 'The people felt instinctively that a new era was about to dawn on them. A new and foreign power had entered into the arena of active politics in the country, and everyone was exercised in mind as to how the country would be affected by it.

'To the vast majority of the common people it was like the opening of a prison door: and no one who witnessed the patient, long-suffering, and toiling mass of humanity that week by week streamed to and from the coast with their produce could refrain from heaving a sigh of gratification on the magnitude of the beneficial results of the short and sharp conflict.'

For the first time in years caravans passed freely through Ijebu-Ode. 'They brought cloths of native manufacture, cotton indigo, palm oil, palm kernels, beads, cattle, poultry, yam flour, pots and plates of native manufacture, calabashes in large quantities, turkeys and pigeons, rubber, etc., and took back mostly salt, cloths and other articles of European manufacture, trade rum, gin, matches, etc.'[23]

The speed with which Ijebu was subjected was not lost on the rest of Yorubaland. The Egba sent emissaries to the Governor to present their apologies for their past closing of the roads. Early in 1893 Sir Gilbert Carter set off on his famous trek in which he effectively brought Yorubaland under British influence if not control. At Abeokuta he made a treaty with the chiefs whereby all disputes between Egba and the British were to be settled by the Governor, human sacrifice was to be abolished, and roads were to be closed only with the consent of the British. In effect a British Protectorate had been established.

On the other hand a special clause was inserted in the treaty to stipulate that as long as the terms of the treaty were observed there would be no question of annexation without the consent of the Egba.

From Abeokuta Sir Gilbert Carter trekked north to Oyo where, after certain difficulties, the Governor was able to draw up a treaty with the Alafin. The British were given free access to all parts of Yorubaland (i.e. under the Alafin's control) and the roads to Lagos were to be kept open. Christianity would be tolerated and human sacrifice abolished. There would be no agreement made by the Alafin with other powers unless by permission of the Governor as representative of the Queen of England. Any disputes between the parties to the treaty were to be referred to the Governor in Lagos. This treaty clearly compromised the Alafin's sovereignty in favour of Britain. From Oyo the Governor continued what was to be a triumphal trek through Ogbomosho to Ilorin, where he succeeded in persuading both Ilorin and Ibadan to break up their respective war camps. Thus ended sixteen years of bitter war.

The only check to this progress through Yorubaland was in Ibadan. The Ibadan refused to sign the agreement Carter drew up for them on the grounds that most of them as warriors had been absent from their town for many years and found it impossible to negotiate such a treaty without giving it deeper consideration. Furthermore, they objected to the idea that they should have a European Resident stationed in their town.

Carter returned to a triumphal reception in Lagos, for his brilliant diplomatic tour had brought an end to nearly a century of fighting, and had once and for all secured the trade of the interior for Lagos. But he could not resist a few words of bitterness about his failure at Ibadan. He even suggested that it was due to the machinations of someone in his own retinue. Johnson rightly dismisses this: 'His Excellency might have allowed such men as govern a town like Ibadan and all its dependants some credit of knowing their own minds and not be swayed by a mere clerk in his office.'[24] Ibadan accepted the treaty, however, in August 1893, after careful assurances by the Governor that he had no intention of interfering with the government of Ibadan.

The treaty with Ibadan declared that although the Alafin would continue to be recognized as 'the King and Head of

Company and Consuls

Yorubaland' Ibadan should become its headquarters; the treaty made with Oyo should be recognized; land should be provided for a railway; and a Resident plus a small constabulary should be appointed. After this treaty there was peace in Yorubaland. A small fracas with Oyo was quickly dealt with by the first Resident, Captain Bower, when he had to take a punitive expedition to Oyo after the Alafin had carried out the emasculation of a man found guilty of a crime for which that punishment was normally meted out. But only Ilorin really remained a thorn in the flesh of the Lagos administration. As we have seen, that problem was finally settled by a punitive expedition despatched by the Royal Niger Company.

The peace Carter achieved was followed up by measures to promote the trade which Britain had always avowed was her main reason for interfering in the politics of Yorubaland. Roads were built and the railway from Lagos to Ibadan was started. Whatever the motives of the British in interfering in Yorubaland, there is no doubt that at the time the Yoruba must have been one of the few African peoples who really welcomed such intervention, for it brought them peace after a century of some of the most complex and seemingly futile wars on the African continent.

CHAPTER XIII

Emirs and Maxims

The system of administration employed by Britain over its various protectorates in Nigeria had so many defects and so many anomalies that it was inevitable that some change should be made. The unpopularity of the Royal Niger Company in the south, and the difficulties of establishing administrative competence over those territories of the north assigned to Britain, led to the withdrawal of the company's charter. In a letter to the Secretary of the Treasury on 15th June 1899, Lord Salisbury gave these reasons for his change of policy:

'The Marquess of Salisbury has for some time past had under consideration the question of approaching the Niger Company with a view to relieving them of their rights and functions of administration on reasonable terms. . . . There are, however, other cogent reasons for the step now contemplated. The West African Frontier Force, now under Imperial officers, calls for direct Imperial control; the situation created towards other firms by the commercial position of the Company, which, although strictly within the right devolving upon it by Charter, has succeeded in establishing a practical monopoly of trade; the manner in which this commercial monopoly presses on the native trader, as exemplified by the rising in Brass, which called for the mission of inquiry entrusted to Sir John Kirk in 1895, are some of the arguments which have influenced his Lordship. . . .'[1]

Probably much more important in Lord Salisbury's reasoning was the critical international situation that had arisen on the Niger, culminating in the French occupation of Bussa in 1897. It became clear that direct governmental control would have to be exercised over the area if the situation was not to get out of hand.

The Niger Company was fully compensated for the loss of its privileged position. The administrative buildings were bought up and a sum of £450,000 was paid as compensation. What is more, the Government undertook to impose royalties on all minerals won in the region bounded by the Niger and a line drawn from Zinder to Yola, and to pay half of these royalties to the company for ninety-nine years. In return the British Government took control of all the company's territories on 1st January 1900. The whole of Nigeria was then reorganized into three administrative areas under the Colonial Office instead of the Foreign Office. The Niger Coast Protectorate which had been transferred to the Colonial Office in April 1899, was included in the new Protectorate of Southern Nigeria, which absorbed former company territory as far north as Idah; Lagos remained an official colony together with a small Protectorate; and a new Protectorate of Northern Nigeria was established bounded by the frontiers agreed at the Anglo-French Convention of 1898. The name Nigeria was chosen by the British Government in preference to such suggestions as 'Niger Sudan', 'Negretia' and even 'Goldesia' in honour of Sir George Taubman Goldie.[2]

In the south the new Protectorate was sufficient of a reality for the administration to set about establishing itself in earnest, though a series of punitive expeditions had to be made before the administration became effective in certain areas. The Protectorate of Northern Nigeria was nothing but a cartographical claim. As Margery Perham wrote of Sir Frederick Lugard's appointment as High Commissioner, 'a colonial governor can seldom have been appointed to a territory so much of which had never even been viewed by himself or any other European'.[3] The British held positions along the banks of the Niger alone and, as the cunning Emir of Kontagora slyly assured his people, were really a species of fish unable to live away from the Niger. It fell to Lugard to prove to the powerful emirs like Kontagora that the white invaders could indeed live a mammalian existence.

Northern Nigeria had been profoundly influenced by the Holy War of Usman dan Fodio, and because of the coherent organization of the Fulani empire presented a formidable opponent for the small forces at Lugard's disposal. In the years that followed the death of the Shehu, the Fulani administration had inevitably lost much of its reforming zeal, becoming increasingly materialistic in outlook. Conditions varied from emirate to emirate. Some, like Kontagora, lived entirely on the proceeds of slave-raiding, and in the process depopulated vast tracts of land. Others, like Kano, lived mainly on their commercial and agricultural activities. There has been a strong tendency, particularly among those who sought to justify British occupation of Northern Nigeria,[4] to talk of the decadence of the Fulani administration in its later years. Certainly it fell from the high standards set by Usman dan Fodio and his son Sultan Bello. In cases like that of Kontagora, often used as a justification for British intervention, affairs were indeed lamentable. In 1880 Ibrahim Nagwamatse, son of the founder of the small emirate of Kontagora, set out on a ruthless campaign to expand his lands. In the course of his conquests he captured thousands of slaves for sale in the northern markets and devastated hundreds of villages, killing anyone unsaleable as a slave and leaving a once populous land so desolate that even today it is one of the most sparsely populated areas of the north. When later he was captured by the British and asked to renounce the slave trade, he taunted: 'Can you stop a cat from mousing? I shall die with a slave in my mouth.'[5]

Certainly the example of Kontagora did much to colour British views of Fulani administration. Major Sharpe, Resident of Kontagora, described his province as denuded of all its inhabitants except old men and babies.[6] It is a contrast therefore to read the notes made by Major Burdon, an early Resident in the north, which show a marked enthusiasm for the Fulani and their administration.[7] He writes: 'What is the attitude of the British Administration towards these states? Briefly it is construction not destruction. Our aim is to rule through existing chiefs, to raise them in the administrative scale, to enlist them on our side in the work of progress and good government. We cannot do without them. To rule directly would require an army of British magistrates . . . which both the general unhealthiness of the country and the present poverty forbid. My hope is that we may make of these born rulers a high type of

British official, working for the good of their subjects in accordance with the ideals of British Empire, but carrying on all that is best in the constitution they have evolved for themselves, the one understood by, and therefore best suited to the people.'[8]

These are not the words of a man who has recognized an empire about to collapse. Unpopular it may have been, but the system of administration was still effective and developing. The materialism of later years should not be confused with inefficiency.

The Fulani empire was organized by Bello and Abdullahi on the pattern outlined by the Shehu in his *Kitab al-Farq*.[9] The provinces, ruled by Emirs, were grouped into an Eastern and Western sector, responsible to Gwandu and Sokoto respectively, with Sokoto supreme, since it was at Sokoto that the Shehu, as Commander of the Faithful, resided.

For the first time since the brief rise of Kebbi to ascendancy in Hausaland in the early sixteenth century, all the Habe kingdoms, with the exception of parts of Gobir, Zamfara and Kebbi, were united under one rule. The old kingdoms were transformed into emirates, with their rulers owing both political and religious allegiance to the Commander of the Faithful at Sokoto. As D. M. Last has pointed out, the Fulani empire was not properly speaking an empire, since its unity depended not so much on force, as on the religious obedience the Emirs or provincial governors owed the Commander of the Faithful at Sokoto. To disobey Sokoto was tantamount to apostasy.[10] The provincial rulers paid tribute to Gwandu or Sokoto, and referred matters of administration to the imperial capitals. The viziers of Gwandu and Sokoto made regular tours of their respective provinces, reviewing administration and settling disputes. Those emirates like Katsina, Kebbi, Gobir, Zamfara and Nupe, where the Fulani administration was not established over all the inhabitants, called frequently on their respective imperial capitals for troops in time of crisis.

In 1817, the Shehu died and there was a brief struggle for power between Bello and Abdullahi for the succession to the religious leadership of the empire. Bello was quickly recognized as his father's successor, taking the title Commander of the Faithful. Administratively, however, the empire remained divided into the two sectors of Sokoto and Gwandu, with Bello continuing to rule Sokoto as Sultan and Abdullahi ruling Gwandu as Emir. Under Bello the Fulani empire was distinguished by its just administration, although it was harassed by a long series of wars with those who were still reluctant to accept the new régime, particularly the Gobirawa and Zamfarawa. Al-Haji Sa'id wrote of Bello in his *History of Sokoto*: 'He gave all of them their just place, for he was upright and pious. He spent from his own earnings and did not spend from the public purse. He had already said of his father at the start of the Holy War, "Shaik, lawful resources are lacking, and it is necessary that you should spend for necessary expenses this money, but, as for myself, I will earn my own living for I am a young man." He was apprenticed to a craft by which means he became independent of the treasury. . . . He was kind to his subjects, most merciful to them, patient, self-controlled, scrupulous concerning their property in possession of the people, and a good administrator. He scrutinized the judges, reversing their judgements which were dictated by their own interests, nor did he give them free rein in their posts.'[11]

Bello was in political terms architect of the empire, but his achievements as an administrator are the more remarkable when one considers that during his reign as Sultan (1817–37), he personally led the Fulani forces into battle against rebels, or against dissident Hausa or Bornu, some forty times. He found time not only to supervise the government of metropolitan Sokoto but of the provinces as well. In addition he wrote a large number of books on a variety of subjects ranging from theology to diseases of the eye, and the history of the Sudan.[12] Clapperton, when he visited Bello at Wurno in 1824, his imperial capital, was very impressed by his learning, particularly his knowledge of early Christian doctrinal disputes. On his second visit in 1826 he gave an Arabic copy of Euclid to Bello, who remarked that his family's copy, brought by a relative from Mecca 'was destroyed when part of his house was burnt down last year' and that he was 'very much obliged to the king of England for sending him so valuable a present'.[13]

It is from the death of Bello that most authorities trace the decline of the Fulani empire, asserting not only a loss in the religious motivation of Jihad and a corresponding increase of wars inspired by the desire for slaves, but also a falling off in standards of learning.[14] They further assert that the Hausa were restive under 'alien' rulers and that the imperial capitals of Sokoto and Gwandu had lost control of the provinces which were effectively independent political units acknowledging only a nominal allegiance to the Commander of the Faithful. This picture has been much influenced by the eye-witness accounts of Barth in the 1850s.

This is, however, a picture that is not borne out by the facts, as Boahen has recently insisted.[15] So far as administration of the empire was concerned it is clear that this remained under the control of Sokoto and Gwandu right up until occupation by the British. Indeed after the death of Sultan Bello there appears to have been a tendency towards greater centralization on the twin capitals of Sokoto and Gwandu. The Emirs of Zaria, for instance, were selected by the Sultans of Sokoto, who usually chose them from among the three families in Zaria, on the recommendations of the electoral council of Zaria. The Sultan was even able to depose the Emir of Zaria in 1860, substituting his own nominee, a man who was not even a member of the families that had so far provided the rulers of Zaria.[16] The Emir of Zaria paid homage as a vassal at the court of Sokoto twice a year, bringing tribute in the forms of slaves, Zaria cloth, horses and cowries. When Zaria's own vassals had complaints they could always seek the intervention of Sokoto. The Waziri (Vizier) of Sokoto, as head of the imperial administration, made frequent tours of Zaria and other vassal emirates, assessing tribute, regulating disputes and checking internal administration.

It is clear from the history of Adamawa and Hammaruwa (Muri),[17] the two provinces most distant from Sokoto, that neither of their Emirs could rule without the sanction of the Commander of the Faithful, to whom, on the death of an Emir, rivals for the succession were sent for his selection. The Waziri of Sokoto toured both Emirates which continued sending tribute to Sokoto until the moment of British occupation.

There were of course exceptions to this general rule. A number of Emirs tried to break away from control by Sokoto. Thus Emir Sidi of Zaria, who was deposed by Sokoto in 1860, had forbidden the entry of the Waziri of Sokoto into his city in an apparent attempt to repudiate his allegiance to the imperial capital. However, when the Sultan summoned him to the court at Wurno to explain his action, he dutifully complied only to be told that he was deposed and a more tractable successor chosen to replace him. He remained in Wurno as a prisoner until he died.[18] Barth, despite the picture he drew of a break-down in imperial control over the provincial governments, nevertheless himself records a similar incident. In the Maradi area, where the former Habe rulers of Katsina had established themselves outside Fulani control, he recorded the following: 'I then rode to Sadiku, the son of the famous M'allem 'Omaro of Ghomaro, who had been eight years Governor of Katsina, after the death of his father, till exciting the fear or wrath of his liege lord in consequence of calumnies representing him as en-deavouring to make himself independent, he was deposed by 'Aliyu, the second successor of Bello, and obliged to seek safety among the enemies of his nation (i.e. Maradi).'[19] Whilst in Katsina Barth also encountered the Galadima of Sokoto, who was concluding a tour of inspection of Zamfara and Katsina, where he had been collecting tribute. But it is clear that Barth was unwilling to recognize this authority of Sokoto as meaning-ful, for when he sought negotiations with Lawal, Lamido of Adamawa (1848–72) in 1851, the latter refused on the grounds that 'he was nothing but a slave of the Sultan of Sokoto', to which Barth replied that Emir Lawal, 'far from being a slave of the Sultan of Sokoto, was almost an independent governor of a large province'.[20] Yet on the death of Lawal, the two claimants to succession both journeyed to Sokoto to seek the choice of the Sultan.[21]

It is not clear why Barth painted the picture of the Fulani empire he did. In a note to the British Government in 1853 he wrote 'it cannot be denied that the Empire of Sokoto if going in the present way, will soon be dissolved, and thrown into pieces'.[22] Clearly, as Boahen has suggested, he over-emphasized the importance of the rebellions against Sokoto authority by the dissident Zamfarawa, Gobirawa, Kebbawa, and Maradi. These were the same rebels that had preoccupied Sultan Bello for so much of his reign, and whilst they did create insecurity in an important part of the empire, there was a vast area that was secure for traders and travellers, as the accounts of travellers like Clapperton and Lander in the twenties, and Vogel in the fifties, bear witness. Also these wars, it must be remembered, did not involve the total population, unless of course they were initiated specifically for slave-raiding. Despite the reports of Barth, these rebels never got the better of Sokoto and Gwandu, and it can be justifiably claimed for the Fulani that they did succeed in creating a large area of peaceful administration covering the greater part of Northern Nigeria in which trade was able to flourish on a much larger scale than it did under the Habe. Barth himself in his account of Kano, which once again had become the leading centre of commerce in the Central Sudan, gives an excellent picture of the improved state of trade under the Fulani régime. No longer involved in the constant wars of the eighteenth century, the former Habe states could now trade easily with each other. Kano quickly regained its former position as terminus of the Sahara caravans, and became the chief emporium of the Fulani Empire.

'The principal commerce of Kano consists in native produce, namely, the cotton cloth woven and dyed here or in the neighbouring towns, in the forms of tobes or *rigona* (sing. *riga*): *turkedi*, or the oblong piece of dress of dark blue colour worn by the women; the *zenne* or plaid, of various colours; and the *rawani baki*, or black litham (Tuareg veil).

'The great advantage of Kano is, that commerce and manufactures go hand in hand, and that almost every family has its share in them. There is really something grand in this kind of industry, which spreads to the north as far as Murzuk, Ghat and even Tripoli; to the west, not only to Timbuktu, but in some degree even as far as the shores of the Atlantic, the very inhabitants of Arguin dressing in the cloth woven and dyed in Kano; to the east, all over Bornu, although there it comes in contact with the native industry of the country; and to the south it maintains a rivalry with the native industry of the Igbira and Igbo, while towards the south-east it invades the whole of Adamawa, and is only limited by the nakedness of pagan *sans-culottes*, who do not wear clothing.

'As for the supply sent to Timbuktu, this is a fact entirely overlooked in Europe, where people speak continually of the fine cotton cloth produced in that town, while, in truth, all the apparel of decent character in Timbuktu is brought either from Kano or from Sansandi.... Besides the cloth produced and dyed in Kano and in the neighbouring villages, there is considerable commerce carried on here with the cloth manufactured in Nyffi or Nupe. . . . The chief articles of native industry, beside cloth, which have a wide market, are principally sandals . . . tanned hides ('kulabu') and red sheep skins, dyed with a juice extracted from the stalks of the holcus, are not unimportant, being sent in great quantities even as far as Tripoli. . . . A very important branch of the native commerce in Kano is certainly the slave trade; but it is extremely difficult to say how many of these unfortunate creatures are exported, as a greater number are carried away by small caravans to Bornu and Nupe than on the direct road to Ghat and Fezzan. . . .'[23]

Whilst it is true that the Fulani empire lost much of its early reforming zeal, there is little justification for the picture of decadence of religious standards and learning given by so many authorities. Though the intellectual brilliance of Bello's court was not paralleled by any of his successors, the histories of Sokoto and Adamawa, to take two examples, make reference to the religious zeal and learning of a number of their rulers including those who reigned in the second half of the century. Thus the Emir Lawal of Adamawa, whom Barth met, is today in Yola 'often regarded as the *beau idéal* of the Fulani administrator: warrior, scholar, and religious ascetic. He enforced a strict code of moral conduct and even of dress. . . .'[24] Lawal also founded many schools in his province. Whilst his successor, Sanda (1872–90), appears to have been weak and indolent, devoted more to affairs in the harem than in the state, Zubeiru, who came to the throne in 1890 and opposed British occupation of his territory, immediately imposed a puritanical régime on the province. A number of Bello's successors were also noted for their piety and learning, in particular his immediate successor Atiku I (1837–42) and Attahiru Ahmadu, who was deposed in 1902 by the British after only one short year's reign.

There is of course another aspect of the Fulani empire that must not be forgotten. Since, like its predecessors, the Habe states, it depended, as indeed did Bornu, on slaves for much of its income, large numbers of peoples on the periphery of the empire suffered greatly at their hands. The case of Kontagora is notorious, but there were many other areas which also lived in perpetual fear of Fulani raids for slaves to be sold to North

Africa or for use as agricultural labour. The insecurity of those areas subjected to these raids is well brought out in Mary Smith's *Baba of Karo*.[25] It was such slaving activities that the British used as one of their main justifications for the conquest of the Fulani empire, effected by Lord Lugard between 1900 and 1906.

The Niger Company had made a number of treaties with the Sultan of Sokoto and the Emir of Gwandu which they claimed gave rights of Protectorate over the Fulani empire. However it seems clear that the Sultan of Sokoto believed that all he was conceding to the British traders was a monopoly of European trade with his empire which was granted in return for an annual payment that he must have considered as a form of tribute.[26] Though the Company used these treaties as a basis for their claim to the Fulani empire and as a means to keep out the rival French, no effective administration had been established in Fulani territory before 1897. In that year the Royal Niger Company constabulary was sent against both Nupe and Ilorin on account of their persistent raids into company territory. A force of 500 men and 25 officers quickly subdued the Nupe forces and a new Emir, likely to be favourable to the company's interests, was installed. The force then marched on to Ilorin, where a treaty was signed whereby the Emir recognized company sovereignty in his state. The Emir of Nupe was forced to concede to the company the southern half of his kingdom which became the province of Kabba. This was the first inroad made by the British into the great Fulani empire.

It was not until the 1st January 1900, however, when the British flag was hoisted at Lokoja, that real attempts were made to establish British control over those territories north of the Niger and Benue assigned her by the Berlin Conference. Though both the Fulani empire and Bornu came within this sphere, the company had control over neither. True, they had drawn up treaties with Sokoto and Gwandu, to whom all other emirates were politically subordinate, but these were mere scraps of paper useful only for the purposes of international diplomacy. At first the new administration headed by Sir Frederick Lugard was in a difficult position, since the bulk of its defence force, the W.A.F.F., had been seconded to the Ashanti campaign. Only Ilorin, Borgu and Kabba were under effective occupation and even there Lugard had continually to assert British authority.[27] To the north lay the slave-raiding kingdom of Kontagora and the emirate of Nupe whose puppet ruler had been deposed by its former ruler, Abu Bekri, a man naturally deeply hostile to the British. These two made plans to attack the W.A.F.F. troops in their Wushishi garrison.

At the same time as he was preparing to deal with Kontagora and Nupe, Lugard was equally engaged in trying to assemble an administration for the vast country he was about to take over. The old company administration was at his disposal but, as Lugard himself complained, this was very rudimentary and certainly not equipped to administer a huge country of nearly 15 million people. Furthermore, nothing he could prepare on the small sum of £135,000 available to him would be sufficient to cope with the administration of so vast an area. To deal with this seemingly impossible situation he formulated his famous policy of indirect rule, that is, rule by the colonial administration through the existing native institutions.

From the very outset Lugard decided that indirect rule was the only method by which the country could be governed, and as a result he has often been credited as its originator. This is an incorrect assumption. It had been used in India and Fiji. His close friend Goldie had already propounded it as a suitable method for governing Nigeria. But Lugard ennobled indirect rule from being just an expedient in times of financial hardship and lack of staff to a complete philosophy of government for Britain's colonial peoples.[28] Before he even reached Nigeria he had decided that his political officers should be called Residents, thereby giving them the status of diplomats rather than administrators. In his first annual report he outlined his system: 'The Fulani rule has been maintained as an experiment, for I am anxious to prove to these people that we have no hostility to them, and only insist on good government and justice, and I am anxious to utilize, if possible, their wonderful intelligence for they are born rulers. . . .'[29] In later years he and his successors were to embroider this makeshift policy into a complete theory of administration.

The immediate problem, as Lugard saw it, however, was still the spread of an effective administration and the promotion of trade. In 1900 he was already advocating the building of a railway without which the north could never be commercially developed. Such a railway would also facilitate the movement of troops. A campaign was therefore first undertaken against the hostile Emirs of Kontagora and Nupe, the main obstacles between him and the conquest of the rich northern emirates. Nupe and Kontagora, having failed to bring Ilorin in on their side, put up stiff resistance against the British, until a full-scale campaign was launched against them in 1901 after the return of the W.A.F.F. troops from the Ashanti campaign in the Gold Coast where they had fought with great distinction. Willcocks, Lugard's right-hand man and commander of these troops, was highly impressed by them. In a letter, to Lugard, he wrote: 'I never served with such fellows. How I love them! Always cheerful, plucky, brave and uncomplaining.'[30] With these well-trained troops Kontagora and Nupe were quickly conquered. Abu Bekri fled northwards and the old company Emir was reinstated. Lugard, at the same time, wrote to the Sultan of Sokoto, Abdurrahman (1891–1902), informing him of this and asked him as overlord of Kontagora to nominate a successor to Nagwamatse.[31] To this letter the Sultan did not reply. By April 1901 eight provinces were established and brought under Lugard's control: Borgu, Ilorin, Kabba, Kontagora, Bida, Zaria, Lower Benue (Nassarawa) and Upper Benue (Muri).

In Yola, the Emir Zubeiru, whom Lugard described as 'a fine type of the Fulani ruler, well educated, but possessed with a religious fanaticism, which rendered him entirely intolerant of European "infidels" ',[32] ordered the representative of the Niger Company to haul down the Union Jack, despite his earlier treaty with the company. An expedition under a Colonel Morland was therefore sent to deal with him. The Emir put up such resistance as he could with the aid of two cannon, but the British forces with their Maxim guns were too great for him. The Emir fled and was murdered by pagans in Adamawa, after attacking German forces in Kamerun. Lugard wrote regretfully of his death: 'I should have wished, had it been possible, to have afforded domicile to this brave though fanatical chief, but he was wholly irrecoverable. . . .'[33]

North of Yola lay Bornu, most of which had been assigned to the British under the terms of the Berlin Conference, though no treaty had been drawn up with the ruler of the thousand-year-old state. After the final abortive revolt of Mai Ibrahim against the Al Kanemi dynasty in 1846, Bornu enjoyed nearly fifty years of comparative security internally. Externally she had arrived at a *modus vivendi* with her enemy, the Fulani empire, which still ruled over lands that once had belonged to Bornu or been tributary to her. But in 1893 Bornu suffered a great upheaval with the invasion of a Sudanese adventurer, Rabeh, who defeated the Bornu army in 1893, occupying the state in the name of the Mahdi, though he did not acknowledge the latter's authority.[34] By 1896 he had brought the whole state under his control. Rabeh had had a chequered career in the Egyptian army and later in the service of the notorious slave-raider, Zubair Pasha, who was imprisoned by the Egyptians for fear of the growing power of his private army. Half of this army was taken over by Rabeh who set off on a whirlwind career of conquest and slave-raiding. Before he won the great prize of Bornu, he had conquered Wadai, Dar Kuti and Bagarimi. In Bornu he proved himself as competent an administrator as a general, dividing the newly acquired state into strictly controlled districts which paid him fixed tribute. His army consisted of 20,000 men, nearly 5,000 of whom were equipped with firearms. In 1892 he attacked Bagarimi, disturbed by the presence of the French officer Gentil in that kingdom. In 1899 he massacred a column led by a Frenchman Brettonet, and ordered the strangling of a Frenchman on a mission to Dikwa, which he had made his headquarters.

Rabeh was fervently anti-European and advocated Holy War against Europe.[35] Well he might have been, for just as he was about to found a third Bornu dynasty, under a much improved administrative system, the final partition of Bornu between the colonial powers of Britain, France and Germany was determined by the Anglo-French Convention of 1898. Zinder, Kanem, Bagarimi and the lands east of the Chari were to be given to France; Dikwa and the territories between the Chari and the Yesderam to the Germans; and the rest to the British.

In 1900 the French sent columns to make good their claims to Bornu, and engaged Rabeh in a fierce battle in which he was killed by one of his former soldiers now serving the French. Gentil then restored the Kanemi dynasty to Dikwa. However, Rabeh's son, Fad-el-Allah, still claimed the throne of Bornu, and appealed to the British for recognition, promising that he would co-operate fully with them. Major McClintock, who had visited Bornu on Lugard's behalf in 1901, was in favour of recognizing Fad-el-Allah, though Lugard doubted whether it would be politic to recognize an avowed enemy of the French. Any indecision on this matter was brought to an abrupt end by a French raid against Gujba, 150 miles within the borders of the agreed British sector of Bornu, in which Fad-el-Allah was killed. The French then demanded 80,000 dollars from Abubakar Garbai, the legitimate Kanemi Shehu, for defeating Rabeh and his son. Only 6,500 dollars remained to be paid when a British task force arrived to take over Bornu. On the way this force subdued Bauchi and established a garrison in the town, hindered only by a self-proclaimed Mahdi, Jibrella of Gombe, who put up extremely brave resistance against the British. In Bornu the British did not have to fight, since they promised Abubakar Garbai the throne of Bornu if he would cease paying the indemnity demanded by the French and submit to their rule, a proposal he gladly accepted. He was eventually established as Shehu at Maiduguri where a British garrison was installed.

The occupation of Northern Nigeria was slow. An expedition had to be undertaken in 1902 against Abuja, where the Emir, descendant of the Habe rulers of Zaria, had closed the trade route to the north. The Magaji of Keffi was the next to be attacked. As the Emir of Zaria's representative and most influential member of the ageing King of Keffi's court, he slaved openly, refusing to recognize the validity of the laws abolishing slavery promulgated by Lugard in April 1901. He actually killed Captain Moloney, the local Resident, with his own hands when the latter tried to persuade him to stop his nefarious practices. He then fled to Kano by way of Zaria, whose Emir still wavered between declaring allegiance to the invading power, or affirming that to his traditional ruler at Sokoto. At the end of the expedition against Keffi, Lugard confidently predicted in his second *Annual Report* that there would be a great increase in trade owing to the pacification of Bornu, Yola and the Benue provinces.[36] But two tasks still confronted Lugard: to render trade routes safe from raiders and to conquer the emirates of the far north. As Lugard remarked in the *Annual Report* for 1902: 'Trade cannot, indeed, be established on a satisfactory basis until the northern Hausa States are included in the "Provinces" of the Protectorate and the trade routes rendered safe for small traders.'[37]

Both Sokoto and Gwandu, the traditional capitals of the Fulani empire, remained hostile to the new administration. When Abdurrahman, the Sultan of Sokoto, eventually communicated with Lugard, he did so in terms which Lugard chose to consider tantamount to a declaration of war. Grave doubts have recently been expressed about the validity of Lugard's interpretation of this letter as an outright declaration of war.[38]

(Translation of Arabic Letter from Sultan of Sokoto to the High Commissioner, seal undecipherable)

'From us to you. I do not consent that any one from you should ever dwell with us. I will never agree with you. I will have nothing ever to do with you. Between us and you there are no dwellings except as between Mussulmans and Unbelievers,— War, as God Almighty has enjoined on us. There is no power or strength save in God on high.

This with salutations.'

Received about May 1902.

Whether or not the Sultan's letter was an authentic declaration of war, Lugard used it as such, and decided the north would have to be taken by conquest, despite the disapproval of the Colonial Office which hoped for a negotiated occupation. He decided first to attack Kano where the Magaji of Keffi had been given asylum by the Emir Aliyu, who observed hopefully, 'If a little town like Keffi could do so much, what could not Kano do?'[39] Lugard was well aware that the whole of the Fulani North, including those states already captured, was awaiting his trial of strength with Kano and Sokoto. As long as Kano retained its reputation for invincibility, and Sokoto remained independent as spiritual overlord of all Fulani Emirs, so long would there be hope of escape from the new administration. If Lugard, who had pathetically small forces at his disposal, showed any sign of wavering, he might have a general uprising on his hands, which it would be impossible to contain.

Lugard had two things in his favour. First, in the words of Hilaire Belloc:

> *Whatever happens we have got*
> *The maxim gun and they have not.*[40]

Secondly, Lugard firmly believed that once the Hausa peasantry saw that he was the real master, they would not put up much of a resistance on behalf of their Fulani rulers. Even so Kano presented a formidable objective. The great city, encircled by enormous walls, deep thorn-filled ditches and cunningly constructed gates, could, under a determined leader, withstand almost indefinite siege. Kano was first to show its cards. The Emir despatched a force against Lugard's garrison at Zaria, only to withdraw on the news of the death of the Sultan of Sokoto. Lugard then sent a force of 1,000 local troops and 50 Europeans, commanded by Colonel Morland, against Kano, despite the strong reservations of the Colonial Office about such an expedition.

Thus, in January 1903, after shelling Bebeji, the first town they came to that offered resistance, Lugard's forces marched in triumph to the gates of Kano, each town capitulating without struggle having seen what happened to Bebeji. The test came at Kano, whose defence had been entrusted to two slaves of the Emir, who had himself gone to Sokoto to consult with the newly elected Sultan, Attahiru Ahmadu, and to draw up another army. The city was quickly taken, and it appeared that the inhabitants, who were Hausa as distinct from their Fulani overlords, were barely concerned about this change of masters. The army brought up by the Emir of Kano was of little effect since his brother, the Wombai, detached his half and refused to fight. The Emir fled across the French border, leaving his army under the command of the Waziri. On 26th February, the Wombai submitted to the British and was installed as Emir. This was the beginning of the end of Fulani resistance. Katsina's intention of submission was then received and *en route* for Sokoto the British took over Gwandu, capital of the Eastern Empire. On the 14th March the Sokoto army was defeated. When the British occupied the town they found that the Sultan had fled. Lugard, arriving on the 19th, called together the Waziri and chiefs and asked them either to recall the fleeing Sultan, Attahiru Ahma-

du, or elect a new one in his stead. In the event, they decided to
choose a new Sultan, Muhammad Attahiru (1903–15). In a
speech approving Attahiru's appointment Lugard made it clear
that the old Empire of Usman dan Fodio was now at an end.

'The old treaties are dead, you have killed them. Now these
are the words which I, the High Commissioner, have to say for
the future. The Fulani in old times under Dan Fodio conquered
this country. They took the right to rule over it, to levy taxes,
to depose kings and to create kings. They in turn have by defeat
lost their rule which has come into the hands of the British. All
these things which I have said the Fulani by conquest took the
right to do now pass to the British. Every Sultan and Emir and
the principal officers of State will be appointed by the High
Commissioner throughout all this country. The High Commissioner will be guided by the usual laws of succession and the
wishes of the people and chiefs but will set them aside if he
desires for good cause to do so. The Emirs and Chiefs who are
appointed will rule over the people as of old time and take such
taxes as are approved by the High Commissioner, but they will
obey the laws of the Governor and will act in accordance with
the advice of the Resident. Buying and selling slaves and en-
slaving people are forbidden. . . . All men are free to worship
God as they please. Mosques and prayer places will be treated
with respect by us. . . . It is the earnest desire of the King of
England that this country shall prosper and grow rich in peace
and in contentment, that the population shall increase and the
ruined towns which abound everywhere shall be built up, and
that war and trouble shall cease. Henceforth no Emir or Chief
shall levy war or fight, but his case will be settled by law, and
if force is necessary Government will employ it. . . . You need
have no fear regarding British rule, it is our wish to learn your
customs and fashion, just as you must learn ours. I have little
fear that we shall agree, for you have always heard that British
rule is just and fair, and people under our King are satisfied.
You must not fear to tell the Resident everything and he will
help and advise you.'[41]

Meanwhile it was essential for Lugard to effect the capture of
both the ex-Sultan of Sokoto and Aliyu the ex-Emir of Kano,
both of whom were potential focal points for opposition to his
régime. The Emir Aliyu was captured shortly after Lugard left

Kano, having fled to the north where he had been seized by
the King of Gobir, ancient foe of the Fulani, who was only too
glad to deliver up this scion of the empire to the European conquerors. This was fortunate for Lugard since had Aliyu been
able to join forces with the ex-Sultan Attahiru Ahmadu, as did
the Magaji of Keffi, Lugard might have been faced with a more
difficult task in consolidating his gains in Northern Nigeria than
he actually did. The ex-Sultan's flight was undertaken as a
hijra, or flight from the infidel. When Usman dan Fodio conquered the Hausa kings in the early nineteenth century, he
prophesied that in the future, at a given sign that would be clear
to all, the faithful would be called upon to undertake the hijra
towards the east. This prophecy was made known through his
daughter, Nana Mariam, and his son, Abubakar Atiku, who
reigned as Sultan from 1837–42. As Muffet has shown, the Emir
Aliyu, when he travelled to Sokoto on the election of the Attahiru Muhammadu as Sultan in 1902, actually suggested that
the time for the hijra had come, and that they should abandon
the country.[42] Throughout the century there had been a number
of occasions when the Moslems had believed the time had come
for the hijra prophesied by the Shehu. But as Muffet records,
when one Emir of Kano in the middle of the century wrote to
Nana Mariam to ask whether people who had begun the
hijra were justified, she answered that the time was not yet
come:

'By Allah's wish, it is better to remain. It is better and safer
to remain where you are, in spite of other longings. . . . The
Shehu, my father, stated that we shall migrate from Hausaland,
but he did not decree the time that this would be. He only
defined the *hijra* for us. . . .'[43]

The ex-Sultan's call to the faithful to follow him in the prophesied hijra to the east gained a response that Lugard had not
bargained for. He had considered the alienation of the Hausa
peasantry from their Fulani rulers an essential factor in the
political situation in the Sokoto empire; yet a large number of
chiefs and peasants abandoned their lands for the long trip
eastwards under the leadership of the Sultan, who as Muffet
has suggested perhaps 'had his roots deeper in the hearts of his
people than was admitted in the hour of his defeat'.[44] Clearly
the exodus, as the *Annual Report* for 1903 stresses, was having a

profound effect on the peasantry[45] and it became evident that it was essential to capture Attahiru Ahmadu if British authority were to be firmly established in the area. The Sultan was finally defeated in a battle after a flight of nearly 575 miles from Sokoto to Burmi, in the course of which he and his followers beat off the British expeditionary force on some six occasions. At Burmi, where the Sultan joined forces with the local Mahdi, and with the Magaji of Keffi and a large number of chiefs from all over the empire, he was finally defeated and killed by the British in a hard fought engagement. Nevertheless his preaching of the hijra still inspired many of his followers. As many as 25,000 people led by his son and Ahmadu of Misau migrated to the Sudan, settling on the Blue Nile where the Fulani settlements are still in existence today.[46]

After the conquest of Sokoto, Lugard was able to get down to the more fundamental task of administration. One cannot but be impressed by the meticulous annual reports he submitted each year, showing how much thought he gave to every problem of administration. Slavery was abolished, but rather than upset the whole social structure of the country, only those who ran away from their masters were deemed free. A dual system of British and Moslem law was instituted. The organization of the provinces was streamlined. Roads were pushed through the bush. Every effort was made to stimulate trade. All this was the most remarkable since for the first three years of his office Lugard was tied down by military expeditions, and handicapped for the whole period by acute shortage of funds. Nevertheless, his policy of indirect rule seemed to be maturing well.

Suddenly, in 1906, it seemed that all Lugard's work was to be destroyed overnight, when news arrived by telegram from Sokoto:

'. . . whole of C Company Mounted Infantry, defeated and annihilated in Satiru. . . . Hillary and Scott, Residents, Blackwood, West African Frontier Force, are I fear killed. Dr. Ellis severely wounded, Sergeant Slack, R.A., and myself and doctor only men remaining most urgent. Signed, Gosling, Sergeant.'[47]

This was a severe blow to Lugard. At a time when his administration seemed to have taken root, white men had been murdered in the heart of the Fulani empire. Would this be a general signal for revolt? Would the Emirs, especially those like

Gwandu and Hadejia who had never really accepted the new administration, now try and overthrow it? They all knew that his forces were tied down suppressing an outbreak of rioting among the Tiv, who had come to the aid of their neighbours the Jukun in a quarrel with local Hausa traders, many of whom had been enslaved. Most serious of all, Major Burdon, the highly competent Resident of Sokoto, was trekking southwards on his way home for leave. What was more, the Sokoto rebels had captured a precious Maxim gun.

It was only later that Lugard learnt the full story of the rising. Two years before, the chief of Satiru, a town some fourteen miles distant from Sokoto, had declared himself the Mahdi. He had been arrested and had died in prison. However, an outlaw from across the border, Dan Makafo, had now persuaded the chief's son, Mallam Isa, to proclaim himself the prophet Jesus. In their excitement the people of Satiru had risen against neighbouring enemy villages, so the Acting Resident went with a small force to quell the rebels. When he tried to treat with them, they rushed his troops, inflicting the casualties outlined in Sergeant Gosling's telegram. It was a touchy moment for British Imperialism in Northern Nigeria. For the first time the white man had been conquered, and a general rising, if led by the Sultan of Sokoto, could well have broken the hold that Lugard had maintained so effectively till then with his shoestring army. Indeed everything depended on Sokoto. 'Had he shown the slightest indecision', wrote Burdon later, 'I have no doubt that the bulk of the "talakawa" (peasantry) would at once have joined the enemy.'[48] As it was, Sokoto remained loyal, possibly because he realized that ultimately the British could always draw on more reserves, possibly because he saw that the success of a revolt led by a 'prophet' would be a threat to his own religious pre-eminence. Maybe he really did feel some loyalty to Lugard. M. G. Smith has suggested that this revolt emphasized the interdependence of the Fulani and British administrations and that therefore a 'tacit agreement grew up that force would not be used'.[49]

With Sokoto's decision to support Lugard, the rising was as good as quashed. A military expedition defeated the rebels, whose ringleaders were put to death. The village of Satiru was razed to the ground, and cursed by the Sultan. The Emir of

Gwandu, who had wavered on the side of the rebels, was deposed, and an expedition was led against the long recalcitrant Emir of Hadejia, who died in the fighting.

Shortly after the Satiru rebellion, Lugard was appointed Governor of Hong Kong. He left behind him a country now firmly under British control. In a final trial of strength the emirs had proved remarkably loyal. Undoubtedly this had much to do with Lugard himself, for he held them in deep respect. It was for his successors to consolidate the vast gains he had made and to regularize the makeshift administration he had so rapidly and successfully established.

CHAPTER XIV

The Unification of Nigeria

On the withdrawal of the Royal Niger Company's charter, the Niger Coast Protectorate and all the company's
territories as far north as Idah were amalgamated into
the new Protectorate of Southern Nigeria. The Lagos Protectorate, like the Protectorate of Southern Nigeria, was brought
under Colonial Office jurisdiction, and comprised all of Yorubaland except the Emirate of Ilorin which was included in the
Protectorate of Northern Nigeria. By 1900 the major areas of
resistance to British authority had been overcome, but in some
areas of the Eastern provinces British authority was only extended with great difficulty. Yorubaland had been brought under
British rule by treaty, Benin had been conquered and the Delta
states had all been subdued in the interests of trade. However, it
took many punitive expeditions to bring the whole of Iboland
effectively under British administration.

The first major operation undertaken by the new Protectorate government was against the Aro, guardians of the famous
Aro Chukwu oracle, which still retained its political influence
over most of the peoples of what used to be the Eastern Region of
Nigeria. The Aro bitterly resented the extension of British
authority over an area in which for more than two centuries the
religious and political supremacy of their oracle had remained
unchallenged. They therefore did as much as they could to frus-
trate the alien administration, particularly by using their religious authority to place embargoes on trade with the Europeans.[1] At first the British had hoped to avoid using force in dealing with the Aro. However, when in June 1901 the latter attacked
some Ibibio villages, carrying off a number of their inhabitants
for sale as slaves on the domestic market, the British decided to

take action. As Anene has put it, 'there were no doubts . . . in the minds of the Protectorate administrators that the one remaining obstacle to the consolidation of imperial rule was the Aro.'[2] The attack on the Ibibio was considered by the Protectorate government as having been aimed at the frustration of trade in the interior. This, together with the continuing role of the Aro in the internal slave trade, gave them the excuse they needed to mount an expedition against the Aro and their oracle. However, as Anene has pointed out, the Colonial Office, while sanctioning the expedition, were not happy about extending the Protectorate by conquest.[3] The expedition met with comparatively little resistance, and entered Arochukwu itself on 24th December 1901. A number of Aro chiefs were hanged, and the oracle was fired. Though the destruction of the basis of Aro authority represented a major step forward in the extension of British authority over Eastern Nigeria, numerous columns, named after the areas they patrolled, were kept on a standing basis. In Ogoja, Owerri, Ibibio, Urhobo and Western Ibo the new government had its most difficult task, often extending control village by village.[4] The local people had the initiative despite their primitive weapons. Great rain forests, meshes of streams and rivers merging into swampland, made rapid communications almost impossible and put the villagers at a great advantage over their well-armed enemies. Thus for the first six years of the Protectorate's life the new administration, particularly in the Eastern provinces, was concerned primarily with the assertion of its authority.

Though some parts of Iboland were not finally brought under British control until as late as 1918, the year 1906, when the Lagos Protectorate was merged with the Protectorate of Southern Nigeria and the north was finally pacified, can be taken as marking the beginning of effective British administration in modern Nigeria. Before then cultural contact with the European, with the exception of the coastal ports and certain towns in Yorubaland, had been of marginal significance. During the three centuries that Europeans had been visiting Nigeria they had made remarkably little cultural impact on the bulk of the local population. This is in marked contrast to the trans-Saharan contact in Northern Nigeria, which resulted in extensive changes in religion, law, architecture, technology and concepts of social stratification. It was only after 1906 that the way of life of the invaders had any appreciable effect on Nigerian society. From then on can be traced the rapid breakdown of the structure of traditional society, as the various peoples of Nigeria were brought under an administration which if not uniform in its application was at least controlled by a single power. Before then the British had been but a handful and their main interest in Nigeria had been economic. With the exception of the missionaries they had neither deliberately nor unconsciously attempted to alter native society except in so far as customs hindered trade, or where practices such as human sacrifice were openly repugnant to them.

The period 1906–12, which preceded the amalgamation of the Northern and Southern Protectorates by Sir Frederick Lugard, is one of the most crucial in the history of Nigeria, for it marks both the beginning of effective administration and the beginning of the rejection of standards and customs that had endured almost intact for many centuries. It was the first time that Nigerians were subjected in any large measure to Western influences, which in the next fifty years were to have such a great effect on Nigerian society. A whole new economic world was to be opened to Nigerians. Christianity, as the official doctrine of the colonial masters, began to spread throughout the pagan areas of both Southern and Northern Nigeria. New forms of administration and justice were introduced. Finally, education in the Western way of life was made available to a wide range of Nigerians as a result of the spread of missions. So although this period appears from the annual reports as a static one, it was in effect the beginning of silent revolution in Nigeria.

Since Britain's overriding interest in Nigeria was economic, it is not surprising that one of the dominant factors tending towards the disintegration of traditional society was the growth of Western-oriented trade. A comparison between trade figures in 1908 and 1910 gives an indication of the extent of this growth in Southern Nigeria. In 1908 exports were valued at £3,094,175 as compared with £4,320,000 in 1910, whilst the figures for imports were respectively £3,076,309 and £5,122,000. Exports consisted mainly of palm products. Trade figures for the North were substantially lower, amounting to little more than £200,000 worth of exports in 1910. Yet significantly in

1911, when the railway reached Kano, figures for ground-nut exports were 19,288 tons compared with a mere 1,179 tons the previous year.[5]

The rapid growth of the Nigerian economy was to have profound effects on the trading structure of Nigerian societies.[6] The installation of the British administration created a huge free trade area, eliminating the dangers that had beset most traders in the past, and depriving many societies of their occupation of exacters of trade tolls. Under British protection traders could move about the country freely with the result that not only did the volume of internal trade rise steeply, but exporting and importing became easier. The most significant innovation by the new administration was the introduction of a new communications system. The slow caravans that trekked from north to south and back, passing along narrow footpaths, often heavily armed against attack, were now replaced by the railway, which if not fast by modern standards cut days off the old journey, and reduced the cost in human carriers. This growth in the internal market was facilitated by the introduction of a common system of portable currency, which, though in many areas it took a long time to replace traditional forms of currency like cowries and iron bars, necessarily overcame many of the obstacles previously presented for inter-ethnic trading. Systematic taxation gave Nigerians motives for producing more than was normally necessary to maintain the family.[7] The introduction of European goods soon stimulated new wants so that in many parts of the country people were beginning to produce a surplus for exchange.

The new money economy brought with it many changes, more marked in smaller societies than, for example, in Hausaland where a developed export trade had been conducted across the desert for many centuries. Wealth soon began to compete with traditional status. Heredity began to give way to acquisition of wealth as the arbiter of influence in the community. New towns began to spring up, or else traditional towns expanded in response both to the demands of trade and the new administration. Here peoples of many tribes mingled, dealing in the same markets, living side by side, and dropping former tribal hostilities and differences in the interest of trade. However, the old static corporate life was slow to be replaced by a life of economic individualism, for it was not undermined to nearly the same extent as in the German Cameroons or certain French territories where efficient plantations were established by alienating indigenously owned land and transferring it either to expatriate individuals or companies. In Nigeria traditional land laws were observed and Europeans were unable to purchase land. Since corporate ownership of land by lineages was fundamental to the traditional structure of most Nigerian societies, the observance of customary land law proved a bulwark against the disruptive elements of the new economic order. At the same time it prevented the economic exploitation of the land by individual Nigerians.

Western economic forces have contributed to the unity of the arbitrary block that is modern Nigeria, and the various ethnic groups comprised within its frontiers have necessarily become more and more dependent on each other as the economy has expanded. Superficially, however, unity was given to the new Nigeria by the establishment of the British administration. Nevertheless, after Lugard's amalgamation of the Northern and Southern Protectorates in 1912, the administrative distinction between the two was maintained. However many local variations there may have been in the administrative system, there was one ultimate factor: there had been a diversion of power from the traditional authorities to the incoming colonial administration. Even in the Northern region where the principles of indirect rule were applied most intensively, the Emir was no longer sovereign and held power by grace of the colonial government. His authority was reduced by the knowledge that, if he stepped over the uncertain boundary of rules for good government laid down by the British, he could be deposed. On the other hand his overlord at Sokoto or Gwandu had exercised a similar restraint on his exercise of power. In one sense his position was made more secure in that the presence of the British reduced threats of deposition from within by rivals.[8]

In the North, Lugard's successors, Sir Percy Girouard and Sir Hesketh Bell, consolidated his policy of indirect rule, though not exactly along the lines he had advocated.[9] The regularization of the Native Courts and the reorganization of the Native Treasuries, known as Beit-el-Mal, whereby the Emir had to submit annual budgets for approval by the administration, both fitted in with Lugard's concept of indirect rule as a dynamic process whereby the Native Authorities would become the instruments of modernization themselves. On the other hand under Girouard and Bell the concept of indirect rule came increasingly to mean a policy of minimal interference by the administration in the affairs of the Native Authorities. Thus while in one sense the Emir, now a salaried official of his own Native Authority, had his power implicitly curtailed by having to submit annual budgets for approval by the British administration, the *laissez-faire* attitude of the latter meant that provided the Emir committed no flagrant abuses of his power he remained very much master in his own house. In the South the Yoruba oba and his courts were similarly subjected to the new concepts of what good government constituted and in a certain sense a diminution of authority inevitably ensued. On the other hand, the focusing of attention by the British on the executive role of the oba gave him authority that he never possessed in the traditional context.[10] In those parts of the East that had been brought under British control the local administration assumed much greater importance than in any other part, and must have proved a revolutionary concept for societies which had conceived political organization at the village level on a largely democratic basis where no one man or group had exclusive power. Furthermore, the introduction of the British system of justice for a large number of matters in the South naturally detracted from the authority of traditional chiefs and broke down many of the sanctions of traditional society. It also provided a place for appeal outside the traditional social system.

Neither the economic nor administrative policy of the government set out deliberately to upset the traditional social structure. Indeed the core of the philosophy of indirect rule as it came to be practised in Nigeria from 1906 onwards was the ensurance of minimum interference with 'native society'. It attempted only to create favourable conditions for trade and to ensure what it considered the basic essentials of human behaviour. By contrast the missionaries, who were excluded from the Moslem areas of the North by Lugard's agreement with the Sultan of Sokoto that he would not interfere with Moslem religion, approached Nigerian societies with a very different attitude. They were convinced that their own society was superior, and also that conversion of the local people would have to be not only from the traditional religion but from the whole way of life which was intertwined with it and supported it. They therefore deliberately set out to change the very structure of traditional society. Until the beginning of the twentieth century they had made only comparatively small inroads into Nigerian society.

Something of the ardour with which the early missionary pursued his self-chosen task is indicated by the career of that remarkable woman missionary Mary Slessor, who is remembered vividly to this day by many of the peoples of Eastern Nigeria. Like her fellows she saw almost nothing that was good in African society, though she never treated the African himself as a man of inferior quality as many other missionaries did.[11]

Mary Slessor left her home in Scotland, where she had worked as a mill girl and had seen the most sordid sides of nineteenth-century industrial life, to serve the Presbyterian mission in Calabar. She arrived there in 1876, and soon became interested in the conversion of the Okoyong people of the Cross River. For the nineteenth-century missionary they presented a considerable challenge: they practised twin murder and human sacrifice on a large scale. Their country was some of the wildest in Nigeria. Nevertheless, against the advice of the other missionaries, Mary Slessor went to live among these people, eating their food, sharing their life so completely that after many setbacks she was able to persuade them of the undesirability of their practices. Such was her standing with the Okoyong that in 1890 she was appointed Vice-Consul for Okoyong by Sir Claude Macdonald, since it was felt that no official could gain their co-operation. In the years that followed she worked in many different parts of the Cross River, earning the deepest respect of the people, for although she was uncompromising about those practices she found repugnant, she had a deep love and respect for the people she was trying to convert. When she died she had made a great impression on a very large number of Eastern Nigerians, many of whose children and grandchildren are amongst the best-educated Nigerians today.

The career of Mary Slessor not only shows what missionaries were fighting, but also how they appreciated that total conversion was necessary. Such an attitude was bound to be disruptive of both those elements which were undesirable on the European scale of moral values and those which gave cohesion to society. The impact of missionaries was more intimately felt by Nigerians than that of administrators. Like Mary Slessor they penetrated the most remote regions, bearing with conditions that would have been intolerable to any other than one who was so whole-heartedly dedicated. In every case they hacked prodigiously away at the very roots of society. Since chiefs or elders were invariably resentful of these intruders, missionaries were often forced to turn to the socially low placed or outcast, who had no deep vested interest in traditional society. Thus a slave, or mother of twins, would be more receptive than a young man destined for important position in the community. Conversion implied for the African a complete rejection of his society. Dancing and drumming were even included in the list of undesirable associations with traditional life. Marriage payment, forming a great bond between two families, polygamy, initiation ceremonies, the basis of a man or woman's education into adulthood, ancestor worship which symbolized the continuing existence of the community, all these were rejected by the true convert. This naturally tended to undermine the structure of the old community. Parental authority, social sanctions were broken down. The convert was necessarily alienated from his community, and indeed was taught to look on its every aspect with contempt. In accepting Christianity he accepted the individualism implicit in its doctrine, which conflicts radically with the corporate concept of African life. He was also taught to believe in the fundamental equality of man before Christ, and the Christian of slave status could use this in argument against his traditional superiors. Later, of course, the Christian convert was to use the same argument in demands for equality with the Europeans. Christianity, whose influence was in the early years restricted to the South, and today affects little more than 20 per cent of the population, had a profound influence on the attitude of the convert towards his own society, for as James Coleman has written, in a searching analysis of missionary impact on traditional society: 'Once the genuine African convert had embraced Christianity, the difficulties of individual adjustment to a socio-political structure incapable of realizing Christian ideals became insuperable.'[12]

Whether the break need have been so dramatic is open to doubt. Subsequent missionaries have felt these early endeavours were too unaccommodating, and implied too great a rupture with the past. Bishop Crowther, who headed the first major experiment in an Africanized mission, believed, like Moslem proselytes, in converting 'the men with influence in the old town so as to win the whole community for the new religion'.[13] But most early missionaries felt that conversion was purely a personal matter, and that no wholesale conversion could be a true conversion. They were not prepared to compromise principles in the light of particular situations. The Moslem proselytizers, on the other hand, probably approaching the problem a little more sceptically, and with a greater appreciation of the realities of African society, made a bee-line for the chief, realizing that once he was converted, the rest of the community would the more readily follow suit. However nominal the conversion might be for the first generation, the succeeding generations would be more likely to be devout Moslems. Bishop Crowther, whilst he never took so calculated an approach as this, undoubtedly as an African realized the difficulties confronting men when asked to give up all their past ways. It was not surprising that his episcopate ended with the Society criticizing him for laxity in supervision and for tolerating heathenish practices amongst his clergy. The mission was purged by a European bishop, and led to a secessionist movement in the Delta, which established the United Native African Church in 1891.[14]

The most radical influence on Nigeria introduced by the British was the Western system of education. Until the end of the nineteenth century education had been conducted at various levels in Nigeria. In the Moslem societies of the North academic education of the Koranic type was fairly widespread. In other societies education of children was essentially directed towards enabling them to take their proper places in the community. There were no societies in the South where reading and writing were understood, so that traditional education was primarily directed towards the acquisition of skills in crafts and agriculture. But since the missionaries were not prepared to modify their educational programmes to suit African needs, academic rather than technical education was given to children.

Early suspicion of education was naturally overcome when it was seen that education was the key to success in the new economic order. The revolutionary effects of education were widespread: English was established as a *lingua franca* so that different tribes now had a common means of communication. Education soon came to be seen as a means not only of economic betterment but of social elevation. It opened doors to an entirely new world, the world of the white man. Since missionaries had a virtual monopoly of schools, they were able to use them as a means of further proselytization, and continued to warn their pupils of the evils of their former way of life.[15]

The North was almost entirely insulated against the revolutionary effects of education by Lugard's promise that missionaries would not be allowed in any Moslem emirate without the Emir's consent. Since the government was neither interested in nor had the money to provide education, for the first years of British administration the only form of education available in the North was that of the Koranic school, except for small schools provided by the C.M.S. missions in Zaria and Bida, and the government school opened outside Kano in 1912.

These revolutionary forces were essentially let loose between 1906 and 1912, a period that in terms of events is really rather dull. They were to influence the subsequent development of Nigeria very profoundly. But one man, in a short but dramatic governorship, was to provide the mould in which the jelly of upheaval was to set. This was Sir Frederick Lugard, nominated in 1912 as Governor-General of Nigeria with the task of amalgamating the Northern and Southern Protectorates. The decisions he made in those years were to influence the canalization of these new forces until, after the Second World War, control of government was slowly taken over from the British administration by the Nigerian nationalists themselves.

The immediate reason for the decision to amalgamate the two Nigerias was economic expediency.[16] The Northern Protectorate was running at a severe deficit, which was being met by a subsidy from the Southern Protectorate, and an Imperial Grant-in-Aid from Britain of about £300,000 a year. This conflicted with the age-old colonial policy that each territory should be self-subsisting. Apart from the fact that it seemed logical to amalgamate the two territories, the one land-locked and the other with a long seaboard, it was felt that the prosperous Southern Protectorate could subsidize its northern neighbour until such time as it became self-supporting. Furthermore, there was the pressing need to co-ordinate railway policy, which at the time was practically non-existent. The Southern track had been started in 1901 and reached the River Niger in the Northern Protectorate at Jebba in 1909. It was to continue to Minna, where a Northern line was being constructed to reach Kano. At the same time, Sir Percy Girouard, the Governor, was intent on extending the Northern line to Baro on the Niger, where goods would be shipped down to the sea on barges. By 1912, then, there were two competing systems, the Minna-Baro-Niger system rivalling the Minna-Jebba-Lagos system, though the former proved less effective than was originally hoped. Ironically Girouard's railway had been built with Southern revenues. Since a new line was envisaged from Port Harcourt through Enugu to the North it was essential that there be more effective co-ordination of railway policy and this could best be ensured through amalgamation.

Amalgamation was finally achieved on 1st January 1914. But in preparing for this day Lugard took a number of decisions that were to influence the whole future of Nigeria. Though the two territories were to be amalgamated, Lugard chose to maintain the distinction between North and South, against the better judgement of men who knew Nigeria well. E. D. Morel, at that time editor of the *African Mail* and a persistent critic of colonial policy, advocated the division of the country into four large provinces.[17] It is essential to take careful note of the schemes proposed to Lugard, for much of the politics of Nigeria before the creation of the twelve states by General Gowon in May 1967 was coloured by dissatisfaction with the present political division of the country, which might have been different if Lugard had listened to Morel or Temple, his Lieutenant-Governor for the North, who himself advocated the division of the country into seven provinces.[18] Morel suggested that the four provinces should comprise a Northern Province, consisting of Kontagora, Sokoto, Katsina, Kano, Zaria Emirate and Bornu; a Central Province corresponding roughly with the Middle Belt state which used to be advocated by the Action Group party and consisting of

The Unification of Nigeria

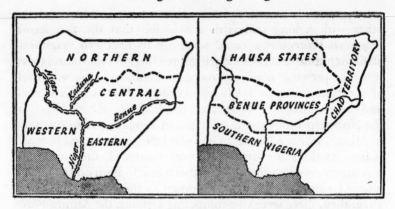

8. Proposed administrative reorganizations of Nigeria, 1914

Bauchi, Plateau, Adamawa and parts of Niger and Benue provinces; a Western Province consisting of the former Western Region, Mid-West State, Ilorin and Borgu; and an Eastern Province that would take in Benue Province as far as the Benue River, together with the former Eastern Region. Temple, who as Lieutenant-Governor of the North was virtually doing himself out of a job by advocating the breakdown of the country into seven provinces, suggested the division of the North into three provinces, and the maintenance of the existing provincial system in the South—Lagos Colony, Eastern, Central and Western Provinces. Neither of these plans was adopted by Lugard, who preferred the existing division partly because he really did not want the break-up of the administration he had devised for the North, partly because he did not want too great an administrative burden thrown on himself. With two responsible Lieutenant-Governors in command of day-to-day administration, he as Governor-General could carry on with general reform. Furthermore, Lugard planned his administration as a continuous one, uninterrupted by leave. During his first tour he spent six months in Nigeria and six months in London at the Colonial Office, and afterwards eight months in Nigeria and four in London, thereby never once letting slip the reins of government.[19] To achieve this unique type of government he had to delegate the main burden of day-to-day administration to his Lieutenant-Governors.

242

The Unification of Nigeria

The Northern and Southern Provinces of Nigeria together retained their status as a British Protectorate, whilst Lagos, the capital, remained a British Colony and its inhabitants had the rights of British citizens. The treaties made with the various Yoruba rulers, except for that with the Alake of Abeokuta, were considered void; for the Chief Justice had found that 'His Majesty had now acquired such complete jurisdiction throughout the Protectorate, with the possible exception of Egbaland, as to be able to legislate in any direction, not only for Europeans and resident non-natives, but for the natives themselves.'[20] Lugard, as we shall see, soon had occasion to bring the semi-independent enclave of Egbaland into line with the other Yoruba kingdoms.

In the general reorganization of Nigeria great powers devolved on the person of the Governor-General. Lugard reduced the already limited powers of the Legislative Council, which in 1906 had been extended to all Southern Nigeria, to a mere cipher by restricting its authority to Lagos Colony alone, and in its place set up an unwieldy Nigerian Council with a majority of officials, and only three nominated Africans from the North and three from the South. As an advisory body, meeting but once a year, it could hardly act as a check on Lugard's powers. Lugard centralized only those departments that he felt necessary for control of overall policy. At every turn he avoided acquisition of a large administration, so that administration was effectively regionalized under the Lieutenant-Governors, a process that only exacerbated the growing differences between the two regions. He amalgamated the Treasury, Railways, Survey, Judiciary, Military, Posts and Telegraphs and Audit. Otherwise everything was left to the Lieutenant-Governors who merely referred to Lugard any matter that seemed to affect Nigeria as a whole. Their budgets were prepared locally and then incorporated in the general budget for the territory. By centralizing the Treasury, Lugard was able to divert revenue that earlier had been properly the South's to balance the Northern deficit.[21] He had few qualms about this since the bulk of the revenue of the South came from a liquor duty, of which he disapproved and which could not be raised in the Mohammedan North. He even hoped to shift his government headquarters from the South to the North which was his spiritual home.

The Unification of Nigeria

The administration of the North remained intact, but the Southern provinces, which had been acquired piecemeal in widely differing circumstances, were reorganized to bring them in line with the North. The three large provinces of the South, where the Provincial Commissioners seemed to have too much power, were broken down into nine provinces with roughly the same population as their northern counterparts. A Resident was placed in charge of each. Bringing the South even more in line with the North, Lugard completely remodelled the judiciary, which had until then been theoretically independent of the executive, though administrators had been commissioners in the district courts of the supreme court, and up till 1914 had presided over native courts, which subsequently they supervised. A supreme court for the whole of Nigeria was established with two divisional courts for the South, one for those provinces west of the Niger and one for those east of the Niger. Under the divisional courts came the provincial courts, presided over by the Residents. A Native Court Ordinance introduced native courts for the South in which cases of indigenous law were heard. Admittedly this system sorted out the judicial chaos that had reigned in the Southern Protectorate before amalgamation, but it raised great objections both in Britain, where the separation of executive and judiciary was held fundamental to good government, and in Nigeria where Lugard's ruling that barristers could not appear in the provincial courts angered the small but vocal group of Nigerian lawyers. Lugard gave as his reason for this ruling that it was designed to restrict 'the fomenting of litigation by lawyers' touts which, by a concensus of opinion, has become a public scandal in the Southern Provinces, with a natural corollary of rendering litigation extremely costly, to the detriment of litigants and the benefit of lawyers'.[22] The greatest objection to Lugard's new scheme was that while it regulated law in the South, it put an end to the attempt to develop a legal system based on that of Britain.

Lugard's most lasting contribution to Nigeria was his development of native administration. Having successfully applied indirect rule in the North, he tried to work out a similar system for what he regarded as the chaotically administered South. Let us look first at the development of native administration in the North.

The Unification of Nigeria

In his *Amalgamation Report*, published in 1920 just after his retirement as Governor-General, Lugard defined indirect rule in Northern Nigeria: 'The system of Native Administration in the separate Government of Northern Nigeria had been based on the authority of the Native Chiefs. The policy of the Government was that these Chiefs should govern their people, not as independent but as dependent Rulers. The orders of Government are not conveyed to the people through them, but emanate from them in accordance, where necessary, with instructions received through the Resident. While they themselves are controlled by Government in matters of policy and of importance, their people are controlled in accordance with that policy by themselves. A political Officer would consider it as irregular to issue direct orders to an individual native, or even to a village head, as a General commanding a division would to a private soldier, except through his commanding officers. The courts administer native law, and are presided over by Native Judges (417 in all). Their punishments do not conform to the Criminal Code, but, on the other hand, native law must not be in opposition to the Ordinances of Government, which are operative everywhere, and the courts . . . are under the close supervision of the District Staff. Their rules of evidence and their procedure are not based on British standards, but their sentences, if manifestly faulty, are subject to revision. Their prisoners are confined in their own gaols, which are under the supervision of the British Staff. The taxes are raised in the name of the native ruler and by his agents, but he surrenders the fixed proportion to Government, and the expenditure of the portion assigned to the Native Administration, from which fixed salaries to all native officials are paid, is subject to the advice of the Resident, and the ultimate control of the Governor. The attitude of the Resident is that of a watchful adviser not of an interfering ruler, but he is ever jealous of the rights of the peasantry, and of any injustice to them.'[23]

The basic pattern laid down by Lugard was developed by his successors, who extended it to the pagan areas of the North. Here, of course, its application was more difficult, for in the absence of a powerful emir some petty chief or influential elder was raised to the status of local ruler and agent for the British administration. Inevitably this meant that the local District

Officer or Resident had considerably greater power than his counterpart in the emirate. As we have seen, Lugard's successors developed indirect rule in directions that Lugard did not feel desirable. Indeed he quarrelled bitterly with Temple, his Lieutenant-Governor in the North, over the question of the independence of Native Treasuries. Lugard felt that the revenues of these treasuries should be included in the general budget for Nigeria, since this would give him control over them. Temple and the Colonial Office opposed this, believing that the essence of indirect rule was minimal interference on the part of the British Government. Inevitably, treasuries that did not come under the control of some central authority gave greater autonomy to individual native authorities, and lessened central control over the Emirs.

The approach of many Northern officers to indirect rule was a static one, which resented any alteration in the system of government of the emirates, whilst Lugard's approach was essentially dynamic, believing as he did that the native administrations could be developed into more and more efficient units of government. Miss Perham, Lugard's official biographer, rightly considers this a fundamental issue in the development of indirect rule in Northern Nigeria and concludes that 'Lugard's policy was at least well worth attempting since, if the new direction he tried to give to policy had been steadily followed by his successors, the Northern region today might have been more uniform in its administration, more centralized, with more fully developed central services. Secondly, it would have presented today rather less of a political contrast with the Southern regions. Thirdly, as the system which many British governments in Africa and elsewhere soon came to regard as the archetype of native administration, it would have been a little less remote both in spirit and form from the more modest realities of these other colonies.'[24]

When Lugard toured Yorubaland and Benin it seemed clear to him that the answer to what he considered the administrative chaos of Southern Nigeria was the introduction of indirect rule on the Northern pattern. The oba and his court surely corresponded to the Emir and his council. Lugard, of course, misconceived the position of the oba in Yoruba society. Whilst the Emir was to a certain extent limited in powers by his counsellors, he was effectively ruler of his emirate. On the other hand, as we have seen, the Yoruba oba was circumscribed in his authority by a large number of checks and balances, effectively only giving voice to a decision that had been arrived at after an intricate process of negotiation and consultation. Certainly he did not possess traditional executive authority that could in any way be construed as measuring up to that possessed by an Emir. No Yoruba oba had ever collected taxes from his people on a regular basis, whilst the Hausa had accepted his ruler's right to taxation for several centuries.[25] Since the levy of taxation was fundamental to the native authority system it meant Lugard had not only to translate his oba into an Emir, but also ask him to levy taxation, hardly a popular measure for a people unaccustomed to it. Lugard sent Richmond Palmer, a trusted Northern Resident, on a tour of the Western Region to report on the feasibility of introducing taxation. Despite protests from Southern officials, which he dismissed as conservatism, Palmer recommended the introduction of taxation to Oyo, Benin and Abeokuta.[26] Lugard received this report with pleasure, though the Colonial Office, bearing in mind the disturbances that followed the introduction of taxation in Sierra Leone, opposed it.

Lugard's first experiment in indirect rule in the South was a success, but the circumstances were rather special. Since the exile of Ovenramwen, after the 1897 massacre, Benin had been without a ruler. When, in 1914, Ovenramwen died in Calabar, his son was installed Oba under the name of Eweka II. Lugard took the opportunity of instituting a native authority for Benin with the Oba at its head. Direct taxation was introduced and accepted by the people. This success is hardly surprising when one remembers how complete the British subjection of Benin had been, and that for over fifteen years they had been without their ruler, the repository of tribal customs.

This early success was not repeated in 1916 when Lugard introduced his native authority for Oyo, with the Alafin at its head. As Miss Perham points out, there were particular difficulties in making an Emir of the Alafin.[27] In the first place, despite his immense spiritual, political and judicial authority, the Alafin was in no easy position to head a native authority. His decisions were always voiced through an intermediary. He never appeared except behind a veil of beads, and only emerged from his palace three times a year. Thus he was virtually *incommunicado* to his people and yet had to run a system of local government that needed his intimate daily attention to every detail of their life. Secondly, though the great city of Ibadan acknowledged the authority of the Alafin, in fact this was more an act of respect than acceptance of political subordination. This city's inclusion in the native authority of the Alafin marked the beginning of many years of tension, ended only in 1934 when Ibadan was made independent.

The first open opposition to the new régime came from the Oyo town of Iseyin, where in October 1916 two representatives of the Oyo N.A., a district head and a native court judge, were murdered. The riots surrounding these incidents were put down with great speed which avoided their repetition in other parts of Yorubaland.

Much more serious was the opposition to Lugard's new policy in Abeokuta, where the native administration system proved particularly irksome. Until 1914 Abeokuta had been a semi-independent state, guaranteed by the treaty of 1893. The Egba United Government, under its Secretary Edun, aided by a British commissioner and missionaries, had developed an administration roughly modelled on the British colonial system. When Lugard became Governor in 1912 he viewed this anomaly with the administrator's distaste. But it was difficult to find an occasion for bringing Abeokuta into line with the other Yoruba states. In 1914 the opportunity came when one of Secretary Edun's opponents, Ponlade, was arrested and died in prison. This led to demonstrations against the Egba United Government, which were sufficiently serious for the Alake and the British Commissioner, P. V. Young, to call on Lagos for troops. As a result tension was increased to such an extent that the troops were ordered to fire on the demonstrators, an incident remembered as the Ijemo massacre. This gave Lugard the excuse to suggest that the Egba United Government's independence could hardly be called a reality if they depended on the Lagos government for support. With the agreement of the Alake he therefore abrogated the treaty and brought Abeokuta into the Protectorate under the same conditions as the other Yoruba states.

The legacy of bitterness from the Ijemo massacre came to a

head with the extension of Lugard's system of indirect rule to Egbaland. In June 1918 the Egba tore up the railway line and looted stations and trains. A number of people were killed, including a chief and one European. The Alake narrowly escaped with his life; 1,000 troops were rushed in and in the ensuing battle over 500 rebels were killed. Indeed, if Nigerian troops had not just returned from the East Africa campaign, the situation might have become extremely serious. The riots were essentially a protest against the introduction of a system of government quite alien to the traditional form. There was bitter resentment against the powers of the district heads, the levying of taxes and the elevation of the Alake to a position of supreme authority where in the past he had merely been *primus inter pares* of the four quarter chiefs of Abeokuta. When the people showed their anger at these innovations they were threatened with troops, a flashback, it seemed, to the Ijemo massacre. A Commission of Inquiry, with one member, a Nigerian barrister, Eric Moore,[28] investigated the riots and laid the blame on the new policy and its unwise application. This was a severe blow to Lugard.

If Lugard had difficulties in applying indirect rule to the West, he found it almost impossible to introduce it in the East. Except for the Delta states there were no chiefs of consequence in the Eastern Region. A system that depended intimately on a fulcrum of authority obviously had no application in so loosely organized a society as that of the Ibo and Ibibio. In the Delta earlier administrators had attempted to use the trading house as a vehicle for administrative edicts, but this meant that they had to acknowledge the existence of slavery, and in effect give support to it, since the houses were based on domestic slavery. Indeed runaway members of houses, under the House Rule Ordinance, might be arrested and restored, and none could employ a member of a house without the consent of the head of the house. Lugard was immediately antipathetic to anything that smacked of slavery, and abolished House Rule, a system which anyway had lost much of its economic and political *raison d'être*. It is, however, significant that in the Delta there was no difficulty in collecting taxes, for before the British administration the house chiefs had imposed tax on their members. The other parts of the East were ruled through courts, which dispensed not only justice but administrative orders. In certain cases individuals with some apparent authority were raised to the status of warrant chiefs, a class that was to incur great unpopularity. Lugard was quite unable to devise any alternative system for the East. This is not surprising when one remembers that all the time he was occupied with the war and the many other problems of administration. Furthermore, the East was still not entirely pacified and in the years from 1912 to 1918 it was still necessary for the Government to despatch punitive expeditions against certain groups.

All these reforms were undertaken during the First World War, in which Nigeria, because of her common frontier with the German Cameroons, played no small part. Until the outbreak of war, Germany had occupied a significant place in Nigeria's external trade. She took 44 per cent of Nigeria's exports and accounted for 14 per cent of her imports. War cut off Nigeria from this important source of trade and the situation was made more serious by shortage of shipping. This, however, was only a temporary phase, for provisions-starved Britain soon found that she needed as much of Nigeria's palm oil as she could get, and trade revived, though towards the end of the war submarine activities off the West Coast made export and import increasingly difficult.

Surprisingly the war was not taken by and large by the Nigerian peoples as an occasion to throw off the colonial yoke. In the Moslem North the Emirs made deep protestations of loyalty and did not waver when Turkey, the leading Moslem power, came into the war on the side of Germany.[29] They were not even affected by the disturbed state of French Niger immediately to the north when, in 1916, the Ouilliminden tribe revolted and besieged Filingue, or when the Touareg chief Kaossen, in league with Senussi chiefs from Tripolitania, besieged Zinder. The Senussi had apparently been goaded into preaching Holy War in Niger and Northern Nigeria by Germans based in Tripolitania and Fezzan so as to embarrass the Anglo-French war effort. Nigerian troops were sent across the border to help the French relieve Zinder.[30]

The only disturbances that could be construed as an attempt to take advantage of the war were the revolt of the Kwale Ibo in modern Asaba division, which was said to have been aggravated by Germans, and a revivalist movement in the Delta, where the Christian 'breakaway' prophet who called himself Elijah II secured a huge following by taking advantage of rumours that Britain was leaving Nigeria because of the war. He claimed to be helping the Germans and promised the Delta peoples independence. This promise had an appeal in the Delta that it might not have held elsewhere because of the temporary collapse, immediately after war broke out, of the palm-oil trade on which most of the people of the Eastern Delta were dependent. The local European traders and administrators were blamed for this collapse. As soon as the palm-oil trade revived the movement faded away.[31]

Nigerian troops played an important role in the war. On the 27th August 1914 a detachment of the Nigeria Regiment was sent to help the Gold Coast Regiment and French troops in German Togo, but arrived after the Germans had been defeated. On the 29th of the same month the Mounted Infantry detachment of the Nigeria Regiment occupied the German post of Tepe in the Cameroons and attacked the important river port of Garua on the Benue. They were defeated the next day in a German counter-attack. In the south of the Cameroons Nigerian forces suffered similar setbacks, a hundred soldiers being killed in an engagement at Nsanakang. It was clear that larger forces were needed to fight in the extremely difficult country of the Cameroons, with its mountains and thick forests.

A combined army was drawn up, consisting of two battalions of the Nigeria Regiment, French Senegalese troops, the Gambia Company, the Sierra Leone Battalion and the Gold Coast Regiment. They invaded the Cameroons after the successful naval bombardment of Duala on 27th September 1914. By Christmas they had driven the Germans back to Yaoundé, and the important town of Edea had been taken together with the capital, Buea. The northern campaign lasted throughout 1915. In June Garua and N'gaounderé were taken, but attempts to capture Mora were unsuccessful. It was not finally until February 1916, after most of the German forces had retreated from Yaoundé to the Spanish territory of the Rio Muni, that it fell to the British.

This long and difficult campaign earned high praise for Nigerian troops from many quarters, but their achievement was perhaps best summed up by one of their officers, Colonel Cunliffe: 'They have been called upon to take part in a great struggle, the rights and wrongs of which they can scarcely have been expected dimly to perceive. They have been through the, to them, extremely novel experience of facing an enemy with modern weapons and led by highly trained officers. Their rations have been scanty, their barefoot marches long and trying, and their fighting at times extremely arduous, yet they have not been found wanting either in discipline, devotion to their officers, or personal courage.'[82]

There was to be no rest for these troops, for almost immediately four battalions were sent off to East Africa together with a large auxiliary carrier corps. No one was more pleased with their performance than the veteran campaigner in Africa, Sir Frederick Lugard. Nevertheless, he wrote to his wife of the Nigerian soldier: 'He also knows how to kill white men, around whom he has been taught to weave a web of sanctity of life. He also knows how to handle bombs and Lewis guns and Maxims —and he has seen white men budge when he stood fast. And altogether he has acquired much knowledge which might be put to uncomfortable use some day.'[83] In fact Lugard's forebodings would have been more appropriate as a commentary on the impact of the Second World War on Nigerians. Fortunately, in the later war, it was not knowledge of weapons that impressed them so much as the realization that they and the white men were fundamentally the same and equal and that they too were quite capable of running their own affairs.

CHAPTER XV

The Rise of Nigerian Nationalism

T he years that followed on Lugard's governorship are superficially some of the dullest in Nigerian history. Yet they mark the emergence of a new class of Africans who began to think of themselves as Nigerians rather than Ibo, Hausa and Yoruba. And it was to be this group, initially confined almost exclusively to Lagos, that wrested control of affairs from the British Government and attained independence for Nigeria in 1960. So, though there are no dramatic upheavals to record during the period between the world wars, though there are few administrative changes to describe, there was the slow, but all-important development of national consciousness amongst peoples of widely varying religious and cultural backgrounds.

When Lugard finally amalgamated the Northern and Southern Protectorates of Nigeria, it might have seemed, as it often did to him, that he was merely lumping together under the same administration groups of mutually incompatible peoples.[1] Certainly his decision to keep the administration of the North and South separate was guided by such thinking. But the British had created a new political unit, and whether they or the peoples under their administration liked it or not, it was inevitable that a certain number of Africans should begin to identify themselves not with their old tribal allegiances, but with the new political entity known as Nigeria. Thus, whilst Lugard's system of indirect rule tended to preserve tribal consciousness, the needs of the new administration were to produce a new class of Africans—clerks, teachers, traders, parsons, doctors and lawyers—who could no longer think in purely tribal by and large they were excluded from office in the native administrations, so that they tended to look towards the central administration for an outlet for their natural desire to have some say in their own affairs. Even if they had been assimilated into the running of local government, it is unlikely that their horizons would have remained for long restricted to the administration of the village or the town.

At first Nigerian nationalism was largely promoted by non-Nigerians, and its focus was on Africa as a whole, rather than on the seemingly artificial units drawn up by the European colonial powers.[2] Men like Edward Blyden from the West Indies, who sought the cultural emancipation of the Negro, or J. P. Jackson, a Liberian, who edited the *Lagos Weekly Record* and constantly attacked the British administration, were at the spearhead of nationalist activity until the twenties. Even Herbert Macaulay, revered today by many as 'the father of Nigerian Nationalism', was a member of the family of that most famous of all freed slaves, Bishop Crowther, a family which had ties all along the West Coast. Indeed Macaulay was agitating against the government in Lagos even before Lugard became Governor General, organizing effective mass protests against the levy of the Lagos water rate which he said was designed to benefit Europeans at the expense of the Lagosians' purse.

But while outbursts like this were of a parish pump character, these early nationalists had a wider aim. As Diké had put it: 'After amalgamation in 1914, what the nationalists fought was the exclusiveness and racial basis of the Crown Colony system of Government. At the beginning, the fight was not so much for self-government, but for a measure of participation in the existing government.'[3]

To this end the National Congress of British West Africa was founded in 1920 in order that peoples of African descent should participate in the government of their own country, an aim in part inspired not only by the writings of New-World Negroes like W. E. Du Bois and his antagonist, Marcus Garvey,[4] but by the declaration of the American President himself on the right of all peoples to self-determination. After its inaugural conference at Accra, led by Casely-Hayford, a well-known Gold Coast lawyer, and attended by representatives of the four British West African colonies, it was decided to send a delega-

tion to the Secretary of State for the Coloni
amongst other things:

1. A legislative council for each territory
   members elected Africans.
2. Control of taxation by African members
   Council.
3. Appointment of and deposition of chiefs by their own
   people.
4. Abolition of racial discrimination in the Civil Service.
5. Establishment of a university in West Africa.[5]

The delegation was treated peremptorily by the Colonial
Secretary, Lord Milner, and after encountering certain financial difficulties returned to Africa, so to speak, empty-handed.
This hardly put the Nigerians in a bargaining position *vis-à-vis*
Sir Hugh Clifford, the new Governor, who roundly denounced
them in the Nigerian Council on 29th December 1920, in terms
that showed how little sympathy the British official had towards
the aspirations of the new African élite.

'It can only be described as farcical to suppose that . . .
continental Nigeria can be represented by a handful of gentlemen drawn from a half-dozen coast towns—men born and bred
in British-administered towns situated on the seashore who, in
the safety of British protection, have peacefully pursued their
studies under British teachers, in British schools, in order to
enable them to become ministers of the Christian religion or
learned in the laws of England, whose eyes are fixed, not upon
African native history or tradition or policy, nor upon their own
tribal obligations and duties to their Natural Rulers which im-
memorial custom should impose on them, but upon political
theories evolved by Europeans to fit a wholly different set of
circumstances, arising out of a wholly different environment,
for the government of peoples who have arrived at a wholly
different stage of civilization. . . .' He was equally critical of the
concept of West African unity: 'That there is or can be in the
visible future such a thing as a "West African Nation" is as
manifest an absurdity as that there is, or can be, an "European
Nation", at all events until the Millennium.'[6]

But perhaps the most significant attack was on the idea that
there could really be a Nigerian nation: 'Assuming . . . that the
impossible were feasible—that this collection of self-contained

mutually independent Native States, separated from one other, as many of them are, by great distances, by differences of history and traditions, and by ethnological, racial, tribal, political, social and religious barriers, were indeed capable of being welded into a single homogeneous nation—a deadly blow would thereby be struck at the very root of national self-government in Nigeria, which secures to each separate people the right to maintain its identity, its individuality, its own chosen form of government, and the peculiar political and social institutions which have been evolved for it by the wisdom and by the accumulated experience of generations of its forebears.'

The author of this violent attack on early African claims to participation in the determination of their own affairs was also the author of the 1922 constitution, which for the first time in British Africa provided for elected African members on a Legislative Council.

As we shall see, this was to be one of the main stimuli to the growth of Nigerian nationalism in the inter-war period.

It has been suggested that Sir Hugh Clifford's apparent change of heart was the result of the activities of the National Congress of British West Africa.[7] But this seems unlikely both from the attitude Sir Hugh himself manifested towards it and its failure to evoke any substantial support when it sent its delegation to England. Anyway, the principle of election had already been introduced for the Lagos Town Council in 1920, before the Congress had produced its Accra resolutions.

Sir Hugh's constitution provided for a new Legislative Council, which would consist of forty-six members, twenty-seven of them officials, and nineteen of them unofficials. Of these unofficials, three members were to be elected by all adult males in Lagos with a residential qualification of twelve months and a gross income of £100 per annum, and one in Calabar. He even went as far as to say that the introduction of the elective principle was but the first step towards eventual self-government and the extension of elections to the backward parts of the Protectorate. Clifford himself declared that he had abolished the old Nigerian council and introduced this more liberal constitution because he liked 'a thing to be real and effective or not to have it at all'.[8]

The first thing the new constitution did was to provide an

official outlet for the ideas of those coastal gentlemen Clifford had so violently attacked. With the prospect of three seats on the Legislative Council, several parties were formed in Lagos, and newspapers were produced to champion their respective causes. In the subsequent election of 1923, Herbert Macaulay's party, the National Democratic Party, took all three seats, as it did again in 1928 and 1933. But the limited application of the new elective principle inevitably restricted nationalist activity to Lagos, since there was little scope for political activity in towns which had no seats on the Legislative Council.[9]

Thus most of the issues that concerned Macaulay in the twenties were essentially Lagos issues. Indeed he devoted almost all his energies in the twenties to what was known as the Eleko question. In 1915 the Eleko, or hereditary ruler of Lagos, was asked by the government to persuade the local people to pay the water rate, a commission he refused to undertake since, though paid a salary by the government in recognition of his special position, he was in fact denied all political power. Piqued, Lugard deprived both him and his white-cap chiefs of their salaries. In 1919, official recognition of the Eleko was withdrawn because he took sides with a Lagos faction that opposed payment of the water rate. Finally in 1920 recognition was withdrawn altogether from Eshugbayi as Eleko, and he was later deported. The 1920 Annual Report records: 'Political intrigues in Lagos resulted in the withdrawal of all official recognition of Eleko, the titular "Prince" of Lagos, who had allowed his position to be exploited by political adventurers.'[10] The foremost amongst these so-called adventurers was Macaulay, who conducted an almost fanatical campaign on Eshugbayi's behalf that seemed at times to monopolize all his political thought.

Nevertheless, he sometimes turned his attentions to larger issues, and the ceaseless attacks on the colonial government in the *Lagos Daily News* did much to inspire others with nationalist zeal. Officially his party did have a national programme, and on occasion he castigated the administration for alleged errors far from the confines of the coastal capital.

The British administration was certainly not greatly worried by Macaulay's activities, especially as they did really only touch on events in Lagos. As far as they were concerned, their main problems lay outside the restricted arena of Lagos politics, particularly in South-Eastern Nigeria where indirect rule was not proving a success.

In the North Lugard's policy, as we have seen, worked smoothly, though not along the lines he had envisaged. Indeed in the North the path indirect rule followed can only be described as retrograde. The emirates were treated more like the Native States of India than as the administrative conveniences they had been for Lugard. Officials emphasized more and more the differences between the North and South, and sought whenever possible to dispense with the services of Southern clerks. This drift did not go unchallenged. In 1924, an article in the *National Review* by a Captain Fitzpatrick, a former political officer in Northern Nigeria, received considerable publicity for the stinging attacks it made on the administration of indirect rule.

'Before the British took over the country, an Emir was an Emir just so long as his hands could guard his head. The system was one of autocracy tempered by assassination. The Emirs today are maintained by British bayonets, so that there are men holding these positions at this time who would not last one week if the bayonets were to cease. . . .' He accused the emirs of corruption and extortion, describing the native authorities as instruments of oppression that were hated by the people. He feared they would be 'fruitful soil for pernicious, seditious, underground propaganda from Egypt'.[11]

One critic of Fitzpatrick asked why he himself had not done anything about the situation.[12] The answer to this—one does not know if Fitzpatrick gave it—demonstrates clearly the character of native administration at that time: official policy, particularly under Sir Graeme Thomson, Governor of Nigeria from 1925 to 1931, was that political officers should interfere as little as possible in Nigeria's 'Indian states'. Nevertheless, Thomson's predecessor, Clifford, had taken measures to tighten up control of administrative policy. The Lieutenant-Governors of both Northern and Southern Nigeria were placed under the Chief Secretary, who was given overall responsibility for the machinery of administration. However, it was not until the appointment of Sir Donald Cameron as Governor in 1931 that any attempt was made to check the growing separatism of the Northern administration and the ever-increasing autonomy of the Emirs.[13]

The Rise of Nigerian Nationalism

The system of indirect rule, however, had proved impossible to apply in Eastern Nigeria and the Ibo, Ijo and Itsekiri areas of the present Mid-West State. Lugard, as we have seen, had been quite unable to devise a satisfactory version of indirect rule for the small societies of Eastern Nigeria. When Clifford became Governor in 1919, one of the first things he did was to order his Secretary for Native Affairs to investigate the situation in the East. In 1922 the Secretary of Native Affairs issued his report strongly criticizing administration there.[14] Indirect rule had been an almost total failure. Despite superficial trappings, the area was in effect administered directly. The warrant chiefs were exceedingly unpopular with the people and were backed up by little, if any, traditional authority. They were generally corrupt. Worse still, the native courts, the main agencies for British administration, were deeply resented. The court clerks and court messengers abused their positions of power so blatantly that they were described in the report as 'licensed libertines'. Despite this early interest in the problem of administration in Eastern Nigeria and the constant references in annual reports to the difficulties it represented, for the rest of Clifford's governorship no action was taken to change it. However, in 1926, after long discussions, it was decided that those people who did not pay taxes, mainly in the Eastern Region and parts of the West, should be forced to pay tax in the form of a poll tax based on a 2½ per cent assessment of their rough annual income. This, however, was to be levied on adult males only.

In 1927 assessment was begun, and sparked off disturbances in the Warri and Kwale areas of the Western Provinces which were said to have had the connivance of certain Lagos leaders. Patrols of up to 300 men were needed to quell them and at one time the police had to fire above the heads of the crowd to disperse the rioters. Elsewhere assessment and collection provoked no open trouble.

However, late in 1929, a certain warrant chief, Okugo, whilst reassessing the taxable wealth of the inhabitants of a village called Oloko, near Aba in Eastern Nigeria, began counting women, children and animals. Rumour quickly spread that this heralded the introduction of taxation of women, for the original poll tax had been preceded by a census, whose purpose had not at the time been divulged to the people. In this densely populated area of Eastern Nigeria, rumour spread quickly and soon the women of Aba and Owerri divisions were up in arms against the administration. Stores were sacked, native courts burnt down and unpopular warrant chiefs attacked. The riots spread to Calabar and Opobo, where, on the 17th December 1929, a riot of such ferocity took place that the police opened fire on the crowd and killed 32 people, wounding a further 31.

The greatest significance of these riots was that they were almost exclusively the acts of women who were able through their age-grade societies to organize themselves far more effectively than any of the local administrators, who were largely ignorant of the structure of indigenous societies, could have imagined. Furthermore, these women were spurred on by the low prices for their farm products because the depression in Europe was already having its effect in Africa.

An official Commission of Inquiry was immediately held on the riots to apportion responsibility for loss of life. It gave speedy exoneration to the officials concerned, but this seemed a vastly unsatisfactory verdict when the scope of the riots was considered.[15] A new commission, with wider membership, was therefore set up to investigate the causes of the riots. Two of its members were African barristers—Sir Kitoyi Ajasa and Mr. Eric Moore. The Commission was asked to discover 'the origin and causes of, and responsibility for the disturbances—and measures taken to restore order, and to make such recommendations as may seem fit.'[16]

As Margery Perham has written, 'whatever view is taken of the findings of this Commission, its activities probably helped to prevent a wedge of bitterness and distrust being driven between the government and the people'. Most remarkable of all was the spectacle of European officials justifying their actions to a commission on which sat two Africans, a situation not a few of them bitterly resented.[17]

The report of the commission in particular condemned the way the administration had concealed the purpose of the census of 1926 which had preceded the introduction of taxation. For this reason, the commission maintained that it was barely surprising that women should have associated the actions of Warrant Chief Okugo with the introduction of tax on themselves,

especially at a time of economic hardship. They
number of the criticisms made earlier by the Se
Affairs against native courts and warrant chie
sion made it clear that there was considerabl
organization of native administration in those
report was a condemnation of the whole system
tion in Eastern Nigeria, which was effectively one of direct rule.
Theoretically the system of administration was one of indirect
rule through the indigenous political institutions, in this case
the warrant chiefs, but these warrant chiefs were mainly men
who appeared to have traditional authority in communities
which in fact were not accustomed to invest executive authority
in a particular individual. It was clear that if indirect rule was
to work in Eastern Nigeria, then the government would have to
discover what in fact were the political institutions of the peoples
of the areas. To do this intensive anthropological investigations
were undertaken in the years 1931 and 1932, so as to ensure
that any future reorganization would take into full account the
natural social organization of the people. By 1935 some 200
reports had been produced, and as a result of the information
contained in them a 'very great variety of units of Native
Authority' were recognized, which only in a few instances consisted of a traditional Chief or Chief in Council . . . 'and for the
most part consisted of Group or Clan Councils or Village
Councils'.[18]

Just after the report of the Commission of Inquiry was published Sir Donald Cameron became Governor of Nigeria, and
having been responsible for the introduction of indirect rule in
Tanganyika, began to examine closely the whole working of
native administration in Nigeria. He was extremely shocked,
not so much by developments in the East, as by the character
of native administration in the North. This had been taken a
step farther on the road towards the creation of 'Indian States'.
Legislation had been mooted whereby *all* inhabitants of an
emirate would be brought under the jurisdiction of the native
authority courts, meaning in fact that Christian Southerners,
expatriate Europeans and Lebanese would be tried before local
Alkali courts instead of under British law. In a speech to the
Legislative Council on 6th March 1933, the new Governor suggested that the administration in the North had departed from

ugard's conception of native authority and that they made feudal monarchy 'the be all and end all' of indirect rule. He attacked the administration for sheltering their Moslem rulers from contact with the outside world:

'I doubt sometimes whether we have done a great deal to impress on the minds of the Native Authorities concerned that the amelioration of the social and economic conditions of a people is one of the primary duties of an administration and that the inspiration to improvement must come from within, from the Native Administration itself.'[19]

Later, Cameron enunciated his own policy for the reform of the native authorities of the North.[20] Nigerian Emirs should be encouraged to travel not only abroad but in other regions of Nigeria. The pagan areas of the North should be developed along their own lines and not as pseudo-emirates. He also abolished certain practices in the native authority prisons such as chaining.

Cameron did not restrict his attention to the North. In the West he made Ibadan independent of Oyo, and suggested that the native authority should have a mixed council in which the educated elements could play their part. As we have seen, the exclusion of the educated Nigerian from participation in both central and local government was one of the main stimuli to early nationalist activity. In 1932, on the installation of the new Oba of Benin, Cameron stressed the fact that the duty of political officers was to train chiefs for the increasing burdens of local administration and to that end he insisted that the Resident sit in on the council and advise on day-to-day conduct of affairs. In the East it was no time for dramatic changes, but for slow and thoughtful reorganization of a system that had been a blatant failure. For the first few years after the Aba riots, the administration spent most of its time collecting information about the people they had been trying to govern, in some parts for nearly thirty years. The 1932 Annual Report admitted: 'It has moreover been emphasized that in the case of primitive communities with European influences, it is necessary that the process of reorganization should be with comparatively small units.'[21] By the end of 1934 no less than 199 reports on local groups had been submitted, and in the light of these and subsequent reports, the native authorities were reorganized to cor-

262

respond with what were described as live units of government, which were often merely small collections of hamlets and villages.

Cameron's major reform was the abolition of Lugard's system of administrative justice. Cameron was particularly critical of a system of law exercised by the administration. 'Change the system of law, if you will, and punish the people by administrative officers exercising a kind of parental correction because the people are primitive; but remember always, pray, if you do so you will thereby be depriving the natives of any judicial court and any judicial system of law.'[22] Lugard himself had justified the administration of British law by political officers on the grounds that they knew the natives better than British-trained lawyers could.[23] Cameron's decision to abolish the provincial courts and limit the powers of the native courts was particularly popular amongst the educated elements. In place of the provincial courts he substituted a High Court for the whole of the Protectorate, under which operated magistrates' courts where lawyers could practise. The introduction of the High Court returned once again to the well-established British principle of the separation of judiciary and executive, though Cameron did envisage that administrative officers with legal experience would act as magistrates. Finally, to emphasize the unity of Nigeria, he abolished the post of Lieutenant-Governor in Northern and Southern Nigeria.

Economically, the period between the wars was a dull one, for the effects of the severe and prolonged depression in Europe made themselves felt on most primary producing countries like Nigeria. A comparison between the export and import figures for 1921, just after the post-war boom had slackened, and those for 1938, just before the demands of a Europe at war made themselves felt in Africa, shows that relatively little economic development had taken place.

	Imports	Exports	Total Trade
1921	10,237,000	8,258,000	18,495,000
1929	13,219,000	17,075,000	30,294,000
1935	7,804,000	11,615,000	19,419,000
1938	8,632,000	9,702,000	18,334,000[24]

On the other hand cotton, which had been grown for local use before the advent of the British and was to be of immense importance to Northern Nigeria in later years, together with groundnuts and cocoa, became increasingly valuable. General wants increased as lists of imports during these years show: they ranged from disinfectant to glassware, ammunition, drugs, china, enamelware, fancy goods, furniture, jewellery, leather goods, rubber goods, textiles, tobacco, cars, soaps, oil, etc.

Perhaps the greatest economic achievement of the administration in the inter-war period was a negative one. In many African countries, notably the Belgian Congo and the German Cameroons, part of which had been attached to Nigeria after the First World War, large banana and oil-palm plantations had been set up, proving themselves economically far more efficient than the rather haphazard farming of bananas and palm trees in Nigeria. However, in Nigeria it had been a principle never to alienate native land, and the establishment of palm plantations in days when government interference in economic affairs was marginal necessarily involved alienation of land to foreign companies. In the Belgian Congo the firm of Lever Brothers had extensive and profitable plantations, and their chairman, Lord Leverhulme, had his eyes on Southern Nigeria for the establishment of similar plantations. In 1924 Lord Leverhulme, at a dinner held by the Liverpool Chamber of Commerce for the Governor of Nigeria, Sir Hugh Clifford, pressed him to permit his company to acquire land and declared:

'I am certain that the West African races have to be treated very much as one would treat children when they are immature and underdeveloped. We have excellent materials. I don't know better materials anywhere for labour in the tropics than the natives of West Africa, but they are not organized. . . . Now the organizing ability is the particular trait and characteristic of the white man. . . . I say this with my little experience, that the African native will be happier, produce the best, and live under the larger conditions of prosperity when his labour is directed and organized by his white brother who has all these million years' start ahead of him.'[25]

Fortunately for Nigeria, Clifford resisted all such attempts to impose Congo paternalist economic theories on Nigeria. But the pressures on Leverhulme's behalf were considerable. Nevertheless, both the Governor and the Chief Secretary assured the people that Lord Leverhulme's views were diametrically opposed to the declared policy of the Government. The criticism made by Captain Fitzpatrick of the system of indirect rule in the North was vaunted by the plantation owners as proof that the present system of government had little to recommend it.

The threat to Nigeria seemed greater when, in 1925, Sumatra emerged as a producer of superior palm oil by plantation methods. Clifford's successor, Sir Graeme Thomson, looked on Leverhulme's policies with a gentler eye. But at the same time the British Government sent out to West Africa Ormsby-Gore, the Parliamentary Under-Secretary for the Colonies, who had backed Clifford partly on the grounds that the introduction of the Congo system would involve government in finding compulsory labour for capitalist profit. In 1926 the matter was effectively closed when the House of Commons gave its support to the system of indirect rule as practised in Nigeria, though educated Nigerians remained fearful of the possibilities of the introduction of a foreign-dominated plantation economy for some time to come.[26]

The nationalist energy generated by Herbert Macaulay for the 1923 elections dissipated in a tangle of Lagos politics from which it was not rescued until the late thirties, when a new generation of Nigerians who looked beyond the narrow political horizons of the capital took over control of the nationalist movement. They were to be the first Pan-Nigerian nationalists, and the outbreak of war in 1939 was to give immense stimulus to their movement for self-government and eventual freedom.

Until the 1930's, most educated Nigerians came from Creole families or from Yoruba families that had been in long contact with Europeans. It was only by the thirties that a wider selection of Nigeria's varied peoples emerged sufficiently educated to compete intellectually with this closed aristocracy.

Appropriately enough, therefore, student organizations were the main instrument in arousing the new spirit of nationalism. Foremost amongst the student organizations abroad was the West African Students' Union, founded in 1925, with the object not only of providing a centre for West African students in London, but also of promoting the understanding of African culture. The founder, a Nigerian called Ladipo Solanke, is often neglected in the annals of Nigerian nationalism. But by providing such a centre, and by his own uncompromising spirit of nationalism, he added a new fire to the movement for colonial emancipation that kept it alive in Nigeria until the return of Dr. Azikiwe from America in 1937. He was an ardent critic of the conduct of administrators in Nigeria, a champion of the glory of the Negro past, a constant writer of letters to the press on subjects concerning West Africa. He made extensive tours of Nigeria and other West African territories to obtain funds for the union, seeking the co-operation of traditional rulers such as the Alake of Abeokuta, who was the patron of W.A.S.U., and the Emir of Kano, who was patron of the Kano branch. By providing this focus for African activity in London, 'from a historical standpoint', as James Coleman has written, 'Solanke was an outstanding figure in the nationalist awakening in Nigeria.'[27]

But it was in Lagos that the next concrete development in nationalist organization took place. In 1936 the Nigerian Youth Movement was formed with Samuel Akinsanya, H. O. Davies, Ernest Ikoli and Dr. J. C. Vaughn at its head. It had grown out of the Lagos Youth Movement, organized to protest against the alleged inferior status of the new Yaba Higher College, which they felt should have been of university standard. One of its early members was Obafemi Awolowo, who subsequently became leader of the Action Group.[28] At first the Nigerian Youth Movement was restricted in its outlook, but on the return of Dr. Nnamdi Azikiwe from America in 1937, it was geared up into a genuine national movement with a broad representation that justified its title 'Nigerian'. Dr. Azikiwe, or 'Zik' as he had always been known to both followers and enemies, was an Ibo who had been educated in America, having collected there an impressive array of degrees, which made him one of the first of his people who could seriously compete with the entrenched Yoruba aristocracy of Lagos. He had proved himself a dynamic personality, running a successful paper in Accra with I. T. A. Wallace-Johnson, and narrowly escaping imprisonment on a charge of sedition. When he arrived in Lagos he founded a paper called the *West African Pilot* which was to be the main outlet for his nationalist activities for the next twenty years. As an active politician he brought something new to Lagos politics:

the interest and participation of the immigrant Ibo and Ibibio people. With Zik's support the Nigerian Youth Movement could genuinely be regarded as representing more than a mere Lagos faction.

Another important spur to this new outburst of nationalist activity was the Italian invasion of Ethiopia, a country which naturally symbolized African independence for all African nationalists. In 1935 a mass meeting was held in Lagos to protest against the Italian action and the Abyssinian Association was formed. Unfortunately, apart from its successful attack on the Cocoa Pool, a monopolistic buying agreement arranged by the major European commercial houses, the Nigerian Youth Movement achieved little that could be called concrete, being rent by internal quarrels. But this was in a way counterbalanced by the outbreak of war in Europe in 1939, which acted as an immense stimulus to nationalist activity. Until the 1939-45 war most Nigerians had been entirely cut off from the outside world. Only the small élite of students who travelled abroad for their studies had any effective contact with the current of ideas of the Western world, or indeed the Communist world. For most Nigerians, the European remained a special kind of being, destined to command, surrounded by apparent wealth in the form of large houses and numerous servants. Few Africans ever attained these heights, and then it was observed they rarely if ever entered into the exclusive domains of the white reservations and were rarely employed in the higher posts of the administration.

One of the most important determinants of the character of the nationalist movement in Nigeria in the inter-war period, was the almost total lack of dialogue between the British administration and the growing educated élite.[29] The majority of British officials, including those responsible for the formulation of policy, believed that there could be no such dialogue. Many officials, particularly those who worked in the provincial administration rather than the secretariat, were quite blunt in their contempt for the educated African. Not that they all considered the African an inferior being. But most of them were ill at ease with the educated African and felt like Sir Alan Burns, a former Chief Secretary of Nigeria, that '. . . the worst effect of education in Nigeria has been the manufacture of bad imita-

The Rise of Nigerian Nationalism

tions of Europeans instead of good Africans'.[30] The more liberal officials subscribed to the view of Lord Lugard that even if one accepted the equality of the African with the European, their cultural and environmental background was such that even when the former were educated, it dictated the social segregation of the two groups.[31] Thus Africans were excluded from the European clubs right up to the early fifties. One coloured official of senior standing in the Colonial Office was refused accommodation in the old Bristol Hotel in 1947, thus causing a great outcry against the administration in the nationalist press.

At the same time the British had to recognize their dependence on the educated classes for staffing the subaltern ranks of the administration. Yet they were not prepared to accept that the more capable members of this class, even those who possessed the requisite educational qualifications, assume senior posts in the administration which would in any way put them in a position of directly governing their uneducated fellow men. They agree with Lord Lugard that it should be 'a cardinal principle of British colonial policy that the interests of a large native population (should) not be subject to the will . . . of a small minority of educated and Europeanized natives who have nothing in common with them, and whose interests are often opposed to theirs. . . .'[32] This same sentiment accounted for the reluctance of the British to allow Nigerians any role in the executive or decision-making process of government. It was only in 1943 that Nigerians were appointed to the Governor of Nigeria's Executive Council, and even then the two so appointed were in the eyes of the nationalists 'safe' government men.[33] The argument that the educated African could not be safely entrusted with the government of his illiterate brothers cut little ice with the nationalists. Many of them came from families with two or three generations of European education. They could remember the day when the senior Bishop of the Anglican Church in Nigeria was an African and the time in 1875 in Lagos when the Head of Police, and Head of Posts and Telegraph, the Registrar of the Supreme Court and the Collector of Customs were all Nigerians.[34] They did not see any merit in the argument that the alien ruler was more likely to be impartial in his dealing with the illiterate masses than the so-called 'alienated' educated African. This situation was the

268

more aggravating to the Nationalists, for whilst the British denied the educated African's ability to govern his fellow men, at the same time they held out, as Coleman has remarked, 'the vision of ultimate control' by allowing a number of them to sit on the Legislative Council to deliberate over the Governor's policy, albeit in a minority position.[35]

How far the demands of the expanding educated classes for greater participation in their own affairs affected the thinking of the Governors of the inter-war period we shall not know until their papers become available for inspection. It appears that Lugard and his successors of the twenties, Thomson and Clifford, did not consider this educated group as in any way presenting a problem in the formulation of overall policy for Nigeria. However the Governors of the thirties, Cameron and Bourdillon, both devoted thought to the role of the educated African in the country. As Miss Perham wrote in 1936, after talking with Cameron, and observing his administration: 'He has done much to gain the interest and support of educated natives for his policy.'[36] Bourdillon, writing towards the end of the war, shortly after he had relinquished his governorship, reflected: 'If there is one lesson which the writer has learned thoroughly in the course of thirty-five years spent in trying to manage other people's affairs for them, it is that on the whole they prefer to manage them themselves.'[37] At the opening of the Yaba College, Sir Donald Cameron declared that future government policy would be to employ more Africans in government, a policy which was applauded by Miss Perham at the time, with one major reservation. Africans could be employed in the service branches of government, they 'should not enter . . . the Administrative service'. Rather they should be encouraged to enter into the 'growing structure of native self-government', i.e. the Native Authorities.[38] Miss Perham, whose ideas on colonial policy did not go unheeded by British officials at the time, had strong reservations about the extension of the powers of the Legislative Council over the administration of Nigeria as a whole. She shared the views of those that feared that the educated African could not be entrusted with the government of those from whom he was supposed to be alienated as a result of his Western education.

Thus she suggested: 'In so far as the political ambitions of the educated are centred upon the Legislative Council, they should be met not by giving them an extension of power over the more backward masses, but by increasing their responsibilities, and therefore their sense of political realities, in urban and other advanced areas.'[39]

Under Cameron and Bourdillon there was growing concern with the role of the educated African and a recognition that his demands were important. But it remained in the realm of discussion rather than of practical policy. It was the war which was to finally prepare the climate for the acceptance by the British Administration of the real facts of the situation, so bluntly stated by Awolowo in his *Path to Nigerian Freedom*.

'It must be realized now and for all time that the articulate minority are destined to rule the country. It is their heritage. It is they who must be trained in the art of government so as to enable them to take over complete control of the affairs of their country. Their numbers will increase, but, like the articulate and politically conscious group in every civilized country, they will always remain in the minority.'[40]

The failure of the British administration to solve the problem of the educated élite by offering it increased participation in the running of the country's affairs in large measure accounts for the virulence of the nationalist attacks on the British administration after the war.[41]

Possibly the greatest effect of Nigeria's participation in the world war was the sudden realization by a large number of ordinary Nigerians, as distinct from the educated élite, that there were Europeans who were different from the privileged colonial administration, who were farmers and private soldiers, traders and shopkeepers, bootblacks and servants like themselves. Nigerian soldiers served alongside white soldiers of their own rank. Allied troops came to Nigeria with no more privileges than Nigerians themselves had. Many Nigerians have testified to the immense impact made by this contact between white and black of similar class. The World War projected Nigerians out of a colonial backwater into a modern world in which, because of the exigencies of war, Nigeria became suddenly important— important as a strategic link in allied defences, as a producer of primary goods essential to feed the starved allied nations, and also as a provider of indispensable troops for the Burma campaigns. Indeed the distinguished anthropologist Meyer Fortes, writing about 'The Impact of the War on British West Africa', said: 'It may well be that the war will prove to have been the outstanding instrument of social progress in West Africa for fifty years.'[42]

Abroad, attitudes towards colonial problems were changing rapidly. The right to empire was being challenged, and within British Government circles themselves there was a certain concern about the administration of the colonies. In 1938 riots in the West Indies had prompted the British Government to set up a Royal Commission to investigate conditions there. One of the main causes of unrest proved to be the very backward economic state of the islands. As a result the British Government established a fund for the West Indies and passed a more general Colonial Development and Welfare Act for her other colonies. Under it, £5 million a year was set aside for colonial development projects together with £500,000 for research.

On the other hand the British Government, headed by Mr. Winston Churchill, seemed impervious to American criticisms of colonialism. The third clause of the Atlantic Charter assured 'the right of all peoples to choose the form of government under which they live . . .'. This was not unnaturally taken by African nationalists to mean that Nigeria would have eventual self-government. But Churchill and his Colonial Secretary, Colonel Oliver Stanley, denied that this clause applied to African dependencies, Churchill declaring that he had no intention of presiding over the break-up of the colonial empire. But American criticisms of colonialism were strong. For instance, *Life* wrote in an editorial: 'Great Britain had better decide to part with her Empire, for the United States is not prepared to fight in order to help her to keep it.'[43] Such criticisms gained some support within the wartime coalition Government in Britain from Labour members, whose Fabian Colonial Bureau kept them up to date on colonial affairs and, in particular, on nationalist aspirations. It was to such organizations as this that West African students in Britain directed their attentions.

Despite early intransigence on the part of the Colonial Secretary, Labour pressure was able to elicit from the Government the promise that British policy in the colonies would be directed towards their political, social and economic development, though no indication was given of a time-table for constitutional advance.

In Nigeria, however, the Nigeria Youth Movement was unable to concentrate the various anti-colonial pressures because of the internal dissensions. Rivalry between Ernest Ikoli and Dr. Azikiwe in 1941 over who should stand for the vacant Legislative Council seat led to the effective demise of the party. Partly this was the result of press rivalry, for Ikoli edited the *Daily Service* which rivalled Zik's *West African Pilot*; partly it was the result of the character of Zik himself who had never been a man to play second fiddle in a political organization. The occasion for the break-up came when Ikoli was put forward for the seat by the party, and Zik counter-proposed Samuel Akinsanya, an Ijebu. Unfortunately for the future of Nigerian nationalism this introduced an element of tribalism that had been largely subdued till then. Ijebu Yoruba were on the whole disliked by other Yoruba, and Zik said that this was the reason why Akinsanya's candidature had not been accepted. Since Zik had all the Ibo solidly behind him this led to a tribal rift in the party, and despite efforts by Obafemi Awolowo to revive the party between 1941 and 1944, it never again rose above petty quarrels. On the other hand, the climate created by the World War and the current of ideas in Lagos was opportune for the creation of a nationalist movement and, on 26th August 1944, Dr. Nnamdi Azikiwe founded the National Council of Nigeria and the Cameroons with himself as Secretary and Herbert Macaulay as President. The N.C.N.C. was not a party in the ordinary sense, but a confederation of trade unions, smaller parties, tribal unions and literary groups. In January 1945 it held its first constitutional convention in which it declared amongst its aims that it intended: 'To achieve internal self-government for Nigeria whereby the people of Nigeria and the Cameroons under British Mandate shall exercise executive legislative and judicial powers.'[44] When a few months later the new Governor of Nigeria, Sir Arthur Richards, presented his constitutional proposals for the country, it was the newly founded N.C.N.C. that led the criticism of its various inadequacies.

CHAPTER XVI

Three Constitutions

The constitutional proposals of Sir Arthur Richards in March 1945, though they were attacked on almost every side by Nigerian nationalists, mark the real turning-point in Nigeria's progress towards independence. The constitution, which came into effect on 1st January 1947, had, according to the Governor, three objects: 'to promote the unity of Nigeria, to provide adequately within that unity for the diverse elements which make up the country and to secure greater participation by Africans in the discussion of their own affairs'.[1] The new Legislative Council was enlarged to forty-four members with a majority of unofficials, twenty-eight as against sixteen officials. Of these twenty-eight, however, only four were elected, the rest being nominated or indirectly elected. The most important feature of the new constitution was the inclusion of the North in the central legislature, a move that in itself could do nothing but further the unity of the country. However, at the same time regional councils were created for the North, East and West. Though they were mainly confined to discussion, their creation has subsequently been severely criticized as being the foundation of tribalism in Nigerian politics. Diké has written: 'Undoubtedly the Richards Constitution is a dividing line in Nigerian Constitutional development. Before it the keynote in Nigerian politics was unification towards a centralized state and the realization of a common nationality. . . . But with the Richards Constitution this tendency towards unification was on the whole arrested. . . .'[2] Sir Arthur Richards might have agreed with these sentiments as far as the two southern provinces were concerned, but he would have argued that the inclusion in the central legislature of the North, so long excluded from participation in national politics, necessitated some degree of regionalization to allow for its very obvious differences from the South. On the other hand, it has been argued that if Sir Arthur really wanted to contain regional and ethnic differences he would have been wiser to have followed the earlier divisions proposed by Morel and Temple, and later advocated by Zik, which would have allowed for regional differences but would also have permitted the creation of a strong central legislature. As it was, he established the basis of a very unwieldy federation with one region twice the size in area and population of the other two.[3]

Sir Arthur obviously conceived of the constitution as allowing for the maximum participation of all sections in the national legislature. In theory there was a link between the smallest native authority and the national representative, since the native authority sent delegates to the regional assembly which, in turn, selected from among its members a delegation to the central Legislative Council.

The constitution was attacked both for its content and for the way in which it was introduced. The newly formed N.C.N.C. regretted 'the unilateral way the whole proposals were prepared without consulting the people and natural rulers of the country. . . . We respectfully suggest that a more democratic approach could have been made to avoid any possible misunderstanding. . . .'[4] Sir Arthur Richards's predecessor, Sir Bernard Bourdillon, himself criticized the peremptory way in which the constitution was introduced,[5] for he had promised Nigerians that they would have a full opportunity to discuss any new constitution, though it must be noted the concept of regional councils was originally his.[6] The particular criticisms, which might not have been so vehement if consultation had taken place, were diverse. The unofficial majorities in central and regional assemblies were attacked as false since many of the so-called unofficials were nominated or quasi-officials like chiefs and native authority members. There was no change in the composition of the Executive Council which remained wholly European. The principle of election, far from being extended, had only been maintained for Lagos and Calabar on the direct intervention of the Colonial Secretary. Curiously enough, in the light of its later policy, attacks were made by the N.C.N.C. on the lack of power delegated to the regional assemblies.

These criticisms which were supported, only less ardently, by the N.Y.M., were accompanied by an effective demonstration of popular discontent. The year of the publication of the new constitution was also the year of the general strike in which Zik played an influential role. The wartime expansion of the economy, following on the increased demand for Nigeria's primary goods, led to a rapid growth of labour unions. In 1940 there were only twelve unions with 4,337 members, by 1944 there were eighty-five with some 30,000.[7] British policy during the war had been to encourage the unions, and in 1942 the Nigerian Trade Union Congress was given official recognition. However, the steep rise in prices during the war led to real economic hardship for wage-earners, many of whom belonged to unions. After complaining bitterly about the regular adjustments of European salaries to the rising cost of living, the Railway, Ports and Telecommunication workers all went on strike, effectively paralysing many of the country's essential services. Though the new constitution was in no way responsible for the strike, the two became associated since Zik, the most ardent critic of the constitution, also backed the strikers through his two papers the *Pilot* and the *Comet*. In certain quarters it was even maintained that he engineered the strike. On July 8th his papers were banned, and shortly afterwards Zik declared that there was an officially backed plot to assassinate him. This was received contemptuously in government circles, but in the country it was widely believed and had the effect of making him a martyr. When, in fact, at the end of the strike a Commission of Inquiry recommended an increase in the cost of living allowance to workers, Zik naturally emerged in the eyes of the public as the champion of a successful strike. He was thus in a strong position to make an all-out attack on the new constitution and the so-called obnoxious ordinances that had been introduced with it. These vested mineral rights and publicly purchased lands in the Crown, and gave the government powers to depose and appoint chiefs. Since land rights and the appointment of chiefs were close to the structure of almost every Nigerian society, Zik could add fuel to his campaign against the constitution, which was little understood by the ordinary people, by warning them that their land and their chiefs were threatened by the government.

During a triumphal tour of the country Zik and his party collected the considerable sum of £13,000, though the tour was marked by tragedy when one member of the entourage, the veteran nationalist, Herbert Macaulay, fell mortally ill. Nevertheless, when the party returned to Lagos it was to a massive reception, and with the money it had collected the N.C.N.C. was able to send to London a delegation led by Zik and composed of men from every part of Nigeria. The Labour Colonial Secretary, Arthur Creech Jones, paid little attention to the delegation, merely advising them to give the constitution a try. Unfortunately there followed financial squabbles, and when the delegation returned home with no definite achievement and a backlog of disputes over money, the N.C.N.C. suffered a real though, as it proved, only a temporary setback.

Meanwhile the Richards constitution had come into effect at the beginning of 1947 and it was envisaged that it would last for nine years with revision after six. It was accompanied by the introduction of an ambitious £55,000,000 ten-year development plan for Nigeria,[8] subsidized from the Colonial Development and Welfare Fund to the tune of £23,000,000. This provided for the extension of rural and urban water supplies, education, communications, town planning, hospitals and agricultural and veterinary research. Under it a department of commerce and industry was set up. At first the application of the plan suffered from lack of qualified staff for the Nigerian administrative service had been very much depleted as a result of the war.

Though Sir Arthur Richards had envisaged that his constitution would last for nine years, the new Governor, Sir John Macpherson, appointed in April 1948, said, after only a few months in the country, that progress had been so good that it was time for a change. He did not make the mistake of his predecessor in foisting a new constitution on the country without consulting the people; if anything he went to the opposite extreme by indulging the country in two years of protracted negotiations on the form the new constitution should take. Macpherson, a young Governor, together with Hugh Foot, his young Chief Secretary, proved very much a new broom in Nigeria. He was responsible for the democratization of local government in the East, and in 1948 appointed a commission to make recommendations about the recruitment and training of Nigerians for the government Senior Service. Eight Nigerians, including Dr. Azikiwe, sat on the commission which recommended that no expatriate should be recruited where a suitable Nigerian was available.[9] Macpherson also appointed four Africans to his Executive Council, and with the appointment of Dr. S. L. Manuwa as first Nigerian Director of Medical Services, this made five, since his post gave him a seat ex-officio.

The people were consulted on their new constitution at every level; a concession, no doubt, strongly influenced by events in the Gold Coast, where riots in February 1948 had forced the government into studying constitutional reform for that country.[10] In Nigeria village councils sent delegates to divisional councils, then to provincial and regional councils, and finally to a general conference at Ibadan.

The decisions made at the Ibadan conference must be seen in the context of the great increase in tribal feeling that had followed the introduction of the Richards constitution. Today the origin of this tribal feeling is the source of much bitterness and recrimination by Nigerian political parties, and it may be long before it can be seen in true perspective.

Fundamentally, as we have seen, there were very considerable differences in the history of the various groups of Nigeria, as well as more points of contact than have generally been supposed. There were latent differences and antagonisms that could be called up by anyone so inclined. The argument over tribalism has been between those who believe that these differences were fixed, and that anyway Nigeria was an arbitrary colonial creation, so that any political settlement should take these factors into account by devolving government on the tribal groups, and those who believe that politics should be worked out in terms of Nigerians rather than Ibo, Hausa and Yoruba, and that this could be achieved if no one resorted to tribal politics.

In fact, originally, the increase in tribal feeling, as Ezera has shown[11], was caused by circumstances rather than design, and only later was it seized upon by politicians. When the British occupied Nigeria they had almost no contact with the large Ibo and Ibibio population of the East, whilst already many Yoruba had received English education and provided a small intellectual *élite* in Lagos. Population pressures and land hunger in the East forced many Ibo and Ibibio to migrate to the cities of the West and North, where they proved remarkably successful as clerks, railway workers and storekeepers. Nearly always they settled in discrete communities, realizing that the key to success under the new administration was Western education, and seeing how far behind the Yoruba they were in this respect, they formed mutual benefit associations in order to give some of their number the advantages of higher education. This tendency to group together was intensified by the close family ties that exist in most African societies and by the fact that in Northern towns Southerners were forced to live outside the walls, in Sabon Garis, or strangers' quarters. Soon these unions began to federate. In 1944, following on the Ibibio State Union, the Pan-Ibo Federal Union was formed. In 1948 Dr. Azikiwe, who had already protested against the Yoruba domination of Lagos politics, became President of this Union. Naturally his opponents retaliated by accusing him of being a tribal politician. Later he even made statements that seemed to confirm this view: 'It would appear that the God of Africa has created the Ibo nation to lead the children of Africa from the bondage of ages. . . .'[12]

Tribal feeling had first come to the fore in the quarrel between Zik and the older members of the Nigerian Youth Movement over the candidature of Samuel Akinsanya for a seat on the Legislative Council. This quarrel resulted in Zik leaving the N.Y.M. with all his Eastern followers, so that the party became effectively a Yoruba-controlled organization.

It was not surprising, therefore, that these tribal unions also interested themselves in political affairs and the Pan-Ibo Union itself was one of the founding members of the N.C.N.C. In 1945 some Yoruba students in London formed the Egbe Omo Oduduwa, or Society of the Descendants of Oduduwa, a cultural organization which soon took on the character of a political party. One of these students was Awolowo, who had already enunciated his own political ideas in *Path to Nigerian Freedom*, which he completed in 1945, though it was not published until 1947.[13] In 1948 the inaugural Conference of Egbe Omo Oduduwa was held at Ife, when Sir Adeyemo Alakija, the President, declared that the 'Yoruba will not be relegated to the background in the future'.[14] Among its objectives was to 'create and actively foster the idea of a single nationalism throughout Yorubaland' and to 'co-operate with existing ethnical and regional associations and such as may exist hereafter, in matters of common interest to all Nigerians, so as thereby to attain to Unity in federation'.[15] The N.C.N.C., at least in theory, always looked to a unitary Nigeria, partly because of the fact of Ibo migration to other parts of the country would be served by a unitary constitution, and partly because its leaders wished to minimize the differences between the various ethnic groups. But the party's policy has never been very fixed on this matter.

In 1948, the intense feelings between Yoruba and Ibo, particularly in Lagos where there was severe danger of communal disorders from July to September, furthered the cause of those elements in the N.C.N.C. who wanted a federal form of government in Nigeria based on small states, and the Ibo State Union was founded as the basis of one of these states.

Until the Richards constitution the North was largely isolated from the South, and since its traditional form of government had largely been preserved there was little opportunity for Western-style politics. However, a few Northerners had received Western education and in 1943 a group of them, including Mallam Abubakar Tafawa Balewa, future Prime Minister of Nigeria, Sa'ad Zungur, the first Northerner to go to Yaba Higher College, and Aminu Kano, present leader of the radical opposition in the North, formed the Bauchi Improvement Association. In 1949, Aminu Kano and Abubakar were among the founders of the Northern People's Congress, a cultural Congress which, like the Egbe Omo Oduduwa, was converted into a political organization to meet the requirements of the new Macpherson constitution.

The three years during which the new constitution was negotiated were dominated by tribal nationalism with the N.P.C. taking the part of the North, the Egbe Omo Oduduwa, which with elements of the old Nigerian Youth Movement became the Action Group, taking the part of the West, and the N.C.N.C., whilst it outwardly preserved its pan-Nigerian aims, taking the part of the East.

At this time, possibly only the extremist Zikist movement could legitimately call itself a pan-Nigerian party. Comprising members from all parts of Nigeria, it was violently anti-colonial, calling on workers to strike and to refuse to pay taxes. In February 1949 ten of its leaders were tried and imprisoned on charges of sedition, and the movement went to earth and might even have petered out but for the notorious Enugu shootings. The miners of the Enugu colliery had staged a go-slow strike in the erroneous belief encouraged by the Zikists that arrears of pay had been withheld from them. The government sent in a detachment of police to collect the dynamite stored in the mine fearful that either the miners would use it or that it might find its way into Zikist hands. The miners in turn feared that the police had been sent to break up the strike and rioted. The European in charge of the detachment ordered his police to fire on the strikers and twenty-one were killed. The news of the massacre was received with great horror all over Nigeria, and the Zikists, whom the government strongly suspected of engineering the strike, seized the opportunity and provoked riots in Aba, Calabar, Onitsha and Port Harcourt.

In the ensuing Commission of Inquiry the police officer responsible for the shooting was adjudged to have acted in all honesty, but to have 'made an error of judgment which fell short of that standard that might be expected from one of his rank and seniority'.[16] To nationalists this seemed too small a penalty for him to pay, and in the Legislative Council Zik demanded unsuccessfully that he be brought back from England to stand trial. The Zikist movement reached a dramatic end when, on 18th February 1950, a Zikist attempted to assassinate Mr. Hugh Foot, the Chief Secretary. Zikists were rounded up and in April 1950 the movement was proscribed.

Meanwhile all over Nigeria discussion of the new constitution was taking place. From March to September 1949 the divisional, provincial and regional conferences had been considering the future constitution, and between October 10th and 21st the drafting committee prepared a preliminary constitution for discussion by the general conference which was convened at Ibadan with all but three of its fifty-three members Nigerians. The drafting committee proposed a federal system of government with a fairly strong central legislature and executive, though considerable powers were to be delegated to the Regions. The central executive or council of state would have six *ex officio* and twelve unofficial members who would be ministers. The composition of the House should be twenty-two from the East and West respectively and thirty from the North by virtue of its larger population. The North, however, insisted on representation equal to that of both the Southern Regions since its population was greater than that of both combined. It also asked that distribution of grants from the central government be made on a *per capita* basis. It wanted no change in the regional boundaries though the drafting committee had recommended that these should be re-examined.

Four minority reports were presented to the general conference.[17] All of them were very important for they contained the seeds of some of the major political disputes of subsequent years. The first minority report, signed by Professor Eyo Ita, Vice-President of the N.C.N.C., and Mazi Mbonu Ojike, attacked the regional basis of government, suggesting that Nigeria should be divided into a larger number of ethnic states. They opposed the creation of Houses of Chiefs, as well as the electoral college system, advocating in a second report that this be replaced by universal adult suffrage. A third minority report opposed the denial of franchise to Southerners resident in the North, whilst a fourth, signed mainly by Western Region members, attacked the proposal that Lagos should be separated from the Western Region.

When the conference's recommendations were sent to the Colonial Secretary, he gave them his general approval and referred the outstanding issues back to the Legislative Council for final solution. A select committee of the Legislature decided that the North should have equal representation with the South, but made no concessions on the major issues raised by the minority reports. In January 1952 the new constitution came into effect, with a central legislature of 148 members, half of them from the North and an executive council of eighteen members, comprising six officials and twelve ministers, four nominated by each regional assembly. In the Regions the assemblies were enlarged and given legislative and financial powers. Each had its own executive council with a majority of African over official members. But neither in any Region nor in the central government was provision made for the post of premier or prime minister. Revenues were to be distributed to the Regions on the principle of need rather than derivation.

In the dry season of 1951–2, Nigeria's first general election was fought by the three major parties: the N.C.N.C. whose domi-

nant policy was the achievement of a unitary Nigeria; the
Action Group, which at first was mainly intent on securing
Western region interests and only later took on a national
character; and the N.P.C., which was transformed half-way
through the election from a cultural organization into a political
party, determined to secure the North for Northerners.[18] The
N.C.N.C. won the East with a large majority; the Action Group
won the West with 49 out of 80 seats (a number of the A.G.
members had stood as N.C.N.C. candidates but subsequently
crossed the carpet); and the N.P.C. swept the North.

Dr. Azikiwe was elected to the Western House as one of the
five members for Lagos, but because of lack of party discipline
he was not elected as a member of the Central House. Since
the other N.C.N.C. members for Lagos refused to stand down
for Zik, this left the Action-Group-dominated Western House
in the position of selecting which two of the five N.C.N.C.
Lagos members they would elect as representatives to the
Central House. Naturally they did not choose Zik, since they
were only too pleased to be able to exclude the national leader
of the N.C.N.C.

The Macpherson constitution, though much more liberal in
its outlook than its predecessor, and much more in keeping with
the desires of Nigerians themselves, was destined for a short life.
Partly this was because of its own deficiencies, partly because
of the political situation at the time. From the party point of
view there was a fundamental difference between the N.C.N.C.
on the one hand, in which important elements wanted a constitution that would give greater powers to the central government, and the Action Group and N.P.C. on the other, both of
whom wanted to retain as much power in the Regions as possible. This was particularly true of the N.P.C. where long administrative separation from the South and relative political
backwardness made their leaders genuinely afraid of Southern
domination, a point which the leader of the N.P.C., the Sardauna of Sokoto, makes very clear in his autobiography.[19]

In effect, the Macpherson constitution was a compromise between these two positions and apportioned power effectively
neither to centre nor to Region. And since, on its promulgation,
it was stated to be only a step towards further constitutional
development, the various parties, despite an initial willingness

to make it work, all the time had their eye on future change. Its particular defect was the position of the ministers. There was no real ministerial responsibility under the constitution since ministers were not directly responsible for their departments, but merely acted as spokesmen on departmental affairs in the Legislature and Council of Ministers, where they were charged 'when a decision had been taken . . . (with) . . . ensuring in association with the appropriate official that effect is given to the decision'.[20] They had no responsibility for the formulation of policy in their own department. Furthermore, ministers were held collectively responsible for all decisions made in the Council of Ministers. In an ordinary party or coalition government this would be a reasonable proviso; but in a council where ministers were elected not by the national legislature but from the regional Houses, and where four African ministers from one Region together with the six European officials could outvote the eight ministers from the other two Regions, there was definite possibility of political deadlock.

The actual breakdown resulted largely from party antagonisms. The N.C.N.C. from the outset was disappointed with the constitution, especially since its own leader had been excluded from the national legislature. In the party there was sharp disagreement between the members holding ministerial office in the Eastern and Central Houses, who wanted to make the constitution work, and those who were disillusioned by Zik's exclusion from the Central House and wanted to withdraw their support. At an N.C.N.C. convention in Jos in December 1952, three N.C.N.C. central ministers were expelled from the party (Dr. Endeley, the Cameroons representative,[21] was not) and when it became apparent that most of the Eastern ministers sympathized with their colleagues at the centre a meeting of the Eastern parliamentary committee of the party asked for the resignation of all nine ministers so that a cabinet reshuffle could take place. The ministers duly signed resignations, but when six of them learnt they were not to be included in the new cabinet they withdrew their resignations. The Legal Secretary accepted their right of withdrawal and so they were able to remain in office only to have every Bill they introduced, including the annual Appropriation Bill, defeated by large majorities. To pass the latter the Lieutenant-Governor, Sir Clem Pleass, was forced to use his reserve powers. The East thus had a minority government, led by the National Independence Party, formed by the dissident Eastern Region ministers and the expelled central ministers.

As far as the N.C.N.C. was concerned the position was intolerable, yet it was the Action Group that precipitated the final breakdown of the constitution. On April 1st an Action Group backbencher, Anthony Enahoro, introduced a private member's Bill demanding self-government in 1956. It was clear that the Northern members would not support this motion,[22] as they did not feel themselves ready for self-government, and in the Council of Ministers the four Northern ministers, together with the six European officials, voted that no minister should participate in the debate. This was opposed by the four Action Group members who felt that they could hardly dissociate themselves from so important a motion by a member of their own party. The N.I.P. ministers abstained. However, according to the doctrine of collective responsibility the Council had to present a united front in the house, so the Action Group ministers resigned. The North tried to push a milder motion asking for self-government as soon as practicable, but both Action Group and N.C.N.C. walked out of the house.

The Northern members were booed by the Lagos crowds and many of them returned to their homes resolved never again to involve themselves in Southern politics, and seriously contemplated secession from the Federation.[23] The position deteriorated when the Action Group, whose leader Awolowo had called the Northern leaders despots and British stooges, announced a tour of Kano, heart of Northern Nigeria. Though the Resident banned it at the last minute, the publicity in its favour had been sufficient to excite deep resentment by local people against the South, though in fact the Northern opposition party, the Northern Elements Progressive Union, welcomed the tour which many have criticized as being an extremely tactless undertaking in the circumstances.[24] The situation was particularly tense in Kano because of the large Southern minority in the Sabon Gari, or strangers' quarter, and from 15th to 19th May there were serious communal riots with an official death roll of 36 killed and 277 wounded,[25] though it is almost certain that the numbers were much larger. Tribal and regional separatism came to a vicious head in those unhappy days and it seemed that Nigeria would split in two.

Shortly after the riots the Northern House of Chiefs and the Northern House of Assembly passed an eight-point programme which in effect demanded the dissolution of the Federation. It devolved government on the regions, which were to be linked only by a Central Agency, of a non-political character, appointed jointly by regional governments. It would be responsible for Defence, External Affairs, Customs and West African Research Unions, and any other matters the regional governments cared to refer to it.[26] The long separation of North from South seemed to have left too deep an impression for their recent political marriage to succeed. The immediate result of the riots and the motion in the Northern House was the realization by the Colonial Secretary, Mr. Oliver Lyttelton, that his earlier complacent statement that what Nigeria 'needs is a period of reflection to let the dust die down'[27] was far from the truth, and almost at once he announced that the Nigerian constitution would be 'redrawn to provide for greater regional autonomy and for the removal of powers of intervention by the centre in matters which could, without detriment to other Regions, be placed entirely within regional competence'.[28]

The various parties sent delegations to the conference in London with many misgivings and with provisos that made its success seem almost impossible. The N.P.C., led by the Sardauna of Sokoto, had already made it clear that the only form in which they would co-operate with the South would be a loose, non-politicized union. The Action Group and the N.C.N.C. in temporary alliance at first refused to go if the N.I.P. attended, and stipulated that if the North were intransigent about the question of self-government they would ask for the creation of a Southern federation which would take self-government in 1956, come what may. Both, however, were agreed on the delegation of residual powers to the regional governments, and as allies they remained tactfully reticent about the question of the status of Lagos. The N.I.P. however opposed self-government in 1956, but advocated the creation of a strong central legislature and the breakdown of the Regions into states.

Against this unpromising background it is remarkable how much agreement was in fact reached by the delegates to the

London conference.[29] The three major parties agreed to a federal constitution in which residual powers would be transferred to the Regions as distinct from the centre as had been the case under the old constitution. Nevertheless, much wider powers were given to the centre than had been envisaged by the Northern delegation. The all-important question of self-government in 1956 was cleverly side-stepped by offering self-government to those Regions that wanted it in 1956, but not to the federation as a whole, thus leaving it open for the North to decide for itself when it was ready for self-government. At the time few had believed that the British Government would make this important concession on a fixed date for self-government.

The most bitter issue of the conference, which broke up the N.C.N.C.-Action Group alliance, was whether Lagos should remain part of the Western Region or become federal territory. The N.P.C. pressed for the latter solution, since it was anxious to ensure that the main outlet for its goods should not be under the control of any other part of the federation. The N.C.N.C., which had many members in Lagos, also felt that a federation should have a true federal capital. The Action Group, however, argued that Lagos was a Yoruba city, and did most of its trade with the Western Region, and as far as the North's fears were concerned both the railways and the ports were under federal control. In the end the three parties agreed to arbitration of the issue by the Colonial Secretary, who decided that Lagos should become federal territory. Despite its agreement to his arbitration, the Action Group bitterly attacked his decision, and for a while it seemed that the resumed constitutional conference in Lagos proposed for January 1954, at which the fiscal arrangements of the federation and the position of the judiciary and civil service were to be decided, would founder over the future of Lagos. However, when the conference opened the Action Group did not raise the Lagos issue but demanded instead that the right to secession be included in the constitution. This was again rejected by the Colonial Secretary, and the Action Group acquiesced in his decision.

Once again a conference about which most people had been very pessimistic was a striking success. The rules for the actual functioning of the federation were settled by the delegates, in particular the delicate problem of distribution of funds between the centre and the Regions.[30] At the 1953 conference Sir Louis Chick had been commissioned to devise a system of revenue allocation based on 'the need, on the one hand, to provide the Federal government and Regional governments with an adequate measure of fiscal autonomy within their own sphere of government, and, on the other, the importance of ensuring that the total revenues available to Nigeria are allocated in such a way that the principle of derivation is followed to the fullest degree compatible with the reasonable needs of the Federal government and the Regional governments'.[31] The conference accepted his basic proposals: that all import, excise and export duties should be federal matters; that all import duties on motor spirits and half the import duty and excise on tobacco should go to the regional governments on the basis of consumption; that half the net proceeds of all other import duties should be distributed to the regional governments on the basis of 40 per cent to the West and 30 per cent each to the East and North; that mining taxes should be collected federally and distributed to the Regions on the basis of derivation; that income tax should also be collected federally and distributed on the basis of derivation. As *West Africa* wrote in its editorial at the time: 'Endorsement of the Chick report means economically as well as politically there will be three Nigerias.' In addition the marketing boards were regionalized, and their combined reserves of £74 million were distributed on a basis of £34 million to the West, £24 million to the North and £15 million to the East. The tendency towards the creation of three Nigerias was consolidated by the regionalization of the civil service and the judiciary, though provision was made for appeals to a Federal Supreme Court. The latter move was bitterly opposed by the Lagos Bar, whilst the former was necessitated by the increase in government responsibility devolved on the Regions.

The constitution agreed on by these two conferences is essentially the constitution under which Nigeria is governed today. Nigeria became a full federation of three Regions, a federal capital, and the quasi-federal territory of the Southern Cameroons, which by agreement of the conferences had been allowed to break away from the Eastern Region. A national legislature of 184 members, half of them representing the North, was to be elected every five years. However, the elections were to take place Region by Region, and the system of election varied from one to the other. The appointment of ministers to the central executive council was not now made by the regional assemblies, but by the leader of the party which gained the majority of seats in each regional federal election. Each Region had the right to three seats on the council. The principle of full ministerial responsibility for departmental affairs was settled though no provision was made for the post of leader of government business. However, in the Regions provision was made for the post of Premier and an all-African Executive Council with the exception of the Governor who remained President. Residual powers were now transferred to the Regions. It was finally promised that the new constitution would be reviewed before August 1956. But the 1954 constitution, despite subsequent changes, had laid down the basic pattern of government for a self-governing Nigeria.

CHAPTER XVII

Independence Achieved

The 1954 constitution marks the end of the nationalist struggle with Britain; for the next six years, until the achievement of independence on 1st October 1960, Nigerian leaders were preoccupied not so much with wresting power from the colonial government as dealing with the day-to-day administration and development of their country as well as settling the basis on which they would co-operate with each other. It was hardly surprising therefore that the year after the new constitution came into effect was a quiet one with ministers taking over departments and learning the basic mechanics of the services for which they were now fully responsible. In the Regions their responsibility was even greater since with the exception of the North there was only one expatriate official in the Regional Executive Council—the Governor. In the federal elections that followed the introduction of the new constitution, the N.P.C. and its allies won 84 of the 90 seats in the North, where the elections were still indirect, though everywhere else they were now direct. The biggest surprise came in the West where the N.C.N.C., having triumphed in the East, won 23 seats to the Action Group's 18, showing that Nigerian politics were not entirely dominated by tribal factors, though it must be pointed out that the N.C.N.C. gained much of its support in the minority area of the Mid-West.[1] In Yoruba areas it gained support because of the unpopularity of the Action Group's taxation policy. However, since the N.C.N.C.'s close ally, the Northern Elements Progressive Union, won no seats in the North, there was still no party with truly national support. The curious situation arose that whilst the N.C.N.C. had the right to choose six federal ministers, having won both the East and West, the N.P.C. had the largest number of seats in the Federal House. This fact curbed the N.P.C. from its original intention of going it alone in the Federal House, for the presence of six N.C.N.C. ministers made coalition between the parties inevitable, if there was to be a government at all. The Action Group, supported by N.I.P. (now U.N.I.P.), formed a small but active opposition.

The agreement of the N.P.C. and the N.C.N.C., whose political views were diametrically opposed on many issues, to work together in the Federal government was perhaps the most signicant development in post-war Nigerian politics since it has proved to be the basis of co-operation in the first five years of independence. It made national unity possible, even if it has meant that both parties have had to compromise their political views.

In 1955 Sir John Macpherson, who had been ultimately responsible for Nigeria during its period of greatest political upheaval and progress, retired. Though the constitution named after him had proved a failure, he left praised by even the most extreme nationalist elements who recognized that Nigeria's accelerated constitutional progress was in no small measure due to his enthusiasm and understanding of the young federation's needs.[2] His successor, Sir James Robertson, turned out to be the ideal man to represent Britain during the final phase of self-government, and happily the improved relations between Nigeria and Britain were crystallized the following year by the royal tour of Queen Elizabeth and the Duke of Edinburgh.

The visit of the Queen seemed somehow to symbolize the unity for which Nigeria was striving. Indeed, as the editorial in *West Africa* remarked at the time, 'the enthusiasm and devotion that the visit has aroused have gone beyond expectation'.[3] The three main leaders called a political truce for the visit, and a bond of goodwill was created not only between Nigerians but between Nigeria and Britain, a bond that seemed far away from the months of 1953 when the N.C.N.C. banned the Coronation ceremonies.

Whilst Nigerian leaders were absorbed in the mechanics of government they also had one eye on the review of the constitution scheduled to take place in September 1956, when it was assumed that both the West and the East would take up the

British promise of self-government in 1956. Indeed the Action Group had published in December 1955 a White Paper, which was approved by the Western House of Assembly, outlining the form self-government would take.[4] However, because of events in the Eastern House of Assembly, the conference had to be postponed.

The N.C.N.C. had long been dogged by instability in the second ranks of its leadership. On 30th April 1956 Mr. E. O. Eyo, the chief whip of the Eastern Region government, tabled a motion in the house accusing Dr. Azikiwe of gross abuse of public office in that he allowed £2 million of public money to be invested in the African Continental Bank in which he had substantial personal interest and which at the time was running at a loss. The debate was refused by the Speaker since the matter was *sub judice* because of a libel action brought by Dr. Azikiwe against Mr. Eyo. Since the Premier would not accede to the Governor of the Region's suggestion that the matter be referred to an independent tribunal, the Colonial Secretary appointed a Commission of Inquiry under the Federal Chief Justice, Sir Stafford Foster-Sutton, which had the effect of delaying the resumed negotiations over the constitution.

Tales of corruption in public life were common in Nigeria at the time and concern over this was obviously one of Mr. Lennox-Boyd's main reasons for ordering the Commission in such delicate circumstances. As far as Dr. Azikiwe's supporters were concerned he was innocent even before he appeared before the tribunal, and the rather mild condemnation of the Commission that his conduct had 'fallen short of the expectations of honest reasonable people' seemed to confirm their view, especially since it was also conceded that Zik's primary motive 'was to make available an indigenous bank with the object of liberalizing credit for the people'.[5] This was not due merely to blind personal following, but to the fact that whatever the rather cold attitude of the British might have been towards the affair, it was felt that Dr. Azikiwe had acted genuinely in the African interest by depositing government money in the African Continental Bank, especially as it was in danger of foundering. For them the bank represented an African achievement, and an attempt to rival the primacy of the British banks, one of which it was observed handled all government accounts. As Kalu Ezera points out, 'Zik's supporters generally believed that the whole affair was a conspiracy by the Colonial Office to discredit and "dethrone" him and to perpetuate British banking monopoly in the country.'[6]

West Africa wrote at the time very perceptively: 'The idea that a man who, like Dr. Azikiwe, has built up a bank and a group of companies, however shaky their finances, should relinquish all control of them when he becomes a Minister, is not universally accepted in Nigeria, where the joint stock company finds unfertile soil.'[7] On the other hand the Commission of Inquiry had the salutary effect of regularizing the affairs of the bank, which, with the National Bank of Nigeria, supported mainly by the Western Region, represents a very considerable entrepreneurial achievement.

Immediately after the Commission's report, delivered on 16th January 1957, Dr. Azikiwe transferred his interest to the Eastern Region government, and went to the country as a trial of strength. He won the election by a comfortable margin of 64 seats to 20 (U.N.I.P. 5, Action Group 13, Independents 2) and was thus in a strong position as chief representative of the N.C.N.C. and the Eastern Region government at the London Conference scheduled for May 1957. Likewise the Action Group had gone to the country in May 1956 so that in the words of Chief Awolowo it 'could go to the next Constitutional Conference fully armed with a mandate of the people in respect of all major issues which will be raised at the conference'.[8]

On 26th March 1957, the Federal House of Representatives, prior to the London conference and just after Ghana had achieved independence, passed a motion asking for independence in 1959. Once again it seemed at first that this might precipitate crisis, for the leader of the opposition, Chief Akintola, moving the motion, had originally asked for independence in 1957, although the North had already made it clear that she would not be hurried into regional self-government. However, the greatly improved relations between the parties were demonstrated clearly when Mr. Jaja Wachuku of the N.C.N.C. asked Chief Akintola whether he would agree to change the date to 1959, which he did, whereupon the House voted it unanimously.

The 1957 conference itself was mainly concerned with the

revision of the constitution of 1954 both in the light of experience in running it and in accordance with foreseen constitutional advance. It was agreed that both the West and the East should have self-government as soon as they wanted it. The Federal House was enlarged to 320 members, who were to be elected directly on the same basis nationally with the exception that suffrage would not be extended to women in the North, in accordance with that Region's Moslem susceptibilities. It was also agreed that there would be appointed a federal Prime Minister with a cabinet drawn from the House of Representatives or the proposed new Senate. The lack of a federal leader of government had hitherto been a major weakness of the constitution, but on the other hand until then it had been difficult to see how the various parties could agree on a Prime Minister, since the three national leaders were in the Regional Houses, and no one party commanded an overall majority. However, experience of working together and recognition of each others' talents made it possible for not only the N.C.N.C., which had been working in coalition with the N.P.C., but also the Action Group to form a national government under Alhaji Abubakar Tafawa Balewa, the former Minister of Transport and Deputy President of the N.P.C. This retiring, but extremely astute Northerner, had already impressed his colleagues as a minister, and in the House his great debating ability had gained him the respect of all legislators. Though in his early days as a national legislator he had talked in terms of Northern separatism, by 1957 he had become as convinced as anyone else of the necessity of national co-operation. In the sense that he was not associated with any of the major tribal groups of Nigeria—unlike most of the Northern leaders he did not come from the Hausa Fulani aristocracy—and as a member of a small tribe, he could in a way, symbolize Nigeria as a whole and not one faction of it.

It might have seemed in 1957 that Nigeria was nearly ready for independence. The North had however refused to be rushed into self-government, on the grounds that Northern cadres were not ready to take over the Region's administration. With eighteen million people to govern and only a handful of university graduates, and probably no more than 2,000 holders of school certificate, the formation of a Northern administration would be dependent on expatriates or Southerners. Moreover, the Regional Premier, the Sardauna of Sokoto, scion of the royal house of Sokoto, fully realized that the tensions existing in the Region between the old forces of aristocracy as represented by the Emirs and their native authorities and the new forces of democracy as represented by the government in Kaduna must on no account clash.[9] The uncertain marriage between the two had to be handled with great care, and the N.P.C. seemed the only organization that could bridge the gap between them. The two Southern Regions had a head start as a result of their greater education, whilst the North, in which early agreements had excluded missionaries who had provided most of the schools in the South, had only just embarked on a large-scale education programme. Thus, before the 1957 conference, it seemed that the Northern reluctance for self-government might well hold up independence for the country as a whole, and it was with considerable relief that delegates heard the Sardauna of Sokoto announce that his Region would in fact become self-governing in 1959.

By far the most complex problem confronting the delegates was that of Nigeria's minority groups, and the demand for the creation of new states that had grown up amongst them. One of the main results of the accentuation of tribal politics in the years of the Macpherson constitution was the increase in the minority reaction against the major tribal groups dominating the political life of the Regions. This minority movement, always potentially existent because of historical and ethnic factors, took the form of political associations seeking the separation of so-called minority areas and the creation of new states. In the Northern Region some people in the predominantly non-Moslem and non-Hausa Middle Belt formed the United Middle Belt Congress. This new party demanded the creation of a separate state for the Middle Belt so that the people could escape from what its leaders alleged was the domination of the Fulani and Hausa. This had certain roots in history for the areas claimed by this party were predominantly those which the cavalry of the Fulani had never conquered. In the Western Region, as a reaction against the allegedly Yoruba-dominated Action Group, the Mid-West State movement was started, supported largely by non-Yoruba-speaking peoples and in particular the people of the old Benin Empire. The N.C.N.C. also supported this movement on the grounds that the only way to create a truly united Nigeria would be to create more states, none of which would be large enough to dominate any of the others. Curiously enough the Action Group itself gave its blessing to this movement, partly because it was beginning to find the Mid-West an electoral and economic liability and partly because it realized that if it were to champion the creation of new states in the Eastern and Northern Regions it could hardly object to the creation of one in the Western Region itself.

In the East the Ibo form a solid core of well over seven million, and are surrounded by three provinces in which other groups predominate: Calabar, Ogoja and Rivers. The movement for the creation of a separate state in the East has been more complex. The main movement has been for the creation of the C.O.R. state or Calabar-Ogoja-Rivers state, but there have been subsidiary movements for the creation of an Ogoja state and a Rivers state including Ijo from both Western and Eastern Nigeria. But in all cases the movements were inspired by fear of the dominant group, and by ethnic chauvinism.

The 1957 Conference referred this knotty matter to a special commission headed by Sir Henry Willink. Its tour of the country was naturally the time for the most vocal outcry of minority groups, and in a sense the whole problem became for a time wildly exaggerated, because of the implicit opportunity the Commission gave to the voicing of all sorts of grievances.

However the Minorities Commission came out very strongly against the creation of new states, because it felt that the fears and problems of minority groups could be better solved within the existing political framework.[10] In each case the Commission found that the cores of the minority movements were too small compared with the area which they claimed for their new state. For instance, they argued that in the West, while most Bini wanted a Mid-West State, by no means all Itsekiri and Ijo felt happy at the prospect of its creation.

Yet the Commission admitted that minority fears of ethnic domination and discrimination in development were real, and proposed that minority areas be set up for both Calabar and the Mid-West. These areas would have special councils, which could keep a watch on regional government activities and could also exercise delegated executive authority. For the Ijo areas of the Niger Delta the Commission recommended the establishment of a special development board on which the regional governments concerned and the Federal government would be represented. However whilst the Commission gave no truck to the creation of a Middle Belt state in the North, it did recommend that a plebiscite be held there to determine whether Ilorin and Kabba wished to remain in the North or join up with the Western Region.

Otherwise the Commission felt that minority fears could be assuaged by the entrenchment of fundamental human rights in the constitution, and by making any amendment to the constitution impossible without the virtual consent of the whole country and in particular the people most intimately affected. Finally, it insisted that the police should remain national rather than be regionalized as the N.P.C. and Action Group had requested.

At the 1958 conference the parties agreed with some reluctance to the acceptance of the minorities report. The Action Group was particularly anxious about the inclusion of the Ilorin and Kabba in the Western Region, and therefore the implementation of the plebiscite recommended by the Commission, but the North, which had agreed to take self-government on 15th March 1959, made it clear that it might be at the price of independence that this point be insisted upon. On the other hand both the Action Group and the N.P.C. had to compromise over the subject of the police. Both had wanted the regionalization of the police, but the N.C.N.C. and the British Government, agreeing for once, saw in the regionalization of the police a danger to political independence, particularly of minorities.

The agreement over the minorities report was, of course, largely influenced by the fact that none of the parties cared to stand out on the issue for fear of being branded as the one that held up independence. The problem still remained and will colour Nigerian politics for some years to come. In retrospect it might seem that the Commission dodged the issue, especially since it was widely known that the British Government would consider the creation of new states as instrumental in delaying the date for independence. But the lines on which the Commission was thinking were made clear by one of its members,

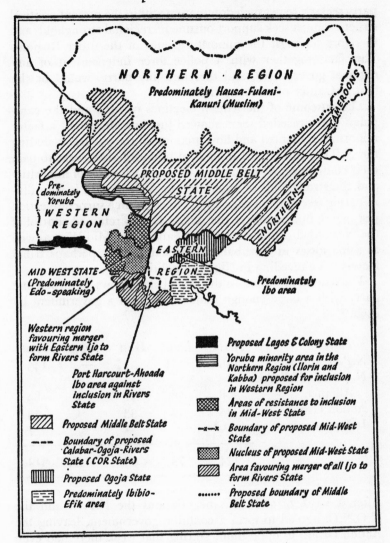

9. The various proposed political reorganizations of Nigeria, 1945–60

Mr. Philip Mason, in a series of articles in *West Africa*.[11] He argued that hopes of the continued unity of Nigeria and justice for individuals must rest initially on the grounds that none of the three major parties could dominate the other and that any party seeking to get such domination within the present political structure must seek support outside its regional stronghold, and therefore amongst the minority groups of the other Regions. This fact, together with a police force independent of any regional government, and therefore any party, would be the best guarantee of minority rights.

The outcome of the federal elections of 1959 and the campaign that preceded them showed just how dominant a factor minorities remained and how anxious all the parties, including the N.P.C. with regard to its own minority area, were to gain their confidence. A comparison of the distribution of minorities and the strongholds of opposition in each Region is very illuminating (see map on page 297). However, in a surprise election just before independence the Action Group retained control of the West, having made significant gains in the Mid-West as well as some losses in Yorubaland, indicating that perhaps tribal factors were receding in Nigerian politics.

The federal elections, as the table below shows, returned one party with a large enough majority to form a government by itself.[12]

Party	North	East	West	Lagos	Total
N.P.C. and allies	135	1†	7‡	—	143
N.C.N.C./N.E.P.U. Alliance	8	58	21	2	89
Action Group	25	14	33	1	73
Independents	6*	—	1	—	7
	174	73	62	3	312

After a week of strenuous negotiations the N.P.C. and the N.C.N.C. agreed to form a coalition government, leaving the Action Group in opposition. During that week there had even been talk of an Action Group—N.C.N.C. alliance, which would have led to the unhappy situation of confronting South and North as Government and Opposition.

* Declared subsequently for N.P.C.
† Niger Delta Congress.
‡ Mabolaje Grand Alliance.

Independence Achieved

Alhaji Abubakar Tafawa Balewa, who was knighted in the New Year Honours, became Prime Minister and Dr. Azikiwe, leader of the N.C.N.C., to the surprise of many, opted for the dignified but in itself politically uninfluential post of President of the newly formed Senate which has an equal number of Senators nominated by each regional government. There was considerable speculation as to whether Dr. Azikiwe would become Nigeria's first African Governor-General, or whether he was waiting for the post of Foreign Minister when Nigeria, on Independence, took over control of external affairs. As it turned out there were no major changes in the government on Independence and Dr. Azikiwe, on the 16th November 1960, became Governor-General of the independent federation.

The rapid political developments that took place in the years from 1945–60 were paralleled by similar developments in the social and economic spheres. The social and economic changes of this period were of the same order as those experienced in the years 1906–12, prior to the amalgamation of Northern and Southern Nigeria. The period between the two world wars by contrast had been one of consolidation of changes already made rather than one of innovation. This was largely dictated by the fact that government revenue was barely sufficient to cover the cost of the general administration of the country. Indeed during the thirties, when world prices for Nigeria's agricultural exports fell to a disastrously low level, cuts in government services had to be made since the funds from which these were paid were in large part derived from duties on exports, and on the imports which the earnings from these exports allowed the country to buy. Yet this is not to minimize the importance of these years in the history of Nigeria, for it was during this period that the nationalistic movement grew up and the future leaders of Nigeria received their education. More important still, during these years was laid the basis of the social and economic transformation of the country that enabled the nationalists to convince Britain in the fifties that they were ready for a self-government which the latter had only envisaged as taking place some time in a distant but unspecified future.

The stimulus for the rapid changes that took place between 1945 and 1960 was Nigeria's involvement in the Second World War. Just as the war had opened up new political horizons for the country, so it provided impetus for economic and social development. Most important of all was the new role assumed by the government in the direction of the country's economy. Hitherto the government had been largely a passive agent in the economic affairs of the country, being guided by the principles of laissez-faire. The economic exploitation of the country was almost entirely in the hands of large import-export companies, in particular the United Africa Company, and the government's main concern was to ensure that the interests of the indigenous population were safeguarded, as in the days when Lord Leverhulme had tried to introduce plantations into the country. Now, in time of war, the colonial administration had to ensure that the Metropolitan government was supplied with as much of the foodstuffs and raw materials produced by the country as possible, and that these should be at low prices. Thus price-controls and wage-ceilings were introduced and the government assumed responsibility for the export of most of Nigeria's agricultural products. Many of these measures hurt indigenous interests[13] but the fact of the government's active participation in the direction of the economy was to be of utmost importance for the post-war years. The government came increasingly to accept that it bore responsibility not only for the regulation of the national economy, but also for its stimulation.

The increased demand for Nigerian raw materials by the allies and the use of Nigeria as a staging-ground in the war effort had an immense economic impact on the country. Exports in the war years more than doubled in value from £10,300,000 to £24,000,000.[14] Associated with this dramatic increase in production was the rapid growth of urban centres like Enugu, Lagos, Kano and Port Harcourt. As far as future economic development was concerned one of the most important effects of the war was the release from military service of a large number of Nigerians who had learned special trades or skills.[15]

The economic expansion resulting from the war continued into the post-war period, not only because of the rising world demand for Nigeria's raw materials, but also because international concern with the morality of colonialism was forcing most colonial powers to pay more attention to the economic development of their colonies for the benefit of their indigenous inhabitants. Thus Britain, who had for long maintained as a cardinal point of colonial policy that her colonies should pay for their own services and provide their own development funds, now accepted, as we have seen, part of the cost of their economic and social development on to her metropolitan budget. In addition to the development funds received from Britain, the Nigerian administration was receiving increasing revenues from duties on imports and exports and thus had at its disposal for the first time the wherewithal to transform Nigeria from the 'colonial backwater' it had been in the thirties into a rapidly modernizing state able to take its place among the independent nations of the world. Yet in 1945 neither the nationalist leaders, who constantly demanded that the administration provide their people with the same services they provided the expatriates in their European reservations, nor the British Government, more conscious of the need for social reform in the colonies now that it was under Labour control, could have envisaged that by 1960 all children of school age in Southern Nigeria would enjoy primary education, free in the Western Region and at a nominal charge in the Eastern Region.

The extent of the economic revolution that took place in the post-war period is brought out in the table below.[16]

Item	1947	1953	1958
Revenue of Governments (£thousands)	£14,193	£51,110	£81,288
Currency in circulation (£thousands)	£23,429	£51,365	£55,118
Bank deposits (£thousands)	£13,697	£31,238	£58,118
Exports (£thousands)	£44,314	£124,232	£135,690
Imports (£thousands)	£32,636	£108,290	£167,074
Railway freight tons (miles—1,000)	571,000	827,000	1,232,000
Cement imports and local manufacture (tons)	107,306	297,436	573,119

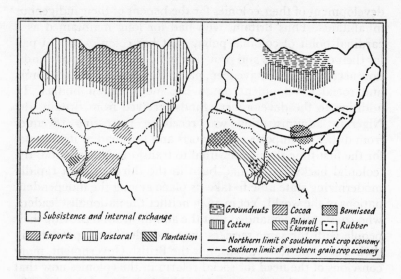

Subsistence and internal exchange
Exports   Pastoral   Plantation

Groundnuts   Cocoa   Benniseed
Cotton   Palm oil E.kernels   Rubber
Northern limit of southern root crop economy
Southern limit of northern grain crop economy

10. **Nigeria's economy in 1960**

The basis of the post-war economic revolution was agriculture, which on the eve of independence still accounted for over 85 per cent of the country's exports.[17] This was the result not so much of the increase in agricultural production, which was considerable, but of the rise in world prices for the export crops produced by Nigeria. Until 1953 this rise was continuous. The balance of Nigeria's exports was accounted for mainly by tin and columbite mined on the Jos plateau. Fortunately for the country as a whole the variety of primary products was sufficiently diverse to avoid the worst effects of the vagaries of the world market, especially after 1953. However the Northern and Eastern regions, which during this period still depended largely on one export crop, were more vulnerable than the West, which was producing palm-oil, rubber, cocoa and timber for export. On average in the years 1956–8 groundnuts, coming exclusively from the North, earned some £30 million a year; palm products from the East and West £33 million; cotton and linters, mainly from the North, £8 million; cocoa from the West, £25 million; and rubber from the West, mainly from the area that is now the Mid-West State, but with some from the East, £7 million.[18]

All crops were bought up by the Statutory Marketing Board established in the immediate post-war years to ensure price stabilization. At the opening of the season, the Marketing Boards fixed the price for purchase of the crop for which they were responsible. If the world price fell below this price, then reserved funds accumulated in favourable years were used to buttress this up. Fortunately up till 1953 prices for all Nigeria's export crop rose steadily so that the Boards were able to accumulate substantial reserves for this purpose. The Marketing Boards so established were: the Nigerian Cocoa Marketing Board (1947), the Nigerian Groundnut Marketing Board (1949), the Nigerian Oil Palm Produce Marketing Board (1949) and the Nigerian Cotton Marketing Board. In the year 1954 these Boards, organized on a national basis and responsible each for the purchase and export of one crop, were dissolved and replaced by Regional Marketing Boards. Under the 1954 constitution agriculture became a regional concern, so that the purchase of agricultural produce had to be reorganized on a regional basis. The assets of the national Marketing Boards were divided among the new regional Marketing Boards, which were responsible for the marketing of all export crops produced within their Regions. However since export was a federal concern under the new constitution, a Central Produce Marketing Board was established to export the crops purchased by the Regional Marketing Boards through their licensed agents.[19]

The large reserves built up by these Boards permitted the Nigerian-dominated governments of the Regions formed in the five years before independence to indulge in a spate of investment spending that left imports exceeding exports by £31 million in 1958, that is only £2 million less than the total value of imports alone in 1947. Thus in the decade before independence imports quadrupled in value, whilst exports only little more than doubled, and remained almost constant in the second five years, a fact that was already giving economists cause for concern before independence.

This expansion in agricultural production was not associated with a significant growth in industry, though industrial centres were created in Lagos, Ikeja, Ibadan, Kano, Kaduna, Aba and Port Harcourt. Before independence the only heavy industries were coal-mining in the East and two major cement works, one in the East and one in the West. Light industry included cigarette factories, breweries, a large textile mill in Kaduna, a huge plywood factory in Sapele and cotton ginneries in the North. Nevertheless in the years before independence the Federal and the Regional Governments were giving top priority to industrial expansion in their development programmes, anxious one day to free Nigeria from her excessive dependence on agriculture for her export income. One of the main hopes in this direction was the exploitation of large oil reserves in the Niger Delta. By 1960, Shell-B.P. had spent something in the range of £60 million on the search for oil and Nigeria was already beginning to export small quantities of crude oil.

Because of the importance of foreign exchange to Nigeria, there is a tendency to think of imports and exports as the sole gauge of her economic well-being. But in the post-war years there was also a remarkable expansion of her internal exchange economy. For instance Nigeria's national income in 1956–7 was estimated at just over £800 million, of which export crops accounted for only £84·4 million, whilst locally consumed foodstuffs were valued at £342·6 million.[20] Revenue from duties on export crops in 1957 brought in over 10 per cent of the total revenue earned by the Federal and Regional Governments.

National income itself rose in the years 1950–1 from an estimated £593·4 million to £812·3 million in 1956–7. Taking into account the different methods used for these two National Income Surveys, and the rise of prices in the intervening years, the increase in National Income probably amounted to about £150 million, that is a growth of not less than 4 per cent a year. Per capita income was estimated at between £25 and £29 per year for 1956–7.[21]

As a result of this rapid economic expansion more and more Nigerians were drawn into participation in the new money economy. This was facilitated by the extension of the country's road system, particularly those roads that gave access to parts of the country far distant from either the railway, which still remained the main artery of the export trade, or from the rivers Niger and Benue, on which a substantial part of Nigeria's trade was carried in the flood seasons. Some idea of the importance of the expansion of the road system is gained by a comparison of the mileages of road in Nigeria in 1946 and 1958. In the former year there were only 25,000 miles of road, with only 700 miles bitumenized. By the latter year 16,000 more miles had been added of which well over 3,000 were bitumenized. Many of these roads led into parts of the country that had only been marginally affected by colonial occupation.[22] Communications were further facilitated by the development of the internal airlines and the great improvement of the posts and telecommunications system.

This new level of economic activity led to a great increase in employment opportunities. Since expatriate workers were extremely expensive to bring out to Nigeria, both the government and the commercial houses looked to educated Nigerians to fill these positions. But since educational opportunities for Africans, particularly at the secondary and university level, had been severely limited before the war, it was difficult to find Nigerians with the appropriate qualifications for these new jobs. Thus the government undertook a great expansion of educational facilities, particularly at the secondary level, and in 1948 the University College of Ibadan was established. At the same time scholarships were provided both by the government and commercial firms for Nigerians to study abroad. Usually Nigerians sent on these scholarships were bonded to work for their sponsors when their training was completed.

Despite this expansion of educational facilities, in 1955 Nigeria was only educating 800 undergraduates and 12,000 secondary school students a year,[23] and most of these came from Southern Nigeria. The need for more clerks, technicians, administrators and professionally qualified men like doctors and engineers, for employment both in government service and in commerce, was a constant problem in the post-war years and severely hampered the execution of governmental development plans. In its expansion of educational opportunities, the government was submitted to great pressure by the nationalists who thought of education as a panacea for most of their country's ills. These nationalists, once they began to assume control of government policy, determined to ensure that there would be places in schools for all Nigerian children. Thus in the West, which in 1957 introduced Universal and Compulsory Free

Primary Education, almost 50 per cent of the current budget is devoted to education. This concern with mass education has inevitably reduced the amount of funds available for higher education, so much more expensive to provide. It has also led to two major problems of the post-independence period, problems that were already manifest before independence. First was the problem of replacing the British civil servants, who, despite the Federal and Regional Governments' declared policy of rapid Nigerianization,[24] in 1956 still occupied most of the technical positions in the government services. In that same year the Colonial Secretary, foreseeing the dangers of a mass exodus of British officials without sufficient Nigerians qualified to replace them, proposed a scheme whereby expatriate civil servants were guaranteed their pension rights by the British Government and alternative employment overseas or in the United Kingdom if they should become redundant. Alternatively they could take their earned pension and a lump-sum compensation reaching a maximum of £10,000 according to service. Unfortunately large numbers of them opted for the second, and in 1958 a new scheme was introduced whereby they could draw 90 per cent of their lump-sum compensation in advance of their retirement as long as they agreed to give one year's notice. Nevertheless, large numbers of British civil servants left the country before independence.

The problem was further exacerbated by the fact that commercial houses, also under political pressure to Nigerianize their managerial staff, were anxious to secure the services of qualified Nigerians. And with the expansion of the economy, the number of posts to be filled was continuously increasing.

Lack of trained manpower was paralleled by an excess in supply of elementary school-leavers, possessing only a Standard VI school leaving certificate. Since the standard of education in many primary schools was poor because of the lack of qualified teachers, these Standard VI certificates often meant that the possessor could read and write but only had a very rudimentary knowledge of the other subjects he had been taught, and was therefore not employable in clerical posts, even if these posts were available. The problem was becoming acute in the years immediately prior to independence when the first products of the universal primary education schemes in the West and East were coming on to the employment market. In 1959, the Ashby report estimated that just over 650,000 children entered primary schools,[25] and in the year of independence 180,000 children left school in Western Nigeria alone.[26] The problem would not have been grave if the primary school-leavers had been prepared to work on the farms as their fathers did. But they preferred to seek their fortunes in the towns where they could use their education to secure jobs as junior clerks, messengers or shop assistants. Thus a single advertisement for the post of messenger could attract upward of five thousand applicants. The problem was partly the result of an education system that was producing children with an elementary education at such a rate that not even the most booming economy in Africa could supply them with the jobs they sought and partly the result of an education system that did nothing to prepare them for a return to the farms where they might use newly acquired knowledge to improve a system of farming which otherwise seemed to them to hold no future. By independence an expert on the problem of school-leavers could write: 'No social and economic problem in Nigeria is so urgent as that of finding employment for the ever-increasing number of school-leavers.'[27]

Thus on the achievement of independence Nigeria was faced with the paradoxical situation that her rapid but uneven expansion of educational facilities had confronted her with two problems: on the one hand the governments had to decide what to do with the vast number of unemployed school-leavers, and on the other they had quickly to provide the higher level manpower—administrators, professional personnel, technicians, teachers, officers in the police and army and the judicial services—which had previously been supplied by the colonial power and without which they could not prosecute their ambitious development schemes.[28] To consider the latter problem the Ashby Commission on Higher Education was appointed in 1959 submitting its report in 1960,[29] in which it advocated an expansion of educational facilities at the secondary, technical and university level that would cost the Federal, and Regional Governments nearly 50 per cent of their recurrent budgets. Furthermore it insisted not only that the present primary educational system be maintained in the South, but that primary education be extended in the North, so that in fact there would result an even greater output of primary school-leavers seeking jobs that did not exist.

This improvement of educational facilities was accompanied by the important if less spectacular extension of other social services. Hospital places more than doubled in the post-war period. A teaching hospital was established at Ibadan, the most advanced in tropical Africa. It even had departments for the training of psychiatric and medical social workers. Water supplies were improved in rural areas as well as towns. In Lagos substantial, if not altogether successful, urban redevelopment was undertaken. This concern with the provision of social services was heightened with the accession of Nigerians to ministerial posts in the Central and Regional Governments after 1951. Now was their opportunity to provide their people with those facilities which they had accused the British of reserving for the expatriate, even though the funds for them were provided by the Nigerian taxpayer.

The second major problem associated with the expansion of the economy in the post-war period was the rapid and often uncontrolled growth of the major urban centres. The problems of uncontrolled growth were most acute in Lagos,[30] but to a greater or lesser extent they were present in Port Harcourt, Enugu, Onitsha, Benin, Ibadan, and Kano. The growth in the population of the towns had been greatly stimulated by the influx of primary school-leavers in search of work. The most pressing problem became the provision of housing for the immigrants. People arrived at a rate faster than houses could be built to accommodate them. In these circumstances there was an open market for speculators who could build sub-standard houses for which they could charge vastly inflated rents. This increase in urban population led to a great strain on municipal services such as water supplies, drainage, and garbage collection, services which often could not be provided on an adequate scale without vast outlays of capital that even large municipalities like Lagos did not have at their disposal. Even a national service such as the Electricity Corporation of Nigeria was hard pressed to ensure a constant supply of electricity for domestic and industrial purposes in some of the major cities. The growth of the population of the major towns and the increase in the number of motor-cars showed how inadequate was the planning of cities that were either pre-colonial in origin or designed by the British in the days when the motor-car was a luxury not enjoyed in Nigeria and horses and bicycles were the common form of transport for the colonial administrator.

It was in these urban centres that the loosening of the traditional bonds which held Nigerian societies together became most acute. This weakening of former ties in no way implied a breakdown in traditional society. For even in the urban centres, where the image of the melting-pot seems most appropriate, traditional ties have proved very resilient. The so-called tribal unions, bringing together people from the same ethnic group, or from the same town or village, remained one of the most important forms of social contact in the cities.[31] They linked the expatriated urban dweller with his people at home and exercised considerable traditional discipline over him, as Chinua Achebe has shown so clearly in his novel *No Longer at Ease*.[32] Even credit unions in the towns were organized on an ethnic basis. It was difficult for the Nigerian in towns to obtain credit from banks or from people other than his own ethnic group, since it was only his own ethnic group that could provide the social controls that would ensure that he would repay money borrowed. Though the immigrant to the towns would meet girls from other ethnic groups, he would rarely marry them. Inter-ethnic marriages were unusual except among the new élite. Yet the towns, particularly those that were important economic centres or seats of government, served as the focus for many new contacts and especially the formation of non-ethnic associations. Though traditional allegiances did not break down, but rather were transformed to meet the new situations presented by town life as exemplified in the credit unions, the immigrants found many new ties of loyalty that cut across ethnic barriers. The most obvious of these were membership in trade unions, sporting associations, literary and debating societies, old boy's clubs and political parties that were not organized on a tribal basis. Apart from membership of a political party, probably the most important cross-ethnic organizations in the towns were those sponsored by the universalist religions.

The two universalist religions, Christianity and Islam, made their greatest progress in the urban centres, particularly those of the South. They also made great headway in the rural areas.

In the East, Christianity remained unchallenged by Islam, whilst the converse was true of the far North. In the Middle Belt and the Western Region, Islam overtook Christianity despite the earlier initiative of the latter religion in much of this area. Islam was particularly successful in Yorubaland,[33] where Christian missions had been active since the middle of the nineteenth century. Islam of course had the great advantage of not being identified with the colonial power and also of being an almost exclusively African controlled religion.[34] Furthermore Islam in West Africa has generally been tolerant of the traditional beliefs and customs of the peoples it converted whereas the Christian missionaries insisted on a complete abandonment of traditional customs even where these were only remotely connected with traditional religion. Although the Anglican Church in Nigeria initially had as its ambition the creation of an African-run Church and had to this end appointed an African, Samuel Ajayi Crowther, as Bishop in 1864, it abandoned this policy in 1890 for one of a missionary church in which leadership would be in the hands of missionary clergy and Africans would only act as their assistants. This latter policy was until very recent years pursued by all the other major Christian churches in Nigeria, notably the Roman Catholics, the Methodists and the Baptists.

Reaction to the abandonment of the so-called 'native church' policy by the Church Missionary Society was swift. In the 1890's a large number of Anglicans broke with the parent church to form an African Church in which they would be governed by their own bishops. Their quarrel with the Church Missionary Society was not only political but also doctrinal, since many Africans felt that the rules and conduct of the Church should be adapted to the realities of Africa. Thus they argued for group baptism, tolerance of polygamy, particularly on the part of first generation converts who had already contracted polygamous marriages, or the use of traditional African music and dance in services. As J. Bertin Webster has shown in his study of the African Churches in Yorubaland, in its resentment of alien control and its quest for a church suited to the local situation, the African Church Movement was a precursor of the nationalist movement.[35] The African churches are still strong, accounting for a large number of Nigerian

Christians, for it was not until the post-war period that the Christian Churches of foreign origin began to Africanize their leadership. Another important development in the Christian Church in Nigeria during the colonial period was the growth of syncretistic churches, notably the *alladura*, which sought to combine elements of traditional religion with those of Christianity.

By independence such was the success of the two universalist religions that nearly two-thirds of the population, then estimated at 36 million, were either Muslim or Christian. Such an estimate is, however, a little misleading for in many cases Islam and Christianity were but a veneer. Indeed traditional religion at least in the rural areas remains remarkably virile. Indigenous religions have of course been at a disadvantage because with rare exceptions none of them are missionary religions and are confined to one particular ethnic group. Their strength depends on regular access to their shrines and priests, so that the emigrant is usually cut off from the life-blood of his religion. An obvious exception to this generalization is the Yoruba religion which has not only survived in the New World among former Yoruba slaves, but has even gained adherents. A Yoruba 'Temple' was recently opened in New York.

The new Nigerian élite is composed almost entirely of adherents of these two universalist religions. This is not surprising given the historic role of Islam in the North and the fact that in the South most education was provided through the missions. For instance in the East primary education is largely in the hands of the Roman Catholic and Anglican churches. This élite has been variously defined,[36] but can for our purposes best be characterized as the group of Nigerians who have taken over the 'Senior service' jobs in government, commerce and industry, that is those posts hitherto reserved exclusively for Europeans, or their equivalents in earning power. Thus of course lawyers would be included in this group, though the law, like the medical profession, was not reserved exclusively to Europeans; so too would the trader or shopkeeper who has established himself independently of the European firms, and yet earned enough to live at the same level as the Nigerian now filling positions formerly held by Europeans.

The emergence of the élite was one of the most dramatic post-war phenomena and was the result not only of the programme of Africanization carried on after 1950, but also of the expansion of educational opportunities. This élite is characterized too by the fact that its earning power is the same as that of its European predecessor, and far above that of the average Nigerian, whether urban worker or peasant farmer.

To begin with this élite tended to accept British cultural norms as the desired ones. There was nothing very unusual about this since the majority of the élite had gained their education in Britain and even when they had obtained higher education in Nigeria the history they learnt was British, the books they read were by English authors. However in the years before independence there was increasing demand for a return to African cultural values. Thus African history was introduced to the curriculum in the University College of Ibadan, the Nigerian Museum was founded, the Nigerian Society for the Promotion of Art and Culture was formed. Fortunately this awakening interest in African as distinct from European culture was paralleled by the emergence of a group of young Nigerian artists and writers who, as recent years have proved, were the precursors of the most virile modern culture in Tropical Africa. Nigeria's most striking achievements have been in the field of creative writing, with poets like Wole Soyinka and J. P. Clark, and novelists like Chinua Achebe, and Cyprian Ekwensi already establishing their reputations before independence. In the field of painting and culture Ben Ewonwu had a long-standing reputation rivalled only by that of the sculptor Felix Idubor. But the really exciting work was coming from a group of young painters, the most notable of whom were Demas Nwoko, Y. Grillo and Jimo Akolo.[37]

The most striking development of all in the post-war years was the rapid politicization of the masses. It is one thing to grant people the vote in what was then still a largely illiterate society, quite another to get them to the polls. Yet in the 1959 Federal Election, as K. J. W. Post shows in the study he made of it, a remarkably high proportion of those eligible to vote actually went to the polls. In some constituencies voting was over 90 per cent of those eligible.[38]

This politicization came about as a result of a number of factors, the most obvious of which were the increased activity and sophistication of the political parties. Education clearly helped.

So too did the radio, which, though politically neutral, informed an increasingly large number of people about the political situation in their country. A similar role was played by the press whether it was identified with a party like *The West African Pilot* or *The Daily Service* (now *The Daily Express*), or independent like *The Daily Times*. Though circulation figures for these papers were comparatively small before independence, each copy was read by a large number of people and its contents conveyed by word of mouth to many more who were illiterate.

Another important factor in the politicization of the masses was the democratization of local government. Thus under the local government law of 1950 the Eastern Region established a system of local government similar to that of Britain, though this was subsequently considerably modified. County Councils, for instance, were abolished and District Officers were given greatly increased powers. In the West the local government law of 1953, whilst it retained traditional members on the councils, introduced effective elected majorities. In the North the Native Authority Ordinance of 1952 abolished the status of sole native authority enjoyed by some Emirs, and in 1954 an amendment authorized the Governor to include a certain number of elected members on the councils, though these have not yet attained very much power on the councils. The development of local government in Nigeria was one of the most interesting features of the post-war years, particularly as there was an increasing devolvement of authority to them, especially in the field of development. Thus the Kano Native Authority, with an annual budget of over £1 million in this period, was responsible for a large number of development programmes. However early optimism about the course of local government in the post-war years has not been justified by events subsequent to independence, with regional governments finding it necessary to withdraw powers from local authorities and to increase supervision of their activities. Many councils have been suspended. Nevertheless elections for local government authorities provided important training for participation in the political process.

The Federation of Nigeria, which became independent on 1st October 1960, was thus a country of great diversity and complexity. The long negotiations over the form independence should take, whilst they clearly exacerbated traditional antagonisms, seemed to indicate to outside observers that the foundations of independent Nigeria were as solidly built as those of any independent African state. Peoples of various groups had been brought into close contact with one another, learnt about common factors as well as differences, begun to think of themselves as Nigerians rather than Hausa, Ibo or Yoruba. Frustrating years of constitutional negotiation and the consequent delay of independence seemed to have had their reward in the formulation of a constitution freely negotiated by Nigerians themselves, and one which up to 1965 seemed, for all its limitations, to have been able, in apparently insoluble crises, to contain the various differences and tensions in the country. As one newspaper put it in 1965 Nigerians seemed to have perfected the art of walking to the brink without falling in. The high hopes that Nigeria, with a population larger than that of the rest of Western and Equatorial Africa put together, would prove a model experiment in African Unity were dashed in 1966. The military *coup d'état* of January 1966 at first looked as though it might put an end to the corruption of the civilian régime and the ethnic tensions which the politicians had fired in order to maintain themselves in power. Alas, within less than six months of power the military régime of Major-General J. T. Aguyi-Ironsi appeared to the northerners in particular to be entrenching one ethnic group in control of the country's destiny: that of the Ibo, of which General Ironsi was a member. The result was the bloody massacre in northern cities of Ibos and other southerners in May and September 1966 which led to a mass exodus to the south of Ibos and many other southern groups. Just as the Ibo leaders of the *coup* had murdered the northern Federal Prime Minister, the Premier of the Northern Region and his political ally the Premier of the Western Region, so in turn northern soldiers assassinated General Ironsi. From then on, despite the protracted efforts of General Ironsi's successor, Colonel (later General) Yakubu Gowon, to hold the country together, the Ibo-dominated Eastern Region seceded from the Federation in May 1967 under the leadership of Colonel Odumegwu Ojukwu, its military governor. Ojukwu declared the Eastern Region the independent republic of Biafra and in July 1967 the armies of the Federation marched on 'Biafra' to put an end to secession.

Independence Achieved

At that time pessimists foresaw the complete break-up of Nigeria. Indeed it looked as though ethnic identity would prevail as a basis for political allegiance. The belief of General Gowon and his military and civilian supporters that the common elements of the past of the various groups of Nigeria and the shared experience of colonial rule were sufficient basis for the survival of Nigeria as a unity was justified by the collapse of Biafra in January 1970 and the successful reintegration of the dissident Ibo in the Federation. While the day when real national unity is achieved may still be far off, the fact that Nigeria survived a bloody civil war in which foreign powers fished to their own advantage with little consideration for the interests of those who were fighting it, has justified those like General Gowon who never lost faith in their belief that in the last analysis *Nigeria* means more to her inhabitants than their former ethnic designations. And though it is too early to write the history of the turbulent decade since independence, perhaps nothing is more indicative of the primacy of Nigeria as a concept than the fact that the erstwhile leaders of the Biafran secession, less than three years after the end of the civil war, are once again walking the corridors of power of the Federal Government of Nigeria.

Summary of Major Events from Independence to the Dissolution of the Federal Parliament in December 1964

1960

November 16th: Dr. Nnamdi Azikiwe, President of the Senate, sworn in as first Nigerian Governor-General and Commander-in-Chief of the Federation, in succession to Sir James Robertson.

December: Nigeria sends troops to help United Nations forces to maintain order in the newly independent Republic of the Congo (Léopoldville).

1961

January: Nigeria breaks off diplomatic relations with France as a result of France carrying out a second atomic test in the Sahara despite the objections of Nigeria and other African states.

February: Northern Cameroons, former U.N. Trust territory under British administration, votes in general plebiscite to join Nigeria, rather than the new Federal Republic of Cameroon.

'Lumumba Riots' in Lagos protest against the murder in prison in the Congo of Patrice Lumumba, first Prime Minister of the Congo (Léopoldville); the Lagos embassies of European countries accused of supporting Lumumba's murderers are damaged.

April: First motion for the creation of the Mid-West State passed in the Federal Parliament.

May: Inquiry ordered by the Federal Government into the affairs of the National Bank (Western Nigeria) is declared illegal by the Lagos High Court; Federal Parliament passes special Act establishing a Tribunal of Inquiry outside the control of the Law Courts.

Monrovia Conference: Nigeria represented by the Prime Minister at conference of moderate African states, called the 'Monrovia Powers', which were opposed to the more radical African states—the 'Casablanca Powers'; Nigeria emphasizes her belief in the moderate policies of the 'Monrovia States'.

August: Conference of all Nigerian Political Parties called by the Prime Minister condemns the Anglo-Nigerian Defence Agreement signed at independence and calls for its abolition; supports idea of political unity among African states; urges Nigeria to try to bring together Casablanca and Monrovia states.

September: Chief Awolowo, leader of the A.G. opposition, demands end to Nigerian Defence pact.

The Peace Corps Incident: First group of American Peace Corps arrives in Nigeria. During their stay in Ibadan University, on 15th October, University undergraduates demonstrate against the Peace Corps as 'colonialists' and demand their immediate return. One member of the Peace Corps had sent home unfavourable descriptions of Nigeria resulting in general outcry against the Peace Corps idea in Nigeria.

October: Federal Supreme Court gives judgment that special Act of Federal Parliament setting up National Bank Inquiry Tribunal is unconstitutional; inquiry suspended indefinitely.

November: N.C.N.C. wins Eastern Region election with 106 seats. A.G. = 15; Dynamic Party = 5; Independents = 20.

Official ban, since 1956, on all Communist publications coming into Nigeria lifted by Federal Government.

December: Prime Minister visits the Republic of Guinea—a member of the Casablanca Group of states—thus beginning reconciliation between Monrovia and Casablanca states.

1962

January: N.C.N.C. Convention at Port Harcourt changes name of Party to 'National Council of Nigerian Citizens'.

Anglo-Nigerian Defence Agreement withdrawn by common consent of Nigeria and Britain.

Lagos Conference of Heads of African and Malagasy States; Charter of Organization of African and Malagasy States drawn up.

March: Six-Year National Development Plan (1962–8) approved by Federal Parliament; austerity measures, including reduction of Ministers' and Federal M.P.s' salaries by 10 per cent, announced by Prime Minister.

April: Western Nigeria Government begins court proceedings to prevent creation of Mid-West State which had by now been approved by all other Governments.

May: First population census in independent Nigeria takes place.

The Western Nigeria Emergency: Rift in A.G. between its Leader, Awolowo, and Deputy Leader and Premier of the Western Region, Chief S. L. Akintola, comes to a head. The Oni of Ife, Governor of the Western Region, asks Alhaji Adegbenro, a supporter of Awolowo, to form government in place of Akintola, who, the Governor insists, has lost his majority in the Western House. Disorder leading to violence in House on the two occasions when Adegbenro tries to present his new government for vote of confidence. Federal Government sends troops to Ibadan and declares state of emergency throughout the region May 29th.

31st May—Senator (Dr.) M. A. Majekodunmi, Federal Minister of Health, appointed sole Administrator of the West, with powers to detain or imprison for maximum of 5 years anyone endangering the peace of the Region; prominent A.G. and N.C.N.C. politicians in the West placed under restriction by the Administrator.

June: Commission of Enquiry set up under Justice G. B. A. Coker to examine the affairs of six Western Nigeria Statutory Corporations.

Independence to December 1964

July: Federal Supreme Court dismisses Western Government motion against the creation of the Mid-West State.

Federal Supreme Court rules that Western Governor's dismissal of Akintola from premiership is unlawful. Adegbenro (the claimant) appeals to the Judicial Committee of Privy Council in London.*

September: *The Treason Trials:* Chief Obafemi Awolowo and 29 others arrested and charged with conspiring to overthrow the Federal Government by force, i.e. 'treasonable felony'. Others arrested include Joseph Tarka, leader of the U.M.B.C., Chike Obi, leader of the Dynamic Party; Chief Anthony Enahoro, A.G. Vice-President, escapes to Ireland, while A.G. Secretary, A. Ikoku, escapes to Ghana.

October: The Action Group wins Lagos Municipal Elections and takes over control of Lagos Municipal Council from the N.C.N.C.

November: The Treason Trials open in Lagos. Federal Government requests British Government to arrest and repatriate Enahoro for trial in Nigeria.

December: *The Census Controversy:* Disagreement over alleged but unpublished results of the National Census; A.G. and N.C.N.C. demand debate in the Federal Parliament; Prime Minister undertakes to look into the matter.

1963

January 1st: *End of Western Nigerian State of Emergency* (*1st Jan.*); Akintola forms new Government by coalition between his new United Peoples Party (U.P.P.) and the Western N.C.N.C.

The Coker Commission Report: Commission of Inquiry under Justice Coker, publishes Report; it condemns Chief Awolowo's direction of the use of public funds; and recommends legal action to recover funds from those who were responsible for the Corporations.

February: Lagos Dock Strike for pay increase from 6 to 12 shillings a day.

* Under the Constitution, such appeals were made by permission of the Federal Supreme Court.

319

Owing to widespread doubts about their accuracy, Prime Minister does not issue official results of census, and decides on a new census.

March: The Moffet Commission of Enquiry's recommendations on the administration of Kano N.A. lead to the deposition of the Emir by the Northern Regional Government.

April: *The Enahoro Affair:* Long and heated controversy in British Parliament and in British and Nigerian Press over British Government's agreement to repatriate Chief Enahoro for trial in Nigeria, and the delays in sending him caused by legal actions in British courts.

29th April: Sir Abubakar, the Prime Minister, announces that Nigeria will become a Republic within the British Commonwealth on October 1st, 1963.

May: End of the Enahoro Affair—British Government sends back Enahoro to face trial in Lagos; trial date fixed.

Privy Council upholds Adegbenro's appointment against Federal Supreme Court's decision (see July 1962); Western House of Assembly passes retroactive law amending the Constitution, with effect from 1960, by removing the Governor's right to dismiss the Premier from office. Akintola remains Premier.

June 3rd: Federal Parliament nullifies Privy Council verdict and endorses action taken by Western House of Assembly.

July: Referendum among Mid-Westerners shows overwhelming support for the creation of the State; results were 579,077 in favour; 7,216 against.

All-Party Conference on a new constitution for the proposed Republic of Nigeria agrees on outline proposals, including one to abolish appeals to the Privy Council; makes tentative suggestions on introducing a 'Preventive Detention Act'.

August: Federal Parliament approves Bill, and Federal Government sets up Interim Administration of the Mid-West under Chief Dennis Osadebay as Administrator.

First World Championship Boxing Contest ever held in West Africa takes place at the Liberty Stadium (Ibadan); Dick Tiger of Nigeria beats Gene Fullmer of U.S.A. and retains his World Middleweight title.

September: Government announces that a fresh census will be held on 5th November 1963.

8th September: *Treason Trials:* Chief A. Enahoro convicted of 'treasonable felony' and jailed for 15 years.

11th September: Chief Awolowo and 18 others convicted of treasonable felony and illegally importing arms into Nigeria; Awolowo jailed for 10 years; others for varying terms of imprisonment.

Call for General Strike for higher wages made by Joint Action Committee of all Trades Unions; strike only avoided on eve of Republic Day, when Government agrees to appoint a Wages Commission of Inquiry.

October 1st: *Republic Day:* Nigeria becomes a Federal Republic within the Commonwealth. New Constitution announced with no major changes. Supreme Court Justice Adeyinka Morgan appointed to head Commission of Enquiry to make recommendations to Government on a national wages policy. The establishment of such a Commission had been one of the conditions made by the Joint Action Committee (J.A.C.) for calling off the general strike.

7th October: A new Party, the Mid-West Democratic Front (M.D.F.) formed to fight forthcoming elections in Mid-West. Allies itself with N.P.C. Leaders: Mr. James Otobo and Apostle Edokpolo.

12th October: African diplomats walk out of dinner attended by Portuguese envoy to Nigeria. Nigerian press demands his expulsion and begins long campaign of criticism against Foreign Minister Jaja Wachuku for his speech to U.N. General Assembly advocating retention of South Africa and Portugal in that organization so that they could answer to the world for their policies.

November 18th: University College, Ibadan, assumes full University status independent of the University of London. Sir Abubakar, the Prime Minister, installed as first Chancellor.

1964

January: N.E.P.U. and U.M.B.C., together with other Northern opposition parties, reported to be negotiating a united opposition party in the North.

8th–10th January: Attempts to introduce motion censuring Foreign Minister Wachuku in Federal House of Representatives fail.

February 4th: Results of Mid-West election held on 3rd February announced: N.C.N.C. = 53; M.D.F. = 11; Action Group (which had contested all seats) = Nil. Mr. Dennis Osadabey, leader of the N.C.N.C. who had been administrator of the Mid-West, becomes first premier.

Northern Progressive Front (N.P.F.) formed by N.E.P.U. and U.M.B.C. with Aminu Kano, leader of N.E.P.U., as President, and Joseph Tarka, leader of U.M.B.C., as Secretary.

24th February: Preliminary results of Population Census announced: Nigeria now has a population of over 55 million compared with 31 million (1952–3 Census). See September 1964 for final results.

Census results rejected by East and Mid-West but accepted by North and West.

March 10th: Nigerian National Democratic Party (N.N.D.P.) formed from Chief Akintola's U.P.P. and a faction of 14 members of the Western N.C.N.C. led by Chief Remi Fani-Kayode. Western House now composed of 52 N.N.D.P., 15 N.C.N.C. and 27 A.G.

April 4th: Nigerian troops leave for Tanganyika to assist Tanganyika government whose army had recently mutinied.

7th–15th April: President Leopold Sédar-Senghor pays State Visit to Nigeria. Delivers address in English to Ibadan University on 'Democracy and Socialism'.

May 15th: Federal Supreme Court discharges four of the seventeen men convicted by the Lagos High Court on charges of treasonable felony. Appeal of Chief Awolowo and others still pending.

18th May: Against background of mounting attacks on the Census results by N.C.N.C. leaders from East and Mid-West as well as by the Action Group, Eastern Region Solicitor-General takes out writ in supreme court to restrain the Federal Government from using the 1963 Census Figures. The fear of the N.C.N.C. is that these results will be used as basis of delimitation of constituencies for forthcoming Federal Election, thus giving a greater number of seats to the North than all the Southern regions combined.

30th May: Because of the tense political situation in the West resulting from the formation of the N.N.D.P. and from the controversy over the Census Results, leading Obas advise Dr. Okpara not to undertake his proposed tour of the region. Dr. Okpara refuses to change his plans and with the Acting Leader of the Action Group, Alhaji Dauda Adegbenro, conducts successful four-day tour. The presence of Adegbenro is taken as presage that the much rumoured N.C.N.C.–A.G. alliance will soon be consolidated.

June 1st: Nationwide strike called by Joint Action Committee (J.A.C.) of the Nigerian trade unions because of delay of government in acting on the recommendations of the Morgan Commission that substantial increases in basic wages be given to workers.

2nd June: E.E.C. (European Economic Community) considers possibility of Nigeria becoming an Associated Member of the Common Market.

3rd June: N.C.N.C. and A.G. announce they will enter into alliance.

Government White Paper rejects Morgan Commission's proposed increases in wages as economically prohibitive and proposes lower scale of increases which J.A.C. rejects. Examples of Morgan and Government proposed increases:

Lagos (highest wage area) Morgan = £12; Government = £9 2s. 6d. per month.

North: Kabba area (lowest wage area) Morgan = £6 10s.; Government = £4 15s. per month.

8th June: Federal Minister of Labour declares that government workers who stay out on strike will be 'dismissed with loss of all privileges'. Private Enterprise follows suit. Workers stay out on strike.

13th June: J.A.C. agrees to call off strike with effect from June 15th on promise that government will negotiate with them on the basis of the Morgan recommendations and that no workers will be penalized.

17th June: Dr. Victor Allen, economist and labour expert from Leeds University, arrested and charged with plotting to overthrow Nigerian government with Nigerian trade union leaders. Houses of three leaders of J.A.C. subsequently searched. But only two leaders of small trade unions not on the J.A.C. are eventually arrested and charged on July 1st.

29th June: Eastern Region suit against the Federal Government concerning the legality of the 1963 Census dismissed by Federal Supreme Court.

Compromise reached between Government and J.A.C.: agreed new wage levels range from £10 high for Lagos to £5·15s. low for Kabba area per month.

July 1st: Chief Awolowo's appeal against his conviction by Lagos High Court on charges of treasonable felony dismissed by Federal Supreme Court along with those of eight other appellants. Three appellants were, however, discharged.

8th July: World Bank announces loan of £29 million for the Niger Dam.

Dr. Okpara announces that the N.C.N.C.–A.G. alliance will contest the Federal elections jointly.

11th July: It is announced the delimitation of constituencies for the Federal Election would be as follows: North = 167; East = 70; West = 57; Mid-West = 14; Lagos = 4.

15th July: N.P.F. announces that its constituent parties, N.E.P.U. and U.M.B.C. will present a single list of candidates for the Federal Elections in the North.

August 20th: Nigerian National Alliance formed by N.P.C., N.N.D.P., M.D.F. and N.D.C. (Niger Delta Congress) to contest forthcoming federal elections.

September: Final Census figures published:

North = 29,758,875 (1952–3 = 16·2 m.).

East = 12,394,462 (1952–3 = 7·2 m.).

West = 10,265,846 } (1952–3 = 6·1 m.).
Mid-West = 2,535,839

Lagos = 665,246 (1952–3 = 0·35 m.).

Total = 55,620,268 (1952–3 = 3·2 m. includes N. & S. Cameroons).

3rd September: Chief Ayo Rosiji and Chief A. M. A. Akinloye, both N.N.D.P. members of the Federal House of Representatives, are appointed Ministers without portfolio, the first members of their party to join the otherwise exclusively N.P.C.–N.C.N.C. coalition.

8th September: Legislation to tighten press laws in Lagos

introduced into Federal House. (Passed 189–22 on September 29th with considerable amendments.)

Italian loan for Niger Dam of $9 million announced. This completes the $42 million sought by Nigeria from overseas to help finance the $72 million project.

October: N.C.N.C., Action Group and N.P.F. (N.E.P.U. and U.M.B.C.) form United Progressive Grand Alliance (U.P.G.A.) to fight Federal Election.

Shell-B.P. predicts Nigeria's Crude Oil production for 1965 will be 6 million tons.

4th October: Meeting of Federal Prime Minister and four Regional Premiers to discuss forthcoming Federal Elections.

9th October: Eight-day long teacher strike called off on promise of establishment of National Joint Negotiation Council to consider their grievances.

22nd October: Dr. Victor Allen sentenced to two months imprisonment for attempting to jump bail.

23rd October: Two-day conference of major political parties reaches agreement on arrangements to ensure that forthcoming Federal Election will be fair.

Rioting and violence in Tiv division, which had occurred throughout the year, reached such a pitch that train services from the East to the North, passing through Tiv, were suspended.

November 10th: Dr. Allen sentenced to one-year's imprisonment with hard labour for conspiring to overthrow the government.

25th November: Federal Minister of Information T.O.S. Benson loses his party's nomination for his constituency in Lagos. Resigns from N.C.N.C.

30th November: Bornu railway extension opened by President Azikiwe.

December 8th: Parliament dissolved. Date for forthcoming Federal Election set for 30th December.

The crisis that ensued over the Federal Election, which brought Nigeria to the brink of disaster, can be seen in retrospect as having prepared the ground for the military *coups* of 15th January and 29th July 1966 which eventually led to

Nigeria's tragic civil war. The events immediately preceding the Election, the year of crisis that followed, and the history of the *coups* and the civil war are far too complex to summarize in the way the first four years of independence have been above. The tragedy of electoral fraud, inter-party fighting ending up in mass murder of opponents and destruction of their property, the assassination of Nigeria's political leaders, the elimination of a substantial portion of her military élite, communal massacres, the re-structuring of the state, secession and finally a bitter three-year civil war can *not* be reduced to a staccato series of dates of major events. So this summary must end here on the eve of six bitter years of crisis from which Nigeria, to the astonishment of the world, and indeed to many Nigerians themselves, emerged a stronger and much more united nation. It will be some time before these six years can be placed in the same historical perspective as the history of Nigeria before it gained its independence. There are, however, two books which give as balanced an account of the period as is possible to give at this time, though both of them required many pages to do it. Walter Schwarz in his *Nigeria* (London, 1968) covers the period from independence up to the secession of the Eastern Region at 2 a.m. on 30th May 1967 (pages 114–301), while John de St. Jorre gives as impartial an account of the civil war as at present possible in his *The Nigerian Civil War* (London, 1972, 391 pages of text). Other books that can be recommended as background to this period are:

Martin Dent, *The Military and Political Process in Nigeria, 1966–68*, London, 1973.

A. H. M. Kirk-Greene, *Crisis and Conflict in Nigeria: A Documentary Sourcebook, 1966–1970*, 2 vols., London, 1971.

Robin A. Luckham, *The Nigerian Military, 1960–1967: A Sociological Analysis of Authority and Revolt*, London, 1971.

John P. Mackintosh, *et al.*, *Nigerian Government and Politics*, London, 1966.

N. J. Miners, *The Nigerian Army 1955–1966*, London, 1971.

John Oyimbo, *Nigeria—Crisis and Beyond*, London, 1971.

S. K. Panter-Brick (ed.), *Nigerian Politics and Military Rule: Prelude to Civil War*, London, 1970.

Independence to December 1964

Michael A. Samuels (ed.), *The Nigeria-Biafra Conflict*, Washington, D.C., 1969.

Ralph Uwechue, *Reflection on the Nigerian Civil War* (revised edition), New York, 1971.

For passionately pro-Biafra accounts, samples are:

Frederick Forsyth, *The Biafra Story*, London, 1969.

Auberon Waugh and Suzanne Cronje, *Biafra: Britain's Shame*, London, 1969.

Samples of Nigerian equivalents of these are:

Robert G. Armstrong, *Nigeria: The Issues at Stake*, Ibadan, 1967.

S. O. O. Amali, *Ibos and their Fellow Nigerians*, Ibadan, 1967.

Robert Collis, *Nigeria in Conflict*, London, 1970.

The most balanced reporting on the civil war is to be found in *West Africa*, which kept a War Diary and in the *Financial Times*, particularly the reports and despatches of Bridget Bloom, formerly on the staff of *West Africa*.

John de St. Jorre has a very full list of Official Pamphlets relating to the war in his selected Bibliography.

Sources: *Africa Diary*
 Africa Digest
 Africa Report
 West Africa

APPENDIX B

Dynasty of the Shehus of Bornu*

SAIFAWA DYNASTY
Mai Dunama Lafiami
k. 1817. Maintained on the
Bornu throne as titular
ruler as was his successor
Ibrahim. The latter was
executed by Shehu Umar
following his complicity
in the Wadai invasion of
1846. His son Ali was
killed fighting the troops
of the Shehu at Minarge
bringing an end to
the 1,000-year rule
of the Saifawa Dynasty.
Shehu Umar then became
ruler in name as well as
in fact but retained the
title of Shehu or
Shaykh.

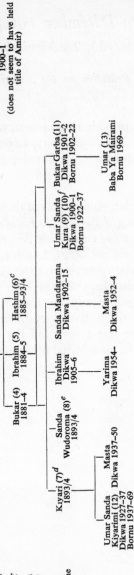

RABEH DYNASTY
Rabeh
1893–1900
(Conquers Bornu in 1893
and installs himself as Amir)

Fadl Allah
1900–1
(does not seem to have held
title of Amir)

Mohammed el-Amin al Kanemi (1)
d. 1837

Umar (2)
1837–81

Abd al-Rahman (3)[a]
1853–4

Abba Masta[b]

Bukar (4)
1881–4

Ibrahim (5)
1884–5

Hashim (6)[c]
1885–93/4

Kiyari (7)[d]
1893/4

Sanda
Wudoroma (8)[e]
1893/4

Ibrahim
Dikwa
1905–6

Sanda Mandarama
Dikwa 1902–15

Umar Sanda
Kura (9) (10)[f]
Dikwa 1900–1
Bornu 1922–37

Bukar Garba (11)
Dikwa 1901–2
Bornu 1902–22

Umar Sanda
Kiyarimi (12)
Dikwa 1927–37
Bornu 1937–69

Masta
Dikwa 1937–50

Yarima
Dikwa 1954–

Masta
Dikwa 1952–4

Umar (13)
Baba Ya Mairami
Bornu 1969–

Bukar
Dikwa 1950–2

a. Abd al-Rahman siezed the throne from his brother in 1853 but was overthrown within a year by Umar's supporters.
b. Abba Masta was chosen as Shehu but the decision of the electors was overruled by Ibrahim backed by the royal gunmen.
c. Hashim was killed on Abba Kiyari's orders following his attempt to come to terms with Rabeh.
d and e. Both Kiyari and his brother Sanda Wudoroma were captured and executed by Rabeh.
Umar Sanda Kura was appointed Shehu by the Foreau expedition in 1899 and deposed by the French authorities on his failure to produce an endemnity of $80,000. Bukar Garbai also failed to collect the endemnity and was enticed to British Bornu where he became the first Shehu thereafter. Until 1915 there were two Shehus, one in German Bornu at Dikwa and one in British Bornu. In recent years it has been customary to refer to the former as Emir of Dikwa.

* I am indebted to Mr. J. E. Lavers for making available to me this dynasty of the Shehus of Bornu in advance of the publication of his own work on Bornu in the nineteenth century.

APPENDIX C

The Sokoto Dynasty

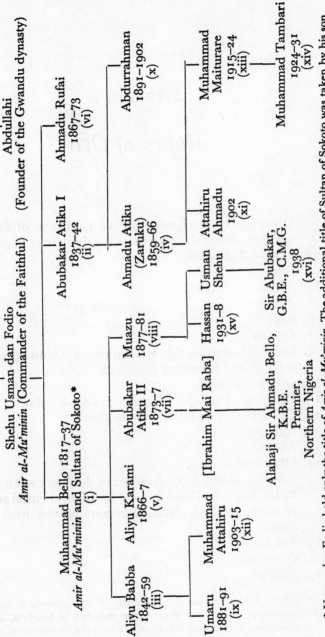

329

Shehu Usman dan Fodio
Amir al-Mu'minin (Commander of the Faithful)

Muhammad Bello 1817–37
Amir al-Mu'minin and Sultan of Sokoto*
(i)

Aliyu Karami 1866–7
(v)

Aliyu Babba 1842–59
(iii)

Umaru 1881–91
(ix)

Muhammad Attahiru 1903–15
(xii)

Abdullahi (Founder of the Gwandu dynasty)

Abubakar Atiku I 1837–42
(ii)

Ahmadu Atiku (Zaruku) 1859–66
(iv)

Ahmadu Rufai 1867–73
(vi)

Abubakar Atiku II 1873–7
(vii)

Muazu 1877–81
(viii)

Abdurrahman 1891–1902
(x)

Attahiru Ahmadu 1902
(xi)

[Ibrahim Mai Raba]

Hassan 1931–8
(xv)

Usman Shehu

Muhammad Maiturare 1915–24
(xiii)

Muhammad Tambari 1924–31
(xiv)

Alahaji Sir Ahmadu Bello, K.B.E., Premier, Northern Nigeria

Sir Abubakar, G.B.E., C.M.G., 1938
(xvi)

* Usman dan Fodio held only the title of *Amir al-Mu'minin*. The additional title of Sultan of Sokoto was taken by his son Bello and all his successors.

APPENDIX D

Alafins of Oyo[*]

1. Oranyan (Oranmiyan)—Son or Grandson of Oduduwa and Founder of the present ruling dynasty of Benin.
2. Ajaka—dethroned.
3. Sango.
4. Ajaka—reinstalled.
5. Aganju.
6. Kori.
7. Oluaso.
8. Onigbogi—conducted evacuation of Oyo-Ile, probably early sixteenth century (Smith).[†]
9. Ofiran (Ofinran).
10. Eguguojo (Egunoju)—founder of Oyo-Igboho.
11. Orompoto—possibly a woman (Smith).
12. Ajiboyede.
13. Abipa.
14. Obalokun, *c*. 1614.
    Oluodo—said to have drowned in the Niger when pursued by the Nupe. Not buried in the Bara [royal burial ground]? Name suppressed. Personal communication from Robert Smith.
15. Ajagbo.
16. Odarawu.
17. Kanran.

[*] This list is based on the list in Johnson, *op. cit.* Appendix B, pp. 669-70. Datings, where given, have their source recorded in brackets. There are several versions of this King list, none of which can be treated as definitive.

[†] Smith 'The Alafin in Exile, *op. cit.*

18. Jayin.
    Interregnum.
19. Ayibi.
20. Osiyago.
21. Ojigi, was reigning in the 1730's (Dalzel).
22. Gberu.
23. Amuniwaiye.
24. Onisile, ?–1754.
25. Labisi, 1754, reigned less than a year (Akinjogbin).†
27. Agbolouje, 1754 (Akinjogbin).
28. Majeogbe, 1754–1770 (Akinjogbin).
29. Abiodun, *c.* 1770–89 (Akinjogbin).
30. Aole (Awole), *c.* 1789–96 (Akinjogbin).
26. Awonbioju (Oduboye), reigned 130 days.
31. Adebo ⎱ *c.* 1796/7.*
32. Maku ⎰
    Interregnum, *c.* 1797–1802.*
33. Majotu, reigned in 1830 (Lander),‡ *c.* 1802–30–1.*
34. Amodo, *c.* 1830–1–*c.* 1833–4.*
35. Oluewu, *c.* 1833–4–*c.* 1835–6.*
36. Atiba, *c.* 1837–59 (Ajayi§). Founder of New Oyo.
37. Adelu, 1859–75.
38. Adeyemi, 1876–1905.
39. Lawani, 1905–11.
40. Ladigbolu I, 1911–44.
41. Adeniran, 1945–56 (deposed).
42. Ladigbolu II, 1956–69.
43. Lamidi Adeyemi II, 1971– . (For two years the Western
    State government and the Oyo kingmakers were in dispute
    as to who should succeed Ladigbolu II.)

† Akinjogbin 'Prelude to the Yoruba Civil Wars', *op. cit.* and *Dahomey and
its Neighbours 1708–1818*, London Ph.D. Thesis, 1963.
    * Law, R.C.C. 'The Chronology of the Yoruba Wars of the Early Nine-
teenth Century: A Reconsideration' *Journal of the Historical Society of Nigeria*,
V, 2, 1970.
    ‡ Lander cited in Ajayi and Smith, *op. cit.*, p. 9.
    § In Ajayi and Smith, *ibid.*

APPENDIX E

British Governors of Nigeria, 1900-1960

Colony of Lagos
Governor
1899-1904: Sir William Macgregor
1904-6: Sir Walter Egerton

Protectorate of Southern Nigeria
High Commissioner
1900-4: Sir Ralph Moor
1904-6: Sir Walter Egerton

Protectorate of Northern Nigeria
High Commissioner Governor
1900-7: Sir Frederick Lugard
1907-9: Sir Percy Girouard*
1909-12: Sir Hesketh Bell
1912-14: Sir Frederick Lugard

Colony and Protectorate of Southern Nigeria
Governor
1906-12: Sir Walter Egerton
1912-14: Sir Frederick Lugard

Colony and Protectorate of Nigeria
Governor-General
1914-19: Sir Frederick Lugard
Governor
1919-25: Sir Hugh Clifford
1925-31: Sir Graeme Thompson
1931-5: Sir Donald Cameron
1935-43: Sir Bernard Bourdillon
1943-8: Sir Arthur Richards
1948-54: Sir John Macpherson
Governor-General
1954: Sir John Macpherson
1954-60: Sir James Robertson

* Girouard's title was changed from High Commissioner to Governor in 1908.

National Ministries to 1960

1951 CONSTITUTION: COUNCIL OF MINISTERS

Northern Region

M. Abubakar Tafawa Balewa, Minister of Works (N.P.C.).

M. Shettima Kashim, Minister of Social Services (N.P.C.).

M. Muhammadu Ribadu, Minister of Natural Resources (N.P.C.).

Alhaji Usuman Nagogo, Emir of Katsina, Minister without Portfolio (N.P.C.).

Eastern Region

Mr. Okoi Arikpo, Minister of Lands, Survey and Development (N.C.N.C.).*

Mr. Eni Njoku, Minister of Mines and Power (N.C.N.C.).

Mr. A. C. Nwapa, Minister of Commerce and Industries (N.C.N.C.).

Western Region

H. H. Sir Adesoji Aderemi, Oni of Ife, Minister without Portfolio (A.G.).

Chief Arthur Prest, Minister of Communications (A.G.).

Chief Bode Thomas, Minister of Transport (A.G.).

Chief S. L. Akintola, Minister of Labour (A.G.).

Southern Cameroons

Dr. E. M. L. Endeley, Minister without Portfolio (N.C.N.C.).*

* Joined N.I.P. on 23rd February 1953.

National Ministries

Members Ex-Officio

The Governor (President of the Council).
The Chief-Secretary to the Government.
The Lieutenant-Governors of the three Regions.
The Attorney-General.
The Financial Secretary.

1954 CONSTITUTION: COUNCIL OF MINISTERS

Northern Region

Mallam Abubakar Tafawa Balewa, Minister of Transport (N.P.C.).
Alhaji Inuwa Wada, Federal Minister (N.P.C.).
Mallam Muhammadu Ribadu, Minister of Land, Mines and Power (N.P.C.).

Western Region

Alhaji Adegoke Adelabu, Minister of Natural Resources and Social Services (N.C.N.C.).
Chief Kola Balogun, Minister of Research and Information (N.C.N.C.).
Chief Festus Okotie-Eboh, Minister of Labour and Welfare (N.C.N.C.).

Eastern Region

Mr. Raymond Njoku, Minister of Trade and Industry (N.C.N.C.).
Dr. K. O. Mbadiwe, Minister of Communications and Aviation (N.C.N.C.).
Mr. M. T. Mbu, Federal Minister (N.C.N.C.).

Southern Cameroons

Mr. Victor Mukete, Federal Minister (N.C.N.C.).

Members Ex-Officio

Governor-General (President)
Chief Secretary
Financial Secretary
Attorney-General

National Ministries

1957 Constitution: National Government

Alhaji Abubakar Tafawa Balewa, Prime Minister and Minister of Finance (N.P.C.).

N.P.C.

Mallam Bukar Dipcharima, Minister of State.
Alhaji Muhammadu Ribadu, Minister of Lagos Affairs, Mines and Power.
Alhaji Inuwa Wada, Minister of Works and Surveys.

N.C.N.C.

Chief Kola Balogun, Minister of Research and Information.
Mr. J. M. Johnson, Minister of Internal Affairs.
Dr. K. O. Mbadiwe, Miniser of Commerce and Industry.
Mr. R. A. Njoku, Minister of Transport.
Mr. Aja Nwachuku, Minister of Education.
Chief Festus Okotie-Eboh, Minister of Labour and Welfare.

A.G.

Chief S. L. Akintola, Minister of Communications and Aviation.
Mr. Ayo Rosiji, Minister of Health.

K.N.C. (Kamerun National Congress)

Mr. Victor Mukete, Minister of State.

1960 Independence Government: N.P.C.–N.C.N.C. Coalition

Alhaji Sir Abubakar Tafawa Balewa, Prime Minister and Minister of Foreign Affairs (N.P.C.).
Mr. T. O. S. Benson, Minister of Information (N.C.N.C.).
Mr. Olu Akinfosile, Minister of Communications (N.C.N.C.).
Mallam Zanna Bukar Dipcharima, Minister of Commerce and Industry (N.P.C.).
Chief J. M. Johnson, Minister of Labour and Welfare (N.C.N.C.).
Mr. Raymond Njoku, Minister of Transport and Aviation (N.C.N.C.).
Mr. Aja Nwachuku, Minister of Education (N.C.N.C.).
Chief Festus Okotie-Eboh, Minister of Finance (N.C.N.C.).
Alhaji Muhammadu Ribadu, Minister of Defence (N.P.C.).

National Ministries

Mallam Usuman Sarki, Minister of Internal Affairs (N.P.C.).

Mallam Maitama Sule, Minister of Mines and Power (N.P.C.).

Mallam Musa Yaradua, Minister of Lagos Affairs (N.P.C.).

Mr. Jaja Wachuku, Minister of Economic Development (N.C.N.C.).

Alhaji Inuwa Wada, Minister of Works and Survey (N.P.C.).

Mallam Waziri Ibrahim, Minister of Health (N.P.C.).

Mallam Shehu Shagari, Minister of Pensions (N.P.C.).

Dr. T. O. Elias, Attorney-General and Minister of Justice.

Dr. M. A. Majekodunmi, Minister of State.

Dr. E. A. Esin, Minister of State (N.C.N.C.).

Mr. Nuhu Bamali, Minister of State (N.P.C.).

Chief F. Omo-Osagie, Minister of State (N.C.N.C.).

Mr. J. C. Obande, Minister of State (N.P.C.).

APPENDIX G

A Note on Major Contributions to the Study of Nigerian History since 1965

Since the publication of the Second Edition of *The Story of Nigeria* in 1966 a number of general histories of Nigeria have been published. By far the best is contained in Thomas Hodgkin's introduction to his second edition of *Nigerian Perspectives: An Historical Anthology* (London, 1973). This provides a concise and stimulating summary of current thinking and research on the history of Nigeria. Walter Schwarz's *Nigeria* (London, 1968) is very useful for the period after independence, which is treated only cursorily in this volume. His book provides incisive insights into the events which led up to the civil war.

The section of Chapter I on the classification of Nigeria's languages which follows closely Joseph H. Greenberg's work on African languages should now be read in conjunction with David Dalby's 'Reflections on the Classification of African Languages with special reference to the work of Sigismund Wilhelm Koelle and Malkolm Guthrie', *African Language Studies*, XI, 1970, in which he expresses reservations about Greenberg's conclusions and argues that for 'historians as well as linguists there is also need to reconsider the implications of the *geographical* distribution of African languages as a separate issue from the question of their detailed inter-relationships'.

A valuable recent contribution to historico-linguistic studies in Nigeria is J. A. Ballard's 'Historical Inferences from the Linguistic Geography of the Nigerian Middle Belt', *Africa*, XLI, 4, October 1971.

A Note on Major Contributions to the

Latest archaeological research in Nigeria is comprehensively treated in Thurstan Shaw's 'Archaeology in Nigeria', *Antiquity*, XLIII, 1969, and has a full bibliography. This should be read in conjunction with his earlier essay, written in 1966, on the archaeology of West Africa in J. F. A. Ajayi and Michael Crowder (eds.), *History of West Africa*, vol. I (London, 1972), in which the prehistory of Nigeria can be seen in the context of that of Nigeria as a whole. Frank Willett's essay on Nigeria in P. L. Shinnie (ed.), *The African Iron Age* (London, 1971), is also a useful survey of the latest archaeological evidence for the Nigerian Iron Age.

A geographical setting for the study of Nigerian history is to be found in Akin L. Mabogunje's 'The Lands and Peoples of Nigeria' in Ajayi and Crowder (eds.), *History of West Africa*, vol. I. W. B. Morgan and J. C. Pugh's *West Africa* (London, 1969), provides a more detailed setting for the history of Nigeria generally. An excellent and provocative background to the study of the development of states in Nigeria is provided by Robin Horton in 'Stateless Societies in the History of West Africa' in the same volume.

For the early history of the savannah states Abdullahi Smith's essay on Hausaland and Bornu before *c.* 1500 in Ajayi and Crowder (eds.), *History of West Africa*, vol. I, is outstanding. The same author has published an excellent detailed study of the early history of one Hausa state, Zazzau (Zaria), in M. J. Mortimore (ed.), *Zaria and its Regions: A Nigerian City and its Environs* (Zaria, 1970). The sixteenth century in Hausaland and Bornu is dealt with in the light of latest research by J. O. Hunwick in 'Hausaland, Bornu and Songhai' in Ajayi and Crowder (eds.), *History of West Africa*, vol. I.

An important reassessment of the history of Bornu during the seventeenth and eighteenth centuries is to be found in J. E. Lavers's 'Islam in the Bornu Caliphate 1600–1800', *Odu*, New Series, No. 5, 1970. Lavers successfully dispels the traditional view that Bornu was in decline during this period.

The best introduction to the early history of Yorubaland is Robert Smith's *Kingdoms of the Yoruba* (London, 1969). Frank Willett's *Ife in the History of West African Sculpture* (London, 1967) is a fine study of the place of Ife art in relation to that of the rest of the Nigerian region. There is a concise survey of the early history of Benin in Alan Ryder's *Benin and the Europeans 1485–1897* (London, 1969). A recent important study of the early history of Benin from the archaeological point of view is Graham Connah's 'Archaeology in Benin', *Journal of African History*, XIII, 1, 1972. See also his 'New Light on the Benin City Walls', *Journal of the Historical Society of Nigeria*, III, 4, 1967.

The early history of the Niger Delta and the Ibo and Ibibio hinterland has been recently reassessed in E. J. Alagoa's 'The Niger-Delta States and their Neighbours 1600–1800' in Ajayi and Crowder (eds.), *History of West Africa*, vol. I. For conflicting views of the rise of the city states of the Niger Delta see Robin Horton's 'From Fishing Village to City State' in Mary Douglas and Phyllis Kaberry (eds.), *Man in Africa* (London, 1969), and E. J. Alagoa's 'Long Distance Trade and States in the Niger Delta', *Journal of African History*, XI, 3, 1970. See also his 'Development of Institutions in the States of the Eastern Niger Delta', *Journal of African History*, XII, 2, 1971. The early history of the peoples of the Upper Benue Basin and the Bauchi Plateau is treated in considerable detail by Sa'ad Abubakar in the Historical Society of Nigeria's *Groundwork of Nigerian History* (forthcoming). Likewise the pre-nineteenth-century history of the peoples of the Niger-Benue valley is treated thoroughly in the same work by Ade Obayemi.

Any general overview of Nigeria's pre-nineteenth-century history has to take into account Philip Curtin's incisive study, *The African Slave Trade: A Census* (Madison, Wisconsin, 1970). This book, together with Ryder's book on Benin and the Europeans, not only renders more precise but sensibly diminishes the importance of the European impact on Nigeria's history before the nineteenth century.

The study of the Jihad of Usman dan Fodio has been inestimably advanced by Murray Last's meticulous study, *The Sokoto Caliphate* (London, 1967). It can be supplemented by R. A. Adeleye's *Power and Diplomacy in Northern Nigeria 1800–1906: The Sokoto Caliphate and its Enemies* (London, 1971), and H. A. S. Johnson's *The Fulani Empire of Sokoto* (London, 1967).

Specific studies of the constituent emirates of the Caliphate are to be found in Sa'ad Abubakar's 'The Emirate of Fombina [Adamawa] 1809–1903' (Ph.D. thesis, Ahmadu Bello University, 1970); M. Mason's 'The Nupe Kingdom in the 19th Century:

A Political History' (Ph.D. thesis, Birmingham, 1970) and his article on 'The Jihad in the South: An Outline of the 19th-Century Nupe Hegemony in North-Eastern Yorubaland and Afenmai', *Journal of the Historical Society of Nigeria*, v, 2, 1970. Yauri, which was in a tributary (*jizya*) relationship to the Caliphate in the nineteenth century has been studied in depth by Madi Adamu in 'A Hausa Government in Decline: Yauri in the 19th Century' (M.A. thesis, Ahmadu Bello University, 1968); Bello Alkali has made a study of Kebbi, Sokoto's enemy throughout the nineteenth century, in 'A Hausa Community in Crisis: Kebbi in the 19th century' (M.A. thesis, Ahmadu Bello University, 1969). Victor W. Low has made a meticulous study of the Emirates of Gombe, Katagum and Hadejia, supplemented with superb maps in *Three Nigerian Emirates* Northwestern, 1972. For a detailed study of one aspect of trade in the Sokoto Caliphate, Kola, see Paul E. Lovejoy's 'The Hausa Kola Trade to the Volta Basin 1700–1900: A Commercial System in the Long-Distance Exchange of West Africa' (Ph.D. thesis, Wisconsin, 1973). There is an excellent analysis of changes in the administrative systems of Hausaland in the nineteenth and twentieth centuries in Murray Last's 'Aspects of Administration and Dissent in Hausaland, 1800–1968', *Africa*, XL, 4, October, 1970. An important contribution to the study of late nineteenth-century history in Sokoto and Bornu is M. A. Al-Haji's 'Mahdism in the Western Sudan with special reference to Northern Nigeria' (Ph.D thesis, Ahmadu Bello University, forthcoming).

The nineteenth-century history of Bornu has had much less attention paid to it than the Sokoto Caliphate. Perhaps the best study of the Shehus is contained in Louis Brenner's *The Shehus of Kukawa: A History of the Al-Kanemi Dynasty of Bornu* (Clarendon, 1973). See also his joint chapter with Ronald Cohen in Ajayi and Crowder (eds.), *History of West Africa*, vol. II.

An important contribution to the nineteenth-century history of the Middle Belt is M. Mason 'Population Density and "Slave-Raiding"—The Case of the Middle Belt of Nigeria' *J.A.H.* X, 4, 1969, pp. 551–564.

The eighteenth- and nineteenth-century history of Oyo has recently been reconsidered in detail. Among the most important reassessments are: R. S. Smith's 'Event and Portent: the fall of

Study of Nigerian History since 1965

Old Oyo, a problem in historical explanation', *Africa*, XLI, 3, July 1971; P. Morton-Williams's 'The Yoruba Kingdom of Oyo' in Daryll Forde and Phyllis Kaberry (eds.), *West African Kingdoms in the Nineteenth Century* (Oxford, 1967); P. Morton-Williams's 'The Oyo Yoruba and the Atlantic Slave Trade 1670–1830', *Journal of the Historical Society of Nigeria*, III, 2, 1964; J. A. Atanda's 'The Fall of the Old Oyo Empire: A Re-Consideration of its Cause', *Journal of the Historical Society of Nigeria*, v, 4, 1971; P. Morton-Williams's 'The Influence of Habitat and Trade on the Politics of Oyo and Ashanti' in Mary Douglas and P. M. Kaberry (eds.), *Man in Africa* (London, 1969). I. A. Akinjogbin's *Dahomey and its Neighbours 1708–1818* (Cambridge, 1967) is useful for a study of Oyo's relationship with its tributary state of Dahomey, though some historians are critical of his analysis of the interrelationship of the Yoruba-Aja states as expressed in his concept of the Ebi social theory. Robin Law, who has recently completed an important thesis on Oyo, has expressed reservations about Akinjogbin's interpretations in a long review of the book in the *Journal of the Historical Society of Nigeria*, IV, 2, June 1968, and two important articles, 'The Constitutional Struggles of Oyo in the Eighteenth Century', *Journal of African History*, XII, 1, 1971, and 'Oyo and its Northern Neighbours', *Kano Studies*, 5, 1972.

The hitherto obscure seventeenth- and eighteenth-century history of Benin from 1600 to the time of the British occupation, has been dealt with in detail by Alan Ryder in his *Benin and the Europeans*.

Apart from the books and articles mentioned above relating to the nineteenth-century history of Nigeria, some important monographs and articles have appeared in the past six years that have greatly helped our understanding of this period. Obaro Ikime's *Merchant Prince of the Niger Delta* (London, 1968) apart from being a study of Nana Olumu, Governor of the Benin River, has valuable information on Itsekiri-Urhobo relations. An excellent study of the relations between the Eastern Yoruba and the Ibadan (Oyo) Empire is contained in S. A. Akintoye's *Revolution and Power Politics in Yorubaland: Ibadan Expansion and the Rise of the Ekiti Parapo* (London, 1971). Akintoye has also published an important article on the relations between the Eastern Yoruba and Benin in 'The Eastern Yoruba and the

341

Benin Kingdom', *Journal of the Historical Society of Nigeria*, IV, 4, 1969. See also his 'The Ondo Road Eastwards of Lagos', *Journal of African History*, X, 4, 1969.

The colonial period of Nigerian history has been comparatively well served in the past six years by microcosmic studies, particularly those concerning aspects of British administration: among these the most notable are Obaro Ikime's *Niger-Delta Rivalry: Itsekiri-Urhobo Relations and the European Presence 1884–1936* (London, 1969); J. A. Atanda's 'The New "Oyo Empire": A Study of British Indirect Rule in Oyo Province 1894–1934' (Ph.D. thesis, Ibadan University, 1967). A. E. Afigbo's doctoral dissertation on 'The Warrant Chief System in Eastern Nigeria 1900–1929' (Ph.D. thesis, Ibadan, 1964) is a major contribution to the understanding of British administration in Nigeria and African reaction to it. The thesis is to be published as *The Warrant Chiefs: Indirect Rule in Southeastern Nigeria 1891–1929* (London, 1973). Philip Igbafe has written an important thesis on 'Benin under British Administration 1897–1938: A Study in Institutional Adaptation' (Ph.D. thesis, Ibadan, 1967). Some of his findings have been published in article form, e.g. 'The District Head System in Benin, 1914–1935', *Odu*, III, 2, and 'British Rule in Benin 1897–1920: Direct or Indirect?', *Journal of the Historical Society of Nigeria*, III, 4, 1967. See also his article on 'The Benin Water Rate Agitation 1937–39: An Example of Social Conflict', *Journal of the Historical Society of Nigeria*, IV, 3. Adamu Fika has written a penetrating study of the reaction of a Northern Nigerian emirate to British administration in 'The Political and Economic Re-orientation of Kano Emirate 1882–1940' (Ph.D. thesis, London, 1973).

The position of the chief under colonial rule is treated with reference to a number of Nigerian examples in Michael Crowder and Obaro Ikime (eds.), *West African Chiefs: Their Changing Status Under Colonial Rule and Independence* (Ife, 1971). Resistance to colonial occupation is considered in Michael Crowder (ed.), *West African Resistance: The Military Response to Colonial Occupation* (London, 1971), in which there is a notable study of the Ijebu expedition of 1892.

British administration in Nigeria has been studied in a provocative book by I. F. Nicholson, *The Administration of Nigeria 1900–1960: Men, Methods and Myths* (Oxford, 1969) while the role of the British Political Officer in Northern Nigeria is dealt with on a broad scale by Robert F. Heussler in *The British in Northern Nigeria* (London, 1968) and on a microcosmic scale by Michael Crowder in *Revolt in Bussa: A Study of British 'Native Administration in Bussa, 1902–1935* (London, 1973). There is a fascinating study of the problems faced by the British in administering the Tiv in David Dorward's 'Early British Administration Among the Tiv', *African Affairs*, 2, 1970. His doctoral thesis on this subject has recently been accepted by Birmingham.

Pioneering work on the study of Nigeria's economic history is contained in A. G. Hopkins's 'An Economic History of Lagos: 1880–1914' (London, Ph.D. thesis, 1964). Hopkins has published many invaluable articles, too numerous to list here. Examples are: 'Economic Aspects of Political Movements in Nigeria and the Gold Coast, 1919–1939', *Journal of African History*, I, 1966; 'The Currency Revolution in South West Nigeria in the late 19th Century', *Journal of the Historical Society of Nigeria*, III, 3; 'R. B. Blaize, Merchant Prince of West Africa', *Tarikh*, I, No. 2, and 'The Lagos Strike of 1897: An Exploration of Nigerian Labour History', *Past and Present*, No. 35, 1969.

An important contribution to our understanding of the recent economic history of Nigeria is R. J. Gavin's 'A History of Economic Development in Nigeria' in *The Groundwork of Nigerian History* (forthcoming). It has a very full bibliography of sources in its notes. Polly Hill's *Studies in Rural Capitalism in West Africa* (London, 1970), and *Rural Hausa: A Village and a Setting* (London, 1972) are vital for the understanding of economic change at the grassroots level over the past ninety years.

Among important recent contributions to the political history of Nigeria are B. J. Dudley's *Parties and Politics in Northern Nigeria* (London, 1968), and C. S. Whitaker's *The Politics of Tradition: Continuity and Change in Northern Nigeria 1946–1966* (Princeton, 1970). Perhaps the best account among many published about the Nigerian civil war, most of which were highly *engagé*, is John de St. Jorre's *The Nigerian Civil War* (London, 1972).

Notes on Chapter I.*

1 A. H. M. Kirk-Greene 'Who coined the name Nigeria?' *West Africa*, 22nd December 1956.

2 Several general histories of Nigeria have been published but so far no full-scale history has been written by a Nigerian. Wale Ademoyega's *The Federation of Nigeria*, London, 1962, is more a general description of the country's geography, politics and resources than a history. D. O. Okonkwo's *History of Nigeria in a New Setting*, Aba (Nigeria), 1961, is essentially designed for schools. The best introduction to Nigerian history is still Thomas Hodgkin's introductory essay to *Nigerian Perspectives*, London, 1960. M. C. English's *An Outline of Nigerian History*, London, 1959, though intended for the junior classes of secondary schools provides a well-balanced introductory survey. Of the two full length histories published so far, Sir Alan Burns's *History of Nigeria*, London, 1962 (6th edition), is essentially an administrative history that pays little attention to pre-European history or to the nationalist period. Sir Rex Niven's *Short History of Nigeria*, London, 1937, almost as long as that of Burns, shows more sympathy for the history of Nigerian peoples before contact with the Europeans. A shortened and substantially revised version of the present work, designed for school certificate candidates, entitled *Nigeria: A Modern History for Schools*, London, 1965, has been prepared by Rex Akpofure and the author. Two general surveys of Nigeria are recommended: K. M. Buchanan and J. C. Pugh *Land and Peoples of Nigeria*, London, 1955, and *Nigeria: The Political and Economic Background*, London, 1960. Reference should also be made to R. J. Harrison Church *West Africa*, London, 1964 (2nd edition).

3 There was considerable controversy in Nigeria over the results for the 1962 census as well as those for 1964. The figures for 1962 were never officially released, whilst those for 1964 gave a population for the country of 55,620,268. The controversy was not so

* *J.A.H.=Journal of African History.*
J.H.S.N.=Journal of the Historical Society of Nigeria.

Notes on Chapter I.

much centred on the plausibility of a 20 million increase over the 1953 census figure of 31,168,000 (for it is generally agreed that that census was inadequately conducted) but over the distribution of population region by region. The 1964 census results give the Northern Region a population greater than that of the combined southern regions, which means that it retains its majority of seats in the house over those of the combined southern regions. The breakdown of the 1964 census figures is as follows:

North	29,758,875
East	12,394,462
West	10,265,846
Mid-West	2,535,839
Federal Territory (Lagos)	665,246
Total:	55,620,268

4 Joseph H. Greenberg *Studies in African Linguistic Classification*, U.S.A., 1955. I have in fact followed in this edition the revised version of Greenberg's book published under the new title, *The Languages of Africa*, in 1963 as a supplement to *The International Journal of American Linguistics*, Part 2, Vol. XXIX, No. 1, 1963.

5 *Ibid.* The author has changed his designation for certain African linguistic families from those used in his earlier work. In so far as Nigeria is concerned the changes are as follows:

   1. Central-Saharan=Nilo-Saharan.
   2. Niger-Congo=Congo-Kordofanian, though Niger Congo still describes a major sub-family of this newly designated branch.
   3. Chad-Afroasiatic=Afro-Asiatic.

6 G. P. Murdock *Africa—Its Peoples and their Culture History*, New York, 1959.

7 Thurstan Shaw 'Field Research in Nigerian Archaeology' *J.H.S.N.*, II, 4, pp. 449–64 is the best up-to-date survey of the present state of archaeological research in Nigeria. See also his *Archaeology and Nigeria*, Ibadan, 1963. Also *Preserving the Past—The Nigerian Museum and its Art Treasures*, Lagos, 1959.

8 Jan Vansina 'Recording the Oral History of the Bakuba—I: Methods' *J.A.H.*, I, 1, 1960, pp. 43–51. For general discussions of the problems confronting the historian of Africa today see J. Vansina, R. Mauny and L.-V. Thomas eds. *The Historian in Tropical Africa*, London, 1964, and K. Onwuka Diké 'The Study of African History' in *The Proceedings of the First International Congress of Africanists*, eds. Lalage Bown and Michael Crowder,

Notes on Chapter I.

London, 1964. Also Vincent Monteil 'La décolonisation de l'Histoire' Supplément au no 142 *Preuves*, December 1962.

9 Vansina 'Bakuba' *op. cit.*, p. 52. In this respect the section on oral history in Murdock *op. cit.*, p. 43 must be treated with extreme caution.

10 H. R. Palmer *The Bornu, Sahara and Sudan*, London, 1936. P. Amaury Talbot *Peoples of Southern Nigeria*, 4 vols., London, 1926. C. K. Meek *A Sudanese Kingdom*, London, 1931.

11 Murdock *op. cit.*, pp. 64–70. See also Roland Portères 'Vieilles Agricultures de l'Afrique intertropicale' *L'Agronomie Tropicale*, V, 1950, pp. 489–507. A useful review article dealing with both Murdock's and Portères' hypotheses is J. D. Fage's 'Anthropology, Botany and History' *J.A.H.*, II, 2, 1961, pp. 299–309.

12 This paragraph is based on Shaw 'Field Research' *op. cit.*, pp. 450–4.

13 *Ibid.*, p. 453.

14 B.E.B. Fagg "Cave Paintings and Rock Gongs of Birnin Kudu" *Proceedings of the Third Pan-African Congress on Pre-History*, Lusaka, 1955.

15 J. Desmond Clark "The Prehistoric Origins of African Culture" *J.A.H.*, V, 2, 1964. pp. 180-1.

16 Dating of the Nok culture has been achieved by the Carbon 14 process, but with present techniques its results can only be considered tentative. See *J.A.H.*, Vol. II, 1, 1960, pp. 137–9. 'Radio Carbon dates for Sub-Saharan Africa' where details of the various radio carbon dates for the Nok culture are given.

17 B. E. B. Fagg: 'The Nok-terracottas in West African Art History' *Actes du 4ᵉ Congrès Pan-Africain de la préhistoire et de l'étude du quaternaire* published by Musée Royal de l'Afrique Centrale, Tervuren, Belgium. Annales série IN—8°, sciences humaines, no. 40, 1962, p. 447.

18 See Greenberg *op. cit.* Greenberg's theory of the origin of the Bantu is challenged by Malcolm Guthrie in 'Some Developments in the Prehistory of the Bantu Languages' *J.A.H.*, III, 2, 1962, pp. 273–82.

19 C. Daryll Forde 'The Culture Map of West Africa—successive adaptations to Tropical Forests and Grasslands' *Trans. New York Acad. Sci.* Ser. II, 15 April 1953, pp. 206–19, reprinted in Simon and Phoebe Ottenberg ed. *The Cultures of Africa*, New York, 1960, pp. 116–39.

Notes on Chapter II.

1 See Roland Oliver and J. D. Fage *A Short History of Africa*, London, 1962, Chapter IV, 'The Sudanic Civilization', pp. 44-52.

For a very useful discussion of the state-building process see Robert G. Armstrong *State Structures in Negro Africa* (unpublished Ph. D. dissertation, University of Chicago 1952, available on microfilm). See also his article 'The Development of Kingdoms in Negro Africa' *J.H.S.N.*, II, 1, December 1960, pp. 27-40.

2 Jean Rouch *La Réligion et La Magie chez les Songhay*, Paris, 1960.

3 In the first edition it was suggested that the Zaghawa were of Berber origin. Since then J. S. Trimingham has suggested that they were in fact a Negro people: *A History of Islam in West Africa*, London, 1962, pp. 104-5. Citing Al-Masuʻdi, Ibn Saʻid, Ibn Khaldun and Al-Idrīsī he concluded, 'At any rate they were distinct from both Berbers and Sudan blacks, like the Teda of today who are probably their descendants.' One of the reasons for believing that the Zaghawa were not of Negro origin was the statement that Mai Selma (*c.* 1193-1210) was the first black ruler of Kanem. Yves Urvoy *L'Histoire de l'Empire de Bornou*, Dakar, 1949, p. 39.

4 J.-P. Lebeuf and Masson-Détourbet *La Civilisation du Tchad*, Paris, 1950 and J.-P. Lebeuf *Archéologie Tchadienne—Les Sao de Cameroun et du Tchad*, Paris, 1962. See also note 40.

5 Trimingham *op cit.*, pp. 105-6.

6 Quoted in Yaqut *Muʻjam*, ii, 932-3.

7 H. R. Palmer *Sudanese Memoirs*, 3 vols., Lagos, 1928 and *The Bornu, Sahara and Sudan*, London, 1936.

8 Urvoy *op. cit.* Trimingham *op. cit.* has a good summary of the history of Kanem-Bornu, and uses Arabic sources extensively. See also E. W. Bovill *The Golden Trade of the Moors*, London, 1955 and his earlier *Caravans of the Old Sahara*, London, 1933. Also: Heinrich Barth *Travels and Discoveries in Northern and Central Africa*, 4 vols., London, 1857; A. Schultze *The Sultanate of Bornu* (trans. P. A. Benton), London, 1913; and Annie M.-D. Lebeuf *Les Populations du Tchad*, Paris, 1959, pp. 33-46.

Notes on Chapter II.

9 The map in *Sudanese Memoirs*, Vol. II places it just to the north-east whilst the map in *Bornu, Sahara and Sudan* places it due east.

10 Urvoy *op. cit.*, p. 27.

11 I am indebted to Dr. A. D. H. Bivar for this discussion of the location of Njimi. Subsequent to the appearance of the first edition of this book, Dr. Bivar with P. L. Shinnie published a detailed account of the location in the 'Old Kanuri Capitals', *J.A.H.*, III, 1, 1962, pp. 1–10.

12 Trimingham *op. cit.*, p. 115 suggests that Ume was the founder of a new dynasty.

13 The dating of the reigns of various kings differs with each authority. Unless otherwise stated I have used Urvoy's dates. Urvoy *op. cit.*

14 Al-Idrisi *History of Africa and Spain*, cited in *ibid.* p. 33.

15 Ibn Khaldun *Histoire des Berbères et des dynasties de l'Afrique septentrionale* tr. M. le Baron de Slane. Algiers, 1854, Vol. II, p. 347.

16 *Ibid.*, Vol. II, p. 109, described Kanem as dominating all the regions of the desert as far as Fezzan.

17 Ahmad ibn 'Abdullah al-Qualqashandi *Subh al-a'sha* written in 1387, Cairo edition 1913–19, viii, pp. 116–18, quoted in Hodgkin *op. cit.*, p. 77–8.

18 Palmer *Sudanese Memoirs*, *op. cit.*, III, p. 109, 'The Kano Chronicle' records that Abdullahi Burja "was the first in Hausaland to give Bornu tsare or gaisuwa. He opened roads from Bornu to Gwanja" (i.e. Gonja in Central (Modern) Ghana).

19 Bivar and Shinnie *op. cit.*, p. 2, state that it was founded in *c.* 1470 which could mean that if we accept the usual dates given for Mai Ali Gazi's reign (1473–1501, by Trimingham *op. cit.*, Urvoy *op. cit.*) it could not have been founded by him. However the authors do not give the source for their dating of the foundation of N'gazargamu, not do they attribute its foundation to Mai Ali Gazi. On the other hand Trimingham who places its foundation at *c.* 1481 does not give a source for this date either.

20 Trimingham *op. cit.*, p. 126.

21 M. G. Smith 'The Beginnings of Hausa Society' *The Historian in Tropical Africa*, London, 1964, p. 346.

22 Palmer *Sudanese Memoirs op. cit.*, III, p. 133, where the Bayajidda legend is cited in *The Daura Girgam*. See also Alhaji Hassan and Mallam Shuaibu Na'ibi *A Chronicle of Abuja* translated and arranged from the Hausa by Frank Heath (2nd edition), Lagos, 1962. Also M. G. Smith *op. cit.*, p. 340.

23 H. R. Palmer 'The Kano Chronicle' *J. Roy. Anthrop. Inst.*, 38,

Notes on Chapter II.

1908, pp. 58–98 and 'History of Katsina' *J. Afr. Soc.*, 26, 103, 1927, pp. 216–36.

24 *Ibid.*

25 In the first edition it was concluded that Islam reached Hausaland 'undoubtedly from Mali'. This is a view shared by a number of historians notably Oliver and Fage *op. cit.*, p. 86, and is based on *The Kano Chronicle*. 'Thus, for example, it was Mande merchants of the fifteenth century who introduced Islam into Hausaland.' However Joseph H. Greenberg argues in 'Linguistic evidence for the influence of the Kanuri on the Hausa' *J.A.H.*, I, 2, 1960, that Islam first reached Hausaland from Bornu. He cites as evidence the fact that certain Hausa words which must have come into use as a result of contact with Islam have Kanuri roots, rather than Arabic or even Mande roots. Thus the word 'write' is of Kanuri origin, and the word 'read', though of ultimate Arabic origin, has been borrowed via Kanuri.

26 The Kano Chronicle places Queen Amina's exploits during the reign of King Burja of Kano (1421–38) Smith *op. cit.*, p. 349. However, the Abuja Chronicle, *op. cit.*, p. 3 places her in the sixteenth century.

27 See J. O. Hunwick 'Religion and state in the Songhay Empire (1464–1591)', a paper contributed to the 5th International African Institute Seminar on 'Islam in Tropical Africa', Ahmadu Bello University, Nigeria, December 1963.

28 Translated from the Arabic by T. H. Baldwin as *The Obligations of Princes*, Beirut, 1932.

29 Leo Africanus *History and Description of Africa*, 3 Vols., London, 1896, trans. John Pory, ed. Robert Brown, III, p. 830.

30 There has been some confusion over the meaning of the word Kanta. Some authorities use it as the personal name of the man who led the Kebbi revolt against the Askia; others use it as the gubernatorial title of the Songhai governor of Kebbi; but consensus seems to favour the opinion that it was the kingly title of the rulers of Kebbi. It is so employed in this edition.

31 Trimingham *op. cit.*, pp. 134–5.

32 Raymond Mauny *Tableau Géographique de l'Ouest Africain au Moyen Age*, Dakar, 1961, p. 434 (Map).

33 *Ibid.*, p. 501.

34 Imam Ahmed ibn Fartua *History of the First Twelve Years of the Reign of Mai Idris of Bornu 1571–1583*, translated from the Arabic by H. R. Palmer. Lagos, Government Printer, 1962. H. R. Palmer *Sudanese Memoirs, op. cit.*, Vol. I includes *The Kanem Wars of Mai Idris Alooma* by Imam Ahmed ibn Fartua.

35 Trimingham *op. cit.*, p. 123.

Notes on Chapter II.

36 Urvoy *op. cit.*, p. 78.

37 See C. K. Meek *A Sudanese Kingdom*, London, 1931, for an account of the Jukun kingdom of Kororofa. Unfortunately historical knowledge of this state is very limited at present.

38 In the Nigerian Census of 1953 the Jukun were not classified separately as an ethnic group. Full details of the 1964 Census, where this situation may have been rectified had not been released at the time of going to press.

39 See 'End of an Empire' *Nigeria Magazine*, No. 64, March, 1960.

40 Additional to note no. 4. Doubt on Lebeuf's dating for the Sao culture has recently been expressed by Paul Ozanne in 'The Diffusion of Smoking in West Africa' *Bulletin of the Institute of African Studies* of the University of Ghana, I, 1, 1966.

Notes on Chapter III.

1 The problem of interpreting Yoruba myths of origin is raised by a number of authors. Probably the best summary is P. C. Lloyd 'Sacred Kingship and Government among the Yoruba' *Africa*, XXX, 3, 1960, pp. 221–37. See also P. C. Lloyd 'Yoruba myths —a sociologist's interpretation' *Odu*, 2, 1956, pp. 20–8; S. O. Biobaku *The Origin of the Yoruba*, Lagos, 1955; Ulli Beier and S. O. Biobaku 'The Use and interpretation of Yoruba myths' *Odu*, 1, 1955, pp. 12–25; Ulli Beier 'Before Oduduwa' *Odu*, 3, 1956, pp. 25–32; and E. Bolaji Idowu *Oludumare: God in Yoruba Belief*, London, 1962.

2 Versions of this myth vary in detail but not in substance. See Peter Morton-Williams 'An outline of the cosmology and the cult organisation of the Oyo Yoruba.' *Africa*, XXXIV, 3, July 1964, pp. 243–62 for a slightly different version of this myth and an interesting discussion of its significance.

3 Samuel Johnson *The History of the Yorubas*, Lagos, 1921, pp. 7–8. Much of the material for this chapter has been derived from Johnson's invaluable book whose main defect is its Oyo bias.

4 Jacob Egharevba *Short History of Benin*, Ibadan, 1960 (2nd edition). For the history of Benin see also R. E. Bradbury and P. C. Lloyd *The Benin Kingdom and the Edo-speaking Peoples etc.*, *plus the Itsekiri*, London, 1959 and R. E. Bradbury 'The historical use of comparative ethnography with special reference to Benin and the Yoruba' *The Historian in Tropical Africa*, London, 1964, pp. 145–64.

5 The Ife bronzes are in fact brasses. See R. Mauny 'A possible source of copper for the oldest brass heads of Ife' *J.H.S.N.*, II, 3, December 1963, pp. 393–5.

6 Frank Willett in 'Ife and its archaeology' *J.A.H.*, I, 2, 1960, pp. 231–48, gives a full account of the history of the discovery of the Ife bronzes and terra-cottas from the time of Leo Frobenius' visit to Ife in 1910 to his own more recent excavations.

7 See *An Introduction to the Art of Ife*, Lagos, 1955, for a general description of the Ife bronzes and terra-cottas, photographs of a number of which are reproduced in this pamphlet.

Notes on Chapter III.

8 Thurstan Shaw 'Field Research in Nigerian Archaeology' *op. cit.*, p. 457.

9 Unpublished. I owe this information to a personal communication by Mr. Morton-Williams who kindly commented on this chapter before it went to press.

10 I have made a number of changes to this section in the early history of Oyo in the light of the Introduction in J. F. Ade Ajayi and Robert Smith *Yoruba Warfare in the Nineteenth Century*, Ibadan and London, 1964, pp. 1–5.

11 *Ibid.*, p. 3.

12 Before the nineteenth century there was no common term for the Yoruba-speaking peoples. They were designated such by European missionaries from the term Yoöba which the Oyo used to describe their dialect of the Yoruba language. Ajayi and Smith *ibid.*, p. 2. Peter Morton-Williams in a personal communication has suggested that it may come from Yarba, the Hausa name for them.

13 Robert Smith 'The Alafin in Exile: A Study of the Igboho Period of Oyo History' *J.A.H.*, VI, 1, 165, pp. 57–77. Mr. Smith very kindly let me see a copy of this paper before it went to press.

14 *Ibid.*, p. 68 and Johnson *op. cit.*, p. 174.

15 Peter Morton-Williams has an excellent analysis of the 'constitution' of Oyo in his article 'The Yoruba Ogboni Cult in Oyo' *Africa*, XXX, 1960, pp. 362–72.

16 See Frank Willett 'Investigations at Old Oyo, 1956–7: An Interim Report' *J.H.S.N.*, II, 1, December 1960, pp. 59–77, where Willett reports that the Afin, or palace, 'covers a very substantial area, probably something of the order of one square mile' (p. 67). The town itself was enclosed by walls the outer of which according to Clapperton was fifteen miles in circumference. (Hugh Clapperton, *Journal of an Expedition into the Interior of Africa from the Bight of Benin to Soccattoo*, London, 1829, p. 58.) The present Afin at Oyo is also enormous, and Robert Smith has suggested that it may in fact reproduce the ground plan and dimensions of that at Old Oyo (Oyo-Ile) (personal communication).

17 R. E. Bradbury 'The Historical Uses of Comparative Ethnography with special reference to Benin and the Yoruba' *op. cit.*, p. 145 ff.

18 P. C. Lloyd 'The Traditional Political System of the Yoruba' *The Southwestern Journal of Anthropology*, X, 4, Winter, 1954, pp. 366–84; also Lloyd 'Sacred Kingship . . .' *op. cit.*

19 Johnson's list of Alafin would make the present Alafin 43rd; Mr. Robert Smith has compiled a list of 45 and in a personal com-

munication with the author writes that in Oyo it is maintained that in all there have been seventy Alafin. See Appendix D.

20 Johnson *op. cit.*, p. 40.

21 S. F. Nadel *A Black Byzantium*, London 1942, Chapter VI and Appendix III. See also note 50 (p. 74) to Robert Smith's 'Igboho' *op. cit.* for a discussion of the dating of Tsoede's reign.

22 Personal communication with the author.

23 Since the publication of the first edition of this book a very useful article has appeared on the origin of kingship in Idah by John Boston entitled 'Notes on the Origin of Igala Kingship' *J.H.S.N.*, II, 3, December 1962.

24 Dennis Williams suggests (see: Smith 'Igboho' *op. cit.*, note 50, p. 74) that the famous Nupe bronzes may be of a considerably later date.

25 Smith *ibid.*, for a full account of the sojourn at Igboho.

26 William Bosman *A New and Accurate Description of the Coast of Guinea*, London, 1705, p. 397.

27 See R. E. Bradbury 'Chronological Problems in the Study of Benin History' *J.H.S.N.*, I, 4, 1959, p. 285, where he suggests that Egharevba's date of 1200 for the beginning of the dynasty is too early (Egharevba *op. cit.*, pp. 85–6). If we accept Bradbury's suggested date 'of not later than 1300' for the foundation of the dynasty, then there is a considerable discrepancy between the suggested date for the foundation of Oyo (Morton-Williams between 1390 and 1440) and that of Benin's new dynasty that has to be resolved. Professor A. F. C. Ryder has cast doubt on the supposed Ife origin of the Benin dynasty in an article entitled 'The Ife-Benin relationship' which appeared in *J.A.H.*, VI, 1, 1965, pp. 25–37, just before this edition went to press.

28 In a paper read to the Department of History, University of Ibadan, seminar on 'Feudalism in Africa', Mr. P. Igbafe, suggested that though it is not certain when primogeniture was introduced to Benin, it was probably at the beginning of the eighteenth century.

29 R. E. Bradbury 'The Rituals of Divine Kingship in Benin' *Nigeria Magazine*, No. 59, 1959.

30 *Ibid.*

31 For this information I am indebted to Mr. P. Igbafe's contribution cited above.

32 The best book available on Benin art is P.J.C. Dark *Benin Art*, London, 1961, with excellent photographs by W. and B. Forman.

33 See Graham Connah 'Archaeological Research in Benin City 1961–1964' *J.H.S.N.*, II, 4, December 1963, pp. 472–3 and map.

1 For the early history of European trade with West Africa see J. W. Blake *European Beginnings in West Africa, 1454–1578,* London, 1937, which should be read in conjunction with the same author's collection of documents covering this period, *Europeans in West Africa,* London, 1942, 2 vols.
See also Bovill *The Golden Trade op. cit.,* pp. 111–20.

2 Ruy de Pina *Chronica del Rey Dom Joao II,* ch. 24, trans. in J. W. Blake *Europeans in West Africa op. cit.,* I, 78–9, reprinted in Hodgkin *Nigerian Perspectives op. cit.,* p. 97.

3 Richard Eden 'The Voyage of M. Thomas Windham to Guinea and the Kingdom of Benin, Anno 1553' in Richard Hakluyt *The Principal Navigations, Voyages, Traffiques and Discoveries of the English Nation,* Glasgow, 1904, vol. VI, p. 149, reprinted in Blake *Europeans in West Africa op. cit.,* II, pp. 314–20.

4 Letter from Duarte Pires to King Manuel of Portugal dated 20th October 1516, trans. in J. W. Blake *ibid.,* I, pp. 123–4.
See also Hodgkin *ibid.,* pp. 99–100.

5 From the account of a 'Voyage from Lisbona to the island of San Thomé south of the Equator, described by a Portuguese pilot and sent to his magnificence Count Rimondo della Torre, gentleman of Verona, and translated from Portuguese into Italian', published in Giovanni Battista Ramusio *Navigazioni e Viaggi,* Venice, 1550. In Blake *ibid.,* I, pp. 150–1 and Hodgkin *ibid.,* pp. 100–1.

6 Eden: 'The Voyage of Thomas Windham, etc.' Blake *ibid.,* I, pp. 148–50.

7 Most authorities agree that 15,000,000 must be treated only as a conservative figure. See Daniel Mannix in collaboration with Malcolm Cowley *Black Cargoes—a History of the Atlantic Slave Trade 1518–1865,* London, 1963, p. 287, and Basil Davidson *Black Mother,* London, 1961, pp. 87–8. The lack of reliable statistics for the trade—some have estimated that as many as 50 million slaves reached the Americas—means that all the figures used here must be treated as very tentative. G. I. Jones in

Notes on Chapter IV.

'European and African Tradition on the Rio Real' *J.A.H.*, IV, 3, 1963, p. 391, has pointed to the danger of uncritical acceptance of contemporary estimates of the extent of the slave trade.

8 For general accounts of the slave trade see: H. A. Wyndham *The Atlantic Slavery*, London, 1935; Elizabeth Donnan *Documents illustrative of the Slave Trade to America*, 4 vols., Washington, 1930–5; Davidson *op. cit.*; Mannix with Cowley *op. cit.*

9 James Welsh *A Voyage to Benin beyond the country of Guinea made by Master James Welsh who set foorth in the yeere 1588*, in Hakluyt *op. cit.*, VI, pp. 456–8.

10 James Barbot *An Abstract of a Voyage to New Calabar River or Rio Real in the year 1699*, trans. and pub. in Churchill *Collection of Voyages and Travels*, 3rd edition, 1744–6, V, p. 459.

11 G. I. Jones 'Native and Trade Currencies in Southern Nigeria during the 18th and 19th Centuries' *Africa*, XXVIII, 1, 1958.

12 Captain Hugh Crow *Memoirs of the late Capt. Hugh Crow*, Liverpool, 1830.

13 Source: personal communication from M. Pierre Verger.

14 I am indebted to M. Pierre Verger for advice on this section. M. Verger is currently preparing a thesis on the slave trade between Brazil and West Africa. He has, however, already published material relevant to this topic, notably: 'Nigeria, Brazil and Cuba' in Michael Crowder ed. *Nigeria 1960—A special Independence Issue of Nigeria Magazine*, Lagos, 1960 and *Bahia and the West Coast Trade 1549–1851*, Ibadan, 1964.

15 Verger 'Nigeria, Brazil and Cuba' *ibid.*, p. 174.

Notes on Chapter V.

1 I am greatly indebted to Mr. Robin Horton for assistance in the preparation of material on the Ijo trading states with both this edition and the first edition. Since the publication of the first edition of this book there has appeared a work of major importance for the history of Nigeria which deals with the relationships between the Ijo and peoples of the Eastern hinterland—G. I. Jones *The Trading States of the Oil Rivers*, London, 1963. Where necessary I have revised or added to the text in the light of Jones's work.

2 E. I. Alagoa *Small Brave City State: A History of Brass Nembe in the Niger Delta*, Ibadan and Wisconsin, 1964, p. 57.

3 There is a very little primary source material for the history of Iboland before the nineteenth century. Some impressions of eighteenth-century Iboland may however be gained from *The Interesting Narrative of the Life of Olaudah Equiano, or Gustavus Vassa, the African, written by himself*, London, 1879, and cited in Thomas Hodgkin's *Nigerian Perspectives op. cit.*, pp. 155–66. It appears however to refer to a Western Ibo society.

4 See C. Thurstan Shaw 'Research Note: Bronzes from Eastern Nigeria—Excavations at Igbo Ukwu' *J.H.S.N.*, II, 1, December 1960, pp. 162–5.

5 Personal communication with the author.

6 The pattern of trading in the hinterland was also altered by the demands of the slave trade. Where there had been no political organization that could offer security of trade throughout the hinterland prior to the slave trade, an oracular cult was founded in Aro Chukwu whose priests were able to use its authority throughout Iboland in order to conduct trade. See S. J. Ottenberg 'Ibo Oracles and Inter-group Relations' *Southwestern Journal of Anthropology*, 14, 3, Autumn 1958, pp. 295–314.

7 G. I. Jones *op. cit.*, p. 177. 'The Kalabari, Bonny and Okrika people maintain that *amanyanabo* should be used to designate only the office of 'king', that is, the chieftaincy of a community which was vested in a single dynasty. They contrast the office of

Notes on Chapter V.

the king with the former office of the village head, called *amadabo* by the Okrika which it replaced.' The *amanyanabo* are of course the kings of contemporary European visitors' reports.

8 Jones *ibid*.

9 P. C. Lloyd 'The Itsekiri Kingdom in the Nineteenth Century; an Outline Social History' *J.A.H.*, IV, 2, 1963, p. 217 writes, 'Itsekiri social structure differed rather markedly from that of the Ijoh towns of Brass, Bonny and Opobo; the term "house" was very little used.'

10 Daryll Forde ed. *Efik Traders of Old Calabar*, London, 1956, p. 141. Chapter by G. I. Jones on 'The Political Organization of Old Calabar', pp. 116–57.

11 Barbot *op. cit.*, V, p. 459.

12 Jones *op. cit.*, pp. 88–101.

13 Ottenberg *op. cit.*, also Jones *ibid.*, various references. At present relatively little is known about the history of the Aro. However Dr. K. O. Diké, with Miss Felicia Ekejiuba, is currently conducting research on the Aro trading settlements in Eastern Nigeria.

14 Olfert Dapper *Description de l'Afrique*, Amsterdam, 1686, cited in Hodgkin *op. cit.*, p. 127.

15 From a letter from David van Nyendael to William Bosman in 1702, published in William Bosman *New and Accurate Description of the Coast of Guinea*, London, 1907 ed., p. 461. For a useful critical discussion of the whole question of Benin's supposed decline in the eighteenth century see James D. Graham 'The Slave Trade, Depopulation and Human Sacrifice in Benin History: The General Approach' *Cahiers d'Etudes Africaines*, V, 2, 18, 1965, pp. 317–34.

16 John Adams *Sketches taken during ten voyages to Africa between the years 1786 and 1800*, Liverpool, n.d., p. 32.

17 Olfert Dapper *op. cit.*, pp. 314–15, cited in Hodgkin *op. cit.*, pp. 130–1.

18 See P. C. Lloyd and A. F. C. Ryder 'Don Domingos, Prince of Warri', *Odu*, 4, 1957.

19 Father Jerome Merolla da Sorrento *A Voyage to the Congo and several other countries in Southern Africk in the year 1682* cited in Hodgkin *op. cit.*, pp. 138–40.

20 Lloyd 'The Itsekiri . . .' *op. cit.*, p. 210.

21 John Adams *op. cit.*, p. 38. G. I. Jones has warned against the uncritical acceptance of Adams's estimates 'Europeans and African Tradition . . .' *op. cit.*, p. 391.

22 W. R. G. Horton 'The Ohu system of slavery in a northern village group' *Africa*, XXIV, 4, October 1954, pp. 311–36.

Notes on Chapter VI.

1 K. Krieger *Geschichte von Zamfara*, Berlin, 1959.
2 Bovill *op. cit.*, pp. 224-5.
3 Thus, in Usman dan Fodio's *Wathiqat ahl al-Sudan*, which may well have been the proclamation of war in the Jihad, it is declared in paragraph xiv: 'And that to make war against the king who is an apostate—who has not abandoned the religion of Islam so far as the professing of it is concerned, and who mingles the observances of Islam with the observances of heathendom, like the kings of Hausaland for the most part—is obligatory by assent, and that to take the government from him by assent.' See A. D. H. Bivar 'The Wathiqat ahl al-Sudan: A manifesto of the Fulani Jihad' *J.A.H.*, IV, 2, 1961, pp. 235-43.
4 A full and excellent discussion of the Fulani Jihads is to be found in H. F. C. Smith 'A Neglected Theme of West African History: the Islamic Revolutions of the 19th Century' *J.H.S.N.*, II, No. 2, 1961. For general background studies of the Fulani see D. J. Stenning *Savannah Nomads*, London, 1959, which deals with the Wodaabe of Western Bornu and Edward Hopen *The Pastoral Fulbe Family in Gwandu*, London, 1958. D. J. Stenning 'Transhumance, Migratory Drift, Migration: Patterns of Pastoral Fulani Nomadism' *J. R. Anthrop. Inst.*, 87, 1957, pp. 57-73. Further works dealing specifically with the Jihad of Usman dan Fodio are: E. J. Arnett *The Rise of the Sokoto Fulani* (paraphrase of *Infaku'l Maisur* of Sultan Bello Muhammad), Kano, 1922. S. J. Hogben *The Muhammadan Emirates of Nigeria*, London, 1930. J. Spencer Trimingham *A History of Islam in West Africa*, Oxford, 1962. Articles in journals are cited in subsequent footnotes.

The main problem confronting the historian of the Jihad is the lack of information about the attitudes of the conquered peoples to the Fulani. No Hausa records of the Jihad appear to have survived, whilst much of the material written by the Fulani on which we now have to rely for want of an alternative source is in the nature of war propaganda.

Notes on Chapter VI.

5 A. H. M. Kirk-Greene *Adamawa Past and Present*, London, 1958, p. 153.

6 See Thomas Hodgkin 'Uthman dan Fodio' in *Nigeria 1960* ed. Michael Crowder, special Independence Issue of *Nigeria Magazine*, pp. 129–36. Also for a detailed account of his early life F. H. El Masri 'The Life of Shehu Usuman dan Fodio before the Jihad' *J.H.S.N.*, II, 4, December 1963, pp. 435–48.

7 H. F. C. Smith 'Muhammad Bello, Amir Al-mu'minin' *Ibadan*, No. 9, June 1960, p. 16.

8 M. Hiskett 'Material relating to the state of learning among the Fulani before their Jihad' *Bulletin of the School of Oriental and African Studies*, 19, 3, 1957.

9 M. G. Smith and M. Muntaka Kumasi *An Account of the Obligations of Withdrawal; being a translation of the 'Bayan Wujub al Hirja allal Ibad' of Shehu Usumanu dan Fodio*, 1959, unpublished, Part I, where Usman dan Fodio writes: '. . . but the countries of Bornu, Kano, Katsina, Songhai, and Malle, as Ahmed Baba shows . . . all these are heathen states without any doubt, since the chiefs . . . are heathen . . . although they practise the religion of Islam, because they are polytheists also. They have obstructed the way of Islam and have put worldly standards before the Faith. In the view of all the 'ulama all this is simply heathen.' See also Usman dan Fodio *Tanbih al-Ikhwan* and also Muhammad Bello *Infaq al Maysur*. The above references are taken from M. G. Smith's 'The Jihad of Shehu dan Fodio—Some Problems' paper presented to the International African Institute Seminar on *Islam in Tropical Africa* held at Zaria, December 1963.

10 M. Hiskett 'Kitab al-Farq' *Bulletin of the School of Oriental and African Studies*, XXII, 3, 1960.

11 M. G. Smith and M. Muntaka Kumasi *op. cit.*, Section 13, cited from M. G. Smith 'The Jihad of Shehu dan Fodio' *op. cit.*

12 For an explanation of the significance of the Sunna see Reuben Levy *The Social Structure of Islam* (2nd edition), London, 1962, pp. 170–1.

13 H. R. Palmer 'An Early Fulani Conception of Islam' *J. Afr. Soc.*, XIII, 1913–14, pp. 407–14 and XIV, 1914–15, pp. 53–9, and pp. 185–92, being a translation of Usman dan Fodio's *Tanbih al-ikhwan* (The Admonition of the Brethren).

14 Hodgkin 'Uthman dan Fodio' *op. cit.*, pp. 131–2.

15 Hiskett 'Material Relating to the Jihad' *op. cit.*

16 See Trimingham *op. cit.*, in particular p. 200. Another argument brought forward by critics of the Jihad in support of their interpretation that it was largely racial in character is the fact that the Habe Hausa rulers were all replaced by Fulanis. However

Notes on Chapter VI.

H. F. C. Smith has shown that in the one case where a Habe ruler, Isiaka Jatau, Sarkin Zazzau, responded to the call of Usman dan Fodio for religious reform, he was allowed to keep his throne and reigned as first Emir of Zaria. 'The Dynastic Chronology of Fulani Zaria' *J.H.S.N.*, II, 2, December 1961, pp. 279–80.

17 This correspondence is printed in Hodgkin *Nigerian Perspectives op. cit.*, pp. 198–205.

18 Nana, daughter of Usman dan Fodio, was to write:

> *Yunfa fled from bare-legged herdsmen.*
> *Who had neither mail nor horseman.*
> *We that had been chased like hares*
> *Can now live in houses.'*

see F. Daniel 'Shehu dan Fodio' *J. Afr. Soc.*, XXV, 1926, p. 281.

19 Arnett *op. cit.*, p. 71.

20 F. W. de St. Croix *The Fulani of Northern Nigeria*, Lagos, 1945, p. 2.

21 H. F. C. Smith *op. cit.*

22 Alhaji Hassan and Mallam Shuaibu Na'ibi *A Chronicle of Abuja op. cit.*, p. 4.

There is no reference to the reign of Isiaka Jatau in the Chronicle, which records that the Shehu's forces 'fell upon the King of Zazzau, Muhammadu Makau on Saturday the tenth day of the month of Zulhaji in the year 1804 whilst he was at the prayer-ground of Idi outside the town' (p. 4). This would suggest that M. Makau was a true Moslem, which if it were so, would bring into question the legitimacy of the Jihad, since it was only lawful to attack those rulers who were by Koranic definition 'pagan'.

23 Smith *ibid.*, p. 280.

24 Urvoy *op. cit.*, p. 103.

25 D. Denham, H. Clapperton, and W. Oudney *Narrative of Travels and Discoveries in Northern and Central Africa, in the years 1822, 1823 and 1824*, London, 1826, cited in Hodgkin *Nigerian Perspectives, op. cit.*, pp. 205–8.

26 *Ibid.*, pp. 214–15, 244. There is an eye-witness account by Major Dixon Denham of the decisive defeat of the Bagirmi army by Bornu in 1824. However the year before Bagirmi had actually invaded Bornu.

27 Isiaka Jatau, First Emir of Zaria, was not of course a flag-bearer. Nor was the Habe ruler of Daura who became a Moslem and accepted the authority of Sokoto. Yakubu is described as non-Fulani in Hogben *op. cit.*, p. 172; but Kirk-Greene *op. cit.*, p. 154 says that the Yakubu was a brother of Buba Yero of Gombe who was definitely Fulani!

Notes on Chapter VI.

28 For the Jihad in Adamawa Province see A. H. M. Kirk-Greene *op. cit.*

29 For the Jihad in Nupe see Hogben *op. cit.* and Nadel *op. cit.*

30 For the Jihad in Ilorin see H. B. Herman-Hodge *Gazetteer of Ilorin Province*, London, 1924, Hogben *op. cit.*, Johnson *op. cit.*

31 I have revised my earlier account of the Jihad in Ilorin in the light of J. F. Ade Ajayi's introduction to 'The Narrative of Samuel Ajayi Crowther' to appear in a collection of African traveller's reports to be edited by Philip Curtin. See also B. G. Martin 'A new Arabic History of Ilorin' *Research Bulletin*, Institute of African Studies, University of Ibadan, Centre of Arabic Documentation, I, 2, January 1965, pp. 20–7.

32 Ajayi *ibid.*

33 Al-Hajj Sa'id *History of Sokoto* trans. C. E. J. Whitting, Kano, 1949, p. 37.

W. E. N. Kensdale 'Field Notes on the Arabic Literature of the Western Sudan' *J. R. Asiatic Soc.*, 1955, 1956 and 1958 lists 83 works by Usman dan Fodio, 75 by Abdullahi dan Fodio, and 93 by Muhammad Bello.

34 Cited in Hodgkin Nigerian Perspectives *op. cit.*, pp. 194–5.

Notes on Chapter VII.

1 Sir Alan Burns *History of Nigeria*, London, 1958, 5th edition, p. 26.
2 Personal communication from Mr. Peter Morton-Williams.
3 I am indebted to Dr. Akin Mabogunje for his advice on the construction of this map.
4 P. C. Lloyd 'The Traditional Politic System of the Yoruba' *op. cit.*, pp. 366–84.
5 Ajayi and Smith *op. cit.*, p. 4.
6 Bosman *op. cit.*, pp. 397–8.
7 Archibald Dalzell *History of Dahomey an Inland Kingdom of Africa*, London, 1800, p. 15.
8 For an interesting discussion of the reasons behind Dahomey's conquest of these coastal states see 'Agaja and the conquest of the coastal Aja states' *J.H.S.N.*, II, 4, 1963, pp. 545–66.
9 Smith 'Alafin in Exile' *op. cit.*, p. 73, citing A. I. Akinjogbin's Ph.D. thesis *Dahomey and its Neighbours 1708–1818*.
10 Dalzell *op. cit.*, p. 157.
11 Johnson *op. cit.*, p. 188.
12 I. A. Akinjogbin 'The Prelude to the Yoruba Civil Wars' (Manuscript).
13 Biobaku *op. cit.*, pp. 8–10.
14 Private communication with Mr. Peter Morton-Williams.
15 Akinjogbin 'Prelude' *op. cit.* All subsequent references to Akinjogbin in this chapter are to this particular paper.
16 J. D. Fage *Introduction to the History of West Africa*, London, 1959, p. 91.
17 Ajayi and Smith *op. cit.*, p. 124.
18 The stress on the constitutional importance of the Oni of Ife is one of the more important points in Akinjogbin's paper *op. cit.*
19 Johnson *op. cit.*, p. 192.
20 See J. F. Ade Ajayi's introduction to 'The Narrative of Samuel Ajayi: Crowther' *op. cit.*
21 Johnson *op. cit.*, pp. 206–7.
22 The date for the fall of Owu is usually given as *c.* 1825. However

Notes on Chapter VII.

Omer-Cooper has suggested that 1827 would be more accurate. See Robert S. Smith 'Ijaiye, the Western Palatinate of the Yoruba' *J.H.S.N.*, II, 3, December 1962, p. 331.

23 John *op. cit.*, p. 189, Ajayi *ibid.*
24 Johnson *ibid.*, p. 196.
25 C. W. Newbury *The Western Slave Coast and its Rulers*, London, 1961, p. 38.
26 Smith 'Ijaiye' *op. cit.*, p. 52.
27 Willett 'Investigations at Old Oyo' *op. cit.*
28 Ajayi and Smith *op. cit.*, p. 29.
29 See: Edouard Dunglas 'La Première attaque des Dahoméennes contre Abeokuta' *Etudes Dahoméennes*, I, 1949, I.F.A.N. See also *Nigeria Magazine*, No. 64, March 1960 where extracts on this paper by Dunglas appear in English. Smith has a most useful analysis of the strategy of the battle of Abeokuta in Ajayi and Smith *op. cit.*, pp. 37–9. I have made a number of changes to the text in the light of Smith's account.

Notes on Chapter VIII.

1 For detailed studies of the movement in Britain for the abolition of the slave trade see: Thomas J. Clarkson *History of the Rise, Progress and Accomplishment of the Abolition of the African Slave Trade*, 2 vols., London, 1808; Sir Reginald Coupland *The British Anti-Slavery Movement*, London, 1933.

2 Eric Williams *Capitalism and Slavery*, London, 1964.

3 A. Falconbridge *An Account of the Slave Trade on the Coast of Africa*, London, 1788. Among other important abolitionist works were: T. Clarkson *Essay on the Slavery and Commerce of the Human Species*, 1788; and J. Newton *Thoughts upon the African Slave Trade* (pamphlet), London, 1788.

4 See Diké *op. cit.*, pp. 11–14.

5 *Captain Canot, or Twenty Years of an African Slaver* ed. by Brantz Meyer, New York, 1854.

6 Lecky *History of England*.

7 The slave trade only became legal for Spaniards in 1789.

8 See Christopher Lloyd *The Navy and the Slave Trade*, London, 1949, on which I have relied heavily in this chapter. Also Mannix with Cowley *op. cit.*, Chapter 9, pp. 191–215; Sir Alan Burns *op. cit.*; *Report of the House of Commons Select Committee on the Slave Trade*, London, 1842; C. W. Newbury *The Western Slave Coast and its Rulers*, Oxford, 1961, Chapter II, pp. 35–48.

9 Source not traced.

10 H. Crow *Memoirs*, London, 1830, p. 137.

11 Cited by Diké *op. cit.*, p. 48.

12 *Ibid.*, p. 67.

13 Burns *op. cit.*, p. 104; Diké *ibid.*, p. 48.

14 Diké *ibid.*, p. 53.

15 W. F. W. Owen *Narrative of a Voyage to Explore the Shores of Africa, Arabia and Madagascar*, New York, 1833.

16 Reprinted in Jones *op. cit.* Appendix B, pp. 221–2.

17 Cited in Christopher Lloyd *op. cit.*

18 See: E. J. Alagoa *op. cit.*, pp. 57–8.

19 Source not traced.

Notes on Chapter IX.

1 See Appendix 'Mortality in West Africa' to Philip D. Curtin *The Image of Africa*, Wisconsin, 1964, pp. 483–7.

2 A. Adu Boahen *Britain, the Sahara and the Western Sudan 1788–1861*, London, 1964, Chapter I, pp. 1–28.

3 *Ibid.*, p. 3.

4 The Proceedings of the African Association have recently been published in a new edition by Robin Hallett ed.: *The Records of the African Association, 1788–1831*, London, 1964.

5 Boahen *op. cit.*, p. 12, shows that whilst the Niger problem was of great concern to the Association 'its solution was not, as is generally supposed, the first concern of the Association'.

6 Leo Africanus *op. cit.*, I, pp. 124–5, but see also III, p. 1096, for a more accurate translation of this vital passage.

7 *Travels of Mungo Park* ed. Ronald Miller, London, 1954, pp. 78–9.

8 *The Proceedings of the Association for Promoting the Discovery of the Interior Parts of Africa*, London, 1790.

9 Miller *op. cit.*, p. 149.

10 'Abstract of Mr. Park's account of his travels and discoveries abridged . . . by B. Edwards . . . also geographical illustrations of Mr. Park's journeys . . . by Major Rennell.' *Proceedings op. cit.*

11 Burns *op. cit.*, p. 78.

12 *Proceedings op. cit.*

13 Miller *op. cit.*, pp. 281–364. See also 'The Death of Mungo Park' *Nigeria Magazine*, No. 71, 1961.

14 James MacQueen *A Geographical and Commercial View of Northern Central Africa*, Edinburgh, 1821.

15 Denham and Clapperton *op. cit.*, cited in Hodgkin *Nigerian Perspectives op. cit.*, p. 211.

16 A. H. M. Kirk-Greene has a useful note in *Man*, nos. 219 and 220, November 1963, on 'Some spears from Bornu, Northern Nigeria' which gives an idea of the weapons used by armies in Northern Nigeria at that period.

17 Denham, Clapperton *op. cit.*, 'Captain Clapperton's Narrative', pp. 51–3, cited in Hodgkin *Nigerian Perspectives op. cit.*, pp. 215–17.

Notes on Chapter IX.

18 *Ibid.*

19 H. Clapperton *Journal of a Second Expedition into the Interior of Africa from the Bight of Benin to Soccatoo*, London, 1829, pp. 196–8.

20 Richard and John Lander *Journal of an Expedition to explore the Course and Termination of the Niger*, London, 1832.

21 MacGregor Laird and R. A. K. Oldfield *Expedition into the Interior of Africa*, 2 vols., London, 1837.

22 Sir Thomas Fowell Buxton *The African Slave Trade and its Remedy*, London, 1839. See also J. Gallagher 'Fowell Buxton and the New African Policy 1832–1842' *Cambridge Historical Journal*, X, 1, 1950, and C. C. Ifemesia 'The "Civilising" Mission of 1841: Aspects of an Episode in Anglo-Nigerian Relations', *J.H.S.N.*, pp. 291–310.

23 Eugene Stock ed. *The History of the Church Missionary Society*, London, 1899, vol. I, p. 45, cited in James Coleman *Nigeria Background to Nationalism*, London, 1958, p. 91.

24 Henri Brunschwig *L'Avènement de l'Afrique* Paris, 1964, p. 70; see also W. Simpson *A Private Journal kept during the Niger Expedition 1841–2 from May, 1841 to June, 1842*, London, 1843.

25 Robert Jamieson *An appeal to the Government and People of Great Britain against the proposed Niger expedition*, London, 1840.

26 J. F. Schön and S. A. Crowther *Journals of the Rev. J. F. Schön and Mr. Samuel Crowther, who with the sanction of Her Majesty's Government, accompanied the expedition up the Niger in 1841, on behalf of the Church Missionary Society*, London, 1842. Also W. Simpson *op. cit.*

27 The best account of Crowther's role in the evangelization of Nigeria is contained in J. F. Ade Ajayi's thesis *Christian Missions and the Making of Nigeria* on which I have relied heavily for material for the second half of this chapter. This thesis has just been published as *Christian Missions in Nigeria 1841–1891: The Making of an Educated Elite*, London, 1965.

28 In the first edition of this book the expedition was described conventionally as a 'disastrous' failure—see for instance J. D. Hargreaves *Prelude to the Partition of West Africa*, London, 1963, who also takes this position. However, subsequent to publication of the first edition there has appeared the important article by C. C. Ifemesia, cited above, in which he shows 'how near to success the expedition was at the time and how it set the pattern for subsequent ventures which eventually led to the British occupation of the entire country (Nigeria) at the turn of the twentieth century'.

29 J. F. Ade Ajayi 'Henry Venn and the Policy of Development' *J.H.S.N.*, I, 4, 1959.

30 Ifemesia *op. cit.*, p. 310.

Notes on Chapter IX.

31 J. F. Ade Ajayi 'The British Occupation of Lagos 1851–1861' *Nigeria Magazine* 69, August 1961, pp. 96–105.

32 Anna Hinderer *Seventeen Years in the Yoruba Country*, London, 1873.

33 Ajayi *Missions* (thesis) *op. cit.*

34 Donald M. Macfarlane *Calabar and the Church of Scotland Mission, 1849–1946*, London, 1946; and Rev. Hugh Goldie *Calabar and its Mission*, London, 1890.

35 See K. Onwuka Diké *Origins of the Niger Mission 1841–1891*, Lagos, 1957; also S. A. Crowther and J. C. Taylor *The Gospel on the Banks of the Niger, Journals and notices of the native missionaries accompanying the Niger Expedition of 1857–9*, London, 1859 and S. A. Crowther, *Journal of an Expedition up the Niger and the Tshadda Rivers undertaken by Macgregor Laird, Esq., in connection with the British Government, in 1854*, London, 1855.

36 J. D. Hargreaves *op. cit.*, p. 4 and Boahen *op. cit.*, pp. 181–215, where there is a full discussion of the origins and achievements of the Central African Mission and its influence in the 1854 Mission.

37 Heinrich Barth *Travels and Discoveries in Northern and Central Africa*, 5 vols., London, 1857. A useful anthology of Barth's writings on Northern Nigeria is A. H. M. Kirk-Greene's *Barth's Travels in Northern Nigeria*, London, 1962.

38 Boahen *op. cit.*, p. 213.

39 W. B. Baikie *Narrative on an Exploring Voyage up the Rivers Kwora and Binue—commonly known as the Niger and Tshadda—in 1854*, London, 1856, also Michael Crowder 'Pioneer of the Niger—W. B. Baikie' *West African Review*, XXVI, 339, December 1955, pp. 1157–61.

40 The much discussed *Africa and the Victorians* by Ronald Robinson and John Gallagher with Alice Denny, London, 1961, which was published after the first edition of this book went to press, has a most useful chapter on 'The Spirit of Victorian Expansion', pp. 1–25, which gives a full account of the attitudes of the society from which these missionaries came to the outside world and Britain's role in it.

Notes on Chapter X.

1 This paragraph has been revised in view of the arguments of Robinson and Gallagher *op. cit.* See pp. 29–30 for particular reference to the Parliamentary Select Committee.

2 Diké *Trade op. cit.*, p. 101.

3 R. S. Smith 'Ijaiye, the Western Palatinate of the Yoruba' *op. cit.*, p. 332.

W. D. McIntyre in 'Commander Glover and the Colony of Lagos, 1861–73' *J.A.H.*, IV, 1, 1963 cites a passage from a Colonial Office minute which brings out the paradoxical position of the humanitarian very nicely: '. . . by encouraging legitimate commerce we may turn serfdom with its loose intermittent obligations, into that unrelenting methodised slavery which is inflicted by a master who sees his way to making a profit of every hour of his slaves' labour.' (Minute by Rogers, 14. XII, 1863, on Glover to Newcastle, 10, xi, 1863, C.O. 147/4.)

4 Diké *ibid*, p. 100–1.

5 G. I. Jones 'Native and Trade Currencies in Southern Nigeria during the 18th and 19th Centuries' *Africa* XXVIII, No. 1, 1958.

See also A. H. M. Kirk-Greene 'The Major Currencies in Nigerian History' *J.H.S.N.*, II, 1, December 1960.

6 K. Onwuka Diké 'John Beecroft 1790–1854: Her Britannic Majesty's Consul to the Bights of Benin and Biafra 1849–54' *J.H.S.N.*, I, 1, December 1956, pp. 5–14.

7 *Ibid.*, p. 14.

8 For Beecroft's role in Bonny affairs I have relied heavily on Diké *Trade op. cit.*, Chapter VII.

9 Jones *Trading States op. cit.*, p. 14.

10 The text of this treaty is printed in Jones *ibid.*, Appendix B, pp. 222–5.

11 J. F. Ade Ajayi 'The British Occupation of Lagos 1851–61' *op. cit.* refutes this view.

12 Ajayi *Missions op. cit.*, p. 38.

Notes on Chapter X.

13 Cited in Ajayi 'British Occupation of Lagos' *op. cit.*

14 Diké *Trade op. cit.*, pp. 137–43. I have modified my original account, based on Diké, in view of Jones *Trading States op. cit.*, pp. 116–20.

15 See Jones *ibid.*, p. 119, where he shows that whilst most of the chiefs of Bonny were against Pepple, they hesitated to have him deported on three grounds: 'What was to happen about the king's debts? What would be the reaction of the Imo river oil markets? Was the deportation of a native of Bonny contrary to their customs and forbidden by their religion?'

16 *Ibid.*, pp. 119–20.

17 T. J. Hutchinson *Ten Years Wandering Among the Ethiopians*, London, 1861, pp. 173–8.

18 See Baikie *op. cit.*

19 Diké *Trade op. cit.*, p. 170.

20 Howard Pedraza *The Story of Lokoja—the first British Settlement in Nigeria*, London, 1960.

21 Cited by Pedraza *ibid.*, p. 55.

22 Diké *Origins of the Niger Mission 1841–1891*, Lagos, 1957, pp. 10–11. See also S. Crowther and J. C. Taylor *The Gospel on the Banks of the Niger*, London, 1859.

23 The Crowther-Townsend dispute is given detailed treatment in Ajayi *Missions op. cit.*

   For an interesting study of the forward-looking ideas of Venn on a large number of subjects relating to the European role in Africa see J. F. Ade Ajayi's 'Henry Venn and the Policy of Development' *op. cit.*

24 Biobaku *op. cit.*, p. 53.

25 I have revised my account of the causes and course of the Ijaye war in the light of Ajayi and Smith *op. cit.*, pp. 76–80, and Smith 'Ijaiye' *op. cit.*, p. 340. The original version was based on Johnson's account in *History of the Yorubas op. cit.*, pp. 331–54.

26 For a detailed account of the course of the war see Ajayi and Smith *ibid.*, pp. 86–122.

27 Biobaku *op. cit.*, pp. 104–5.

   In preparation for the secondment of this force to the Egba, a Captain A. T. Jones of the 2nd West India Regiment was sent to Abeokuta where he made a report on the military situation in that area, which is published as an appendix in Ajayi and Smith *op. cit.*, entitled 'Captain Jones's Report on the Egba Army in 1861', pp. 129–40.

28 Cited in Biobaku *op. cit.*, p. 68.

29 Burns *op. cit.*, p. 126.

Notes on Chapter X.

30 Since the first edition of this book was published a very useful article on Glover has appeared. See W. D. McIntyre 'Glover and Lagos' op. cit.

31 Ajayi *Christian Missions op. cit.*, p. 201.

32 Biobaku *op. cit.*, p. 77.

Notes on Chapter XI.

1 I have relied heavily on Biobaku *op. cit.*, pp. 73–95 for my account on Glover's activities in Lagos and Yorubaland. See also McIntyre *op. cit.* Glover's wife wrote a full-length biography of her husband: Lady Glover *Life of Sir John Hawley Glover*, London, 1897.

2 Biobaku *ibid.*, pp. 79–80.

3 *Ibid.*, Map No. 4. 'A Sketch showing Trade Routes to the Interior from Lagos' reproduced from Commander Glover's coloured plan in C.O. 147/21, 1872.

4 *Ibid.*, p. 95.

5 Johnson *op. cit.*, p. 416.

6 Notes as to source mislaid.

7 There is a full account of the early career of Jaja and his rise to power in Bonny in Diké *Trade op. cit.*, C.X., pp. 182–202. See also G. I. Jones *Trading States op. cit.*, pp. 127–32.

8 Jones *ibid.* suggests this date from a letter from Consul Richard Burton to the Foreign Office, p. 128.

9 *Ibid.*, pp. 128–9.

10 Cited in Diké *ibid.*, p. 194. F.O. 84/1326, No. 27, Granville to Livingstone, 3 Aug. 1870.

11 P. C. Lloyd 'The Itsekiri' *op. cit.*, pp. 212–23.

12 *Ibid.*, p. 224.

13 See Pedrarza *op. cit.*, pp. 67–74 also Burns *op. cit.*, p. 139.

14 Diké *Niger Mission op. cit.*, pp. 16–18.

15 Macfarlane *op. cit.*

16 See J. E. Flint *Sir George Goldie and the Making of Nigeria*, London, 1960, for a study of Goldie's career in Nigeria and for an excellent account of British policy in the Niger region. Unfortunately Goldie made it impossible for anyone to write a full-scale biography of him for he had a passionate hatred of any publicity about himself. However something of the complexity of his character emerges in the pages of the book and also in Lady Dorothy Wellesley's impressionistic *Sir George Goldie—Founder of Nigeria*, London, 1934.

17 He was, however, not the first Englishman in Nigeria to have made this appreciation, for Baikie and Glover had both expressed concern over French ambitions to the Foreign Office as early as 1859. See McIntyre *op. cit.*, pp. 59–60.

18 *London Gazette*, 5th June 1885. See Burns *op. cit.*, p. 145.

Notes on Chapter XII.

1 The principal clauses of the Charter are reproduced in Burns *op. cit.*, pp. 152–3.

2 For the history of the Royal Niger Company's activities I have relied heavily on Flint *op. cit.* Also see Cook *op. cit.*, Chapter III, pp. 79–114 and Burns *op. cit.*, Chapter XIII, pp. 151–64.

3 Burns *ibid.*, pp. 157–8.

4 Mary Kingsley *West African Studies*, London, 1901 (2nd Edn.), p. 308.

5 Cited in Wellesley *op. cit.*, p. 21.

6 See J. Lombard 'Un système politique traditionnel de type féodal: les Bariba du Nord-Dahomey. Aperçu sur l'organisation sociale et le pouvoir central.' *Bulletin de l'I.F.A.N.*, T. XIX, sér. B, Nos, 3–4, 1957, pp. 464–506.

7 See *The Diaries of Lord Lugard, Vol. 4, Nigeria, 1894–5 and 1898* ed. Margery Perham and Mary Bull, London, 1963. Extracts of the diary are published in Herman-Hodge *Gazetteer of Ilorin Province op. cit.* There is a full account of the race to Nikki in the first volume of Margery Perham's biography of Lugard *Lugard: The Years of Adventure 1855–1898*, London, 1956.

8 *Diaries of Lord Lugard ibid.*, IV, p. 143.

9 Perham *Lugard I ibid.*, p. 537.

10 Cited in Cook *op. cit.*, p. 61.

11 The full text of the letter is reproduced in *Burns op. cit.*, p. 149.

12 The full text of this treaty is reproduced in *ibid.*, Appendix J, pp. 326–8.

13 Cook *op. cit.*, p. 66.

14 P. C. Lloyd 'The Itsekiri' *op. cit.*, p. 229.

15 Cook *op. cit.*, p. 72.

16 Flint *op. cit.*, Chapter 7, pp. 129–55, has a full account of Macdonald's investigation.

17 *Ibid.*, Chapter 9, pp. 187–215 has a full account of the war between Brass and the R.N.C.

18 Edun Akenzua 'The British Occupation of Benin' *Nigeria Magazine*, No. 59, 1960. See also James D. Graham 'The Slave Trade . . . in Benin History' *op. cit.*

Notes on Chapter XII.

19 H. Ling Roth *Great Benin—Its Customs, Art and Horrors*, London, 1903. See also Alan Boisragon *The Benin Massacre*, London, 1897 and R. H. Bacon *Benin, the City of Blood*, London, 1897

20 Cited in Johnson *op. cit.*, p. 547.

21 *Ibid.*, p. 593.

22 *Ibid.*, pp. 613–14.

23 *Ibid.*, p. 623.

24 *Ibid.*, p. 632.

Notes on Chapter XIII.

1 Cited in Burns *op. cit.*, p. 162-3 from *Papers relating to the Surrender of the Charter of the Royal Niger Company, 1899* (C. 9372).

2 Wellesley *op. cit.*, pp. 98-9.

3 Perham *Lugard II, op. cit.*, p. 27.

4 See for example Lady Lugard *A Tropical Dependency*, London, 1905, in particular Chapter 43, pp. 399-407.

5 Cited by Burns *op. cit.*, p. 177, no source given.

6 *Annual Report for Northern Nigeria*, 1902, p. 43.

7 J. A. Burdon 'The Fulani Emirates of Northern Nigeria' *J. Roy. Geo. Soc.*, VI, December 1904, pp. 636-51.

8 *Ibid.*, p. 649.

9 M. Hiskett '*Kitab al-Farq*' *op. cit.*

10 D. M. Last in a paper entitled 'Notes on a Muslim Caliphate, with special reference to Sokoto' presented to the Seminar on Feudalism in the Department of History, University of Ibadan, 26th October 1963.

11 Al-Hajj Sa'id *op. cit.*, p. 11.

12 For an excellent short biographical study of Sultan Bello, see H. F. C. Smith 'Muhammad Bello, Amir Al-mu'minin', *Ibadan*, 9, June 1960.

13 H. Clapperton *Journal of a Second Expedition into the Interior of Africa etc.*, London, 1829, pp. 196-8.

14 For instance Lady Lugard *op. cit.*, Trimingham *op. cit.*, p. 205 where he writes, ' 'Atīq (Bello's successor) a rigid puritan, attempted some reforms, but the religious enthusiasm of the Fulbe had ebbed, for only 'Uthmān and a few of his original followers were moved by genuine religious conviction. The fruits of power sapped the vital energies that had brought such success and the *jihād* degenerated into undisguised slave-raiding which, together with perpetual wars, ruined and depopulated vast areas. During the reign of 'Alī (1842-59) power passed completely into the hands of the provincial governors whose number 'Alī had increased, and as independent rulers they recognised only the religious authority of the ruler of Sokoto.'

Notes on Chapter XIII.

See also Lord Lugard's *Reports on Northern Nigeria* for 1900, 1901, 1902.

15 Boahen *op. cit.*, Appendix IV, 'Political Conditions in the Western Sudan in the First Half of the Nineteenth Century', pp. 219–47.

16 M. G. Smith *Government in Zazzau op. cit.*, pp. 163–6.

17 A. H. M. Kirk-Greene *Adamawa Past and Present op. cit.*, pp. 125–65.

18 M. G. Smith *ibid.*, pp. 159–64.

19 Barth *op. cit.* (New York, 1857 edition), III, p. 81.

20 *Ibid.*, II, pp. 186–7.

21 Kirk-Greene *ibid.*, p. 140.

22 Boahen *op. cit.*, p. 241 (F.O. 101/34, Barth to F.O., 28, January 1853).

23 Barth *op. cit.*, I, pp. 510–15.

24 Kirk-Greene *ibid.*, pp. 139–40.

25 Mary Smith *Baba of Karo*, London, 1954.

26 Cook *op. cit.*, p. 155. The 1885 Treaty between the Sultan of Sokoto (Omaru, 1881–91) and Joseph Thompson, on behalf of the National African Company is reproduced in Burns *op. cit.*, Appendix G, pp. 322–3.

27 For Lugard's conquest of Northern Nigeria I have relied mainly on Perham *Lugard I, op. cit.*, C. W. J. Orr *The Making of Northern Nigeria*, London, 1911, and Lugard's own Annual Reports.

28 Lugard *The Dual Mandate in Tropical Africa*, London, 1923. See also Perham *Lugard II, op. cit.*, pp. 138–73.

29 *Annual Report for Northern Nigeria 1901*. Report for period January 1901–March 1901, p. 15.

30 Cited in Perham *ibid.*, p. 45.

31 See *Annual Report for Northern Nigeria 1901 op. cit.*, p. 15.

32 *Ibid.*, p. 7.

33 *Annual Report for Northern Nigeria 1902*, p. 10.

34 Saburi Biobaku and Mohammad Al-Hajj 'The Sudanese Mahidiyya and the Niger-Chad Region', p. 13. Paper presented to the Seminar on Islam in Tropical Africa (cited). The authors show how the Mahdi was in correspondence with both Bornu and Sokoto demanding both recognition and support.

35 For Rabeh's career see Urvoy *op. cit.*, Schultze *op. cit.* and E. Gentil *La Chute de l'Empire de Rabeh*, Paris, 1902.

36 *Annual Report for Northern Nigeria, 1901*, p. 15.

37 *Ibid.*, p. 15.

38 D. J. M. Muffett in *Concerning Brave Captains*, London, 1964, pp. 34–51.

39 Lady Lugard *op. cit.*, p. 441.

Notes on Chapter XIII.

40 Hilaire Belloc in *The Modern Traveller* cited in Perham *Lugard II*, *op. cit.*, p. 45.

41 *Annual Report for Northern Nigeria 1902*, Appendix III, p. 105.

42 Muffet *op. cit.*, pp. 143–212.

43 *Ibid.*, p. 147.

44 *Ibid.*, p. 137.

45 *Annual Report for Northern Nigeria 1903*.

46 Biobaku and Al-Hajj *op. cit.*, p. 15.

47 Perham *Lugard II op. cit.*, p. 252.

48 Cited *ibid.*, p. 258, from Cmd. 3620, p. 19.

49 M. G. Smith *op. cit.*, pp. 205–6.

Notes on Chapter XIV.

Notes on Chapter XIII.

45 *Annual Report for Northern Nigeria 1902*.

1 J. C. Anene 'The Protectorate Government of Southern Nigeria
  and the Aros 1900–1902' *J.H.S.N.*, I, 1, December 1956, pp.
  20–6. Unfortunately in writing on the Aro in the first edition I
  missed this article. I have now revised my earlier account in
  view of this additional material.
2 *Ibid.*, p. 21.
3 *Ibid.*, p. 26.
4 See Burns *op. cit.*, p. 210. Also for a short passage on the pacification of Urhobo see 'The Establishment of British Administration
  in the Urhobo Country (1891–1913) *J.H.S.N.*, I, 3, December
  1958, pp. 198–200.
5 *Colonial Annual Reports for Southern Nigeria* for 1908 and 1910.
6 There is an excellent and very full account of the impact of
  Western economic forces on Nigerian society in James Coleman
  Nigeria: Background to Nationalism, London, 1958, pp. 63–90.
7 Direct taxation, which was unknown in most parts of Southern
  Nigeria, was conceived by Lugard and other British administrators, to be useful not so much for raising revenue for government (for this could always be obtained by duties on imports and
  exports), but because of its alleged 'moral benefits'. Taxation
  forced the African to work more than was necessary to
  satisfy his immediate wants. Since work was considered morally
  good, then taxation, which forced the African to work more, was
  morally beneficial. Of course it was also beneficial to the colonial
  power, anxious to exploit the country's economic resources,
  since in order to raise funds for the payment of taxes, the African
  had to grow cash crops, which like cocoa, were often of no use to
  him for personal consumption. See Lord Lugard *The Dual
  Mandate in Tropical Africa*, London, 1922, Chapter XII, pp.
  230–55.
8 Captain J. F. J. Fitzpatrick 'Nigeria's Curse—The Native
  Administration' *National Review*, No. 502, December 1924, p.
  618.
9 See Mary Bull 'Indirect Rule in Northern Nigeria 1906–1911'

Notes on Chapter XIV.

Essays in Imperial Government (presented to Margery Perham), ed. Kenneth Robinson and Frederick Madden, Oxford, 1963.

10 P. C. Lloyd 'Kings, Chiefs and Local Government' *West Africa*, Saturday, 31st January 1953.

11 For a full length biography of Mary Slessor on which much of this section is based, see W. P. Livingstone *Mary Slessor of Calabar*, 4th edition, London, 1935. Also 'Mary Slessor' *Nigeria Magazine*, No. 58, 1958.

12 James S. Coleman *op. cit.*, p. 101. I am much in debt to Professor Coleman's chapter on 'Christianity and Missionaries', pp. 91–112, for this section on missionary impact on Nigeria and also to discussions with Mr. Robin Horton.

13 Ajayi *Missions op. cit.*, p. 225–6.

14 *Ibid.*, pp. 253–4.

15 See Coleman *op. cit.*, Chapter 5, 'Western Education', pp. 113–40 for a full discussion of the impact of Western education on Nigerian societies.

16 For a full discussion of the economics and politics of 'amalgamation' see Perham *Lugard II op. cit.*, Chapter XX: 'The Creation of Nigeria', pp. 408–21. Also *Nigeria: Report by Sir F. D. Lugard on the Amalgamation of Northern and Southern Nigeria and Administration, 1912–1919*, Cmd. 468, London, 1920, and Cook *op. cit.*, pp. 190–211.

17 E. D. Morel *Nigeria, its Peoples and Problems*, 2nd edition, London, 1912, pp. 201–10.

18 See Perham *ibid.*, p. 414.

19 *Ibid.*, Chapter XIX, pp. 377–407.

20 *Report on Amalgamation op. cit.*, p. 12.

21 Perham *ibid.*, pp. 418–20.

22 Cited by Cook *op. cit.*, p. 207, no source given.

23 *Report on Amalgamation op. cit.*, p. 14–15.

24 Perham *ibid.*, pp. 487–8.

25 Of course direct taxation was not altogether foreign to the Yoruba since it was introduced to Ilorin by the Fulani after 1830.

26 This report is not a published one, existing only in typescript: 'Reports of a Tour in the Southern Provinces in 1914 by H. R. Palmer' cited by Margery Perham from the Lugard Papers. Perham *ibid.*, p. 444.

27 *Ibid.*, pp. 445–7.

28 Lugard shared many of the prejudices against mixing with educated Africans current among the British at the time. (See Lord Lugard *The Dual Mandate op. cit.*, p. 87, where he cites an article he wrote in the *Edinburgh Review* of April 1921: 'Here, then, is the true conception of the inter-relation of colour: complete uni-

379

formity in ideals, absolute equality in the paths of knowledge and culture, equal opportunity for those who strive, equal admiration for those who achieve; in matters social and racial a separate path, each pursuing his own inherited traditions, preserving his own race-purity and race-pride; equality in things spiritual, agreed divergence in the physical and material.') However, he not only appointed Moore to this Commission of Enquiry but also made Henry Carr Resident of Lagos. He was also a close personal friend of Sir Kitoye Ajasa, publisher of the pro-Government *Nigerian Pioneer*, see Coleman *op. cit.*, p. 185 and 453, n. 12.

29 See Burns *op. cit.*, p. 217 where the letters of the Shehu of Bornu and the Lamido of Adamawa to Lugard are printed. See also Burns for a detailed account of the course of the war (pp. 216–24). Perham discusses Lugard's role in the Nigerian war effort in Chapter XXVII of *Lugard II*, *op. cit.* For the conquest of the Cameroons and Nigeria's military role in it, see W. O. Henderson *Studies in German Colonial History*, Chicago, 1962, Chapter VIII, pp. 96–108. Also *Statistics of the Military Effort of the British Empire during the Great War 1914–1920*, London, 1922.

30 'Les sénoussistes pendant la guerre 1914–1918' in *Les Troupes coloniales pendant la guerre 1914–1918*, Paris, 1931, pp. 483–98.

31 Information supplied in a personal communication from Mr. Robin Horton.

32 Cited by Burns *op. cit.*, p. 221. Source not given.

33 Letter dated 19th June 1918, cited by Perham *Lugard II*, *op. cit.*, p. 549.

Notes on Chapter XV.

1 See Perham *Lugard II*, *op. cit.*, Chapter XIX: 'The Two Nigerias, 1912–1914', pp. 377–407.
2 I have relied heavily in this chapter on Coleman's admirable study of the growth of Nigerian nationalism, *op. cit.*
3 K. Onwuka Diké *100 Years of British Rule in Nigeria 1851–1951*, Lagos, 1957, p. 35.
4 Coleman *ibid.*, pp. 188–92. For a biography of Garvey see Edmund David Cronan *Black Moses—The Story of Marcus Garvey and the Universal Negro Improvement Association*, Wisconsin, (U.S.A.) 1955.
5 Kalu Ezera *Constitutional Developments in Nigeria*, London, 1960, p. 24, cited from Martin Wight *The Gold Coast Legislative Council*, London, 1946, p. 27.
6 Address by the Governor *Nigerian Council* (Gvt. Records of Proceedings of Council, Lagos), 29th December 1920, p. 20.
7 Ezera *op. cit.*, pp. 26–7; Coleman *op. cit.*, p. 196–7. Coleman stresses that it will be impossible to assess the influence of nationalist agitation on Clifford's decision until we have access to the relevant official papers.
8 *Proceedings of the Nigerian Council*, 1923, p. 4, cited in Cook *op. cit.*, p. 247.
9 See Coleman *op. cit.*, for a more detailed account. Also J. F. Ade Ajayi *Milestones in Nigerian History*, Ibadan, 1962, pp. 28–38; Diké *100 Years of British Rule op. cit.*, pp. 33–42; Burns *op. cit.* for official attitudes to the nationalists; Perham *Lugard II*, *op. cit.*, Chapter XXIX, pp. 581–606; Raymond L. Buell *The Native Problem in Africa*, 2 vols., New York, 1928; Joan Wheare *Nigerian Legislative Council*, 1949; Obafemi Awolowo *The Path to Nigerian Freedom*, London, 1946; Nnamdi Azikiwe *Renascent Africa*, London, 1937.
10 Nigeria, *Annual Report* for 1920, p. 6.
11 Fitzpatrick 'Nigeria's Curse' *op. cit.*, p. 618.
12 Source not traced.
13 I have relied heavily on Margery Perham *Native Administration in*

Notes on Chapter XV.

Nigeria, London, 1937, for my account of the working of indirect rule in Nigeria in the inter-war period. See also Lord Hailey *Native Administration in the British African Territories*, London, 1951, Pts. III and IV. Also L. P. Mair *Native Policies in Africa*, London, 1936.

14 *Report on the Eastern Provinces by the Secretary of Native Affairs*, Lagos, 1922.

15 *Report of a Commission of Enquiry appointed to inquire into certain incidents at Opobo, Abak and Utu-Ekpo in December, 1929*, Sessional Paper, No. 12 of 1930, Lagos, 1930.

16 *Report of a Commission of Enquiry appointed to inquire into the Disturbances in the Calabar and Owerri Provinces, December, 1929*, Sessional Paper, No. 28 of 1930, Lagos, 1930.

17 Perham *Native Administration op. cit.*, p. 215 (1962 edition).

18 Hailey *ibid.*, pt. III, p. 160.

19 *Supplement to Gazette Extraordinary*, 6th March 1933, p. 17, cited in Perham *ibid.*, p. 332.

20 *Principles of Native Administration and their Application*, Lagos, 1934.

21 *Annual Report for 1932*, Lagos.

22 See *Report of the Commission of Inquiry into the Administration of Justice in Kenya, Uganda, and the Tanganyika Territory, in Municipal Matters, May 1933 and Correspondence arising out of the Report*, Cmd. 4623, 1934, p. 134–5, cited in Perham *ibid.*, p. 338.

23 Lugard *Dual Mandate op. cit.*, pp. 544–5.

24 *Nigerian Handbook*, 2nd edition, Lagos, 1953.

25 *West Africa*, 26th July 1924.

26 *Debate in House of Commons*, 29th July 1926, Hansard, 198, p. 2399, etc. See particularly speech of Mr. Snell, who makes a strong attack on the plantation system in Africa.

27 Coleman *op. cit.*, p. 207.

28 For his own account of the history of the Nigerian Youth Movement see Obafemi Awolowo *Awo—The Autobiography of Chief Obafemi Awolowo*, London, 1960, pp. 113–59.

29 In the preparation of this section I am much indebted to Mr. Richard Gleicher who has been undertaking research on the memoirs and other writings of British officials who served in Nigeria from 1900–40.

30 Burns *op. cit.*, p. 258.

31 Lugard *Dual Mandate op. cit.*, p. 87.

32 *Report on Amalgamation op. cit.*, p. 19.

33 Coleman *op. cit.*, p. 153.

34 J. F. Ade Ajayi *Milestones in Nigerian History*, Ibadan, 1962, p. 24.

35 Coleman *op. cit.*, p. 161.

36 Perham *Native Administration op. cit.*, p. 343.

Notes on Chapter XV.

37 Sir Bernard Bourdillon *The Future of the Colonial Empire*, London, 1945, p. 56.

38 Perham *ibid.*, p. 361.

39 *Ibid.*, p. 362.

40 Obafemi Awolowo *Nigerian Freedom op. cit.*, p. 63. It is interesting to note that Lucy Mair had recognized this fact, though without enthusiasm, as early as 1936 in her *Native Policies in Africa op. cit.*, pp. 283-6.

41 W. R. Crocker *Self-Government for the Colonies*, London, 1949, Chapter 6, pp. 43-62, where he cites some of the more virulent of the post-war nationalist abuses.

42 Meyer Fortes 'The Impact of the War on British West Africa', *International Affairs*, XXI, 2, April, 1945, pp. 206-19.

43 *Life*, 10th October 1942, cited in Lord Hailey *An African Survey Revised (1956)*, London, 1957, p. 245.

44 *The Constitution of the N.C.N.C.*, Lagos, 1945, p. 1.

Notes on Chapter XVI.

1 *Proposals for the Revision of the Constitution of Nigeria:* Cmd. 6599 (1945), p. 6.
2 K. Onwuka Diké *100 Years of British Rule in Nigeria 1851–1951*, Lagos, 1957, p. 43.
3 For a fuller discussion of the Richards Constitution, and the two constitutions that followed it in 1951 and 1954, see Ezera, *Constitutional Developments in Nigeria*, London, 1960, Coleman *op. cit.*, Eme Awa, *Federal Government in Nigeria*, Berkeley and Los Angeles, 1964, pp. 17–24.
4 *N.C.N.C. Memorandum on the New Constitution of Nigeria*, Lagos, 1945.
5 Sir Bernard Bourdillon 'Nigeria's New Constitution' *United Empire*, XXXVII, 2, March-April, 1946, pp. 76–80.
6 Ezera *op. cit.*, p. 65; see also Sir Bernard Bourdillon *Memorandum on the Future Political Development in Nigeria*, Lagos, 1939.
7 Coleman *op. cit.*, p. 258.
8 See *A Ten Year Plan of Development and Welfare for Nigeria*, Lagos, 1946.
9 *Report of the Commission appointed by His Excellency the Governor to make recommendations about the recruitment and training of Nigerians for Senior Posts in the Government Service of Nigeria*, Lagos, 1948.
10 See David Apter *The Gold Coast in Transition*, Princeton (U.S.A.), 1955, pp. 169–74 or Apter *Ghana in Transition* (revised edition of the above), New York, 1963, pp. 169–74.
11 Ezera *op. cit.*, pp. 89–96. See also Coleman *op. cit.*, Chapter XVI 'The Ibo and Yoruba Strands in Nigerian Nationalism', pp. 332–52.
12 Cited by Ezera *op. cit.*, p. 91, from *The West African Pilot* of 8th July 1949.
13 Awolowo *Nigerian Freedom op. cit.*, p. 173.
14 Cited in Coleman *op. cit.*, p. 346.
15 *Ibid.*, pp. 344–5 from *The Constitution of the Egbe Omo Oduduwa*, Ijebu-Ode, 1948, pp. 5–6.
16 *Proceedings of the Commission of Enquiry into the Disorders in the*

Notes on Chapter XVI.

Eastern Provinces of Nigeria, Lagos, 1950, see Ezera *op. cit.*, pp. 97–100.

17 Ezera *op. cit.*, pp. 118–20.

18 For an admirable study of the development of political parties in Nigeria see Richard Sklar *Nigerian Political Parties—Power in an Emergent Nation*, Princeton (U.S.A.), 1963.

19 See Sir Ahmadu Bello, Sardauna of Sokoto, *My Life*, London, 1962, pp. 110–12.

20 *Nigeria (Constitution) Order-in-Council, 1951*, Section 162, p. 58.

21 Included in the four ministers elected from the East.

22 See the Sardauna of Sokoto's own account of the Northern position in his autobiography *op. cit.*, pp. 110–48.

23 *Ibid.*, pp. 135–6.

24 See for instance Ezera *op. cit.*, p. 171.

25 *Report on the Kano Disturbances, 16th, 17th, 18th and 19th May, 1953*, Kaduna, 1953, p. 21.

26 For full details of the eight-point programme see *My Life op. cit.*, pp. 143–4.

27 Source not traced.

28 *Hansard* v. 515, p. 2263, 21st May 1953. Debate in House of Commons.

29 *Report by the Conference on the Nigerian Constitution held in London in July and August, 1953*, Cmd. 8934, London, 1953.

30 *Report on the Resumed Conference on the Nigerian Constitution held in Lagos in January and February, 1954*, Cmd. 9050, London, 1954.

31 *Report of the Fiscal Commissioner on the Financial Effects of the Proposed new constitutional arrangements*, Cmd. 9026, London, 1953.

Notes on Chapter XVII.

1 The figures for the results of the federal election in both the North and East are inaccurate in the first edition. I have revised these in the light of Richard Sklar *op. cit.*, p. 35. The actual figures are *North*: N.P.C.=79, Allies=5, Independents=4, Action Group=1, Middle Belt People's Party=1; *East*: N.C.N.C.=32, U.N.I.P.=4, Action Group=3, Independents= 3; *West*: N.C.N.C.=23, Action Group=18, Commoners' Liberal Party=1; *Southern Cameroons*: K.N.C.=5; *Lagos*: N.C.N.C.=1, Action Group=1.

2 *West Africa* 'Sir John and Nigeria', 16th April 1955, pp. 337–8.

3 *West Africa* 'Eyes on Nigeria', 4th February 1956, p. 97.

4 *Self-Government for the Western Region*. Sessional Paper No. 3 of 1955, Ibadan, 1955.

5 *Proceedings of the Tribunal appointed to inquire into Allegations of improper conduct by the Premier of the Eastern Region of Nigeria in connection with the affairs of the African Continental Bank, Limited, and other relevant matters, August-November, 1956*, Lagos, 1957, also *Report of the Tribunal appointed to inquire into allegations reflecting on the Official Conduct of the Premier of, and certain persons holding Ministerial and other Public Offices in, the Eastern Region of Nigeria*. Cmd. 51, London, 1957, p. 42.

6 Ezera *op. cit.*, pp. 230–1.

7 *West Africa* 'The Bank Report' 19th January 1957, p. 49. Sklar *op. cit.*, pp. 143–89 has an excellent section on the N.C.N.C. and the African Continental Bank.

8 *West Africa* 'Polling in West Africa', 26th May 1956, p. 315.

9 Michael Crowder 'Political Tensions in Northern Nigeria' *West Africa*, 11th and 18th January 1958.

10 *Report of the Commission appointed to enquire into the fears of Minorities and the means of allaying them*. Cmd. 505, London, 1958.

11 Philip Mason *West Africa* 'Conference and Minorities Commission': I 'Prospects of Permanence' 22nd November 1958, p. 1115; II 'Safeguards for Citizens' 29th November 1958, p. 1135.

12 Revised figures. There was an inaccuracy in the table in the first edition. See Sklar *op. cit.*, pp. 36–7. Since the appearance of the

first edition K. W. J. Post has published an excellent study of
The Nigerian Federal Election of 1959, London, 1963.

13 Coleman *op. cit.*, p. 252.

14 *The Economic Development of Nigeria* (International Bank for Reconstruction and Development), Baltimore, 1955, p. 666.

15 Coleman *ibid.*, p. 254.

16 Adapted from the table 'Selected Indicators of Economic
Growth' in *Economy Survey of Nigeria, 1959*, Lagos, 1959.

17 Material for this section is based on *The Economic Survey of
Nigeria, op. cit.* and *Nigeria: The Political and Economic Background*
(Royal Institute of International Affairs), London 1960.
'Nigeria Gets Ready for 1960' *New Commonwealth*, July 1959, pp.
434-7 and 'One Sixth of Africa's Market' *New Commonwealth*,
July 1960, pp. 425-31.

18 *Economic Survey ibid*, p. 27.

19 For a full and critical discussion of national marketing boards see
P. T. Bauer *West African Trade*, London, 1963, (2nd edition) in
particular Part V, pp. 263-343.

20 *Economic Survey op. cit.*, p. 22.

21 *Ibid.*, p. 17.

22 For a study of the impact of the road on traditional societies, see
Joyce Cary *Mister Johnson*, London, 1939.

23 'Nigeria Works It Out' *Economist*, 7th July 1962, p. 42.

24 See Sir Sidney Phillipson and S. O. Adebo *Nigerianisation of the
Civil Service: A Review of Policy and Machinery*, Lagos, 1954, and
*Report of the Commission to make Recommendations about the Recruit-
ment and Training of Nigerians for the Senior Posts of Government*,
Lagos, 1948, and *Statement of Policy on the Nigerianisation of the
Federal Public Service and the Higher Training of Nigerians, 1956—60*,
Lagos, 1956.

25 *Investment in Education: Report of the Commission on Higher Education
in Nigeria* (Chairman: Sir Eric Ashby), Lagos, 1960.

26 Archibald Callaway 'School Leavers in the Developing Economy
of Nigeria' in *The Nigerian Political Scene* ed. Taylor Cole and
Robert Tilman, London, 1962.

27 Callaway *ibid*. For a treatment of the problem on a pan-African
scale see the same author's 'Unemployment among African
School Leavers' *Journal of Modern African Studies*, I, 3, 1965,
pp. 351-71.

28 Fred J. Harbison 'Human Resources and Economic Development in Cole and Tilman *op. cit.*, pp. 210-16.

29 Ashby *op. cit.*

30 For a study of urban problems in Lagos see Peter Marris *Family
and Social Change in an African City*, London, 1961.

Notes on Chapter XVII.

31 For studies of the role of voluntary associations in the modern cities see Kenneth Little 'West African Urbanization as a Social Process' in *Cahiers d'Etudes Africaines*, III, 1960, pp. 90–102, reprinted in W. J. Hanna *Independent Black Africa*, Chicago, 1964, pp. 137–48 and Immanuel Wallerstein 'Voluntary Associations' in Coleman and Rosberg *Political Parties and National Integration in Tropical Africa*, Berkeley and Los Angeles, 1964, pp. 413–43. For a comprehensive study of Credit Unions see Shirley Ardener 'The Comparative Study of Rotating Credit Unions' *Journal of the Royal Anthropological Institute*, Vol. 94, Pt. II, 1964.

32 Chinua Achebe *No Longer at Ease*, London, 1960.

33 J. S. Trimingham, *Islam in West Africa* (report to the C.M.S. & Methodist Church Council), London, 1953.

34 J. S. Trimingham *Islam in West Africa*, London 1959, chapter 'The Process of Religious Change', pp. 24–40. The only exception was of course the Pakistani directed Ahmaddiyya movement in Yorubaland.

35 J. Bertin Webster, *The African Churches among the Yoruba*, London, 1964, p. 193.

36 See for instance the Introduction in Hugh H. Smythe and Mabel M. Smythe *The New Nigerian Elite*, Stanford, 1960.

37 See Michael Crowder 'New Nigerian Artists and Writers' in *Prospect*. Roger Bannister ed., Hutchinson, 1963, pp. 147–53.

38 Post *op. cit.*, tables on pp. 351, 353 and 355.

Bibliography

Ajayi, J. F. Ade *Milestones in Nigerian History*, Ibadan, 1962.

Ajayi, J. F. Ade and Smith, Robert *Yoruba Warfare in the Nineteenth Century*, London and Ibadan, 1964.

Ajayi, J. F. Ade *Christian Missions in Nigeria 1841–1891: The Making of an Educated Elite*, London, 1965.

Alagoa, E. J. *The Small Brave City State—A History of Brass-Nembe in the Niger Delta*, Ibadan and Wisconsin, 1964.

Alimen, H. *The Prehistory of Africa*, London, 1957.

Armstrong, Robert G. *State Structures in Negro Africa*, unpublished Ph.D. dissertation, Chicago University, available on microfilm.

Arnett, E. J. *The Rise of the Sokoto Fulani (Paraphrase of Infaku'l Maisuri of Sultan Bello Muhammad)*, Kano, 1922.

Austin, Dennis *West Africa and the Commonwealth*, London, 1957.

Awa, E. O. *Federal Government in Nigeria*, Berkeley and Los Angeles, 1964.

Awolowo, Obafemi *Path to Nigerian Freedom*, London, 1947.

Awolowo, Obafemi *Awo: The Autobiography of Chief Obafemi Awolowo*, London, 1960.

Azikiwe, Nnamdi *Renascent Africa*, Lagos, 1937.

Azikiwe, Nnamdi *Zik*, London, 1961.

Baikie, William B. *Narrative of an Exploring Voyage up the Rivers Kw'ora and Binue (commonly known as the Niger and Tsadda) in 1854*, London, 1856.

Barth, Heinrich *Travels and Discoveries in Northern and Central Africa*, London, 5 vols., 1857–8.

Bauer, P. T. *West African Trade*, London, 1963 (2nd edition)

Bello, Sir Ahmadu, Sardauna of Sokoto *My Life*, London, 1962.

Biobaku, S. O. *The Egba and their Neighbours, 1832–1872*, London, 1957.

Biobaku, S. O. *The Origin of the Yorubas*, Lagos, 1955.

Bibliography

Blake, J. W. *Europeans in West Africa, 1450–1560*, 2 vols., London, 1942.

Blake, J. W. *European Beginnings in West Africa*, London, 1937.

Boahen, Adu *Britain, The Sahara and the Western Sudan, 1788–1861*, London, 1964.

Bohannan, Laura and Paul, *The Tiv of Central Nigeria*, London, 1953.

Bovill, E. W. *The Golden Trade of the Moors*, London, 1955.

Bovill, E. W. *Caravans of the Old Sahara*, London, 1933.

Bown, Lalage and Crowder, Michael (ed.), *Proceedings of the First International Congress of Africanists*, London, 1964.

Bradbury, R. E. and Lloyd, Peter C. *The Benin People and Edo-speaking Peoples, etc., plus the Itsekiri*, London, 1959.

Buchanan, K. M. and Pugh, J. C. *Land and People in Nigeria*, London, 1955.

Buell, R. L. *The Native Problem in Africa*, 2 vols., New York, 1928.

Burdon, J. A. *Historical Notes on Certain Emirates and Tribes (Nigeria, Northern Provinces)*, London, 1909.

Burns, Sir Alan C. *History of Nigeria*, London, 1956.

Buxton, T. F. *The African Slave Trade and its Remedy*, London, 1839.

Cameron, Donald *Principles of Native Administration and their Application*, Lagos, 1934.

Cary, Joyce *Britain and West Africa*, London, 1940.

Church, R. J. Harrison *West Africa*, London, 1957.

Clapperton, Hugh *Journal of a Second Expedition into the Interior of Africa, etc.*, London, 1829.

Coleman, James *Nigeria: Background to Nationalism*, Berkeley and Los Angeles, 1958.

Cook, Arthur N. *British Enterprise in Nigeria*, New York, 1943.

Cowan, L. Gray *Local Government in West Africa*, New York, 1958.

Crocker, W. R. *Nigeria: A Critique of British Colonial Administration*, London, 1936.

Cronan, E. D. *Black Moses—the story of Marcus Garvey and the Negro Improvement Association*, Wisconsin, 1955.

Crowther, S. A. *Journals of an Expedition up the Niger and Tshadda Rivers, etc.*, London, 1855.

Davidson, Basil *Old Africa Rediscovered*, London, 1959.

Bibliography

Davidson, Basil *Black Mother*, London, 1961.

Davidson, Basil and Ademola, A. (Editors) *The New West Africa*, London, 1953.

Davies, J. G. *The Biu Book*, Nigeria, 1956.

Denham, D. Clapperton, H. and Oudney, N., *Narrative of Travels and Discoveries in Northern and Central Africa in the Years 1822, 1823 and 1824*, London, 1826.

Diké, K. Onwuka *Trade and Politics in the Niger Delta, 1830–1885*, London, 1956.

Diké, K. Onwuka *100 Years of British Rule in Nigeria, 1851–1951*, Lagos, 1957.

Diké, K. Onwuka *Origins of the Niger Mission, 1841–1891*, Lagos, 1957.

East, Rupert (ed.) *Akiga's Story*, London, 1939.

Egharevba, J. U. *A Short History of Benin*, Lagos, 1936.

English, M. C. *An Outline of Nigerian History*, London, 1959.

Ezera, Kalu *Constitutional Developments in Nigeria*, London, 1960.

Fage, J. D. *An Introduction to the History of West Africa*, London, 1955.

Fartua, Imam Ahmed ibn *History of the First Twelve Years of the Reign of the Mai Idris Alooma of Bornu*, trans. with Introduction and Notes by H. R. Palmer, Lagos, 1926.

Flint, J. E. *Sir George Goldie and the Making of Nigeria*, London, 1960.

Forde, Daryll *The Yoruba-Speaking Peoples of South-Western Nigeria*, London, 1951.

Forde, Daryll ed. *Efik Traders of Old Calabar*, London, 1956.

Forde, Daryll and Jones, G. I. *The Ibo and Ibibio-Speaking Peoples of South-Eastern Nigeria*, London, 1950.

Forde, Daryll and others *Peoples of the Niger-Benue Confluence*, London, 1955.

Fortes, Meyer and Evans-Pritchard, E. E. *African Political Systems*, London, 1940.

Geary, William N. M. *Nigeria Under British Rule*, London, 1927.

Greenberg, Joseph *Studies in African Linguistic Classification*, U.S.A., 1955.

Greenberg, Joseph H. *The Languages of Africa International Journal of American Linguistics*, XXIX, 1, Pt. II, Jan. 1963, Bloomington, 1963.

Bibliography

Hailey, Lord *Native Administration in British African Territories*, 5 vols., London, 1951.

Hailey, Lord *An African Survey*, London, 1938.

Hailey, Lord *An African Survey Revised, 1956*, London, 1957.

Hancock, W. K. *Survey of British Commonwealth Affairs*, 2 vols., Oxford, 1942.

Hargreaves, J. D. *Prelude to the Partition of West Africa*, London, 1963.

Harris, John *Books about Nigeria* (4th edition), Ibadan, 1963.

Harris, Philip *Local Government in Southern Nigeria*, London, 1957.

Hassan and Shu'aibu (trans. F. Heath) *A Chronicle of Abuja*, Ibadan, 1952.

Herman-Hodge, H. B. *Gazetteer of Ilorin Province*, London, 1929.

Hodgkin, Thomas *Nationalism in Colonial Africa*, London, 1956.

Hodgkin, Thomas *Nigerian Perspectives*, London, 1960.

Hogben, S. J. *The Muhammedan Emirates of Nigeria*, London, 1930.

Hopen, Edward *The Pastoral Fulbe Family in Gwandu*, London, 1959.

Howard, C. and Plumb, J. H. *West African Explorers*, London, 1952.

Hutchinson, T. J. *Ten Year's Wandering among the Ethiopians*, London, 1861.

Ibn Battuta (trans. H. A. R. Gibb) *Travels in Asia and Africa, 1325-1354*, London, 1953.

Idowu, E. Bolaji *Oludomare—God in Yoruba Belief*, London, 1962.

International Bank for Reconstruction and Development *The Economic Development of Nigeria*, U.S.A., 1955.

Johnson, Samuel *The History of the Yorubas*, Lagos, 1937.

Jones, G. I. *The Trading States of the Oil Rivers*, London, 1963.

Kingsley, Mary *West African Studies*, London, 1901, (2nd edition)

Kirk-Greene, A. H. M. *Adamawa, Past and Present*, London, 1958.

Kirk-Greene, A. H. M. *Barth's Travels in Nigeria*, London, 1962.

Krieger, K. *Geschichte von Zamfara*, Berlin, 1959.

Laird, Macgregor and Oldfield, R. A. K. *Narrative of an Expedition to the Interior of Africa in 1832, 1833 and 1834*, London, 1837.

Lander, Richard and John *Journals of an Expedition to Explore the Course and Termination of the Niger, etc.*, London, 1832.

Langa Langa *Up Against it in Nigeria*, London, 1922.

Livingstone, W. P. *Mary Slessor of Calabar*, London, 1933.

Bibliography

Lloyd, Christopher *The Navy and the Slave Trade*, London, 1949.

Lugard, F. D. *The Dual Mandate in British Tropical Africa*. Edinburgh, 1929.

Lugard, F. D. *Report on the Amalgamation of Northern and Southern Nigeria and Administration*, London, 1920.

Lugard, F. D. *Political Memoranda*, London, 1906.

Lugard, Lady *A Tropical Dependency*, London, 1905.

Macfarlane, Donald M. *Calabar: and the Church of Scotland Mission, 1846–1946*, London, 1946.

McPhee, Allan, *The Economic Revolution in West Africa*, London, 1926.

Mair, L. P. *Native Policies in Africa*, London, 1935.

Mannix, Daniel P. with Cowley, Malcolm *Black Cargoes*, London, 1963.

Mauny, Raymond *Tableau Géographique de l'Ouest Africain au Moyen Age*, Dakar, 1961.

Meek, C. K. *Northern Tribes of Nigeria*, London, 1925.

Meek, C. K. *A Sudanese Kingdom*, London, 1931.

Mockler-Ferryman, A. F. *British Nigeria*, London, 1902.

Morel, E. D. *Nigeria: Its Peoples and Problems*, London, 1912.

Murdock, G. P. *Africa—Its Peoples and Their Culture History*, Dakar, 1961, New York, 1959.

Muffet, D. J. M. *Concerning Brave Captains*, London, 1964.

Nadel, S. F. *A Black Byzantium*, London, 1942.

Newbury, C. W. *The Western Slave Coast and its Rulers*, Oxford, 1961.

Nigeria, *The Nigeria Handbook*, London, 1953.

Niven, C. R. *A Short History of Nigeria*, London, 1937.

Niven, C. R. *A Short History of the Yoruba Peoples*, London, 1958.

Oliver, Roland *Sir Harry Johnston and the Scramble for Africa*, London, 1957.

Oliver, Roland and Fage, J. D. *A Short History of Africa*, London, 1962.

Orikpo, Akoi *Who Are the Nigerians?* Lagos, 1958.

Orr, C. W. J. *The Making of Northern Nigeria*, London, 1911.

Palmer, H. R. *The Bornu, Sahara and Sudan*, London, 1936.

Palmer, H. R. *History of the first twelve years of the reign of Mai Idris Alooma of Bornu (1571–1583) by his Imam, Ahmed ben Fartua*, Lagos, 1926.

Palmer, H. R. *Sudanese Memoirs*, 3 vols., Lagos, 1928.

Bibliography

Park, Mungo *Travels in the Interior Districts of Africa, in 1795, 1796 and 1797, etc.*, London, 1799.

Park, Mungo *Journal of a mission to the interior of Africa in the year 1805, etc.*, London, 1815.

Parrinder, Geoffrey *The Story of Ketu—An Ancient Yoruba Kingdom*, Ibadan, 1956.

Pedler, F. J. *West Africa*, London, 1951.

Pedrarza, Howard J. *Borioboola-Gha: The Story of Lokoja, the first British Settlement in Nigeria*, London, 1960.

Perham, Margery *The Native Economies of Nigeria*, London, 1946.

Perham, Margery *Native Administration in Nigeria*, London, 1937.

Perham, Margery *Lugard: The Years of Adventure, 1858–1898*, London, 1960.

Perham, Margery *Lugard: The Years of Authority, 1899–1945*, London, 1960.

Perham, Margery and Bull, Mary *The Diaries of Lord Lugard*, Vol. IV, London, 1963.

Post, K. J. W. *The Nigerian Federal Election of 1959*, London, 1963.

Prest, A. R. and Stewart, I. A. *The National Income of Nigeria*, London, 1953.

Robinson, Ronald and Gallagher, John with Denny, Alice *Africa and the Victorians*, London, 1961.

Roth, Henry L. *Great Benin: its Customs, Art and Horrors*, Halifax, 1903.

Royal Institute of International Affairs *Nigeria: The Political and Economic Background*, London, 1960.

St. Croix, F. W. de *The Fulani of Northern Nigeria*, Lagos, 1944.

Schöen, Jacob F., and Crowther, S. A. *Journals of an Expedition up the Niger in 1841*, London, 1842.

Schultze, A. (trans. P. A. Benton) *The Sultanate of Bornu*, London, 1913.

Shaw, Thurstan *Archaeology and Nigeria*, Ibadan, 1964.

Sklar, Richard *Nigerian Political Parties*, Princeton, 1963.

Smith, Mary *Baba of Karo*, London, 1954.

Smith, M. G. *Government in Zazzau*, London, 1960.

Stenning, Derek *Savannah Nomads*, London, 1959.

Talbot, P. Amaury *The Peoples of Southern Nigeria*, Vol. I *Historical Notes*, London, 1926.

Temple, C. L. *Notes on the Tribes, Provinces, Emirates and States of Northern Nigeria*, Lagos, 1922.

Bibliography

Thorp, Ellen *Ladder of Bones*, London, 1959.

Trimingham, J. Spencer *Islam in West Africa*, London, 1959.

Trimingham, J. Spencer *A History of Islam in West Africa*, London, 1962.

Urvoy, Yves *Histoire de l'Empire du Bornou*, 1949, Paris.

Vansina, J. Mauny R. and Thomas, L.-V. *The Historian in Tropical Africa*, London, 1964.

Wellesley, Lady Dorothy *Sir George Goldie: Founder of Nigeria*, London, 1934.

Westermann, Diedrich and Bryan, M. A. *Languages of West Africa*, London, 1952.

Wheare, Joan *The Nigerian Legislative Council*, London, 1950.

Whitting, C. E. (translation of) *History of Sokoto* by Al-Hajj Sa'id, Kano, 1949.

ARTICLES

Ajayi, J. F. Ade 'Nineteenth Century Origins of Nigerian Nationalism' *J.H.S.N.*, II, 2, 1961. 'Henry Venn and the Policy of Development' *J.H.S.N.*, I, 4, 1959. 'The British Occupation of Lagos 1851–1861' *Nigeria Magazine*, No. 69, August, 1961.

Akinjogbin, I. A. 'The Prelude to the Yoruba Civil Wars of the Nineteenth Century', *Odu*, new series, no. 2.

Anene, J. C. 'The Southern Nigerian Protectorate and the Aros, 1900–02' *J.H.S.N.*, I, 1, 1956.

Armstrong, J. G. 'The Development of Negro Kingdoms in Africa' *J.H.S.N.*, II, 1, 1960.

Beier, Ulli 'Before Oduduwa' *Odu*, 3, 1956.

Beier, Ulli and Biobaku, S. O. 'The Use and Interpretation of Myths' *Odu*, 1, 1955.

Biobaku, S. O. 'The problem of traditional history with special reference to Yoruba traditions' *J.H.S.N.*, I, 1.

Bivar, A. D. H. 'Wathiqat ahl al-Sudan: a Manifesto of the Fulani Jihad' *J.A.H.*, II, 2, 1961.

Bivar, A. D. H. and P. L. Shinnie 'Old Kanuri Capitals' *J.A.H.*, III, 1, 1962.

Boston, J. 'Notes on the Origin of the Igala' *J.H.S.N.*, II, 3, 1962.

Bourdillon, Bernard, 'Nigeria's New Constitution' *United Empire*, XXXVI, 2, March-April 1946.

Bibliography

Bradbury, R. E. 'Chronological Problems in Benin History' *J.H.S.N.*, I, 4, 1959.

Bull, Mary 'Indirect Rule in Northern Nigeria, 1906–11' in *Essays in Imperial Government*, ed. Kenneth Robinson and Frederick Madden, Oxford, 1963.

Burdon, John A. 'Sokoto History: tables of dates and genealogy' *J. Afr. Soc.*, 6, 24th July 1907.

Clark, J. Desmond 'The Spread of Food Production in Sub-Saharan Africa' *J.A.H.*, III, 2, 1962. 'The Prehistoric Origins of African Culture' *J.A.H.*, V, 2, 1964.

Dunglas, E. 'La première attaque des Dahoméens contre Abeokuta, 1851' *Etudes Dahoméennes*, I, 1948 and XX, 1957.

Fortes, M. 'The impact of the war on British West Africa' *International Affairs*, 21st April 1945.

Fagg, Bernard 'A life-size terra-cotta head from Nok' *Man* 95, 1956. 'The Nok culture' *West African Review*, December, 1956. 'The Nok Cultures in Pre-history' *J.H.S.N.*, I, 4, 1959.

Forde, Daryll 'The cultural map of West Africa' trans. *New York Acad. Sci.*, *Ser.* 2, 15th April 1953.

Gertzel, C. 'Relations between African and European Traders in the Niger Delta, 1880–1896' *J.A.H.*, III, 2, 1962.

Greenberg, J. H. 'Linguistic Evidence for the Influence of Kanuri on Hausa' *J.A.H.*, I, 2, 1960.

Hambly, Wilfrid D. 'Culture areas of Nigeria' *Chicago: Field Museum of Natural History* (Anthropological Series XXXI, 3), 1953.

Hiskett, M. 'Material relating to the state of learning among the Fulani before their Jihad' *Bull. of the School of Oriental and African Studies*, XIX, 3, 1957. 'The Kano Chronicle' *Journal of the Royal Asiatic Soc.* XXX, 1957. 'Kitab al-Farq' *Bull. of the School of Oriental and African Studies*, XXII, 23, 1960.

Hodgkin, Thomas ' 'Uthman dan Fodio' *Nigeria* 1960, Special Independence Issue of *Nigeria Magazine*, October 1960.

Horton, W. R. G. 'The Ohu system of slavery in a northern Ibo village-group' *Africa*, XXIV, 3, 1954.

Ifemesia, C. C. 'The "Civilising" Mission of 1841' *J.H.S.N.*, II, 3, December 1962.

Jones, G. I. 'Native and Trade Currencies in Southern Nigeria during the 18th and 19th Centuries' *Africa*, XXVIII, 1,

1958. 'European and African Tradition on the Rio Real'
J.A.H., IV, 3, 1963.

Kirk-Greene, A. H. M. 'Who coined the name Nigeria?' *West
Africa*, 22nd December 1956.

Lloyd, Peter C. 'The traditional political system of the
Yoruba' *South-Western Jour. Anthrop.* X, 4, Winter 1954. 'The
Itsekiri and the 19th Century; an Outline Social History'
J.A.H. IV, 2, 1963.

Lloyd, P. C. and Ryder, A. F. C. 'Don Domingos, Prince of
Warri—Portuguese contact with the Itsekiri' *Odu*, 1954.

Lugard, Frederick D. 'Expedition to Borgu' *Geog. Journal*, 6,
1895.

Morton-Williams, P. 'Some Yoruba Kingdoms under Modern
Conditions' *J. Afr. Admin.*, 7th October 1955. 'The Yoruba
Ogboni Cult in Oyo' *Africa*, XXX, 4, 1960. 'An Outline of
the Cosmology and Cult Organisation of the Oyo Yoruba'
Africa, XXXIV, 3, July 1964.

Palmer, H. R. 'The Bornu Girgam' *J. Afr. Soc.* XII, 45,
October 1912. 'An early Fulani conception of Islam' *J. Afr.
Soc.* XIII, 52, July 1914; XIV, 53, October 1914; XV, 54,
January 1915. 'The Kano Chronicle' *J. Roy. Anthrop. Inst.*
XXXVIII, 1908. 'History of Katsina' *J. Afr. Soc.* XXVI, 103,
1927.

Perry, Ruth 'New Sources for research in Nigerian history'
Africa XXV, 3, 1955.

Ryder, A. F. C. 'Missionary Activity in the Kingdom of Warri
to the Early Nineteenth Century' *J.H.S.N.*, II, 1, 1960.

Smith, H. F. C. 'The Dynastic Chronology of Fulani Zaria'
J.H.S.N., II, 2, 1961. 'A neglected theme in West African
History: the Islamic Revolutions of the Nineteenth Century' *J.H.S.N.*, II, 2, 1961. 'Muhammad Bello, Amir Al—
mu'minin' *Ibadan*, 9, June 1960.

Smith, Robert 'Ijaiye, the Western Palatinate of the Yoruba'
J.H.S.N., II, 3, 1962. 'The Alafin in Exile' *J.A.H.*, VI, 2,
1965.

Smith, M. G. 'The Origins of Hausa Society' in *The Historian
in Tropical Africa, op. cit.*

Urvoy, Yves 'Chronologie du Bornou' *J. Soc. Africanistes*, 11,
1941, 21–32.

Verger, Pierre 'Yoruba influences in Brazil' *Odu*, 2, 1955, 3–11.

Bibliography

'Nigeria, Brazil and Cuba' *Nigeria*, 1960. Special Independence Issue of *Nigeria Magazine*, October 1960.

Willett, F. 'Investigations at Old Oyo' *J.H.S.N.*, II, 1, 1960. 'Ife and its Archaeology' *J.A.H.*, I, 2, 1960.

GOVERNMENT PUBLICATIONS

Northern Nigeria
Annual Reports: 1900–1 through to 1912.

Southern Nigeria
Annual Reports: 1899–1900 through to 1913.

Nigeria/British Government 1914–1960
Annual Reports: 1915 onwards.
Political Memoranda, Lagos, 1918.

Report by Sir F. D. Lugard on the Amalgamation of Northern and Southern Nigerian Administration 1912–19, (1919) Cmd. 468, XXXVI, 609.

Report on a Tour of the Eastern Provinces by the Secretary for Native Affairs, Lagos, 1923.

Report of a Commission of Enquiry appointed to enquire into certain incidents at Opobo, Abak and Utu-Etim-Ekpo in December, 1929. Sessional Paper No. 12 of 1930, Lagos, 1930.

Report of the Commission of Enquiry appointed to enquire into the Disturbances in the Calabar and Owerri Provinces, December, 1929. Sessional Paper No. 28 of 1930, Lagos, 1930.

The Principles of Native Administration and their Application, Lagos, 1934.

Report of the Commission to make recommendations about the Recruitment and Training of Nigerians for Senior Posts in the Government Service, Lagos, 1948.

Report of the Commission of Enquiry into the Disorders in the Eastern Provinces of Nigeria, Lagos, 1950.

Proceedings of the General Conference on Review of the Constitution, January, 1950, Lagos, 1950.

Report on the Kano Disturbances, Lagos, 1953.

Sir Sidney Phillipson and S. O. Adebo Nigerisation of the Civil Service, Lagos, 1954.

Report by the Conference on the Nigerian Constitution held in

Bibliography

London in July and August, 1953. Cmd. 8934, London, 1953.

Report by the Resumed Conference on the Nigerian Constitution held in Lagos in January and February, 1954. Cmd. 9050, London, 1954.

Report by the Nigerian Constitutional Conference held in London in May and June, 1957. Cmd. 207, London, 1957.

Report of the Tribunal appointed to inquire into allegations reflecting on the Official Conduct of the Premier of, and certain persons holding Ministerial and other Public Offices in the Eastern Region of Nigeria. Cmd. 51, London, 1957.

Report of the Resumed Nigeria Constitutional Conference held in London in September and October, 1958. Lagos, 1958.

Commission appointed to Enquire into the Fears of Minorities and the Means of Allaying them. Cmd. 505, London, 1958.

JOURNALS, ETC.

Africa: International African Institute, London.

African Affairs: Royal African Society, London.

Bulletin of the School of Oriental and African Studies: University of London, London.

Journal of African Administration: H.M.S.O., London.

Journal of African History: Cambridge University Press.

Journal of the Historical Society of Nigeria: Ibadan University Press.

New Commonwealth: London.

Nigeria Magazine: Exhibition Centre, Lagos.

Odu: Ibadan.

West Africa: London.

West African Review (ceased publication): London.

Index

Note: Material in summary form at the end of the book is not indexed.

Aba, riots in, 259–60, 262, 280; as industrial centre, 303

Abd al-Salam, Emir of Ilorin, 95, 105, 106, 120, 121; as critic of Holy War, 98

Abd-al-Salam, disciple of Usman dan Fodio, 95, 98

Abdullahi Bongia, King of Kano city state, 42

Abdullahi, successor to Rimfa of Kano, 46

Abdullahi, brother of Usman dan Fodio, 95, 97, 99, 102; expels King of Kebbi, 101; rules western Fulani empire, 102, 213

Abdurrahman, Sultan of Sokoto, 221, 224

Abeokuta: emergence of, 119; Egba and other communities of, 120; Dahomey attacks, 122–3; missionaries in, 143, 144, 156, 165; missionary troubles after 1850's, 167–9; French 1887 mission to, 191, 204; missions expelled from, 175; returned Sierra Leone slaves in, 143; key role of in Lagos troubles, 169, 174; Townsend defends against Lagos, 172; Carter in, 207–8; resists Lugard, 248–9

Abiodun, *see* Alafins of Oyo

Abipa, *see* Alafins of Oyo

Aboh, mid-19th c. trading post, 162

Abolitionists, *see* Slave trade

Abomey, siege of (Dahomey-Oyo strife), 112

Abubakar, *see* Balewa

Abubakar Atiku, Sultan of Sokoto, 227

Abubakar Garbai (Kanemi Shehu), French demands on, 223

Abu Bekri (Nupe), 220; Lugard's men defeat, 221

Abuja, 31, 101; *Chronicle* of, 100; British 1902 expedition against, 223; terracottas of, 33

Abuyazidu (Bayajidda) tradition of Hausa States' foundation, 43–4

Abyssinian Association, founding of, 267

Accra: Jaja's trial at, 198; National Congress of British West Africa at, 254; Accra Resolutions, 254–5

Achebe, Chinua, *No Longer at Ease*, 309, 312

Acheulean period (Earlier African Stone Age), 30

Action Group: and Nigeria's first general election, 282 seqq.; 'Middle Belt' proposal of, 241; initial interests of, 282–4; opposes federal solution for Lagos, 286; in Western Nigeria, 289; taxation policy of, 289; after 1959, 290 seqq.; issues White Paper on self-government, 291; alleged Yoruba domination of, 294; and movement for Mid-Western state, 295; reaction of to Minorities' Report of 1958, 296; in opposition after 1959 federal elections, 298

Adahoozu, King of Dahomey, 113

Adamawa: as Fulani eastward limit, 92, 104; language group of, 26; town Fulani of, 100; Emirs of, 215–16; histories of, 218; murder of Zubeiru in, 221; and proposed division of Nigeria, 242

Adams, Capt. John, on Ibo slaves, 89; on Benin's decline, 89

Ade Ajayi, Professor J. F., 10, 11, 14; and Smith, Robert, *Yoruba Warfare in the Nineteenth Century*, 12; *Christian Missions in Nigeria, 1841–1891*, 13, 19; *The Making of an Educated Elite*, 13; quoted or cited, 20, 105–6, 114, 117, 168

Adebo, *see* Alafins of Oyo

Adegun, and the Oyo breakdown, 116

Adele, Oba of Lagos, 156

Adelu, *see* Alafins of Oyo

Adhwey, France annexes, 186

Adimu (of Ife), 54, 55

Adola, Oba of Benin, 202

Index

Afonja Kakanfo, Ilorin revolt of, 105, 108, 113, 116; effects of, 117

African Association, founded 1788, 134; and Abolition, 135

African Church Movement, as precursor of nationalism, 310

African Continental Bank, 291–2

African Mail, 241

Agades, 92, 100

Agaie, Emirs of (Nupe), 105

Aghwey, France annexes, 186

Ago Oja, site, new capital of Oyo, 121; split with Ikoyi, Gbogun, weakening Yoruba against Fulani, 120

Ague festival, Benin, 202

Aguyi-Ironsi, Major-General A. J., 314

Ahmadu of Misau, in the 1903 *hijira*, 228

Ahmed Baba, Timbuktu historian, work of, 46

Ahmed ibn Fartua, *see* Imam

Air, early 16th-c. conquest of, 47

Ais Kili N'guirmamaramama, a Bornu ruler (woman), 49

Ajaka, son of Oranmiyan of Oyo, 59, 60

Ajasa, Sir Kitoyi, African barrister, 260

Ajayi, Dr., *see* Ade Ajayi; quoted or cited, 105–6, 114, 117, 168

Ajayi, *see* Crowther

Ajele, Oyo empire officials, 58

Ajiboyede, finally defeats Nupe, 61

Ajogbu, *see* Alafins of Oyo

Akassa: Court of Equity, 154; Goldie's bombardment of, 186; Royal Niger Company's post at, 190; Lugard starts from, 193; Brassmen attack, 201

Akinjogbin, Dr. A. I., 'Prelude to the Yoruba Civil Wars', 12–13, 14, 20, 117, 331 n.; on Oyo breakdown, 113, 114, 116

Akinsanya, Samuel (Nigerian Youth Movement), 266, 272, 278

Akintola, Chief, in road toward independence, 292

Akitoye, King of Lagos, 13, 144, 150; deposes Kosoko, 144, 155; and Consul Benjamin Campbell, 166

Akolo, Jimo, Nigerian painter, 312

Akpofure, Rex, 14

Aku Creoles in new (Yoruba) towns, 143

Alafins of Oyo, 13, 54, 56, 167–8, 204, 205, 208; a record of, 59–62; lists of, 330–1; as 'companions of the gods', 57; 17th-c. power of, 108, 113–14; and the Ibadan-Ijaye wars, 170; and the Ibadan-Egba wars, 177; fear outcome for Yoruba peoples of civil wars, 175; French 1887 negotiations with, 191–2; final treaty with Carter, 208; after the August 1893 treaty, 208–9; and

Lugard's innovations, 247–8; Abiodun, 112, 114; Abipa, successor to Ajiboyede, 62; Adebo, 117–18; Adelu, 167–8; Ajiboyede, 61; Ajogbu, 62; Amodo, 121; Aole (Awole), 115–16; Atiba, founder of New Oyo, 121, 167; with Kori, founder of Ede, 60; Labisi, 112; Maku, 105, 118; Ojigi, 62, 111; Olewu, in alliance with Egunoju, 61, 62; Borgu, 121; Onigborgi, 60, 61; Oranmiyan, 55, 56; Sango (deified), 58, 59, 60

Alake of Abeokuta: Lugard respects treaty with, 243; and Ijemo massacre, 249; as patron of West African Students' Union, 266

Alaketu of Ketu, 54

Alakija, Sir Adeyemo, 278

Alali, Regent of Bonny, preceding King William Dapple Pepple, 155, 179

Albert, Sudan, Wilberforce, missionary ships to Niger, 141

Albert, Prince Consort, supports missions, 141, 145

Al-Bukhari, 106

Alburkah and *Quorra*, first iron trade steamships in Niger trade, 140

Alecto (gunboat) against Nana, 200

Alexander Miller Bros. and Co. (Glasgow) in Niger trade, 184

Al-hajj Umar ibn Said, Western Sudan, 96

Al-Hajj Umar ibn Sa'id, author of *History of Sokoto*, on learned women of Bello's reign, 106; on Bello, 214

Aliu Baba (Sultan of Sokoto), 107

Aliyu, Emir of Kano, against Lugard, 224, 226

Alkalawa, capital of Gobir, 102

Al-Kanemi, in power in Bornu, 13, 14, 103, 104; effects religious revival in Bornu, 97; defeats Fulani, 102–4; writes to George IV, 137–8; receives Denham and Clapperton, 137

Alladura (syncretistic churches in Nigeria), 311

Allen, Commander William, on Niger expeditions, 141, 142

Al-Maghili, *Obligations of Princes*, 45, 46

Alwassa, Fulani defeat at, 99

Amakiri, of New Calabar, King William Pepple attacks, 159

Amalgamated Association (European Traders) against Jaja's monopoly, 197

Amalgamation Report, Lugard's, 1919, 245

Amanyanabo, role of in Ijo culture, 80, 81, 83; trade profits of, 86

Amazons of Dahomey, 122, 123, 144

Americas, discovery of as stimulus to

Index

slave trade, 72; intake of slaves by, from Nigerian ports, 72; U.S.A. abolishes slavery, 1808, 127; see Slave trade

Amina, Queen of Zaria, 45, 51

Amir al-mu'minin defined, 96

Amodo, see Alafins of Oyo

Andoni country, Jaja's retreat to, 180

Anglo-African (newspaper), 171

Anglo-French Convention of 1898, 211; partition of Bornu at, 222

Angola, slave exports from, 72

Anka, capital of Zamfara, 92, 99

Anna Pepple house, of Bonny, 130, 159, 179

Anti-Slavery patrols, 140; see West Coast; Itsekiri impoverished by, 181

Aole, see Alafins of Oyo

Apomo, destruction of in Owo war, 115–16, 117

Arab learning, early influence of, 46; see Moslem

Ardo Lerlima, a Fulani leader, 102

Are title, 122 n.; Are of Ijaye, see Kurumi

Are Ona Kakanfo, titled slave (Oyo), 58, 105, 117, 122 n.

Aremo title (crown prince of Oyo), 57; Aremo Egunoju, 61

Arguin, 217

Argungu, Fulani checked at, 101

Armstrong, Professor R. G., 14

Aro people, opposed to British, 232–3; as Ibo subsection, 86; Aro of Arochukwu as Delta ports' slave controllers, 86–9

Aro Chukwu oracle, 77, 231

Asaba: Lander brothers at, 139; Goldie bombards, 186; as headquarters of Royal Niger Company, 190; in first World War, 250–1

Ashanti kingdom, matriarchy in, 41; Ashanti wars of 1875, 219; Jaja's role in, 196

Ashby Commission on Higher Education, 1959, 307–8; on primary education in Western Nigeria, 1959, 307

Askia, Daud, of Songhai, 48

Askia Ishaq II, Songhai power declines under, 48

Askia Muhammad I of Songhai, 47

Ata of Igala, 61

Atiba, see Alafins of Oyo

Atiku I, Bello's successor, 218

Atlantic slave trade, 66–78; for detail, see Slave trade

Attahiru Ahmadu, Sultan of Sokoto, 218, 225; *hijira* of, 227–8

Australia, discovery of, 135

Auyo, Fulani conquer in Holy War, 101

d'Aveiro, João Affonso, reaches Benin in 1486, 66

Awaye people, Ibadan attack, 170

Awolowo, Obafemi (Action Group and Nigerian Youth Movement), 266, 272, 292; criticizes Northern leaders, 284; *Path to Nigerian Freedom*, 270, 278

Awujale of Ijebuland, see Ijebu

Azikiwe, Dr. Nnamdi ('Zik'), background of, 266–7; returns from America in 1937, 266; rivalry with Ikoli for Legislative Council seat, 272; founds National Council of Nigeria and the Cameroons, 272; role in 1945 general strike, 275; triumphal tour after strike, 275–6; in London, on Macpherson's 1948 commission, 276; opposes Yoruba domination of Lagos politics, 278; elected as a member for Lagos, 282; Eyo's accusation against, 291; January 1957 ascendancy of, 292; becomes president of Senate, 1959, 299; becomes Governor-General of independent Federation, Nov. 1960, 299

Baba Goro b. al Hajj Muhammad b. al-Hajj al-Aminu of Kano, historian, 46

Badagry: as slaver port, 118, 129; as Egba trade outlet, 166; missionaries in, 143–4; opposing Akitoye's claims, 156; Freeman annexes, 170

Bagarimi: Rabeh attacks, 222; France takes over, 222

Bahia (Brazil), Yoruba slaves in, 78

Baikie, Dr. (Niger explorer) as trade pioneer, 134; the 1854 expedition, 147, 148, 162; the three motives of the 1857 *Dayspring* expedition, 164; wreck of *Dayspring* at Jebba, 162–3; achievements and death of, 163. *See also* Lokoja

Bakuba, 27

Bale of Gbogun, see Gbogun

Balewa, Sir Abubakar Tafawa (Northern Nigeria), 279; in the 1957 talks, 294; as Prime Minister after 1959 Federal elections, 299; knighted, 299

Banana and palm-oil plantings, inter-Wars, 264

Banks, Sir Joseph, founds African Association, 135

Bantu languages of Equatorial Africa, 26

Banza Bakwai (seven 'bastard' Hausa states), 43

Baptist mission, 143

Barbari, King of Gobir (Hausa state), 91; attacks Zamfara, 92

Barber, Capt. J. W. B., see Lander

Barbot, James, late 17th-c. trader to Bonny, 75; on Delta States trading conditions, 84–5

Index

Bariba, Oyo loses, 113

Barquq, Mamluk Sultan, 42

Barruwa (Lake Chad), 192

Barth, Heinrich, early 19th-century explorer, 134, 147; sees Hausaland potential, 163; on the Emirs, 216; on Kano, 217; describes Hausa after Bello's death, 215; misrepresents Fulani Empire, especially Sokoto, 215, 216, 217

Basorun (of Oyo), 57; threatens Alafin supremacy, 121, 122

Batedo War, 122

Batu (ethnic group), 26

Bauchi, British subdue, 223; and proposed division of Nigeria, 242; Bauchi Improvement Association, 279

Bawa, King of Gobir, successor to Barbari, 92

Bawo, son of Bayajidda, in Hausa tradition, 43

Bayajidda, *see* Abuyazidu

Beecroft, John, British Consul (Bights of Benin and Biafra, 1849), 154–9; aids Egba against Dahomey, 123; slave treaty with Pepple, 1850, 155; and King William Dappa Pepple's exile, 159; establishes Benin river governorship, 181

Beeswax trade, 129, 153

Bebeji, Lugard shells, 225

Beit-el-Mal, the Native Treasuries, 235–6

Belgian Congo, banana and oil developments in, 264

Bell, Sir Hesketh, succeeds Lugard in north, 235–6

Bello, Sultan of Sokoto, son of Usman dan Fodio, 97, 99, 102, 212, 216; quoted, 44, 99; revival of learning under, 106; and Clapperton, 139; as architect of Fulani Empire after struggle with Abdullahi, 213, 214; some successors of, 218, 326

Beni-Saif (nomadic group), 39, 50

Benin: King list of, 14; early kings of Empire, 54; major research scheme into history of, 28; old kingdom of, 21; Bight of, 128, 136, 137, and *see* Beecroft, Bights; bronzes; terracottas, 55, 203; carvings in wood and ivory, 64; coronation ritual, 63; secular art generally, 64; bronzes taken to Britain after Phillips incident, 203; Benin kingdom, degree of matriarchy in, 41; foundation of Benin and Oyo twin kingdoms, 56; achieves independence, 57; later contacts with Oyo, 62; Eweka I strengthens kingdom of, 62; migrations from, under Ewuare the Great, 63; at height of power, 63; name changed to Edo, 64; Benin city as trade centre, and caravan terminus, 64–6; Portuguese arrive in, 66; export of slaves from (with Lagos), 72; James Welsh's 1588 voyage to, 75; eastward migrations from, 87; and Onitsha, 87; later 17th-c. prosperity of, 87–8; Benin River Court of Equity, 154; and Glover's conference (interior rulers, 1871), 176; Beecroft explores river, 154; Benin River governorship established, 1851, 181; comes under British protection, 1884, 182; Nana's river monopoly, 200; at last trade centre against Protectorate, 202; fall of, as last stage before British occupation of Southern Nigeria, 203; human sacrifice in, 202, 203; expansion problems of in 1950's, 308

Benue-Congo sub-family of languages, 26

Benue and Niger 1854 expedition, 147; *see* Barth; Barth identified Benue river with Tschadda, 147; Benue under Lugard, 221

Berbers, in Sahara trading, 29

Bere festival, Oyo, 61

Beri-Beri, Yakubu halts Buba Yero at, 104

Berlin Conference and Treaty (and parcelling of West Africa), 187, 188, 196, 197, 219, 221

Biafra, secession of, 314; collapse of, 315

'Bible and Plough' policy, 142, 145

Bida, Fulani rule Nupe from, 105; C.M.S. missions in, 240; under Lugard, 221

Bights division, in West Coast anti-slavery patrols, 127, 128, 131

Bikorom, successor to Biri, *see* Mais of Bornu

Bini, *see* Evian

Biobaku, Dr. S. O., *The Egba and their Neighbours*, 19, 113; on Glover's departure, 176

Biram, foundation of state of, 43

Biri, Moslem king of Kanem, *see* Mais of Bornu

Birni (early states centred on walled cities), 43

Birnin Kebbi, capital of Kebbi, 101

Birnin Kudu rock paintings, 31

Birnin Zamfara, 92; *see* Zamfara

Bismarck, as supporter of Niger Navigation Act, 187

Bivar, Dr. David, 19

Blackhall, Governor-in-Chief (West African Settlements), 174

Blyden, Edward as promoter of Nigerian nationalism, 254

Index

Boahen, Adu, *Britain and Sahara and the Western Sudan, 1788–1861*, 13, 135; quoted, 215, 216, on aims of African Association, 135

Bojador, Cape, 66, 67

Bonny, slave port, 72, 75, 79, 128; monarchical system in, 83; king's role in slave trade, 159; after Opobo's death, 130; slave-trade abolition treaties with, 130; Court of Equity, 153–4; refuses resettling freed slaves, 147; as richest palm-oil port, 129, 152; Beecroft's work in, 1853, 158–9; Church of Scotland rebuffed in, 165; in the Jaja-Oko Jumbo rivalry, 179–81; France sends gunboat to, 186; lizard worship in, 184

Borgu, as province of Mali, 47; as Oyo's rival, 56; in continuous wars with Oyo, 61, 116; defeat Oyo (consequences of this), 114; as Ibadan's ally in Ijaye wars, 170; role of, in British-French rivalry, 192–4; British control of becomes effective, 219; under Lugard, 221

Bororoje (cattle Fulani) in Holy War, 97

Bornu: Shehu of Bornu dynasty (table), 328; ancient kingdom of, 21, 28; historians of, 28, 46, 47; Kanem empire extends into, 41, 42; occupation of completed under Mai Ali Gazi (16th-c.), 42; reconstituted empire of, involved in Hausa history, 47; as quasi-overlord of Hausaland, 47–8; under Mai Idris Alooma, 49; slave governors of, 74; Mandara defeat, 90; nomads constantly threaten, 90; later 18th-c. decline of, 90–1; Al-Kanemi's religious revival in, 97; successes and defeats against Fulani, 102–3; saved by Al-Kanemi, 103; small emirates carved out of, 102; in 1830, 106; explorers in, 137; British consulate established in, 139; dependence of on earnings from slave trading, 218; assigned to Britain at Berlin Conference, 221; Rabeh invades, 222; history of after 1846, 222–3; British take over, 223; *see also* Al-Kanemi

Bosman, William, describes Oyo's standing army, 111

Bourdillon, Sir Bernard: on role of educated Africans, 269–70; as critic of Sir Arthur Richards's constitution, 274

Bowen's mission (Baptist) in Abeokuta, 144–5; his *Grammar and Vocabulary of the Yoruba Language*, 165

Bower, Captain (Resident, Abeokuta) in fracas with Oyo, 209

Bown, Miss Lalage, 14

Bradbury, Dr. R. E., 19

Brand's consulship, Lagos, during Ibadan-Ijaye wars, 168

Brandenburgers, in slave trade, 73

Brass (Nembe) as slaving state, 79; exports slaves to Brazil and Cuba, 131; R.N.C. discrimination against, 190; divided political authority in, 83; in palm oil trade, 152, 183; attacks New Calabar, 179; Courts of Equity, 154; Goldie bombards, 186; the 1896 disturbances against British trade monopoly, 190; in trade conflict with Royal Niger Company, 201

Brazil: results of Dutch conquest of, 73; Yoruba slaves in, 77–8; slave revolts in, 77; gains slaves from Yoruba and other wars, 129, 131

Brettonet, Rabeh defeats, 222

Bristol: slave-trade-based prosperity of, 73; abolition fails to affect adversely, 126

Britain: in the slave trade, *see* slave trade; and abolition, 124–33; real economic interest of, in stopping slave trade, 126; changing attitudes of, to West African chiefs, 129–33; establishes Protectorate over Nigeria, 132 seqq.; and the Brazil slaves (trade considerations), 132; trade needs of, in early 19th c., 134; loses American colonies, 135; after Niger opening, 140 seqq.; trade methods after 1950, 150; role of Select Committee of 1865, 150; the pre-Protectorate rule, 173–87; strong enough to cope with Yoruba troubles, 179; recognizes claims of Opobo, 181; proclaims Protectorate over Niger Districts, 187; agrees Dahomey-Lagos boundary with France, 192; crisis in relations with France in West Africa, 192–6; completes occupation of Southern Nigeria, 203; first foothold of, in Yorubaland, 205; troubles with Ijebu, 205–6; virtual final establishment of Protectorate, 207; finally quells Ijebu, 207; first inroads against Fulani by, 219 seqq.; overriding economic interests of, 233; *see* Lugard, individual names of explorers, missionaries, *also* Appendix for summary of events; British governors of Nigeria, 1900–60, 332

British Anti-slavery patrols, 118; *see* Slave trade

British West Indian colonies, slaves in, 76, 77

Index

Brohemie, as 'arsenal' and Nana's headquarters, 200

Brokensha, Dr. David, 14

Bronzes, see Benin; see Idah; Ife, 55; Nupe, 61

Brown, Roland, 20

Buba Yero, Emir of Gombe (Bornu), Fulani leader, 102, 104

Buea, in War I, 251

Bulala people, Kanem, 42, 47; Bornu hold on weakens, 48

Burdon, Major (Resident, Northern Nigeria), 212, 229

Burmi, in the 1903 *hijira*, 228

Burns, Sir Alan, on some effects of education in Nigeria, 267–8

Burton, Sir Richard, on role of slaves in legitimate trade, 152; as Consul at Fernando Po, 202

Bussa people, 31; pebble tools of, 30; Askia Muhammad I invades, and Askia Daud sacks, 47–8; and the Borgu question, 192–3; Goldie opposes Chamberlain in respect of treaty with, 195; French 1897 occupation of territory of, 210; Bussa Rapids, Mungo Park murdered at, 137, 139

Buxton, Sir Thomas Fowell, abolitionist, 141, 143; *The African Slave Trade and its Remedy*, 140

Calabar: see Slave trade; in palm oil trade, 128, 129; virtual end of slave trading in Old Calabar, 133; Church of Scotland missions in, 143, 145–6; missions generally, 145, 184; after 'open competition', 160–1; destruction of Old Town, 160–1; Mary Slessor's work in, see Slessor; Sir A. Richards maintains principle of election in, 274; riots in, after Enugu shootings, 280; proposal for Calabar-Ogoja-Rivers state, 295. See also New Calabar, Old Calabar.

Cameron, Sir Donald, governorship of (Northern Nigeria), 258, 261–2; abolishes Lugard's system of administering justice, 263; at opening of Yaba College, 269; and role of African élite, 269

Cameroons, republic of, 23, 33; Southern, 18; foothill languages, 26; Germany declares Protectorate over, 187; Germans, traditional land laws flouted by, 235; at time of War I, 250, 251; German, War I, 264; Southern, as quasi-Federal territory, 287

Campbell, Benjamin, first British Consul at Lagos, 1853, 166–7; in negotiations with Diare, 182

Cannibalism, 201

Canot, Théodore, French slave trader, on commercial motives behind Britain's abolition measures, 126

Caravan routes, trans-Saharan, and Hausa politics, 45 seqq.

Carter, Sir Gilbert, governorship of Lagos: and Ijebu strife, 206–7; treats with Alafin Oyo, 208; trade after peace of, 209

Carthaginians, in gold trade with West Africa, 66

Casely-Hayford, Mr. Gold Coast lawyer, 254

Central Africa Mission, 147

Central African Trading Co., London, in Niger trade, 184

Central Produce Marketing Board of Nigeria, 303

Chad, Lake (and region): early arrival of nomad Zaghawa in, 36; 11th–12th c. extension of Kanem power in, 40–1; Lake discovered, 137

Chamba people, 104

Chamberlain, the Rt. Hon. Joseph, and the Nikki affair, 195–6; Goldie disagrees with, 195

Chari river, 222

Chanomi, successor to Diare (Itsekiri), 182

Chick, Sir Louis, allocates revenues, Federal and Regional (Chick Report), 287

Christianity, and cross-ethnic organization of new communities, 309–11; see also Conversion, total

Church Missionary Society, 143, 171, 240; earliest ventures of, 141–3; as political influence, 145; expands beyond Yorubaland, 146; founding Niger Mission, 164; roots of the opposition to Campbell, 166–7; moves headquarters to Lagos Island, 175; 'native church policy' of, 310. See also *Dayspring*

Church of Scotland, missionaries of in Old Calabar, 143, 145, 146

Churchill, Winston, American criticisms of as colonialist, 271

Civil Service, problem of replacing British, 306

Clapperton, Hugh (Niger explorer), as early trade pioneer, 134, 137, 138; on decline of Mais of Bornu, 103; joins Denham, 138; second expedition of, 138–9; sees Hausaland potential, 163; visits Bello at Wurno, 214, 216; death of, 139

Index

Clark, Professor Desmond, 14, 31

Clark, J. P., Nigerian poet, 312

Clarkson, Thomas, English abolitionist, 125; in African Association, 135

Clifford, Sir Hugh, 256-8; denounces nascent nationalism, 255; elective principle as envisaged by, 256-7; investigates failure of 'indirect rule' in Eastern Nigeria, 259; resists the Leverhulme plantation plans, 264; and the African élite, 269

Cocoa, 302, 303; Cocoa Pool attacked by N.Y.M., 267

Coleman, Professor James, 19; *Nigeria Background to Nationalism*, 19; on total conversion, 238; quoted, 266, 270

Colonial Development and Welfare Fund, and Act, 271, 276

Columbite mines, Jos plateau, 24, 302

Comet, edited by Azikiwe, 275

'Comey' (Customs) payments (Europe and the Delta kings), 86

Commerell, Commodore J. E., secures Opobo-Bonny peace, 181

Compagnie du Sénégal et de la Côte Occidentale d'Afrique, 185

Compagnie Française de l'Afrique Équatoriale, 185

Congo Association (Leopold, King of the Belgians), 187

Congo-Kordofanian family of languages, 26, 345

Conversion, total, as disruptive influence, 238, 239

Cook, E. L., *British Enterprise in Nigeria*, 199

Cotonou, French annex, 186

Cotton, 24, 303, 304; of Northern Nigeria, 264

Courts of Equity, the 1873 regularizing of, 183

Cowries as currency, 205, 215, 234; coins replace in mid-19th c., 162

Creech Jones, Arthur, and N.C.N.C. delegation, 276

Creek Town, Old Calabar, 83; Church of Scotland missions in (and in Duke Town), 146

Crockett, Davy, 145

Cross River, Beecroft explores, 154; Church of Scotland in, 165; the Akuna-Ibo incident of 1893, 199-200; Cross River language group, 26; *see also* Slessor, Mary

Crow, Captain Hugh, in slave trade, 76, 128

Crowther, the Rev. Samuel, later Bishop, 141, 142, 148, 310; is ordained, 143; becomes Bishop of the Niger, 142; Lord Palmerston receives, 145; early difficulties of, in Niger Mission, 164; in Baikie's 1857 expedition, 164; in the Lokoja incident, 182; missions of persecuted in Bonny, 184; view of conversion, 239; West Coast family ties, 254; his *Grammar and Vocabulary of the Nupe Language*, 165

Cuba: Efik and Ibibio slaves in, 78; slaves from Brass in, 131; slaves from Fulani, Yoruba and other wars in, 77, 129; sugar plantation slavery in, 132

Cunliffe, Colonel, on Nigerian regiments in War I, 251-2

Dahomey, 23, 28, 110, 171; Ajobu makes war on, 62; the Amazons of, *see* Amazons; as perpetually troublesome to Oyo in 18th c., 111; invades Great Ardra, 111; Oyo defeats, 112; slaving ports of, 114-15; interest of in Owu wars, 119; 19th-c. slave-trade prosperity of, 122; attacks Abeokuta in 1851, 144-5; tension with Egba, 1857, 167; against Ibadan, 168; threaten Egba afresh in 1863, 171; French base at, 191; French conquer in 1892, 192; Lagos fears French activities in, 203; invades Oyo, 1887, 204; *see* Slave

Daily Service (*Daily Express*) of Africa (ed. Ikoli), 272, 313

Dalzell, on Dahomey's victory at Great Ardra, 111

Dan Makafo, outlaw, in Satiru rising, 229

Dan Yahaya, Fulani victory of, 101

Danes in slave trade, 73; declare illegality of in 1804, 127

Dapper, O. (*Description de l'Afrique*), on Gwatto slave trade, 87; on Warri's independence, 88

Darfur, 26

Dar Kuti, Rabeh conquers, 222

'Dash' in trade, 86

Daud, *see* Askia Daud

Daura (one of the 'Seven Hausa States'), 43, 51; early ironworks of, 44

Davies, H. O., and N.Y.M., 266

Dayspring, wrecked on Juju Rock, Jebba, 162, 163, 164; *see* Baikie

Decœur, in race to Nikki against Lugard, 193-4

Degel (Gobir), 94, 95

Delta States, *see* Niger Delta

Index

Dendi Marshes, 49

Denham, D., on Bornu in 1820's, 103; on the Clapperton-Oudney Niger expedition, 137

Denman, Captain, destroys slavers' barracoons, 1839, 131

Denton's governorship, as successor to Maloney, 206

Diare (Itsekiri), 181; makes agreement with Beecroft, 181, 182

Diké, Dr. K. O., 10; *Trade and Politics in the Niger Delta*, 19; *A Hundred Years of British Rule in Nigeria*, 254, 273; quoted, 128; on Beecroft, 154; on traders taking over from explorers, 162; on earliest nationalist fight against Crown Colony system, 254; on Richards's Constitution, 273

Dikwa, Germany acquires in 1898, 222

Docemo, ruler of Lagos, 166, 168, 169; cedes Lagos to British, 152

Domingo, Antonio, Olu of Warri, 88

Doornboos, Martin, 14

Dried fish, connection of with slave trading, 81

Duala, 1914 naval bombardment of, 251

Du Bois, W. E., 254

Dugu, Beni-Saif leader, 39

Duke Town, Beecroft modifies Egbo tyranny in, 83; 158;

Dunama, Moslem king, Kanem, 40

Dutch in slave trade, 73

Dutsin Wake, battle of, 92

Dynastic disputes, as distorters of history, 27–8

'Eastern Route' (Lagos to interior), 176

Ebrohimi, as Olumi's headquarters, 182

Ebute Metta, 174

Ede, Alafin Kori founds, 60

Edea, in War I, 251

Eden, Richard, on hazards of early West African trade, 71

Edinburgh Review, and early Niger missions, 142

Edo, *see* Benin; Edo-speaking peoples of Western Region, 26, 53

Edoni, son of Oguola, King of Benin, 63

Education: missions' role, 165, 184; nationalist and European attitudes to educated African, 267–9; introduction of western, 239–40; today's expansion, 305–6; reasons for Northern backwardness, 294, 302; *see also* Élite, emergence of

Edun, Yoruba general defeated by Fulani, 120

Edun, Secretary of Egba United Government, 248

Edwards, Bryan, Secretary of African Association, 135

Effon (in Ekiti Confederation against Ibadan), 177

Efik people, of the Eastern Region, 26; language of, *see* Goldie, Waddell; trading state of, *see* Old Calabar, *also* 79, 84; slaves, in Cuba, 78; ill treatment of slaves by, 146, 157; *see also* Egbo.

Egba, Egbaland, 56; declare independence from Oyo, 1780's, 113; Egba-Owu battles after fall of Owu, 119; in slave trade at time of Owu wars, 119; settle at Abeokuta, 120; receive aid from Britain, 123; pass law abolishing human sacrifice, 146; serious position of, in 1860's, 168–9; obstructing Glover in free trade from Lagos, 171, 175; Freeman's blockade of, 170; persist in blocking Lagos-Ibadan road, 173; main object of, 177; block all trade with Lagos, 205; finally submit to British, 207; Lugard's indirect rule in, 243, 248–9; *see also* Ibadan-Egba wars

Egba-Alake, 120

Egba-Oke-Ona, 120

Egba United Board of Management, 174

Egba United Government, resists Lugard, 248

Egbado (Oyo-controlled), 56; seek British protection, 205

Egbe Omo Oduduwa (Society of the Descendants of Oduduwa), 278

Egbo Society, Old Calabar, as real power in Old Calabar, 83; re-created in Cuba by Efik and Ibibio slaves, 78; harsh government by, 157–8; unifies Efik settlements, 84; passes law abolishing human sacrifice, 1850, 146

Egharevba, Chief Jacob, 54; *Short History of Benin*, 14

Egunuju, Aremo, 61, 62

Egypt, Kanem influence extends to, 13th c., 40; extends own influence to Nubia, Ethiopia, in ancient times, 29–30

Ekiti people (and country), *see also* Ijesha: independent of Oyo, 57; successfully eludes Alafin's control, 110; is placed under Ibadan, 121; Ilorin attack, 122; Ibadan slave-raiding in, 176; the Ekiti-Parapo confederation against Ibadan, 177, 178; in fighting behind Lagos, 203, 204

Ekwensi, Cyprian: Nigerian novelist, 312

Elective principle, 256–7

Index

Electricity Corporation of Nigeria, 308

Eleko question (Lagos), 257

Elijah II (prophet in Delta, during War I), 251

Élite, emergence of an, 267–70; and return to African Cultural norms, 312; at time of independence, 312

Elizabeth, Queen, and Prince Philip, in Nigeria, 1956, 290

El Maghili, *Instructions in the Obligations of Princes*, 46

Emaye (Benin river), 181; house of, 182

Emirs, Emirates: Cameron hopes of liberalizing, 262; after 1899, 210–30; increasing autonomy of, in 1930's, 258; and Northern backwardness, 294

Employment of school-leavers, 1959 problem, 307

Enahoro, Anthony, of Action Group, 284

Endeley, Dr., Cameroons representative on N.C.N.C., 283

'Enogie', chiefs of Benin, 62

Enugu shootings, 280; Enugu as increasingly important urban centre, 300; expansion problems of 1950's, 308

Enwonwu, Ben, Nigerian painter, 312

Epe: as Kosoko's retreat, 166; Freeman destroys, 170; Carter's punitive expedition against Ijebu at, 207

Equipment Treaty, in abolition of slavery, 129–30

Eshugbayi, Eleko, hereditary ruler of Lagos, 257

Esilogun-Adele dispute (Lagos, 1811), 156–7

Ethiopia, Italy invades, 267

Eunuchs as provincial governors, 57, 74

Evian (Bini leader), 54

Ewedo (Ife dynasty ruler in Benin), 62–3

Eweka I, first Ife king in Benin, 62

Eweka II, Oba of Benin, 247

Ewuare, the Great, Ogun, contact with Europe, 63, 66

Explorers, 134–40; *see* Gomes, Niger, and named explorers

Eyambe V, king of Duke Town, 146

Eyo, E. O., accuses Azikiwe, 291

Eyo Honesty, King of Bonny, Creek Town, 146; in oil trade irregularities, 160; in 'trust' trade dispute, 160, 161

Ezera, Dr. Kalu, *Constitutional Developments in Nigeria*, 19, 291–2

Fabian Colonial Bureau, 271

Fad-el-Allah, Rabeh's son, claims Bornu, 222–3

Fagg, Bernard, 19; on Nok culture, 31, 32

Falconbridge, Dr., on slaver conditions 125

Federal-Regional revenue allocation, 1953, 287; Federal Supreme Court, 287

Fernando Po, trade with Portugal ousting Benin, 71; and Palmerston's aspirations, 131; Beecroft in, 154; Akitoye in, 157; consulate transferred from, to Old Calabar, 183

Ferry, Jules, Prime Minister of France, annexations by in Africa, 186; 'le Tonkinois', 191

Fezzan, 36, 218; under Kanem influence by 13th c., 40, 41

Fiji, early indirect rule in, 220

Filingué besieged by Ouilliminden tribe, 250

Fitri, Lake, 39

Fitzpatrick, Captain, attacks indirect rule, 258, 264

Flegel, Herr, seeks treaties with Sokoto and Gwandu, 187

Foot, Hugh, Chief Secretary to Sir John Macpherson, 276; assassination attempt on, 280

Foote's consulship, Lagos, and Porto Novo incident, 168

Forde, Professor Daryll, 14, 33

Fortes, Meyer, on Second War and West Africa, 271

Fortified villages, ancient, 31

Foster-Sutton, Sir Stafford, Federal Chief Justice, 291

'Four provinces' proposal, Morel's, 241–2

Fourah Bay Institute, Freetown, 147

Fox, Charles James, in African Association, 135; favours Abolitionist cause, 125

France, *see also* Decœur, Ferry, Mizon, Nikki; in slave-trade, after Treaty of Utrecht, 73; West Indian colonies of, slave revolts in, 77; makes 'free labour' contracts, 167; Lugard against, *see* Lugard, Lord; as trade rival in Delta, 179, 185 seqq.; Protectorate over Niger districts as move against, 179; Goldie opposed to, 186; resents Niger Company, 190; as constant threat, 191; attempts treaty with Alafin of Oyo, 205; makes good her claim to Bornu, 222–3

'Free labour', 1857 French scheme, 167

Free trade areas under early British administration, 234

Freeman, Henry Stanhope, first Governor of Lagos colony, 169

Index

Freeman, Thomas Birch, head of Gold Coast Methodist Mission, Badagry, 143

Freetown, as freed slaves' settlement, 128; Fourah Bay Institute, 147

Fulani, people and Empire, languages of, 26; cattle Fulani, 92, 99; 'Holy War' of, see Usman dan Fodio; Holy War extends to Brazil (Moslem slave revolts), 78; as chief upholders of Islam in Western Sudan, 92; Hausaland way of life of, 93; establish hegemony throughout Northern Nigeria, 96; and El Kanemi, 97–8; secret of strength of, 99; 18th-c. social organization of, 100; progress by 1830, 102, 106–7; 'Fulani Pax', 106; as menace to declining Oyo empire, 116; and the Yoruba wars, 122, 129; Goldie's treaty agreement with, 192; and Lugard, 212–19; Barth misrepresents, 215, 216–17; income of, from slavery, 218; Britain's foothold in, 219; Lugard's last conquests in, 224–5; present-day Blue Nile settlements, 228; see also Sokoto Caliphate

Gaha (Basorun) of Oyo, 108, 112, 113; son of, leads attack on Oyo, 118

Gaiser, G. L., invades Lagos trade, 186

Gaisuwa (bribe giving) in Habe kingdoms, 95

Galadima of Sokoto, 41, 48, 216

Gallwey, Vice-consul (Benin river), 1892, 202

Galvão, Antonio, 66

Gambarou, summer palace (Bornu), 90

Gambia Company (regiment) in War I, 251

Gambia river, pre-exploration view of, 135

Gamergum, Idris Alooma takes, 49

Gao, port of Niger, 47

Garin Gabbas, in Holy War, 101

Garni Kujala, defeat of Bulala of Kanem at, 47

Garua, in War I, 251

Garvey, Marcus, 254

Gatarwa, Fulani conquer in Holy War, 101

Gavin, Dr. R. J., 11

Gbagura towns, destroyed after Owu wars, 119

Gbebe mission station, 164

Gbodo, Ilorin defeated at, 122

Gbogun, and Oyo breakdown, 116, 118; Fulani conquest of, 120

'Gbonka' the (Oyo army commander), 60

Gentil, French officer in Bagirmi, restores Kanemi dynasty to Dikwa, 222

George IV, contact with Bornu, 137–8

Germany: in trade rivalry, Delta and West Coast, in 1870's, 185–7; Protectorate of, see Cameroons; resents Niger Company, 190; the 1886 boundary agreement with, 191; getting established in Togoland, 193; in Nigeria's export trade before 1914, 250

Gezo, King of Dahomey, declares independence of Oyo, 113; as slave-trader, 123, 144, 155

Ghana (former Gold Coast), achieves independence, 292

Ghana (and successor Mali) as empires, position of in Western Sudan, 35

Ghat, 217, 218

Gimbana, Yunfa attacks (early days of Holy War), 95

Girouard, Sir Percy, successor in North to Lord Lugard, 235, 236, 241

Glover, Lieut., in Baikie's search for route to Lagos, 163; role of, after Lagos annexation, 169–70; becomes Lieutenant-Governor and Administrator responsible to Blackhall, in Lagos, 171–2; and the Yoruba civil war, 173 seqq.; blockades Egba supply lines, 1865, 174; and the Egba-Ijebu road-blockings, 176; and the Jaja-Bonny strife, 181

Gobir (Hausa state), 43, 44; in war with Katsina, 45; growth to power, 52; in strife with Kano, 91; Fulani attack on, 97–8; Zamfara attacks, 97; in later stages of Holy War, 99–100; the 1830 position, 106; rebelling against Sokoto, resists Bello, 213–16; delivers ex-Emir Aliyu to Lugard, 226

Gold Coast Regiment (War I), 251

Goldie, the Rev. G., Cross River Mission of, 184; studies of Efik language by, 165

Goldie, Sir George T., 'founder of modern Nigeria', 185, 186, 187, 191, 211; makes treaties with local chiefs and Germany, 187; and French colonial expansion, 192; claims Borgu for Royal Niger Company, 193; conquests of Nupe, Ilorin, 195; supports idea of indirect rule, 220

Gollmer, Herr, German missionary to Abeokuta, 144

Gombe (Bornu), emirate, 102, 104

Gomes, Fernão, Portuguese explorer, 67–8

Goshawk, H.M.S., and the deporting of Jaja, 198

Index

Gosling, Sergt., reports on Satiru incident, 228, 229

Gowon, General Yakubu, creation of the 12 states, 241; and Biafran secession, 314–15

Granville, Lord, on European interference in 1870, 180–1; learns of further trouble with Jaja, 197

Granville Sharp, *see* Sharp

Great Ardra, 111

Great Britain, *see* Britain

Greeks in Africa, in ancient times, 30

Greenberg, Joseph H., *Studies in African Linguistic Classification*, 26, 33

Griffeth, Robert, 13

Grillo, Y., Nigerian painter, 312

Groundnuts, 24, 234, 264, 302, 303

Guangara state (possibly Katsina Laka), 48

Gudu, Usman dan Fodio's flight to, 95

Guinea, 1725 Moslem revolts in, 93

Guinea coast, French slavers on, 73

Gujba (British Bornu), raided by French, 223

'Gumsu' title, 41

Gwandu (*see also* Flegel and Niger Company), as Fulani headquarter, 399, 102; Emirs of, 105, 213, 229–30; Gwandu-Sokoto divisions of Fulani empire, 213–14; and Britain, 214, 215, 217; submits to Lugard, 225

Gwari (Hausa 'bastard' state), 44

Gwatto, slave port for Benin, 87; in pepper trade, 69

Gwoni Mukhtar, Fulani leader, 102; Al Kanemi's army kills, 103

Habe kingdoms and kings, before the Holy War, 92, 95; power of, exceeding Alafins', 111; raid cattle of Fulani in Hausaland, 100; books of, Fulani accused of destroying, 106; Usman dan Fodio against, 93–4; kingdoms united, 213; in trade after 18th-c. wars, 217; dependence of, on income from slaving, 218

Hadejia, Fulani wrest from Bornu, 101, 104

Hadejia, Emir, 229, 230

Haiti, origin of voodoo in, 78

Hammaruwa, Emirs of, 215

Hanno the Carthaginian, 66

Harding, the Rev. T. (C.M.S.), 207

Hausa, Hausaland, 41; Hausa Bakwai (Seven States), 43; Chad basin immigrants enter, 42; early development of states, 43; Mohammedan foothold in, 44–6; by late 15th-c., 46; Askia

Muhammad of Songhai's successes in, 47; Barbary merchants in, 48; early Yoruba trade with, 60; rule through slaves, 74; and Brazil slaves' revolt, 78; seven 'bastard' states of, 43–4, 91; concerned with Sahara desert trade, 90; rise of Fulani in, 92; climactic moments in Fulani domination of, 96, 97, 100, 101, 102; explorers among, 137; Baikie's route to, 163; after Bello's death, 214–15; Lugard's final conquests in, 224–9; documentary history of, 28; language of, 26; *see* Schön

Havana, slave revolts in, 77

Hearn & Cuthbertson, trading in Old Calabar, 161

Henry the Navigator, 67

Hewett, Consul, in treaty agreements with Nana, 182; and treaties of protection, 187; treaty with Jaja, 196

Higgins, Henry, Acting Colonial Secretary, at end of Yoruba civil wars, 204

Hinderer, Mr. and Mrs. (C.M.S.), 145

Hiskett, M., translator of *Kitab-al-Farq*, 94, 95; on intellectual superiority of leading Fulani, 97

Hodgkin, Thomas, 19; on Usman dan Fodio, 96

Hoenigsberg affair, Nupe, 191

Hogben, S. J., 18

Holt, Mr. J., Liverpool trader, on Ibuno incident, 197

Hong Kong, Lugard's governorship of, 229

Hope Waddell's Calabar mission, 145–6; *Efik Vocabulary*, 165

Horton, Robin, 10, 14, 20; on Ijo society, 81

Houghton, Major, Niger explorer, 135

House and House rule, development of in Ijo society, 81, 82; Lugard abolishes in Delta States, 249

Human sacrifice, 83, 88, 146, 160, 202, 206, 207, 208

Hunwick, J. O., 14, 38 n.

Hutchinson, T. J. (Consul), succeeds Lynslager, 161; *Ten Years' Wandering among the Ethiopians*, 160

Hutton, Thomas, & Son, in early trade with Abeokuta and Badagry, 144

Hutt's Select Committee, 132–3

Ibadan, emergence of, 119; post-1829 mixed settlement, 119; the Batedo war, with Ijaye, 1844, 122; defeat Ilorin at Gbodo and Oshogbo, 122; allies of Oyo in support of Alafin Adelu, 167–8; 1858 renewal of Ibadan-Ijebu wars,

Index

Ibadan—*cont.*
167–8; Ibadan-Egba war analysed, 177; hoping for direct trade with Lagos, 177; surrounded by hostile armies, 177; powers of survival of, 178; decisive Ibadan-Egba battles of 1865, 171; at height of power, 176–7; continue strife with Ekiti Parapo, 203; Ibadan-Ilorin endless war, 205; and Carter, 208; finally break up war camps, 208; resists Alafin of Oyo's authority, 248; Cameron separates from Oyo, 262; Ibadan Conference of 1948, 277; as industrial centre, 303; University College of, established, 1948, 305; African history introduced to U.C. curriculum, 312; teaching hospital founded, 308; in 1950's expansion problems, 308

Ibami mission, established in 1879, 184

Ibibio, of the Eastern Region, 26; slaves of, in Cuba, 78; in trade with Ijo, 80; Ibo, Ibibio, as successful town workers, 277–8; Ibibio State Union, 278

Ibn al-Sabbagh (Katsina), historian, 46

Ibn Battuta, historian, 45

Ibn Khaldun, historian, 41

Ibo, Iboland, 21; as slave source, 80–1, 89; thieves as slaves, 74–5; tribal organization in 18th-c., 77; capture Lander brothers, 139; slaves settle in Calabar, 147; slaves and missions, 164; punitive expeditions against, 231–3; indirect rule fails in Ibo areas of Western Nigeria, 259; 1940's rivalry with Ijebu, 272; Ibo State Union, 279; strength of today, in Eastern Nigeria, 295; massacre of in 1966, 314; reintegration into Federation, 315

Ibrahim Nagwamatse, Emir of Kontagora, as ruthless slaver, 212

Ibrahim Zaki, Fulani leader, enemy of Bornu, 102, 103

Ibuno (Ibeno) incident, 196–7

Idah, 211; Benin's influence extends to, 64; Beecroft reaches, 154; bronze casting arts of, 61; as Ata of Igala's capital, 61

Idoma, position of in 1830, 106

Idris, son of Jumada, 105

Idris Alooma, King of Bornu, army of, 49–50

Idubor, Felix, Nigerian sculptor, 312

Ife, kingdom of, 21; bronzes of, 61; Oduduwa legend of creation of, *see* Oduduwa; the Ife, Oyo and Benin states south of the Niger, 53; analysis of art of, 55; importance of to Benin and Yorubaland, 58; Ife dynasty in

Benin, 62 seqq.; relations of with Oyo during Yoruba civil wars, 110; as Yoruba province, 115; deserted, 121; role of, in Ibadan's wars, 177; destroyed by Modakeke and Ibadan, 178; in Yoruba civil wars, 119; inaugural Conference of the Egbe Omo Oduduwa in, 278–9

Ifemesia, C. C., 'The "civilizing" mission of 1841', 13, 142–3

Ifole riot, 175

Igala, 61

Igbajo war of 1867 (Ibadan against Ilesha), 174

Igbessa, on Lagos trade route, 176

Igboho, 121

Ijaw (Western) tribe, 63

Ijaye: role of, in New Oyo, *see* Kurumi; Yoruba Mission Station at, 165; Are of, as traditionalist, 167; Ogun river claims of, 168; Ijaye wars after annexation of Lagos, 170

Ijebu, 56–7; Alafin's power restricted in, 110; as Yoruba province, 115; in slave trade at time of Owu wars, 119; resist missions, 145; as middlemen and opponents of free trade, 177, 204; the Ijebu-Ife-Oyo settlement at Ibadan, 119; hoping to destroy Abeokuta, 120; and the 1850's Ibadan-Ijaye troubles, 168, 170; in the road-to-Lagos strife with Glover, 175, 205; makes peace with Ibadan, 178; Denton attempts to pacify, 206; the Ijebu-Ode trade route to Lagos and Ibadan, 176, 206, 207

Ijebu-Remo, Egba attack, 168, 170

Ijemo massacre of 1914, 248–9

Ijesha, Ijeshaland, Oyo at war with, 60; Ilorin fails to quell, 120; under Ibadan, 121; in alliance against Ibadan with Egba, Ekiti and Ilorin, 177; as middlemen, 178

Ijo: groups, language, 26; as original preponderating Delta group, 79; bring in slaves from Ibo, 80–1; slave-trading villages, 81–2; exports, 80; failure of indirect rule among, 259; Willinck Commission proposal for, 295

Ikeja, as industrial centre, 303

Ikirun, 204

Ikoli, Ernest (N.Y.M.), 266; in rivalry with Azikiwe, 272

Ikorodu, in 1850's wars of Ibadan-Ijaye, 168; Egba besiege, 171; Glover defeats Egba at, 175

Ikotana mission, Cross river, 184

Ikoyi, obliterated after sack of Old Oyo, 119

Index

Ilari, 58, 118

Ilaro (Egba capital), Yoruba mission at, 175; Maloney's British garrison at, 205

Ile-Ibinnu, becomes Ubini (Benin), 63

Ile Ife, as 'origin of life', creation myth of Yoruba, 53; as 'heaven of the kings of Benin', 59; *see* Ife

Ilesha, 58; Dahomey wages war on, 122; as Ibadan's ally in 1860's, 167–8; at end of civil wars, 174

Ilo, 47; French establish residence at, 195; British at, 196

Ilorin, 56, 113; first Fulani Emir of, 105; aims to carry Jihad into Yorubaland, 119; makes important Yorubaland conquests, 120; in brief alliance with Ibadan, 122, 167–8; Goldie captures for Company, 195; opposes Ibadan-Offa alliance, 204; last Yorubaland faction to negotiate, 203–4; as persisting opponents of R.N. Company, 208, 209, 219; British occupation becomes effective, 219; under Lugard, 219; emirate of included in Northern Nigeria Protectorate, 231; and the 1957 Conference, 296

Iluku, 121

Imam Ahmed ibn Fartua (chronicler), 49

India, as British trade outlet, 135; early indirect rule in, 220

Indirect rule (*see also* Goldie, Lugard), introduced into Nigeria, 235 seqq.; modifications of Lugard's, 236; for Northern Nigeria, Lugard defines, 245; failure of, Southern Nigeria, 258–9; Cameron's form of, 261; Fitzpatrick criticizes, 264

Indonesia, ancient East Coast trade with, 30

Industrialization, 24, 304

Inna Gharka, learned woman, mother of Bello, 106

Investigator, H.M.S., in Lokoja incident, 182

Iperu wars (Egba defeat Iperu), 170–1

Iron, in the early cultures, 31, 44; iron bars as currency, 75, 234

Ironsi, Major-General Aguyi, *see* Aguyi-Ironsi, Major-General

Isaaco, servant to Mungo Park, 137

Isaga, Yoruba Mission at, 165; Dahomey overcomes on path to Abeokuta, 123

Iseyin riots, against Lugard's Oyo policy, 248; Yoruba Mission at, 165

Isiaka Jatau, Habe ruler, becomes first Emir of Zaria, 100

Islam, reaches Hausa, 40, 61–2; and attitude to slavery, 45; early Sudanese states' contact with, 35–6; Idris Alooma's devotion to, 49; influencing Fulani clans, 92; dilution of by Habe rulers, 94; and Hausaland's indigenous religion, 94; in 18th, 19th c., 96; and breakup of Oyo empire, 116; and Northern Nigerian missionaries, 148; in new urban communities, 309–11; Lugard's agreements concerning, 236, 240. *See* Moslem missions

Ita, Professor Eyo, criticizes regional basis of government, 281

Italy invades Ethiopia, 267

Itsekiri, kingdom of Warri: source of slaves, 79; its role as slaving port, 88; economic trials of, after Abolition, 181; Oil Rivers Protectorate control over, 200

Ivory trade, 75, 87, 129, 137, 152; carvings (Benin), 64

Iwe-Irohin, Yoruba Mission newspaper, 165; role of, in Iperu wars, 171

Iwere, 115

Iwo, Maku's unsuccessful war against, 118

Iyase, 63, 64

Jackson, J. P., editor of *Lagos Weekly Record*, 254

Jaja, founder of Opobo, 84; as head of Anna Pepple house, Bonny, 179; declares his independence, 180; relations with British, when King of Opobo, 196; 1884 treaty, 196–7; Johnston brings to trial, 198; importance of, in Nigerian history, 200

Jakpa, Ologbotsere headquarters, 181, 182

Jamaica, slave revolts in, 77

James Pinnock & Co., Liverpool, in Niger trade, 184

Jameson, Robert, *An Appeal against the Proposed Niger Expedition* (against Fowell Buxton's ideas), 141

Jebba, as limit of Niger Company's establishment, 192; Lugard in, 193–4; as railway terminal, 241; see *Dayspring*

Jemaa terracotta, 32

Jengi, Etsu Nupe at, 105

Jibrella of Gombe (Mahdi), resists British, 223

John II of Portugal ('Lord of Guinea'), 68, 69

Johnson, Mr., Secretary of Egba United Board of Management, 174

413

Johnson, the Rev. Samuel, *History of the Yorubas*, 13, 56, 57, 59, 60, 203, 205, 207, 330; on end of Alafin despotism, 112; and the Lagos trade strife, 203; on Ijebu's trade tyranny, 206; on the 1893 Carter-Ibadan treaty, 208; on outbreak of Owu wars of 1812, 116-17

Johnston, Consul H. H., in negotiations with Jaja, 197-8

Jones, G. I., *The Trading States of the Oil Rivers*, 12, 86; on house rule (Ijo), 82, 83; on king's role in Bonny trade, 159-60; on Jaja's manœuvres, 180

Jos plateau: ancient fortified villages, archaeological finds, 30, 31; possible Stone Age footbridges of, 27; terracotta head from, 28; and 1952 N.C.N.C. convention, 283; position of in 1830; 106

José, Domingo, slave trader, supports Akitoye against Kosoko, 156

Journal of African History, 14

Journal of the Historical Society of Nigeria, 13

Judar Pasha, of Morocco, invades Timbuktu, 48

Juju Rock, Jebba, *see Dayspring*

Jukun kingdom, of Kororofa, ancient Sudanese state, 35; degree of matriarchy in, 41; people of, 50; in decline, 51; Fulani attacks on begin, 80; Emir of Muri infiltrates, 104

Jumada, cousin of Majia (Nupe), 104-5

Kabba province (created from southern half of Nupe kingdom), 219; Lugard controls, 221; after 1957 Conference, 296

Kaduna; regional government and emirates, 294; as industrial centre, 303, 304

Kagara, 32

Kaiama, in the race to Nikki, Lugard at, 193-4; French take over, 195

Kaigama, army leader under Mais of Bornu, 41

Kakanfo, Oyo army leader's title, *see* Are Ona Kakanfo; K. Oyabi in Abiodun's quelling of Gaha, 112; K. Kurunmi of Ijayi, 121

Kalabari people, of the Ijo, 26

Kamerun, 221, *see* Cameroons

Kanajeji, a king of Kano, 45

Kanem: ancient, 21; Zaghawa kingdom as precursor of, 37; in 12th-14th c., 40; Moslem infiltration of, 40-2; becomes Kanem-Bornu, 35, 37, 42; early detachment of, from Hausaland, 43; *see* Al-Kanemi, Idris Alooma;

France takes over in 1898, 222; first capital of, 39

Kanem-Bornu Empire, early development of, 35; Urvoy's history of, 37 seqq.

Kanembu (of old Kanem), nomad foes of Fulani, 102-4

Kano (Hausa state), 23, 35, 42, 43; traditions of (Kano chronicle), 44, 50; disputing pre-eminence with Katsina, 44; early ironworks of, 44; 15th-c. power of, 45; agricultural wealth of, 46; mid-16th-c. population of, 48; Ibn Battuta on Kano-Katsina wars, 45; Askia Daud invades, 48; Jukun, Fulani, Zamfara attacks on, 51 seqq.; commercial wealth of declines, 48-52; Zamfara conquest of, 1900, 91; falls to Fulani, 101; Clapperton visits, 138; Baikie visits, 1862, 163; shelters Magaji of Keffi, 223; railway reaches, 1911, 234, 241; agricultural and commercial importance of, 212; Barth's account of Fulani improvements in, 217; Emir supports W.A.S.U., 266; 'Sabon Gari' (Strangers' Quarter) of, 284; Awolowo's proposed tour of, 284; 1952 riots in, 284-5; rapid economic development of, 1940's, 300-3; expansion problems, 1950's, 308

Kano, Aminu, radical leader, 279

Kanta, governor of Kebbi, 47-8; *see* Kebbi

Kanuri people, N.E. Nigeria, 26, 53; ancient Kanuri-Hausa contacts with Arabs, 27, 28-9

Kaossen, Touareg chief, 250

Karari, first Kebbi king of Argungu, 101

Katagum, Bornu emirate founded, 102

Katsina, ancient Sudanese state, 35, 44; traditions of, 44; earthworks of, 45; Islam's high prestige in, in 16th c., 48; commercial wealth of, 48; profits from Songhai decline, 51; controls early 18th-c. caravan routes, 90; falls to Fulani, 1807, 101; separated from Maradi in 1900's, 102; nature of emirate of, 213; submits to Lugard, 225

Katsina Ala, 32

Katsina Laka, 48

'Katunga', as name for Oyo, 56

Kazaure, Fulani conquer, 101

Kebbi (Hausa 'bastard state'), 44, 213; against Songhai, Bornu, 47-8; in Holy War, 94, 99; position of, in 1830, 106; in rebellion against Sokoto, 216

Index

Keffi, Magaji of, against British, 223; and death of Captain Moloney, 223; joins Attahiru Ahmadu, 227, 228

Ketu, Yoruba kingdom, Dahomey, 28, 54, 176

Kiawa (a Katsina town), 92

'Kingmakers' of Benin, 63, 64

Kingsley, Mary, *West African Studies*, 190

Kirk, Sir John, reports on Brass disturbances, 190, 201

Kishi (Yorubaland), 121; Lugard's treaty with, 194; French take, 195

Kisoki (Hausa king), 46

Kisra legend (Hausa and Bornu history), 28

Kitab al-Farq, by Usman dan Fodio, 95, 213

Koelle, the Rev. S. W., of C.M.S., *Grammar of the Bornu or Kanuri Language*, 165

Kontagora, Emir of, as large-scale slaver, 212, 218, 220; hostile to Lugard, 211, 221

Kori, Alafin of Oyo, founder of Ede, 60

Korofofa (Jukun), Hausa 'bastard state', 30, 35, 44, 50, 51; as one of Queen Amina's tributaries, 45, 51; people of, 50; in decline, 51

Kosoko, King of Lagos, usurper, deposition of, 144, 145, 150, 156, 165–6; interferes with trade, 166–7; strife with, 165–70

Kuka (Bornu), *see* Tyrwhitt

Kurumi, Are of Ijaye, 121, 122, 122 n., 167, 170

Kwa language, 26

Kwa Ibo, Jaja attacks for free trading, 196–7

Kwale Ibo revolt (during War I), 250–1; poll-tax revolts, 259

Kwana, France shells, 192

Labisi, Alafin of Oyo, 112

Lada, Bulala defeated at, 47

Lafiagi, Emirs of, 103

Lagos (*see also* Akitoye, Esilogun, Kosoko, Mahin), Benin's influence in, 64; as slaving port, 118, 129, 133; returned slaves in, 78, 143; trade importance of, 152; succession dispute after 1811, 156–7; trade begins to extend behind coast, 162 seqq.; Kosoko overthrown, 165–6; full-time consuls in, after 1853, 166; missionary troubles in, 166–7; Docemo cedes to Britain, 169–70; roots of Abeokuta conflict, 174; five routes from, to interior, 175–6; disruption of interior trade by 1885, 178, 179; becomes self-administrating in 1886, 203; after 1899, 211; the Protectorate comes under Colonial Office jurisdiction, 231; remains a British colony, 243; as centre of nascent nationalism, 253; importance of water-rate levy in, 254; early nationalist issues in, 257; Cameroon abolishes Lugard's system of administrative justice in, 263; Lagos Youth Movement develops into N.Y.M., 266; Sir A. Richards maintains principle of election in, 274; minority groups' disputes in, 285, 286; rapid economic development in, after War II, 300; as industrial centre, 303; the 1950's urban development in, 308; introduction of principle of election into Town Council, 256. *See also* Lyttelton

Lagos Daily News, 257

Lagos Weekly Record, 254

Laird, Macgregor, in Niger trading, mid-19th-c., 140, 162–4; first venture fails, 163; factories of attacked, 163–4; results of arrival of, 158

Lakanle, leader of Oyo Ibadan, 1829, 119

Lake, Captain Thomas, and the Lander brothers, 139

Lambert, Nicholas, in early pepper trade, 72

Lander, Richard and John (explorers), 134, 139, 216

Languages, 24–6; study of indigenous, translations into, after 1850's, 165

Last, D. M., on nature of Fulani Empire, 213

Lavers, J. E., 11

Lawal, Lamido of Adamawa, Fulani administrator, 216, 218

Lawrence, Professor A. W., on the Benin art style, 55

Lebeuf, J. P. and Masson-Détourbet, archaeologists in Chad region, 37, 347

Lecky, on some abolitionists' motives, 126–7

Lekki, Freeman annexes from Kosoko, 170

Lennox-Boyd, The Rt. Hon. A., and the 1956 Azikiwe enquiry, 291

Leo Africanus, 47, 135

Leo X, Pope, 250

Leopold, King of the Belgians, and the Congo Association, 187

Lever Bros., in Belgian Congo, 264; Lord Leverhulme's plantations schemes, 264, 300

Levinge, Lieut. (West African Naval Squadron), 128

Life magazine, quoted, 271

Linguistic affiliations, 24–5

Liverpool, in slave trade, 73, 126, 161; in palm-oil trade, 152–3; and the Macgregor Laird ventures, 158, 162; traders' troubles, 163–4; government limits traders' interests, 172; alliance of with Delta middlemen broken, 184; resent Niger Company, 190

Livingstone, Consul, in Jaja affair, 180

Lizard worship, Bonny abandons, 184

Lloyd, Dr. Peter, 19; on the Warri, 88–9

Lodder, Lieut., mediates between Ibadan and Ijaye, 168

Lokoja, mission site (Crowther's), 147, 148; mid-19th-c. trading posts of, 162; Baikie at, 163; consulate established in, 182; significance of incidents (ransoming of Crowther, etc.), 183; British flag hoisted at, Jan. 1900, 219

'Long Juju', *see* Aro Chukwu

Lugard, Sir Frederick, later Lord, 21; Margery Perham's biography of, 19; as amalgamator of Northern and Southern Protectorates, 21, 235, 240, 253; in the 'race to Nikki' with France, 192–6; beats Decœur, 194; in early 1900's (Bornu and Fulani difficulties), 211, 212, 219–20; policy of indirect rule of, 220 seqq.; eight provinces controlled by, by 1901, 221; tasks of after Bornu's defeat, 223–4; and the Sultan of Sokoto, 224; takes Kano, 225; announces end of Usman dan Fodio's empire, 225–6; surprised by Attahiru Ahmadu's *hijira*, 227–8; after conquest of Sokoto, 228–9; as Governor of Hong Kong, 229; and the amalgamated Protectorates, 235 seqq.; sets up Nigeria Council, 1906, 243; North as 'spiritual home' of, 243, 258; reorganizes judiciary, 244; contribution of assessed, 244–6; his own definition of indirect rule, 245; on Nigerian troops in War I, 252; tribal consciousness preserved in indirect rule of, 253; and the educated African, 268, 269

Lynslager, Consul, warns King Eyo on trading irregularities, 160; destroys Old Calabar, 161

Lyttelton, Mr. Oliver, on revision of constitution, 285; decides on Lagos's federal status, 286

Mabogunje, Akin, 20

Mabolaje Grand Alliance, 298

Macaulay, Herbert, 'father of Nigerian nationalism', 254, 257; in the N.C.N.C., 272; succeeded by pan-Nigerian nationalists, 265; death of, 276

McClintock, Major, and Fad-el-Allah (Bornu), 223

Macdonald, Sir Claude, Governor of Oils River Protectorate, 199, 201–2; appoints Mary Slessor Vice-consul, 237

McKoskry, Acting Consul at Lagos, 169

Macleod, J. M., Consul at Lokoja, 182

Macpherson, Sir John, Governor of Nigeria, 276; shortlived Constitution of, 276-7, 282; retires, 1955, 290

McQueen's Niger theory, 137

Maghreb, gold of the, 66, 67

Magira, Queen Mother (ancient Kanem), 41

Mahin beach, near Lagos, German foothold at, 186

Maiduguri, British garrison, 223

Mais of Bornu (Kanem), 40–2; ruling council of, 41; learned, of later 18th century, 90; under Fulani attack, 102–3; Mais: Abu Amr Uthman b. Idris, 42; Ahmed, 102, 103; Ali Gazi, 42; Ali, successor of Idris Alooma, 50; Bikorom, 40; Biri, 40; Dala, 49; Dunama, 49, 103; Dunama Dibbalemi, 42; Ibrahim, 104, 221–2; Idris (A.D. 1600), 39; Idris Alooma, 49, 50, 51; Idris Katakarmabe, 47; Kashim Biri, 40; Umar ibn Idris, 42; Umarmi, 51; Ume, 40

Majia, son and successor of Muhammadu of Nupe, 104

Maku, *see* Alafins

Malaria, in early Niger expeditions, 140, 142; *see* Quinine

Malaysian food plants, spread of through Guinea Coast, 30, 33

Mali, ancient empire of Western Sudan, 35, 40, 41, 45; early sway of, over Western Hausaland, 43; Songhai becomes independent of, 47

'Mallam' defined, 46; Mallams: Alimi, ally of Kakanfo Afonja, 105, 106; Dendo (as Nupeland ruler, at time of Jihad), 105; Isa, in Satiru rising, 229; Jibril, Moslem teacher, 93; Makau, of Zaria, 100, 101; Musa, Zaria, 100

Mandara people, in wars with Bornu, 49, 90

Manila house of Bonny, 130

Mansfield, Lord Chief Justice, in Slavery judgment, 124–5

Manuwa, Dr. S. L., first Nigerian Director of Medical Services, 277

Mao, in Kanem, 39

Maradi, Habe kings of, and allies, 101;

Index

harass Fulani, 101; in rebellion against Sokoto, 216
Marata (Gobir), 93
Marghi people, Bornu conquers, 49
Marketing Boards (1940's) replaced by Regional Marketing Boards, 1954, 303
Marroki, King of Zamfara, 91, 92
Martinique, *see* Ouidah
Masaba, King of Nupe, 171; Baikie's friendship with, 163; and European trade, 183; envoy of, murdered, 174
Mason, Philip, quoted 297–8
Matriarchy, and Koranic requirements, 41
Mauny, R., 38 n.
Maye (Chief), Ibadan, 119, 120
Meek, C. K., 29
Meroë, as ancient cultural crossroads, 30
Merolla da Sorrento, Father Jerom, 88
Methodist missions, 143
Middle Passage (in slave trade), 72, 74, 81, 89, 119, 124
Mid-West State Movement (minority group, mainly non-Yoruba), 242, 294–5
Millet, as subsistence crop, 24, 37
Milner, Lord, and early nationalist aspirations, 255
Mineral rights, Azikiwe's opposition to vesting of in Crown, 275
Minna-Baro-Niger railway system, 241
Minna-Jebba-Lagos railway system, 241
Minorities Report (Willinck), 1958 Conference reluctantly accepts, 296
Miriam (learned woman), 107
Missau, lost to Bornu, 104
Missionaries, missions, 140–9, 236–9; influence of on Warri, 88–9; *see* Church Missionary Society, Church of Scotland, Methodist missions, Roman Catholics; three-prong approach in Nigeria, 143; combining commercial and philanthropic interests, 146–7; destroying African culture, 148; some benefits of education of, 148, 149; the 1850–65 expansion throughout Southern Nigeria, 165; press war in Iperu wars, 170–1; early exclusion of from North limits Northern progress, 294; *see also* Ajayi, Baptist missions, Crowther, Gollmer, Hinderer, Ibami, Ikotana, Isaga, *Iwe-Orohin*, Koelle, Olubi, Schön, Slessor, Townsend, Venn, Yoruba
Mizon, Lieut., sails up Yola for French, 192
Modakeke, Oyo build walled town of, 121; at war with Ife, 178; in faction beyond Lagos, 203, 204

Moddibo Adama, 104
Mohammed Korau of Katsina, Hausa king converted to Islam, 44; *see also* Muhammad
Moloney, Governor of Lagos, 203; 1890 mission to Ilorin, 205; nature of administration of, 206
Monitor lizards, worship of, 184
Monopoly clause, 1886 Royal Niger Company, 188
Moor, Acting Consul-general, 200
Moore, Eric, African barrister, 260; blames Lugard's policy for Ijemo massacre, 249
Mora, in War I, 251
Morel, E. D., 274; opposes Lugard's North-South distinction, 241; proposes four provinces, 241–2
Morland, Col., Lugard sends against Yola, 221
Morocco leather, 24
Morton-Williams, Peter, 13, 14, 19; on destruction of Old Oyo by Nupe, 61; on early history of Oyo, 55
Moslem law: developing Sudanese states adopt, 36; and the Holy War, *see* Usman dan Fodio; justifications for war, 93; foothold of in all Hausa states, 45–6; Moslem areas of North, 236; effect of Moslem exclusion of missionaries, 240; Moslem North and War I, 250; in 1950's, 293
Muffet, D. J. M., *Concerning Brave Captains*, 13; on Emir Aliyu's hijira suggestion, 227
Muhallabi, Arab historian, 37
Muhammad b. Ahmad, Timbuktu divine, 48
Muhammad Ahmad ibn Abdullah (Tue Mahdi), 96
Muhammad Attahiru, Sultan of Sokoto approved by Lugard, 225
Muhammad Etsu, of Nupe, 104
Muhammad Fodi, King of Kebbi, 101
Muhammad Gao (Songhai), 48
Muhammad Ibn Abd-Al-Wahbab (Saudi Arabia), 96
Muhammad ibn Ali al-Sanusi (Cyrenaica), 96
Muhammad Ibn Masanih (Katsina), historian, 46
Muhammad Kukuna, King of Kano, 51
Muhammad Rimfa, Kano's greatest king, 45; offers titles to eunuchs and slaves, 46, 47
Muhammad Zaki, King of Kano, 51
Murdock, G., *Africa, its People and their Cultural History*, 29

Index

Muri (Emirate of) (Adamawa), 104; French at, in 1891, 192; under Lugard, 221

Murzuk, 217

Mussoro, Chad region, 39–40

Na Alhaji, Fulani leader, 101

Nadel, Dr. S. F., *A Black Byzantium* (on the Nupe people), 60–1

Nafata, King of Gobir, 94

Nagwamatse of Kontagora, 221

Nana, Governor of Nenue river, challenger of Niger Coast protectorate, 182, 199, 200–1; importance of, in Nigerian history, 200–1

Nana, Maryam, prophesies *hijira*, 227

Napoleon III, a contract with house of Régis Aîné, 167

Napoleonic wars, 135

Nassarawa (Lower Benue), under Lugard's control, 221

National Africa Company, formed in 1882, 186

National Congress of British West Africa, founded 1920, 254–6

National Council for Nigeria and the Cameroons (N.C.N.C.), founded by Azikiwe, 1944, 272, 278–86; relations of, with Action Group, 285, 286, 289; attitude of, to Sir Arthur Richards's constitution, 274; chooses six Federal ministers, 289; in association with Northern People's Congress in Federal government, 290 seqq.; boycotts Coronation ceremonies, 290; leadership troubles, 291; Pan-Ibo Union as founder-members, 278

National Democratic Party (Herbert Macaulay's), 257

National Independence Party, 284; becomes United N.I.P., 290; basis of rivalry with N.C.N.C., 286

National Review, 258

Native Authority Ordinance, 1952, and status of Emirs, 313

Native Court Ordinance (Lugard), 244

Native courts, criticisms of, 259, 261; Cameroon limits, 263

Naturalism, in Ife art, 55

Navy treaties, with coastal chiefs, 130–2

Nelson, steamer, sunk in Niger, 183

Nembe, (Brass) group of the Ijo, 26, *see aslo* Brass

Netherlands, abolish slave trading, 127

New Calabar, slave port, 72, 75; compared with Old Calabar, 84; and the Aro oracle, 87; in palm-oil trade, 152;

monarchical system of, 83; Court of Equity, 154

New Oyo, foundation of, 120, 121

N'gaoundéré, in War I, 251

N'gazargamu, Bornu's new 15th-c. capital, Yobe river, 42; taken by Al Kanemi, 102, 103

N'guigmi, 39

Nguru, Galadima's capital, Kanta's defeat of Bornu at, 48; sacked by Fulani, 102

Niger Coast Protectorate, in 1899, 211; amalgamated with Protectorate of Southern Nigeria, 211, 231

Niger Company (Royal Niger Company), and the Consuls, 188–209; charter terms, 188–9; constabulary of, 219; established on Oil Rivers, 192; moves into Nupe, Ilorin, 195, 219; and French claim to Borgu, 193; and Oil Rivers British trade generally, 199; after 1895, 201; charter of withdrawn, 210, 231; compensation given to, 211; treaties with Gwandu and Sokoto, 219

Niger Delta, old city states of, 21; slave-trade ports of, 73 seqq.; development of House rule in, 81; societies of, lasting features, 148; ports as trade outlet after 1850, 152; trade of, 79–89; middlmen in trade of, 152–3, 183–4; middlemen resent Niger Company's increasing power, 196; radical trade change in, after 1865, 161; opposition to Laird's new-style trading in, 162; British consolidation in hinterland, 173 seqq.; French rivalry in, 185, 186; Jaja's power in, 179–81; Goldie's re-organization in, 185–6; Sir Claude Macdonald's and Johnston's attitude to, 199; the oil trade competition in, after 1865, 173; petroleum oil reserves, 304; Lugard abolishes House rule in, 249; Lugard's indirect rule in, 249–50; *see also* Beecroft

Niger Delta Congress, 298

Niger (river and region), the language group (Niger-Congo), 25–6; Kanem influence extends to middle Niger, 13th c., 40; the Niger-Northern Nigeria Anglo-French 1900's boundary, 102; the legendary river, 134; explorers after 1788, 134 seqq.; Mungo Park discovers eastward flow of, 136; Lander brothers find source of, 139; *see also* Peddie, Denham, Clapperton; new trade possibilities of realized, 140; 1841 expedition to, by Society for the Extinction of the Slave Trade, 141; Niger Mission, beginnings of, 142; the

Barth-Richardson-Overweg expedition to, in 1854, 147; Baikie's work in, 147; Beecroft's penetration as far as Idah, 154; Niger Mission, 141–2; *and see* Crowther; missionary position by 1880, 184; Baikie's demonstration of Niger as highway to interior, 163; 'Niger Districts' defined, 187; Britain's 1885 Protectorate over Districts, 173; revision of Niger Navigation Act, 1884, 187; French denied access to navigable stretch, 196; trade situation in 1878, 184

Nigeria: early history of, 27 seqq.; physical features, 23; modern political divisions, 23; as independent federation (Lugard's amalgamation), 21, 253; as sovereign federation, October 1960, 23; early forest belt subsistence crops in, 24; constant ethnographic pattern, 26–7; ethnic and linguistic divisions, 24–6; oral and documentary history, 27, 28, 29; Stone Age traces in, 29–32; origins of Northern, 35; tribal groups today, 24–5; rise of Arab learning in, 46; cultural exchanges with Brazil through slavery, 77, 78; Nigerians as slaves, *see* Slave trade; arrival of first Europeans in Benin, 66; Barth explores North, 147; early missionary traders in, 165; Britain's first annexations in, 162; first footholds, 184; *and see* Lugard; alien rule begins, 173–87; Fulani administration in North, 106–7, 217; role of missionaries, traders, explorers, 88–9, 134–49, 165, 170–1, 236–9; three areas of British interest after 1865, 173 seqq.; the late 19th-c. resistance to British, 196 seqq.; *see also* Poll tax; British occupation of Southern, completed 1897, 203; name chosen (and alternatives), 211; extent of Southern Protectorate by 1899, 211; Holy War's effect on Northern, 211–12; Satiru crisis in Northern settlement, 228; Iboland brought under British administration, 232–3; unification of, 231–52; native courts regularized in, 235; Niger Coast Protectorate absorbed, 1899–1900, 231; the 1906 merging with Lagos Protectorate, and crucial 1906 events, 233–4, 240; Ilorin Emirate absorbed in Northern Protectorate, 231; Cameroon in, 258–63, 269; the 1908–10 trade figures, 233; Western education in, 239–40, 305; the breakdown of traditions after 1906, 233; Lugard's 1912 plans for, 235–45; Lu-

gard's successes in North, 235–6; development of native administrations in North, 244–6; the 1912 amalgamation and the birth of national consciousness, 253; railways in, 24, 209, 241, 301, 304; 1914 proposals for, 241; Lugard introduces indirect rule to South, West, East, 246 seqq.; Lugard sets up Nigerian Council, 243; Nigerian troops in War I, 250–2; pioneers of nationalism, 254; the 1929 Poll tax riots (East), 260; indirect rule fails in East, 261; Nigeria's 'Indian states', 258, 261; Northern discriminations against South under indirect rule, 258, 278; inter-Wars trade figures, 263; students' organization abroad, 265, 267; Azikiwe's support for N.Y.M., 266–7; Nigerians in War II, 270; background to 1954 Constitution, 273 seqq., 280, 281; Nigerian Trades Union Congress officially recognized, 1942, 275; rise of nationalism, 253–72; North-South rivalries in 1950's, 277 seqq.; trouble with minority groups comes to head, 281, 284–6; the 'right to secede' issue, 287; the 1954 Constitution, 287–8; independence achieved, 289–314; Northern People's Congress, election successes of, 289; the minority groups in 1957, 281, 294–8; the first general election, 281–2; Federation of three regions, 273–88; role of Central Agency, 285; significance of Northern eight-point programme, 285; agreed system of elections after Federation, 288; Regional Executive Council, 289; the 1945–60 proposals, 293–8; outcome of 1959 Federal elections, 298 seqq.; Middle Belt State proposed, 294–7; social and economic developments after last war, 299–305; agriculture at present, 302 seqq.; new Marketing Boards, 303; the 1956–7 national income, 304; new light industries, 304; education, health, Civil Service, etc., 305–7; local government democratized, 313; population (1962–4 census), 334–5; Federal election of 1964, 322–5; the new élite, 311; Nigerian Museum founded, 312; Society for the Promotion of Art and Culture founded, 312; national ministries after 1951 listed, 333–6; British Governors of, 1900–60 (listed), 332

Njimi, first Kanem capital, 39, 40

Nok, and Congo basin, similarities in art of, 33; Nok late Stone Age culture, 31, 32

Index

Northern Elements Progressive Union, 284; after 1959, 289
Northern House of Assembly, House of Chiefs, 285
Northern People's Congress, foundation of, 279; securing North for the Northerners, 282; conditions of, for co-operation with South, 282
Nsanakang, in War I, 251
Nubia, rise of, in Meroitic civilization 30, 37
Nuh, Songhai ruler, 49
Nupe (Hausa 'bastard state'), 26; as ancient Sudanese state, 35; associated states (Bayajidda legend), 44; as Ife rival, 56; invade Yorubaland, 60; destroys Old Oyo, 60–1; continuous wars with, 61; Fulani seek foothold in, 104; secure independence from Oyo, 113, 114, 116, 118; Barth seeks trade route to, 163; Ibadan's 1870's invasion of, 176; Goldie and, 186, 195; nature of Emirate of, 213; as persistent raiders into Niger Company territory, 219; cede southern half to Company, 219; hostility of Emirs of, to Lugard, 221
Nupe bronzes, 61
Nupe language, see Crowther
Nupe (Nyffi) cloth, 218
Nur al-Albab, by Usman dan Fodio, 106–7
Nurse, Capt., destroys slavers' barracoons, 1841, 131–2
Nwoko, Demas, Nigerian painter, 312

Oban mission, 1879, 184
Obas of Benin, 54, 55, 59; token burials of, in Ife, 59; focal role of, 64; death of Oba Ovenramwen and restoration of dynasty by Lugard under indirect rule, 246, 247
Oduduwa conquest myth of Ife, 53
Offa, in civil wars, 178
Ofinran (Ofonran), successor to Onigbogi, 61
Ogbomosho, Yoruba mission station, 165, 208
Ogboni, role of (Oyo), 110–11; Ogboni Society (secret society checking Oyo Mesi's power), 58, 110
Ogiamwe, son of Evian, 54; enemy in Benin of Eweka I, 63
Ogiso (early kings of Benin), 54
Ogoja, 232, 295; resists unification, 232
Ogun, Ewuare the Great, of Benin, 63
Ogun River, in Ibadan–Ijaye wars, 168–9; E.U.B.M. proposed customs post on, 174
Oguola, king of Benin, 63

Ohen, son of Oguola, king of Benin, 63
Oil, see Palm oil
Oil Rivers, 97; states of, 188; Royal Niger Company established on, 192; Protectorate of (after 1887), 188, 190, 199
Ojigi, Alafins of Oyo, see Alafins
Ojike, Mazi Mbonu, attacks regional basis of 1949 Constitution, 281
Ojukwu, Colonel Odumegwu, 314
Okba ben Nafi, conqueror of Fezzan, 36
Okeho, in 1850's Ogun River troubles, 168
Oke Igbo, chief of (Oni-Elect of Ife) in Ibadan wars, 177
Oke-Igbo (town) on Lagos trade route, 176, 177
Oko-Jumbo, adviser to George Pepple, 179
Okoyong people of Cross River, Mary Slessor among, 237
Okrika people (and Ijo trading town), 26, 79, 84; attack New Calabar, 179; Jaja and, 180
Okugo of Oloko, poll-tax blunder of, 259–60, 261
Old Calabar: as slave port, 72; see also Slave trade; pattern of House rule in, 83; in palm-oil trade, 152; slave rebellion in (Beecroft intervenes), 157; Court of Equity, 154; Fernando Po consulate transferred to, 183
Olinda, Eyo Honesty's free-trade ship, 161
Ologbotsere, house of (Benin river), 181, 182;
Olorun myth, see Oduduwa
Olowu of Owu, 54
Olubi, the Rev. D. (C.M.S.), 206, 207
Oluewu, see Alafins
Olumu, Benin trader and governor of Benin river, 182
Olupopo of Popo, 54
Oluyole, see Basorun
Ondo, on Lagos trade route, 177; Alafin's powers curbed in, 110
Oni of Ife, 55, 59, 63; sanctions installation of Alafins, 115; and outbreak of Owu war, 117; humbles Oyo refugees, 121
Onigbogi, see Alafins
Onikoyi, King, and outbreak of Owu war, 116
Onisabe of Sabe, 54
Onitsha Ibo people, 63, 80; migrate to the Niger, 87; missionaries to, 148, 164; mid-19th-c. trading posts, 162; trading houses and missions burnt down, 184; riots, after Enugu shootings, 280; 1950's expansion problems, 308

Index

Opobo, King of Bonny, 128, 129, 130

Opobo state, founded by former slave Jaja, 84; after his declaration of independence from Bonny, 180; Britain recognizes, 181; Court of Equity, 154

Oral tradition, interpretation of, 27–8

Orangun of Ila, 54

Oranmiyan, King of Benin, 54, 56, 63, 64; as king of Oyo, 55, 56; as descendant of Oduduwa, 54, 59

Ormsby-Gore's 'Congo system' investigation, 265

Orompotu, brother and successor of Egunojo, 61

Oshogbo, Ilorin defeated at, by Ibadan, 122

Osi Efa, battle representative of Alafin of Oyo, 58

Otta, Dahomey captures, 122

Oudney, N., 137, 138

Ouilliminden tribe, 1916 revolt of against French, 250

Ovenramwen, Oba (Benin), 203; asked to abandon human sacrifice, 202; succeeded by Eweka II, 247

Overpopulation and the slave trade, 89

Overweg, explorer (*see also* Barth, Richardson), 147

Owen, Captain, and Opobo of Bonny, 129

Owerri, riots in, 1929, 260

Owome (New Calabar), Delta slave trading state, 79

Owu people of Yoruba, 58, 115; Olowu of, 54; Owu wars of 1812, 116–17; impact of wars of 1821, 116; the 1827 fall of, 118, 119

Oyo, Yoruba empire of, 21; early history, 55–62; legendary kings of, 59; Benin and Oyo as twin kingdoms, 56; capital returns to original site, 62; as caravan terminus, 66; empire in decline, 105; 18th-c. recovery, 108; extent of 18th-c. authority of, 110; dominates Dahomey, 110; seeking westward expansion, 110–13; spiritual and constitutional relationships, 115; the 1797 end of empire, 116; at start of wars, 119; split with Ikoyi, Gbogun, 120; Yoruba mission to, 165; as Ibadan's ally, 167–70; slave-trade monopoly of, at outbreak of Owu war, *see* Ajayi, Akinjogbin; Dahomey invades, 1887, 204; in alliance with Lagos against French, 205

Oyo Igboho, town founded by Egunojo, 61

Oyo Mesi, powers of, 57, 58; rejecting of kings by, 108

Ozo title of Ibo, 77

Paine, Thomas, *The Rights of Man*, 125

Palma: port given to Kosoko by Campbell, 166; Freeman annexes from Kosoko, 170

Palmer, Richmond, emissary of Lord Lugard, 247; writings of, 18, 29, 37, 39

Palmerston, Lord, 157; hopes for Fernando Po as oil base, 131; and the Lagos troubles, 156–7

Palm-oil trade, 24, 152, 180, 302; extent of Britain's, 128–31; the connection with Abolition, 126, 129, 131, 133; growing in importance, 148; attack on Porto Novo after embargo on, 168; 1856 exports from Egbaland, 167; cut-throat nature of, 179, 183, 184; 'Palm-oil ruffians', 133, 153; French threat to, 1887, 191; value, in 1888, 203; inter - war developments, 264; Sumatra's 1925 superiority, 265

Pan-Ibo Federal Union, 1944, 278

Pan-Nigerian nationalism, 265

Park, Mungo, 135; in Niger exploration, 136–7; murder of, 137

Patani, Goldie's measures against, 186; attack French in 1889, 192

Pategi (Nupe), 105

Peddie, Major (explorer), 137

Peel, Sir Robert, reduces import duty on sugar, 132

Pepper expedition to Benin, 71–2

Pepple dynasty of Bonny, 76, 83; George, 179; Opobo, 128; William Dappa, 130, 131, 155, 159; in exile in England, and death of, 158–60, 179; the Manila Pepple faction, 159, 180

Perham, Margery, in *Lugard* and other works, 19; on background to Nikki treaty, 194; on Lugard in Northern Nigeria, 211; on indirect rule, 246; on Lugard's Oyo difficulties, 247; on 1929 enquiry into poll-tax riots, 260; on Cameroon's support of educated Africans, 269–70

Pettiford, American sharp-shooter, 170

Phillips, the Rev. C., 202–3

Philomel, H.M.S., in Nana affair, 200

Phoebe, H.M.S., in Nana affair, 200

Phoenicians, in Africa, 30, 66

Pitt, William, supports Abolition, 125; backs African Association, 135

Pleass, Sir Clem, 283–4

Pleiad, trading vessel, 150

Index

Poll-tax, introduced 1926 to Eastern Nigeria, 259–60

Polygamy, C.M.S. approach to, 310

Ponlade, opponent of Edun, 248

Pope Hennessy, Governor (West African settlements), 176

Popo, France annexes, 186

Port Harcourt: proposed railway from, 241; riots in, after Enugu shootings, 280; economic developments in, 300, 303, 308

Porto Novo, 62, 111; France annexes, 186; Glover's measures against, 171, 176

Portuguese: reach Benin, 66; effects of the 1580 union with Spain, 72 (*see also* Spain); influence of, in Warri, 88–9

Possoo, Epe ruler, 170

Post, K. J. W., 19; study of 1959 Federal election by, 312

Presbyterian mission, Calabar, *see* Slessor, Mary

Protectorate of Southern Nigeria, comes under Colonial Office, 231

Qua River Blood Men (slave uprising), 157–8

'Queen's Dominions' in West Equatorial Africa, 165

Quinine, 142, 147, 180

Rabba, Nupe capital, 105; Fulani struggle to remain in, 104–5

Rabeh, Sudanese adventurer in Bornu, 1893, 222

Rainbow, in Niger trade, 1859 attack on, 163

Rajada (on Niger), 105

Rakah, port of, 139

Rano, Hausa industrial state, 43, 44

Reichard, Herr, geographer on Niger, 136

Rennell, Major, Niger theory of, 136, 137

Richards, Sir Arthur, Governor of Nigeria, 272, 274; constitutional proposals of, 273, 276

Richardson, James (explorer), 147

Rio Pongos, 131

Rivers State proposal (Calabar–Ogoja–Rivers state), 295

Robertson, Sir James, succeeds Macpherson, 290

Robinson, R. and Gallagher, J., *Africa and the Victorians*, 13

Robins, Chief Willy Tom (Calabar), 161

Roman catholicism in Nigeria, 310, 311

Roth, Henry Ling, *Great Benin: its Customs, Arts and Horrors*, 203

Rowe, Governor-General, 1883, on trade wars behind Lagos, 178

Royal Niger Company, *see* Niger Company

Rubber of Eastern Nigeria, 302

Rudkin, Prof. Harry, 10

Russell, Lord John, and the Hutt Committee, 132

Sabon Birni, 92

'Sabon Garis', 278

Sabongari, Usman's base camp at, 99

Saif dynasty (Bornu), 103

Saifawa dynasty, 42

Saki, (Shaki), 121; Yoruba Mission station at, 165; defeats Ijaye troops, 168

Salisbury, Lord, 196; on Niger Company's withdrawn charter, 210

Salt, role of, in slave trade, 81

Sanda, Emir, successor of Lawal of Adamawa, 218

Sandam, overlords of, 101

Sango (of Oyo), 58, 59, 60

Sango shrine ceremonies (Oyo), 115 n.

Sangoan age, 30

São peoples, 37, 42

São Thomé, Portuguese trade with, ousting Benin, 71

Sapele plywood, 304

Sardauna of Sokoto and N.P.C., 294

Sarkin Zazzau, kings of Ajuba, 101

Satiru incident (crisis in Northern Nigeria pacification), 228

Say-Barruwa line (British-French), 192–3

Schön, the Rev. F. J., missionary, 141, 142, 147; *Grammar of the Hausa Language*, 165

'Scramble' sales of slaves, 76

Secession right, Action Group claims, 286

Select Committee of 1865 (British West Coast trade), 150, 151, 152, 171–2, 182

Self-government: the 1956 provisions, 285, 286, 288, 290 seqq.; Northern reluctance to adopt, 293–4

Semellé, Comte de, in Niger trade struggle, 185–6

'Semi-Bantu' linguistic sub-family, 26

Senegal, Senegal river, 47, 135

Senussi 'Holy War', 250

Sequiera, Ruy de, reaches Benin in 1472, 66

Serer language, 26

'Seven provinces' proposal, *see* Temple

Shagamu, in Lagos-Ibadan trade, 205

Shari river, Denham confuses with Benue, 139

Shari'a, introduced (replacing customary law) by Mai Idris Alooma, 49, 93, 96

Sharp, Granville, anti-slavery crusade of, 124, 125

Sharpe, Major, resident at Kontagora, 212

Shaw, Flora, later Lady Lugard, 21

Shaw, Professor Thurstan, 10, 14, 27, 31

Shehu Ahmadu (Western Sudan), 96

Sidi, rebellious Emir of Zaria, 215–16

Sierra Leone, missionaries' freed slave settlement in, 140, 141, 142; disturbances in, following introduction of taxes, 247; Sierra Leone battalion in War I, 251

Simpson, W., of 1841 missionary expedition, 141

Simpson, W. H., 183

Slaves, slave trade: Atlantic, 61–78; various African attitudes to, 74, 75; early trade, Sudanese states, 36; British in early coastal trade, 72; slave status, in African social system, 74; arrangements between European and African dealers, 74; European moral attitude to, 74; nature of goods exchanged for, 75; murders of weak slaves, 75; slaver-ship conditions, 75–6; repatriated slaves as slave dealers, 78; and political structure of Niger Delta, 79 seqq.; and depopulation, 89; slave raiding after Jihad, 107; and fall of Dahomey (various interpretations), 114–15; Britain abolishes, 124–33 (*see* Sharp, Buxton, Wilberforce); Spain-Portugal anti-slavery agreements, with Britain, 127; countries ready to abolish, 127; and sugar legislation, 132; African Association and, 135; attacked at its economic roots, 140; in decline after 1850, 152; Slave trade increase through legitimate trading, 153; Kontagora as large-scale trader, 212, 218, 220; slave trade of Kano (Barth), 218; Fulani dependence on income from, 218–19; as element in background to Yoruba civil wars, 178; late raiding by Nupe, 195; later surreptitious involvement of Nana (Benin River), in, 200; Ilorin in, 204; Lugard's attitude to the freeing of slaves, 228

Slessor, Mary (missionary in Eastern Nigeria), 237, 238

Smith, Abdullahi, 10

Smith, Mary, *Baba of Karo*, 219

Smith, M. G., cited, 229; on development of savannah-land states, 43

Smith, Oliver, Queen's Advocate, 204

Smith, Robert, 11, 12, 13, 14; 'The Alafin in Exile', 14, 330 n.; on slavery's increase through legitimate trade, 153

Society for the Abolition of the Slave Trade, 1787, and the Freetown settlement, 125, 128

Society for the Extinction of the Slave Trade and the Civilization of Africa, 141

Society for the Suppression of Human Sacrifices in Calabar, 146

Sodeke, of Abeokuta, 119, 143

Sokoto, 214, 215, 216, 217; as ancient savannah power, 21; progress by 1830, 106–7; Moslem divines at court of, 106; Clapperton in, 138; and the control of Borgu, 193; Emirs responsible to, 213; histories of, 218; Lugard's war on, 224–5; finally decides to support Lugard, 229; Sardauna of, leader of N.P.C., 282; self-government situation, 1959, 294; Sardauna of, as Regional Premier, Northern Nigeria, 294. *See also* Bello, Flegel, Niger Company, Usman dan Fodio, Fulani Empire

Solagberu, ally of Abd al-Salam (Holy War), 106

Solanke, Ladipo, founder of West African Students' Union, 265–6

Somersett v. Knowles case, 124–5

Songhai empire of Gao, 47; as a leading power in Western Sudan, 35; 16th-c. invasions by, in 15th–16th c., 47; influence of ends, 48; late 16th-c. collapse of, 92

Sonni Ali, king of Songhai, 47

Soyenbola, Onikoyi of Ikoyi, 120

Soyinka, Wole, Nigerian poet, 312

Spain and Portugal, and slave trade, 127, 128, 129, 130

Stanley, Col. Oliver, Colonial Secretary, 271–2

Stock, Eugene, *History of the Church Missionary Society*, 141

Students' organizations, 265, 267

Sugar-slavery link, 73, 132; Sugar Act, 132

Sultan of Sockatoo, 1875–6 attacks on, 183

Sulumanu, Emir of Kano, 1807, 101

Sumatra, palm oil of, 265

Sweden, abolishes slavery in 1813, 127

Tabkin Kwatto, Fulani beat Gobir at, 98

Tada bronzes (Nupe), 61

'Talakawa' (Hausa 'common people'), 97

Talbot, Amaury, 29

Index

Tanbih al-ikhwan by Usman dan Fodio, 95–6

Tapa (Nupe), lost to Oyo, 113

Taubman, *see* Goldie

Taxation: early (Kano and Bornu), 40, 46, 50; Fulani resentment of, by Habe, 95, 97; under British, 234, 245, 247; *see also* Poll tax

Taylor, the Rev. J. C., in *Dayspring*, 164

Temple, Lieut.-Governor (North Nigeria), 274; advocates 'seven provinces' solution, 241, 242; Lugard disagrees with, over Native Treasuries, 246

Tepe, in War I, 251

Thompson, Joseph, defeats German aspirations in Sokoto, 187

Thomson, Sir Graeme, Governor of Nigeria, 258; and the Leverhulme policies, 265; and the educated African, 269

Tié (possible first capital of Kanem), 39

Timber trade: alternative to slave trade, 128, 129; modern exports, 301

Timbuktu, 48; Mungo Park journeys to Bussa from, 135

Times, The, on early Niger missions, 142

Timi, hunter, in Oyo history, 60

Tin Mines of Jos plateau, 24, 302

Tinubu, Madam, Docemo expels, 167

Tiv people, of Middle Belt, 26, 29; riot in support of Jukun, 228

Togoland, German, 56, 251

Tonking disaster (to France), 191

Torodbe clan of the Fulani, 92, 93

'Town chiefs', 64

Townsend, Henry (missionary) of Badagry and Abeokuta, 143, 144; repels Dahomey attackers, 144; opposes Crowther's bishopric, 165; attitude of to Alake, 145; and the inter-tribal wars generally, 171; resents Glover's aims in Abeokuta, 172

Trade: see Slave trade; growth of legitimate, 150–72; effect on of 1850's–1860's tribal wars, 171; freedom of, under Niger Company charter, 188; free trade areas under early British administration, 234; *see* Niger Delta, Trusts

Tribal feeling (Yoruba against Ibo) and Federation, 277–9

Tribal unions, and town immigrants, 309

Trinidad, Yoruba slaves in, 77

Tripoli, as Arab merchants' base, 48, 139; Kano goods sent to, 217, 218; as Denham-Clapperton expedition's base, 137

Tripolitania, in War I, 250

'Trust' or credit goods, in Delta trade, 153, 161

Tryon, Lieut., at Bonny, 130

Tschadda river, 147

Tsetse fly, 34, 110

Tsoede, king of Nupe, probable destroyer of Old Oyo, 61

Tsuntsuwa, Usman dan Fodio defeated at, 98

Tuareg people, 41, 50; against Hausa, 44; against Fulani, 99, 100; veils worn by, 217

Tunis, Kanem influence extends to, 40

'Turkedi' defined, 217

Turkey, in War I, 250

Twi-speaking people, of modern Ghana, 26

Twin murder, in Calabar, 146

Tyrwhitt, as both consul and explorer (Kuka), 139

Ubini, *see* Ile-Ibinnu (Benin)

Udagbedo, King of Benin, son of Oguola, 63

Umar, Sheikh, son of Al Karemi, 104

Umaru of Hadeija, a Fulani leader, 101

Umaru Dallaji, Fulani leader, first Emir of Katsina, 101

Umaru Dumyawa, Fulani leader, 101

Umoru, King of Nupe, and the French traders, 185

United African Company, Goldie welds trading companies into, 185; at time of second World War, 300

United Middle Belt Congress (minority group), 294

United Native African Church, founded 1891, 239

U.N.I.P. replaces N.I.P., 290, 293

Urban population increases, 1950's, 307–9

Urhobo tribe, 63

Urvoy, Yves, *Histoire de l'Empire de Bornou*, 18, 37, 50, 103

Usama, one-time Benin capital, 62

Usman dan Fodio, leader of Jihad (Holy War), 28, 46, 90–107; adherents of, 95; motives of, 93–5; early life of, 93–4; three phases of war, 98; *see also* Holy War; high standards set by, 212; for writings of, *see Kitab-al-Farq, Nur al-Albab, Tanbih al-Ikhwan*

Utrecht, Treaty of, slave trade affected by, 73

Uwaifiokun, Benin usurper, 63, 64

Uyanga Mission, 1879, 184

Uzama kingmakers, as check to power of Oba, 64

Index

Van Nyendael, on Benin's early 18th-c. decline, 88

Vansina, Dr. J., 10, 27, 28

Vaughn, Dr. J. C. (N.Y.M.), 266

Vellacott, George, 20

Venn, Henry (C.M.S.), 142, 164, 165; supports Crowther, 142

Verger, M. Pierre, 20; on returned slaves of Lagos's 'Brazilian Quarter', 78

Victoria, Queen: interested in C.M.S., 145; rewards Jaja of Opobo, 196

Von Pittkamer, in Nupe affair, 191

Voodoo, African, surviving in Haiti, 78

Wachuku, Mr. Jaja (N.C.N.C.), 292

Wadai, 36; Idris Alooma partially conquers, 49; Sherif of, 104; Rabeh conquers in 1893, 222

Waddell, Hope, student of Efik language, 165; in Calabar, 1846, 145-6

Wallace-Johnson, I.T.A., co-editor with Azikiwe of Accra, 266

Warrant chiefs, 250

Warri, Itsekiri kingdom, founding of, 88; pattern of house rule in, 83; independent of Benin, 88; Catholic faith in, 88-9; secessionist movement from, 181; comes under British protection in 1884, 182; 1927 poll-tax troubles, 259

Webster, J. Bertin, on African churches in Yorubaland, 310

Wedgwood, Josiah, as founder-member of African Association, 135

Welsh, James, 16th-c. trader to Benin, 75

West Africa, 287, 290, 292, 297-8

West African Company (Manchester), in Niger trade, 184

West African Frontier Force, 195, 210, 219, 220, 221

West African Pilot, 266, 272, 275, 313

West African Squadron (anti-slave patrol), 132, 133, 157

West African Students' Union, founded 1925, 265-6

West Coast anti-slavery patrols, position of by 1840's, 127, 130-1

West Indies: effects of Spanish rule in, 72-3; 17th-c. demand for slaves in, 73; slaves making wealth of, 125; 1938 riots in, 271

Western Delta, British progress in, 182-5

Western Ibo tribe, 63

Western Ijo, partly under British protection, 1884, 182

Western Slave Coast, 118

White, James, 13

Widgeon, H.M.S., in Nana attack, 200

Widows, seclusion of (Calabar), 146

Wilberforce, William, 125, 126; and the Hutt committee, 132; in African Association, 135

Willcocks, Captain, as right-hand man to Lugard, 221

Willink, Sir Henry (1957 Commission on Minority Groups), 295-8

Windham, Captain, on Portugal's influence in Benin, 71—2

Wolof language, 26

Wombai, the, of Kano (Lugard's time), 225

Wood, the Rev. J. B., at Abeokuta, and Ekiti-Parapo strife with Ibadan, 178

Wurno, 216

Wushishi garrison, W.A.F.F.'s, 220

Wydah, Dahomey attacks, 111-12

Yaba Higher College, 266, 269, 279

Yaji, King of Kano: converted to Islam, 45; attacks Kororofa, 50

Yakubu, Emir of Bauchi, 104

Yakubu, King of Kano, 45

Yam crops, 24, 30, 33

Yamusa, Fulani leader, attacks Zaria, 100-1

Yandaka area, 101

Yaoundé, in War I, 251

Yauri (Hausa 'bastard' state), 44

Yeri, 41

Yerima, provincial governor of Yeri, 41

Yesderam, Germans acquire, 1898, 222

Yola, Emirate of (Adamawa), 104, 147, 162, 211; French penetrate, 192; Lugard's conquest of, 221

Yoruba, Yorubaland (see also Ife, Oyo), 26-8, 30, 44, 53, 56, 59, 176; ancient Nok art of, 32; creation myth, 53; explanation of military successes of, 58; a Hausa history of, in Katsina, 59; early trading with Hausa, 60; slaves from civil wars of, 72; tribal organization of, 77; fighting following death of Abiodun, 112 seqq.; status obtainable by slaves in, 74; Fulani seeking foothold in, 104; seek to expel Fulani from Ilorin, 120, see Fulani; advance of missions in, 143, 152; missions after 1850, 165; Lagos as gate to, 152; major wars of, 108-23, 176 seqq.; the climactic incident of civil wars of, 171; end of civil wars, 204; the French threats from Dahomey, 203; comes under effective British

Yoruba—*cont.*
control, 205–7; under British control by treaty, 231; later position of Obas in, 246–7; strength of in Action Group, 294; the October 1960 independence, 273; Yoruba Temple in New York, 311

Young, P. V., British Commissioner, 248

Young, Sir William, of African Association, 135

Yunfa, King of Gobir, 94, 95; death of, 102

Zaghawa nomads, 36–7; kingdom of, as precursor of Kanem Empire, 37; in Lake Chad region, 36–7

Zamfara (Hausa 'bastard state'), 44, 47, 52, 102; rivalling Katsina, 91–2; in the Holy War, 97; unites with Gobir against Fulani, 99; nature of Emirate, 213–14; resists Bello, 214; rebels against Sokoto, 216

Zani Gharka (learned woman), 106

Zanna (title), 51

Zaria, 47; Emirs of, 100, 215; as Hausa slave raiding state, 44, 45; becomes tributary to Jukun, 51; Baikie seeks trade route to, 163; under Lugard's control, 221; C.M.S. missions to, 240

Zazzau (Zaria), 43, 100. *See* Zaria

Zenne (plaid), 217

'Zik', *see* Azikiwe; Zikist movement, 279–80

Zinder, 104; France acquires in 1898, 222; Kaossen and Senussi besiege, 250 and Senussi besiege, 250

Zubair Pasha, slave raider, 222

Zubeiru, Emir of Yola, 218, 222

Zuguma (Nupe), 105

Zungur, Sa'ad, 279